# How to Read GREEK SCULPTURE

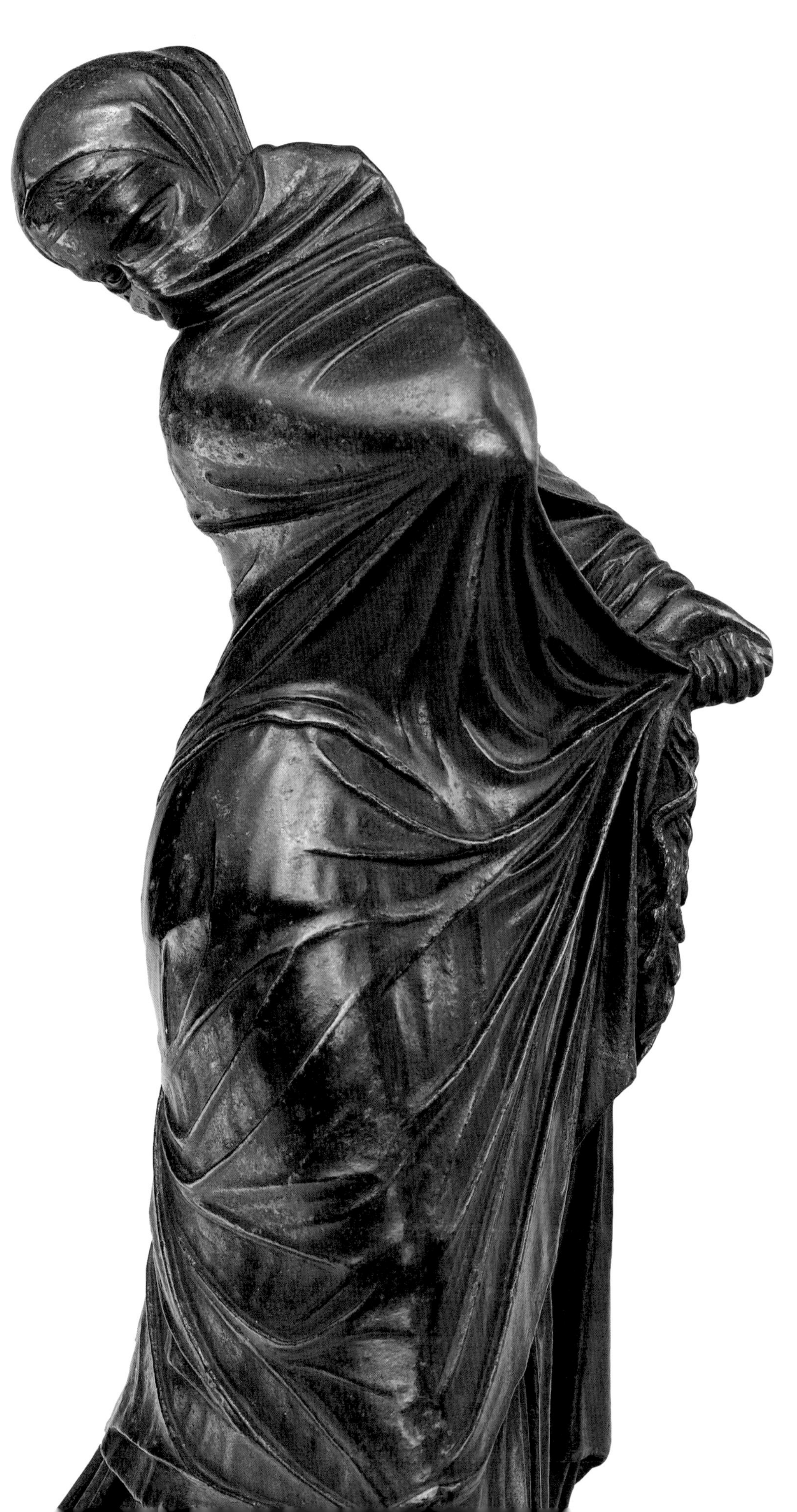

# How to Read GREEK SCULPTURE

Seán Hemingway

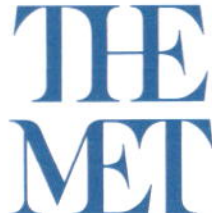

The Metropolitan Museum of Art, New York
Distributed by Yale University Press, New Haven and London

This publication is made possible by James and Mary Hyde Ottaway, the Jenny Boondas Fund, and the Friends of Greek and Roman Art: Philodoroi.

Published by The Metropolitan Museum of Art, New York
Mark Polizzotti, Publisher and Editor in Chief
Peter Antony, Chief Production Manager
Michael Sittenfeld, Senior Managing Editor

Edited by Margaret Donovan
Designed by Cindy Hwang and Rita Jules, Miko McGinty Inc.
Production by Christopher Zichello
Image acquisitions and permissions by Josephine Rodriguez-Massop
Maps by Pamlyn Smith

Unless otherwise noted, all works are in the collection of The Metropolitan Museum of Art, New York. Photographs of works in the collection are by Paul H. Lachenauer, Oi-Cheong Lee, Juan Trujillo, Katherine Dahab, and Eugenia B. Tinsley, Imaging Department, The Metropolitan Museum of Art, unless otherwise noted.

Additional photography credits: Image by Dorothy H. Abramitis: fig. 33; bpk Bildagentur/Staatliche Museen/Johannes Kramer/Art Resource, NY: fig. 40; ©President and Fellows of Harvard College: fig. 52; Drawing by Seán Hemingway: fig. 14; Image © The Metropolitan Museum of Art: figs. 1–5, 8, 10, 11a–f, 12, 13, 15, 17–24, 26–32, 34–38, 41–46, 50, 51, 54–56, 58–61, nos. 1–3, 5–11, 13–18, 20, 22, 23, 26, 28–35, 37–40; Image © The Metropolitan Museum of Art, photo by Katherine Dahab: fig. 16, no. 36; Image © The Metropolitan Museum of Art, photo by Paul Lachenauer: figs. 6, 7, 25, nos. 4, 12, 19, 23, 24, 25; Image © The Metropolitan Museum of Art, photo by Oi-Cheong Lee: figs. 39, 53, 57; Image © The Metropolitan Museum of Art, photo by Eugenia Burnett Tinsley: no. 21; Image © The Metropolitan Museum of Art, photo by Juan Trujillo: fig. 9, no. 27; Photograph © 2021 Museum of Fine Arts, Boston: fig. 48; Image by Pavol Roskovensky: figs. 47, 62

Typeset in Aktiv Grotesk, Documenta, and Le Monde Livre by Tina Henderson
Printed on 150gsm Perigord
Color separations, printing, and binding by Trifolio S.r.l., Verona, Italy

Front cover: Head of a horned youth wearing a diadem, Greek, late 4th or early 3rd century B.C. (detail, no. 30); back cover: Relief with a dancing maenad, Roman, copy of a Greek relief of ca. 425–400 B.C. (detail, no. 21)

Additional illustrations: p. 2, Statuette of a dancer (detail, no. 32); p. 6, Statuette of a horse (detail, no. 40); p. 8, Statue of a *kouros* (youth) (no. 6), with Fragment of a stele of a hoplite (no. 10) and Stele of a youth and young girl (no. 9), on display in the Judy and Michael H. Steinhardt Gallery for Greek Art of the 6th Century B.C. at The Metropolitan Museum of Art; pp. 46–47, Stele of a family group (detail, no. 25); p. 164, Statuette of a horse (no. 40)


First printing



The Metropolitan Museum of Art
1000 Fifth Avenue
New York, New York 10028
metmuseum.org

Distributed by
Yale University Press, New Haven and London
yalebooks.com/art
yalebooks.co.uk

Cataloguing-in-Publication Data is available from the Library of Congress.
ISBN 978-1-58839-723-2

# CONTENTS

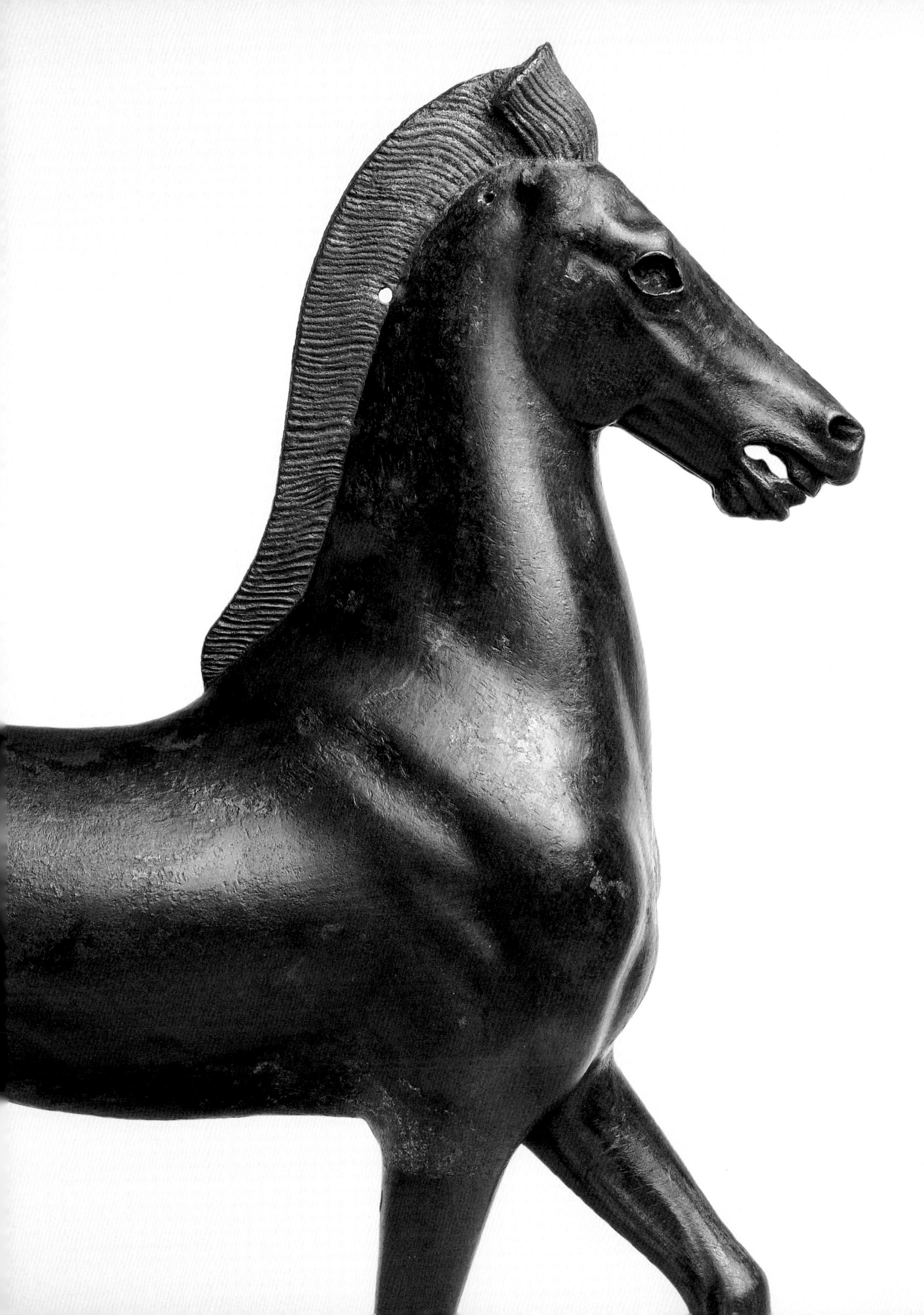

# DIRECTOR'S FOREWORD

The sculptural tradition developed by the ancient Greeks over the span of eight centuries is justifiably considered one of the most remarkable achievements in Western art. In their earliest works, Greek sculptors emphasized the essence of form with a reductive mathematical precision that displayed an understanding of the very building blocks of life. From this sense of order and a devotion to excellence in their craft, they charted a trajectory toward an idealized naturalism that became a hallmark of the sculpture of the Classical Age. Following on the unprecedented conquests of Alexander the Great, sculptors during the Hellenistic Age adopted a new internationalism that led to a host of different styles.

The works selected for inclusion in this book by Seán Hemingway, John A. and Carole O. Moran Curator in Charge of the Department of Greek and Roman Art, are drawn from his own in-depth work with The Met collection over a period of more than twenty years. They offer a thought-provoking account of the wonders achieved by Greek sculptors. Featured are sculptures in a wide variety of media and subjects that span the everyday to the divine as well as the rich mythic world that intertwined the two in ancient Greece. Among the works selected are representations of athletes, children, domesticated animals, and people dancing or deep in thought, all reminding us of the long thread of our shared humanity. They illustrate how, over two millennia ago, Greek artists captured so brilliantly many of the fundamental aspects of the human condition.

This book, the tenth in a series, is the second devoted to Greek art. It follows on the very successful *How to Read Greek Vases* by Joan R. Mertens, Curator Emerita in the Department of Greek and Roman Art, and is organized in the same fashion. Vases and sculptures represent two of the great strengths in The Met's holdings of ancient Greek art, which are beautifully displayed in the majestic Beaux-Arts galleries designed for the Greek and Roman collection, immediately south of the Museum's Great Hall. I encourage our readers to visit these galleries, where they will be able to look anew at the remarkable sculptures presented here and at a multitude of others on display.

We gratefully acknowledge James and Mary Hyde Ottaway, the Jenny Boondas Fund, and the Friends of Greek and Roman Art: Philodoroi for support that made this book possible.

Max Hollein
Marina Kellen French Director
The Metropolitan Museum of Art

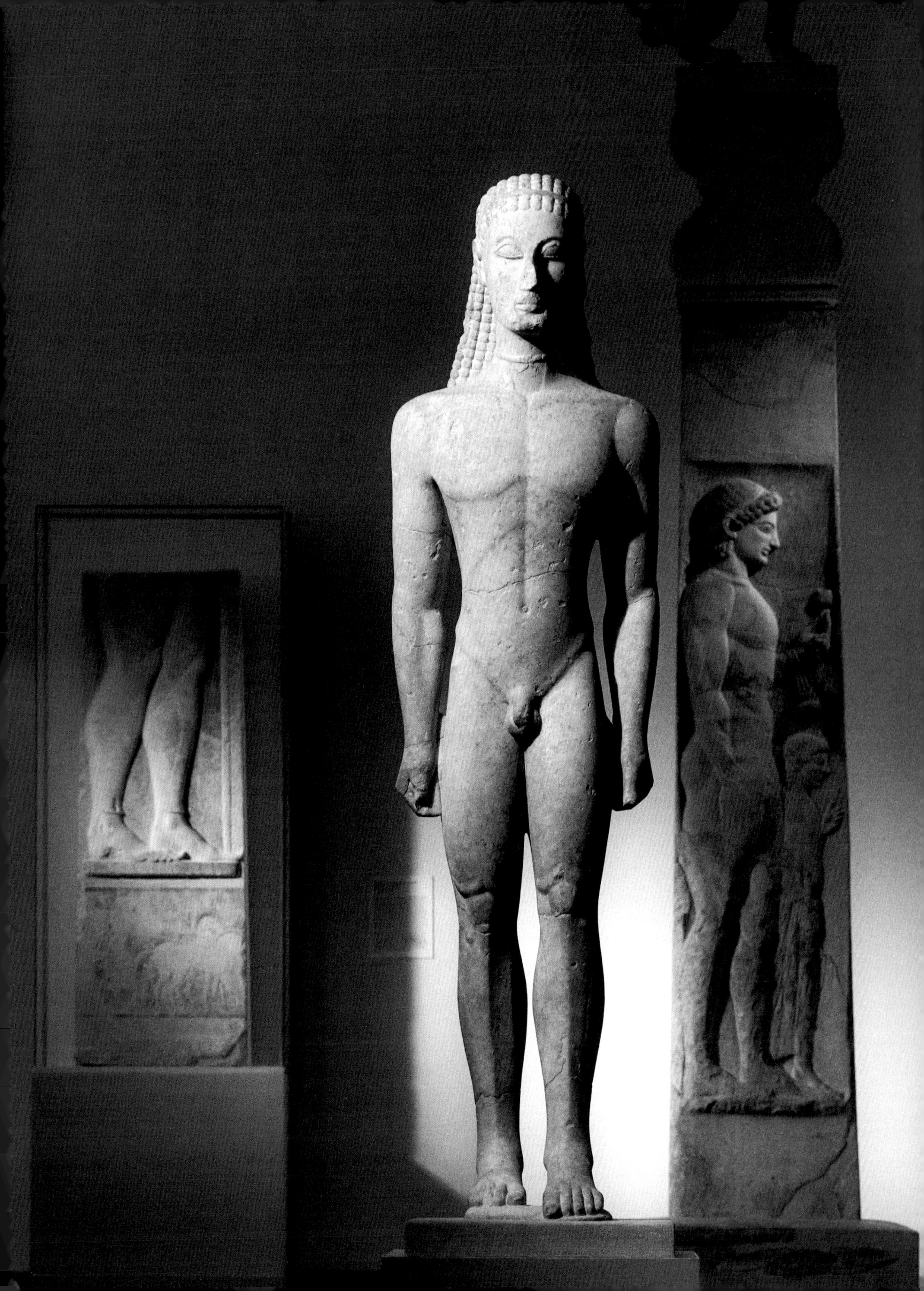

# ACKNOWLEDGMENTS

It is a pleasure to acknowledge here the numerous individuals who have helped with this publication. My first thanks are to Daniel H. Weiss, President and Chief Executive Officer, and Max Hollein, Marina Kellen French Director, The Metropolitan Museum of Art, for their support. I thank Carlos A. Picón, former Curator in Charge of the Department of Greek and Roman Art, for initially encouraging me to undertake the project. I am grateful to Mark Polizzotti, Publisher and Editor in Chief, and his team, including Peter Antony, Rachel High, Gwen Roginsky, and Michael Sittenfeld, for their collaboration, and particularly to Production Manager Chris Zichello, Image Acquisitions Specialist Josephine Rodriguez-Massop, and my editor, Margaret Donovan, for her thoughtful review of my text, which led to significant improvements. Special thanks to Cindy Hwang and Rita Jules of Miko McGinty Inc. for their beautiful design work. The generosity of James and Mary Hyde Ottaway, the Jenny Boondas Fund, and the Friends of Greek and Roman Art: Philodoroi made this volume possible.

In the Department of Greek and Roman Art, I would like to acknowledge Michael J. Baran, Katherine Daniels, Debbie T. Kuo, Sarah E. Lepinski, Lenka Maskova, Joan R. Mertens, Maya B. Muratov, Pavol Roskovensky, Jennifer S. Soupios, and Sarah Szeliga. In 2016–17, at the outset of the project, Madeleine Glennon, a Curatorial Studies Fellow working under my supervision, kindly assisted with preliminary research on the sculptures. My hat is off to Barbara J. Bridgers, former Head of the Imaging Department; William Scott Geffert, General Manager; and their team, especially the Museum's photographers, notably Paul H. Lachenauer, Oi-Cheong Lee, Juan Trujillo, Katherine Dahab, and Eugenia B. Tinsley, who have made such excellent images to accompany the text. For technical discussions and numerous collaborations on the sculptures featured in this book, I am grateful to Dorothy H. Abramitis in the Department of Objects Conservation, as well as to Marco Leona, David H. Koch Scientist in Charge, and Federico Caró, Research Scientist, in the Department of Scientific Research.

My own pursuits in the study of ancient sculpture have been encouraged by a number of generous mentors and colleagues. Among these, I would like to single out Brunilde S. Ridgway, along with Colette Czapski Hemingway, Carol C. Mattusch, Elizabeth J. Milleker, David G. Mitten, Andrew Stewart, and Paul Zanker. In addition, I want to thank the following individuals: Amy Brauer; Jennifer Brown; Sharon H. Cott; Stephen L. Gavel; Patrick and Carol Hemingway; Valerie M. Hemingway; John A. and Carole O. Moran; Rebecca Noonan Murray; Meredith Reiss; Jeff L. Rosenheim, Joyce Frank Menschel Curator in Charge, Department of Photographs; Bruce J. Schwartz; and Shelby White. A special note of appreciation goes to my wife, Colette, and daughter, Anouk, for their support and understanding as I wrote this book largely at home during the COVID-19 pandemic.

Seán Hemingway
John A. and Carole O. Moran Curator in Charge
Department of Greek and Roman Art

# GREECE AND ASIA MINOR

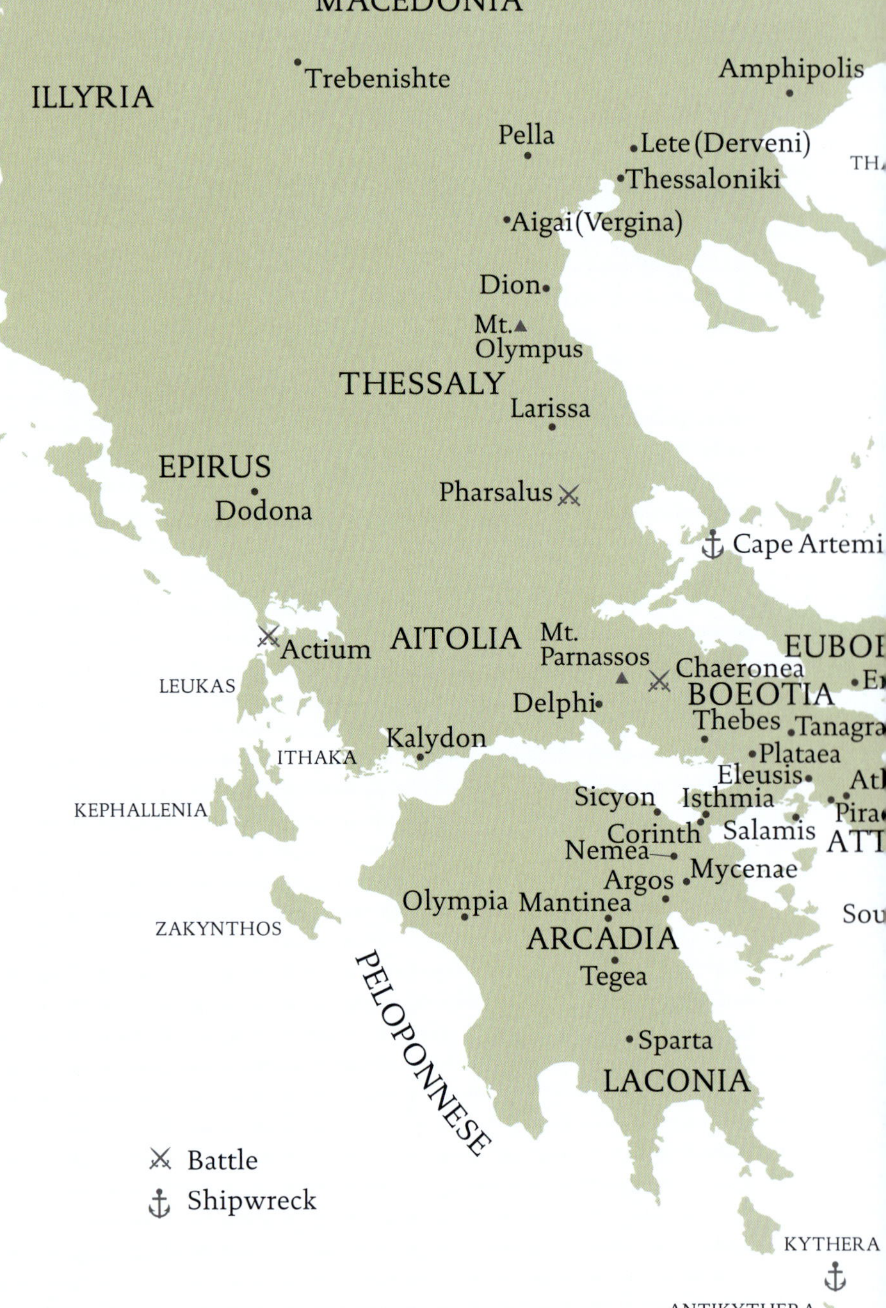

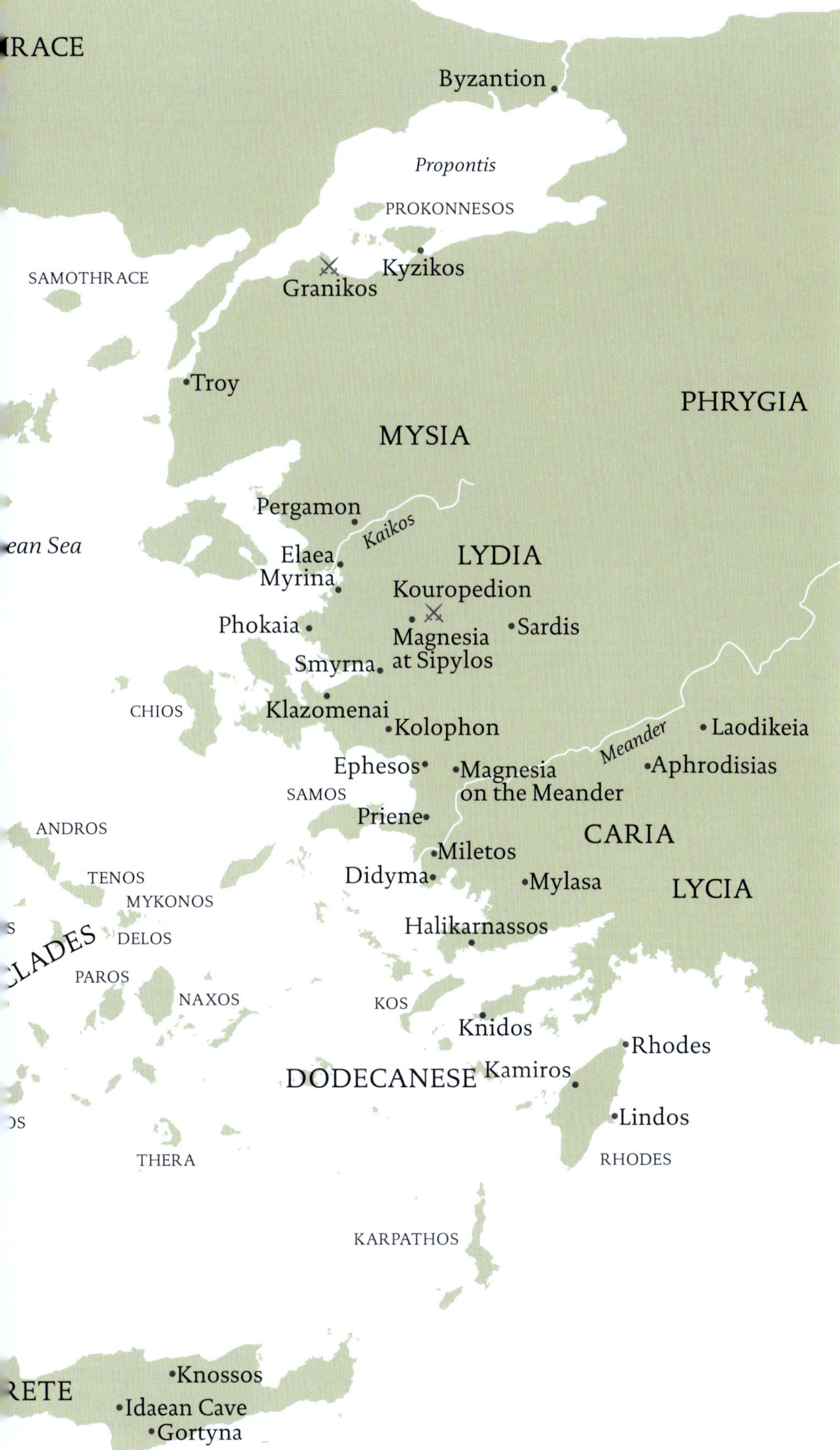

RACE
Byzantion
Propontis
PROKONNESOS
SAMOTHRACE
Kyzikos
Granikos
Troy
PHRYGIA
MYSIA
Pergamon
Kaikos
ean Sea
Elaea
LYDIA
Myrina
Kouropedion
Phokaia
Sardis
Magnesia
at Sipylos
Smyrna
CHIOS
Klazomenai
Kolophon
Laodikeia
Meander
Ephesos
Magnesia
on the Meander
Aphrodisias
SAMOS
Priene
ANDROS
CARIA
Miletos
TENOS
Didyma
Mylasa
LYCIA
MYKONOS
LADES
DELOS
Halikarnassos
PAROS
NAXOS
KOS
Knidos
Rhodes
Kamiros
DODECANESE
Lindos
THERA
RHODES
KARPATHOS
Knossos
RETE
Idaean Cave
Gortyna

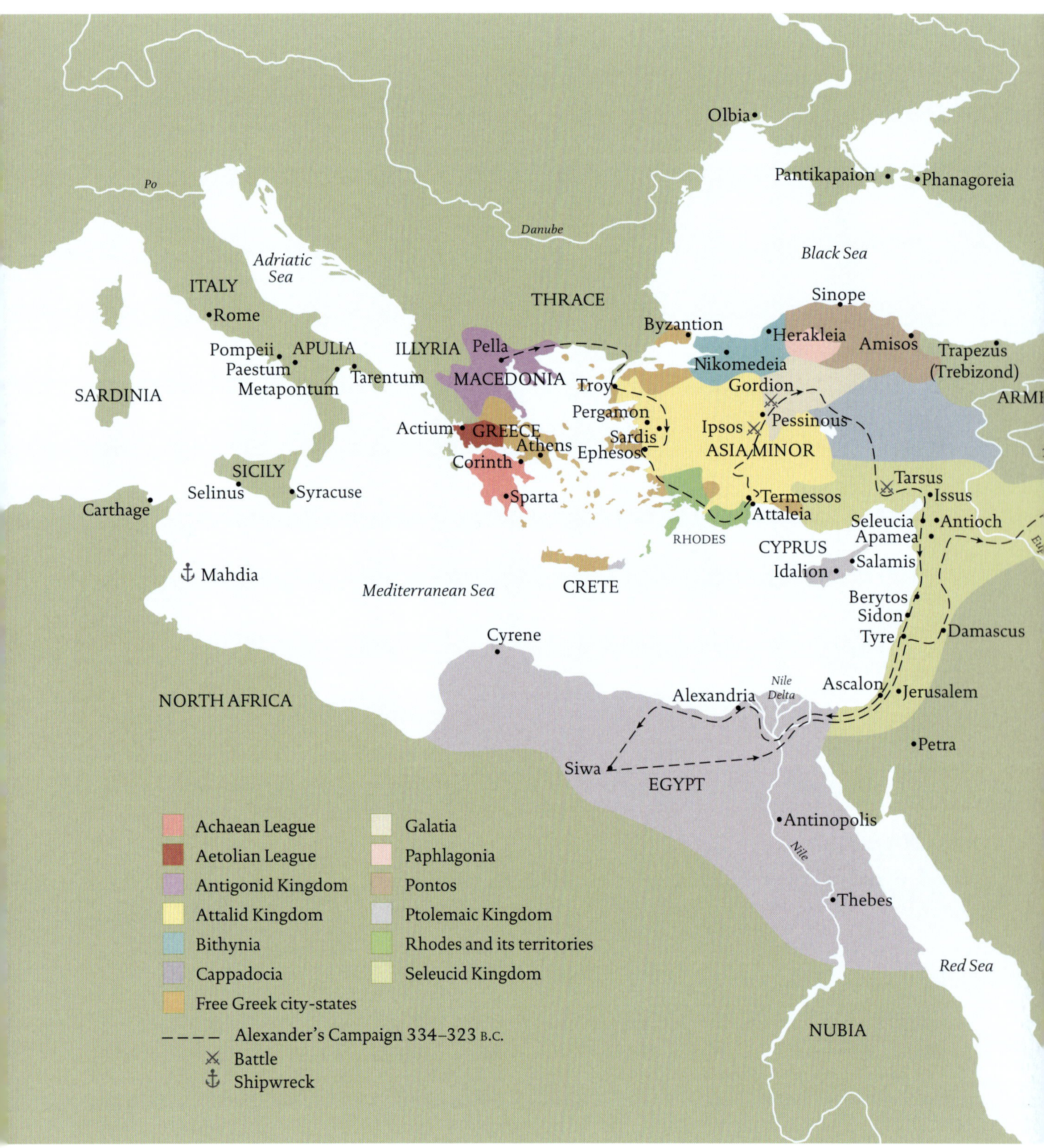


# HELLENISTIC KINGDOMS, CA. 185 B.C.

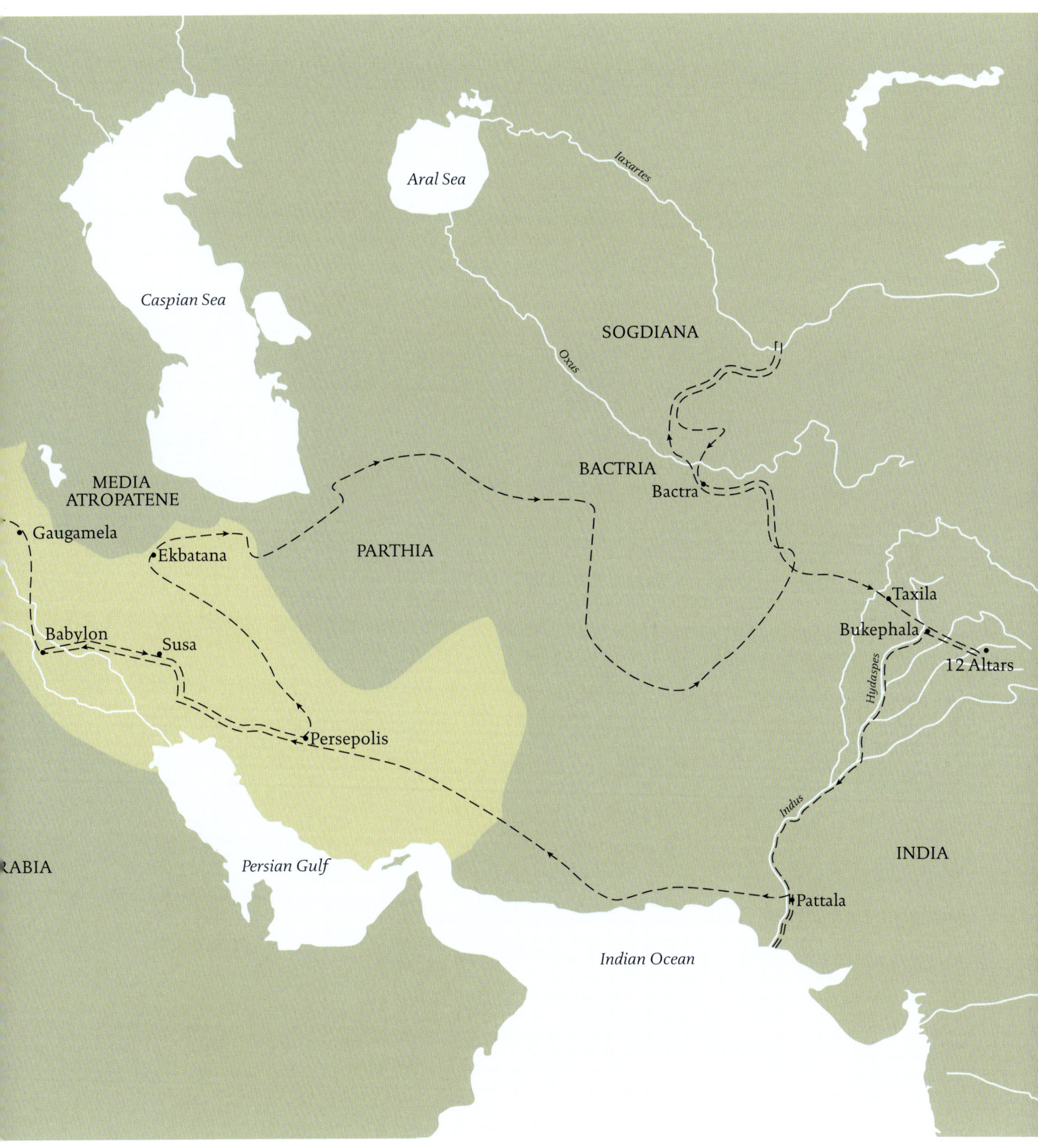
Aral Sea
Iaxartes
Caspian Sea
SOGDIANA
Oxus
MEDIA
ATROPATENE
BACTRIA
Bactra
Gaugamela
Ekbatana
PARTHIA
Taxila
Bukephala
Babylon
Susa
12 Altars
Hydaspes
Persepolis
Indus
INDIA
RABIA
Persian Gulf
Pattala
Indian Ocean

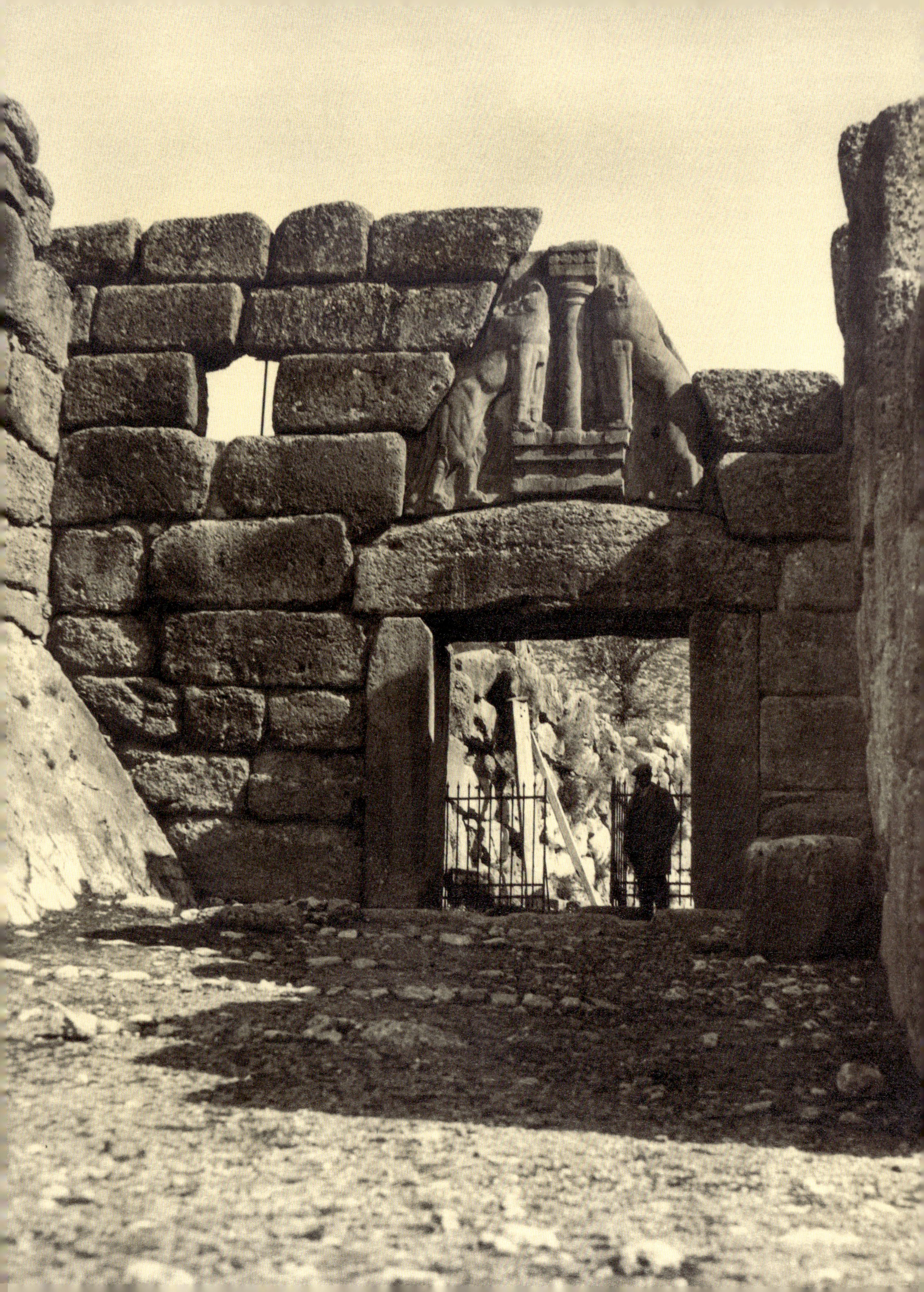

# Introduction

The achievements of Greek sculptors rank among the greatest and most recognizable accomplishments in the history of art. This book aims to present their successes in broad strokes through close examination of a selection of sculptures in the collection of The Metropolitan Museum of Art. While the emphasis of similar studies has traditionally been upon large-scale works of stone and bronze as well as upon the lost masterpieces of gold and ivory sculpture, a broader approach is taken here. We consider a wider variety of small-scale works in bronze, gold, ivory, terracotta, and stone along with a selection of artifacts—mostly utensils and vessels but also architectural elements—that incorporate sculpture into their forms with considerable effectiveness. This is not, therefore, a comprehensive overview of the subject but a more selective survey of a group of sculptures (nos. 1–40) that nonetheless yields interesting results.

Sculpture is by its nature three-dimensional, and knowledge of ancient Greek examples derives in large part from close study and firsthand observation. The excellent photographs presented here provide useful and carefully chosen vantage points, but if you wish to continue on your own journey toward becoming literate in the subject you will want to come to the Museum, where you can see the works for yourself from the many perspectives they offer. Indeed, seek out as many other original ancient Greek sculptures as you can. It will be time well spent, and the cumulative knowledge that you acquire will enable you to hone your eye and your appreciation for these wondrous works of art. The study of Greek sculpture and the ancient culture that fostered its creation can be a rewarding lifetime pursuit.

Our era of concern is roughly eight centuries, from the Geometric period, beginning about 900 B.C., through the Hellenistic Age, ending in 31 B.C. There are earlier traditions of sculpture in Greece, notably the marble sculptures of the Neolithic and Early Bronze Ages in the Cyclades as well as the diverse sculptural arts of Minoan Crete and Mycenaean Greece, but for the most part these are far removed from the works under consideration here. To be sure, the Lion Gate at Mycenae (fig. 1), which has remained visible since its construction in the fourteenth century B.C., must have impressed ancient Greeks as a marvel from an earlier age of heroes, and other sculptural relics would have surfaced from time to time, but they are the exception rather than the norm. The impoverished centuries after the collapse of the Mycenaean palaces have long been known as a dark age. In many ways, the dawn of the first millennium B.C. heralded a new epoch for Greek sculpture.

Fig. 1. Martin Birnbaum. *Mycenae—Gate of the Lions*, ca. 1957. Photogravure, image: 9 7/16 × 6 13/16 in. (23.9 × 17.2 cm). Gift of the artist, 1957 (57.562.5)

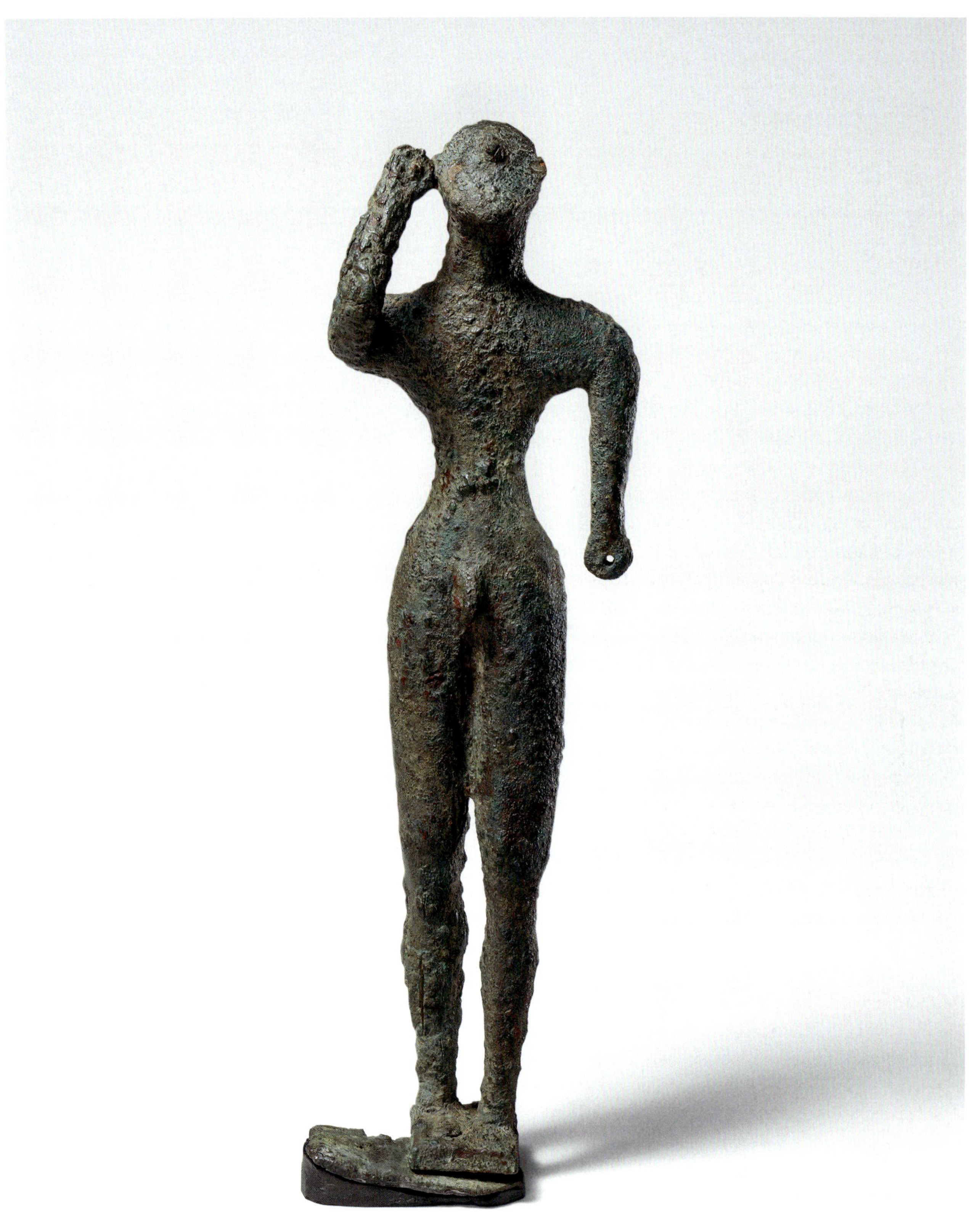

Fig. 2. Statuette of a warrior. Greek, Geometric period, ca. 750–700 B.C. Bronze, H. 6⅞ in. (17.5 cm). Fletcher Fund, 1936 (36.11.8)

## GEOMETRIC PERIOD

It was during the Geometric period (ca. 900–700 B.C.) that the primary institutions of Greek civilization were established. The major Greek city-states, such as Athens, Corinth, and Sparta, began to flourish, and the first Panhellenic (literally, "for all Greeks") sanctuaries were created with their elaborate festivals and competitions that brought those city-states together. Inspired in part by the Phoenician script, the Greek alphabet was developed, and writing quickly spread, enabling rich oral histories of myths and legends to be recorded in a more permanent fashion. The eighth century B.C. is the time of Homer, the great poet whose epic accounts of the Trojan War and the travels of the long-suffering hero Odysseus are enduring sources of inspiration for Greek art and culture.

Geometric art takes its name from the pottery of the period, which is decorated with rectilinear and curvilinear designs. The sculpture of the time also reflects this interest in geometry, not just in the use of designs but in the elements used to create form. At the core of Geometric sculpture is the manifestation of order and rhythm, a fundamental aspect of Greek art throughout antiquity. Many of the best sculptures that survive from this era are small bronze statuettes. The bronze horse that begins our selection of sculptures is a particularly fine specimen (no. 1). Another superlative example is a bronze warrior of the second half of the eighth century B.C. who stands tall, with his right arm raised, and originally held a spear ready to strike (fig. 2). With a minimum amount of modeling, the artist has reduced the human form to its essence. Certain stylistic elements, such as his long legs and the shape of his broad chest, echo Minoan conventions, and the sculpture was most likely made by a Cretan artist. The rectangular base that the warrior stands on has pins affixing it to a thin sheet of metal. This feature indicates that the figure originally decorated the rim of a large bronze cauldron with ring handles, a popular type of votive dedication at Greek sanctuaries in this period.

A small statuette in The Met collection presents a rare image from this early period of a Greek artisan at work (fig. 3). The figure, which originally held a mallet in his right hand, sits with one knee raised as he steadies and shapes a bronze helmet on a support. Such bronzesmiths produced a variety of metalwork, including sculptures. The first large-scale ancient Greek bronze statues were made in the Geometric period from hammered sheet metal by a technique known as *sphyrelaton* (literally, "hammer-driven"). The process of their manufacture would have been very similar to that employed in making armor. This small statuette was probably created as a votive dedication at a sanctuary to thank the gods for the completion of a successful commission.

Of the thousands of early Greek bronze horse statuettes known today, most have been found at sanctuaries, especially Olympia, the most sacred site devoted to Zeus, father of the Olympian gods. Single horses are particularly common (no. 1), but groups of up to four also exist. A tender image of a mare and her foal may have been a thank offering dedicated at a sanctuary for the successful birthing of a purebred steed (fig. 4). Less austere than other works of the period, it reflects the more personal subjects that characterize many small Geometric bronzes. Numerous other animals and a variety of human types

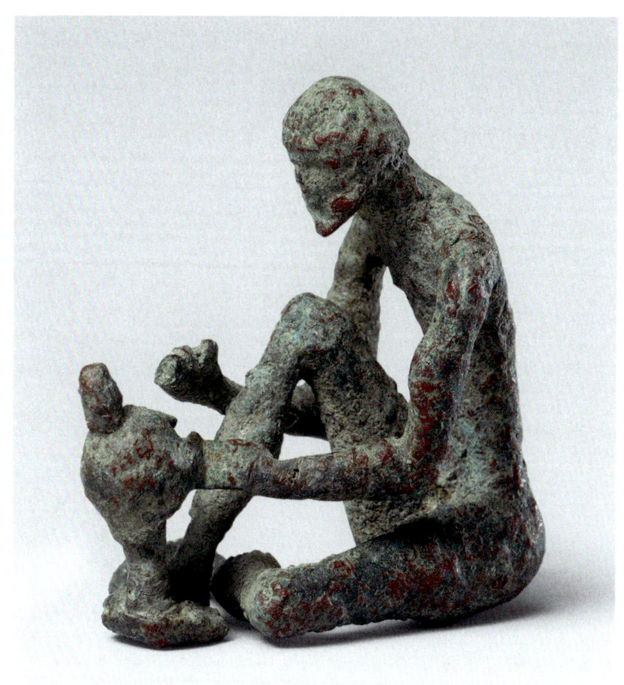

Fig. 3. Statuette of an armorer working on a helmet. Greek, Geometric period, late 8th–early 7th century B.C. Bronze, H. 2 in. (5.1 cm). Fletcher Fund, 1942 (42.11.42)

were also made. With their minimalist forms, the specific meanings of Geometric small-scale bronze sculptures are often hard to pin down. This is especially true of the more complex groups (no. 2), which are much rarer and often represent mythological scenes.

## ARCHAIC PERIOD

During the seventh and sixth centuries B.C., a dramatic change occurred in Greek sculpture that ushered in the Archaic period (ca. 700–480 B.C.). The abstract Geometric style of the preceding period was supplanted by more naturalistic renderings that were strongly influenced by greatly expanded contacts with the Near East and Egypt. Greek settlements along the coast of Asia Minor, trading posts set up in the Nile Delta of Egypt and in the Levant, major colonies established at sites across the Mediterranean, and contact with itinerant artists, notably on Cyprus and Crete, all inspired Greek sculptors to adopt a new repertoire of iconography and to work in the broader range of materials that became available through newly established trade networks (no. 3).

Fantastic mythological creatures such as griffins (no. 4) and Sphinxes became popular subjects, especially as guardian figures. Although derived from Near Eastern and Egyptian prototypes, these subjects were transformed by Greek sculptors who made them their own by developing distinct stylistic features. A bronze foot in the form of a Sphinx presents the salient elements that appealed to Greek sculptors (fig. 5). This creature—almost always female in Greece, unlike in Egypt—comprises the head of a beautiful woman and a body that combines those of a lion and an eagle. With its block cut and rows of curls, the hairstyle of this Sphinx is known as Daedalic, a fashion popular on Crete and the Greek islands in the seventh century B.C. The foot itself was one of several that would have supported a large shallow basin. Its overt frontal pose and inlaid pupils add to its strength and power to ward off evil.

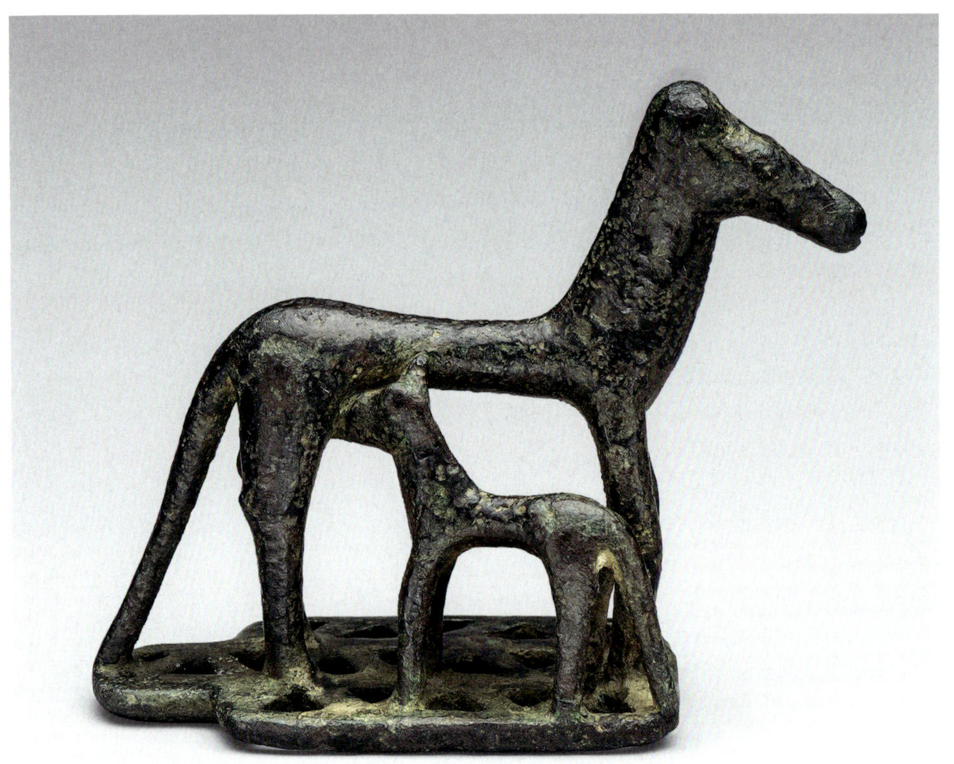

Fig. 4. Statuette of a mare and foal. Greek, Geometric period, late 8th century B.C. Bronze, H. 3⅞ in. (9.8 cm). Gift of Mrs. Frederick M. Stafford, in memory of Mr. Frederick M. Stafford, 1999 (1999.526)

Fig. 5. Foot in the form of a Sphinx. Greek, Archaic period, ca. 600 B.C. Bronze, H. 10⅞ in. (27.6 cm). Gift from the family of Howard J. Barnet, in his memory, 2000 (2000.660)

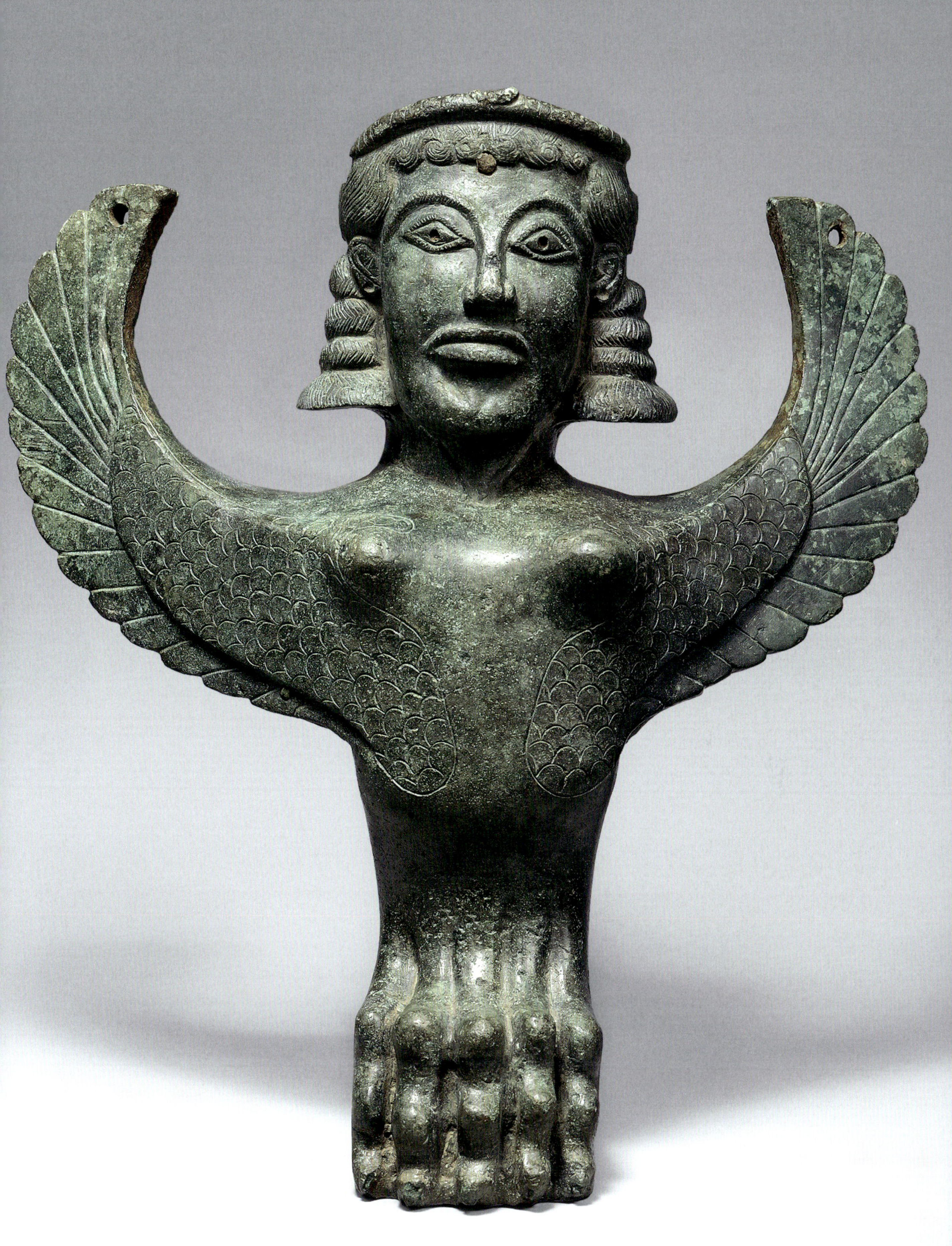

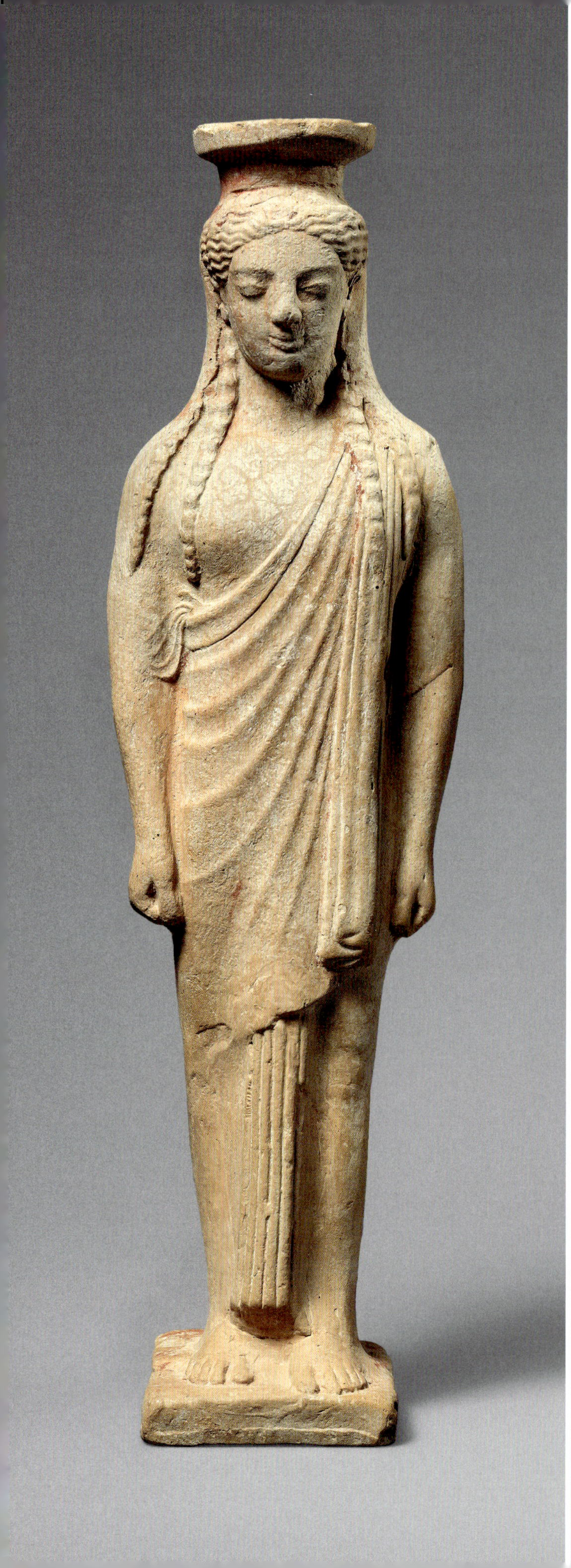

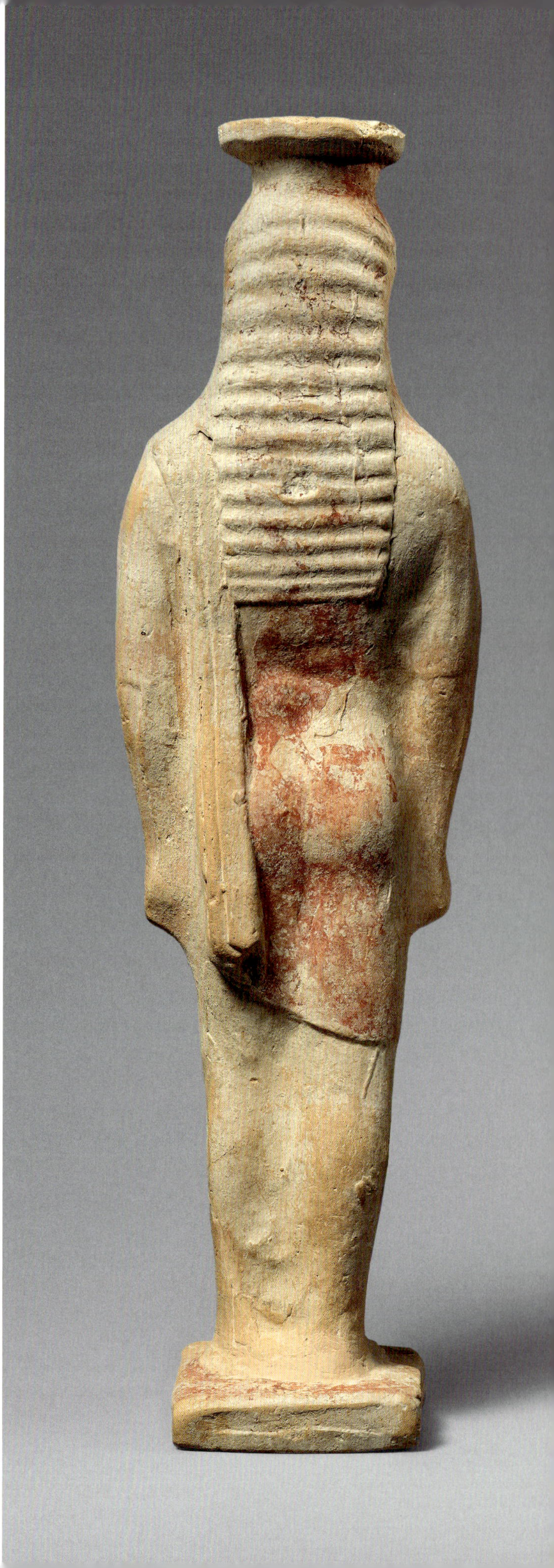

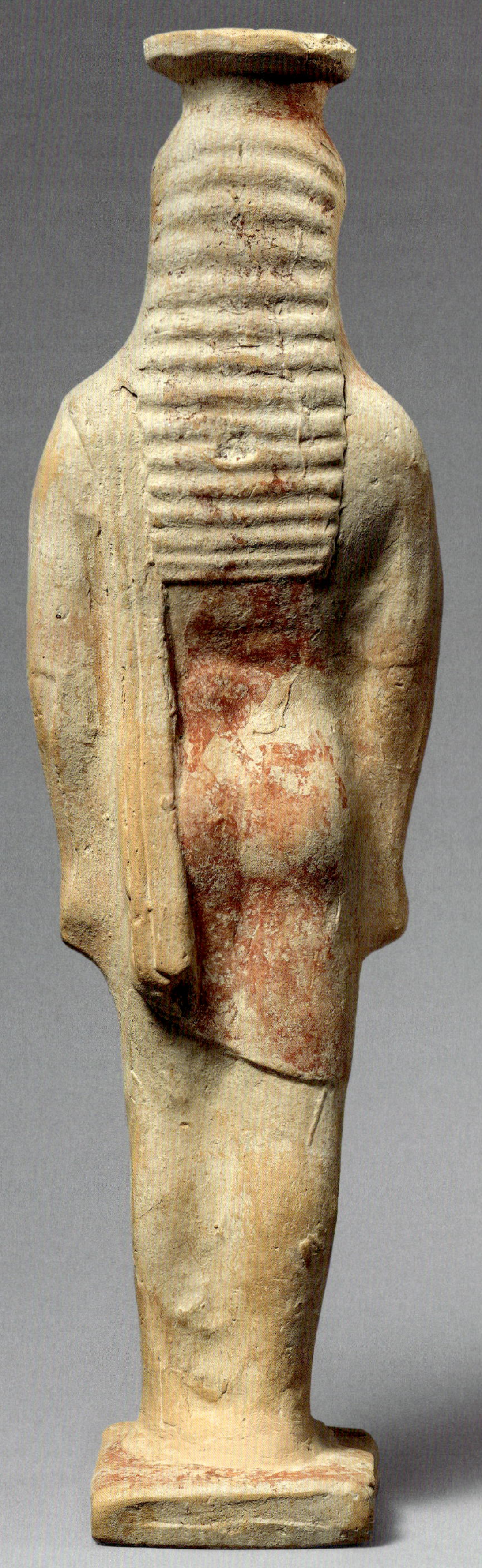

During the sixth century B.C., representations of the nude standing youth (*kouros*) and the draped standing female figure (*kore*) were the predominant forms of freestanding Greek sculpture. Like all monumental sculptures of their day, the statues had religious significance, as dedications in sanctuaries or as tomb markers that served as permanent memorials to the dead. The New York Kouros is one of the earliest examples preserved today from the region of Attica (no. 6). The monumental scale of these works and their use of stone were inspired by Egyptian precedents, and the New York Kouros is remarkable for its adoption of an Egyptian canon of proportions that makes the association still more explicit.

Variations in the representation of youths and maidens in the Archaic period provide a good example of how even basic issues of identification can be difficult with Greek sculpture. A terracotta alabastron (perfume vase) in the form of a standing figure wearing a chiton (long garment) covered by a himation (cloak) was long identified as an image of a *kore* (fig. 6). However, further study of the type and consideration of other representations from the eastern Greek islands and the coast of Asia Minor made it clear that a youth is represented. Young men generally wore their hair long (fig. 7), and social mores in the Greek East led to different fashion trends and distinct sculptural types of male representation.

Sculpture played an important role in the decoration of Greek architecture. In the sixth century B.C., monumental temples were erected in stone throughout the Greek world, and the upper elements of their facades as well as their roofs were embellished with sculpture. Two orders dominated: the Doric, prevalent in mainland Greece and its colonies, and the Ionic, favored in the Greek settlements along the coast of Asia Minor and in the Dodecanese Islands. In Doric architecture, the pediment, a triangular space beneath the gables of the roof, was often the primary location for sculptural adornment. A series of pediments belonging to temples and shrines on the Athenian Acropolis excavated in the late nineteenth century provide good examples of the powerful, mythic subjects featured in the Archaic period. Emile

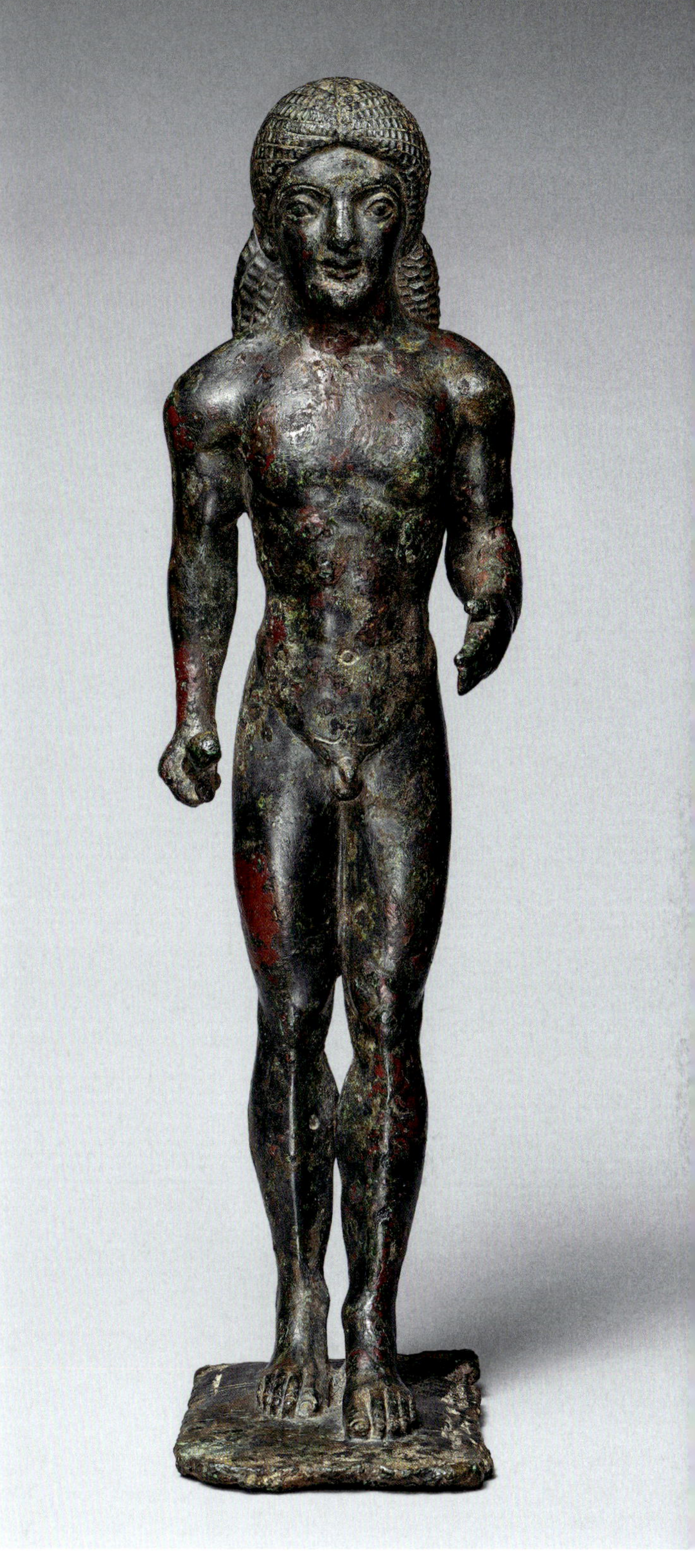

Fig. 7. Statuette of a *kouros* (youth). Greek, Archaic period, ca. 550–525 B.C. Bronze, H. 6 in. (15.2 cm). Bequest of Walter C. Baker, 1971 (1972.118.101)

Fig. 6. Alabastron (perfume vase) in the form of a youth. East Greek, Archaic period, mid-6th century B.C. Terracotta, H. 10½ in. (26.7 cm). Fletcher Fund, 1935 (35.11.4)

Gilliéron's watercolor paintings of the Acropolis limestone pediments record their vibrant colors, including red, blue, black, green, and ocher, at the time of their discovery, before they were altered by prolonged exposure to the elements. Look, for example, at "Bluebeard," which originally filled one triangular end of a pediment decorating a large temple on the Acropolis (fig. 8). This fantastic triple-bodied beast with feathered wings and a snaky tail is shown holding the attributes of water, sky, and earth in its hands. The bold colors were applied without a stucco undercoating, and the strong palette enabled the artists to bring out details of the sculptural decoration that otherwise would have been difficult to see from a significant distance, as was necessary for sculpture displayed high on a building.

It is important to remember that most ancient Greek sculpture was colorful. Today, the paint is rarely well preserved, although The Met collection has a number of unusually vibrant Archaic examples (see, for instance, nos. 9 and 10). A Sphinx that crowns a tall funerary marker, or stele, is remarkable for its extensive traces of polychromy (no. 9). Standing ready to pounce on any who would desecrate the tomb, the figure has brightly colored wings and wears a necklace and diadem decorated with a meander pattern (fig. 9). Scientific studies of sculpture employing an array of techniques have furthered the understanding and appreciation of the kinds of pigments used for ancient Greek sculpture and have helped us to recreate their original appearance.

Most of the time, Greek sculpture survives in a fragmentary state. You must become versed in looking at fragments in order to understand the information they impart and to reconstruct them in your mind's eye. See, for example, a marble relief representing a youth, of which only the head is preserved (fig. 10). He wears a fillet, and the precise snail curls of the hair around his forehead and the nape of his neck contrast with the smooth area above the band, where the hair was most likely rendered with paint. Traces of the red undercoat are still visible. The fragment may well represent an athlete, but it is difficult to know for certain. Comparison with other,

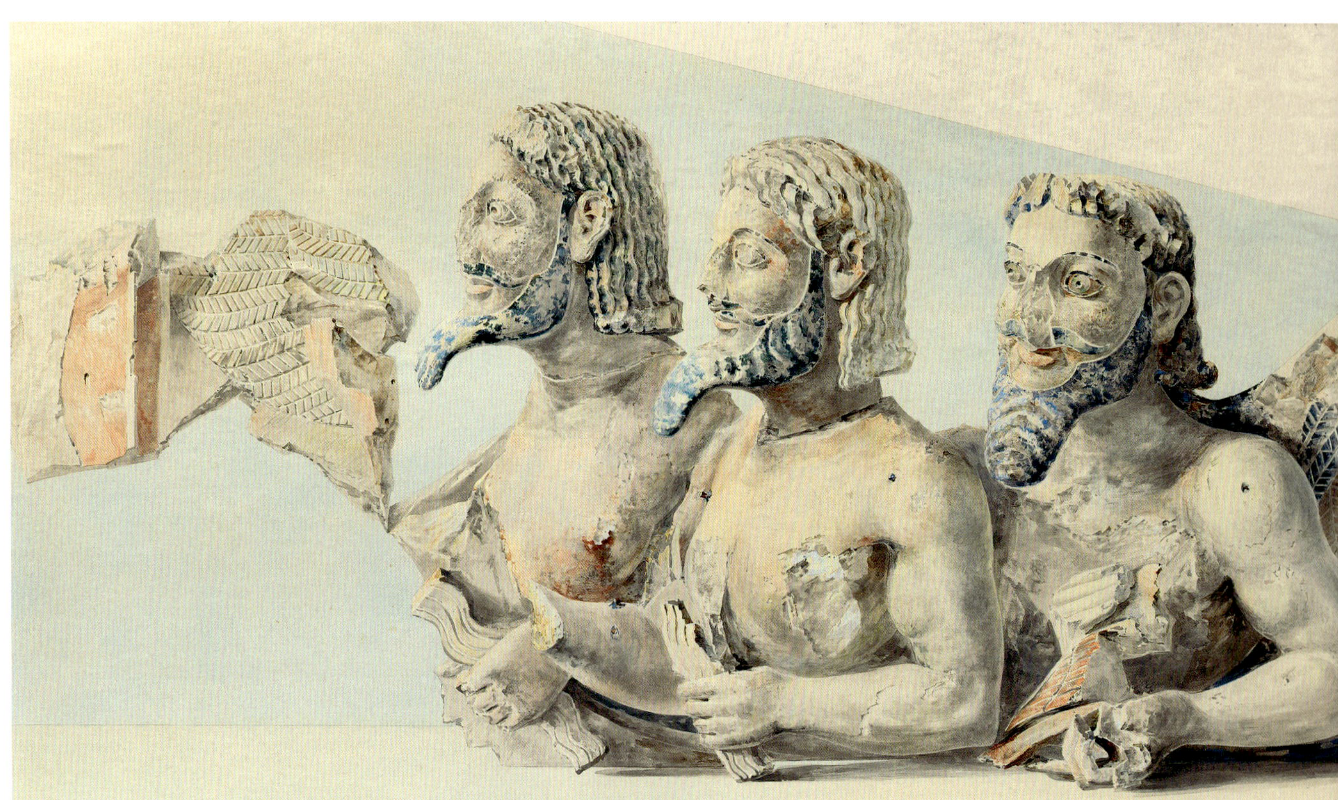

Fig. 8. Emile Gilliéron (1850–1924). Winged three-bodied creature, commonly known as "Bluebeard," from the Athenian Acropolis, 1919. Watercolor, graphite, and crayon, 39⅞ in. × 11 ft. 1 in. (101.3 × 337.8 cm). Dodge Fund, 1919 (19.195.1)

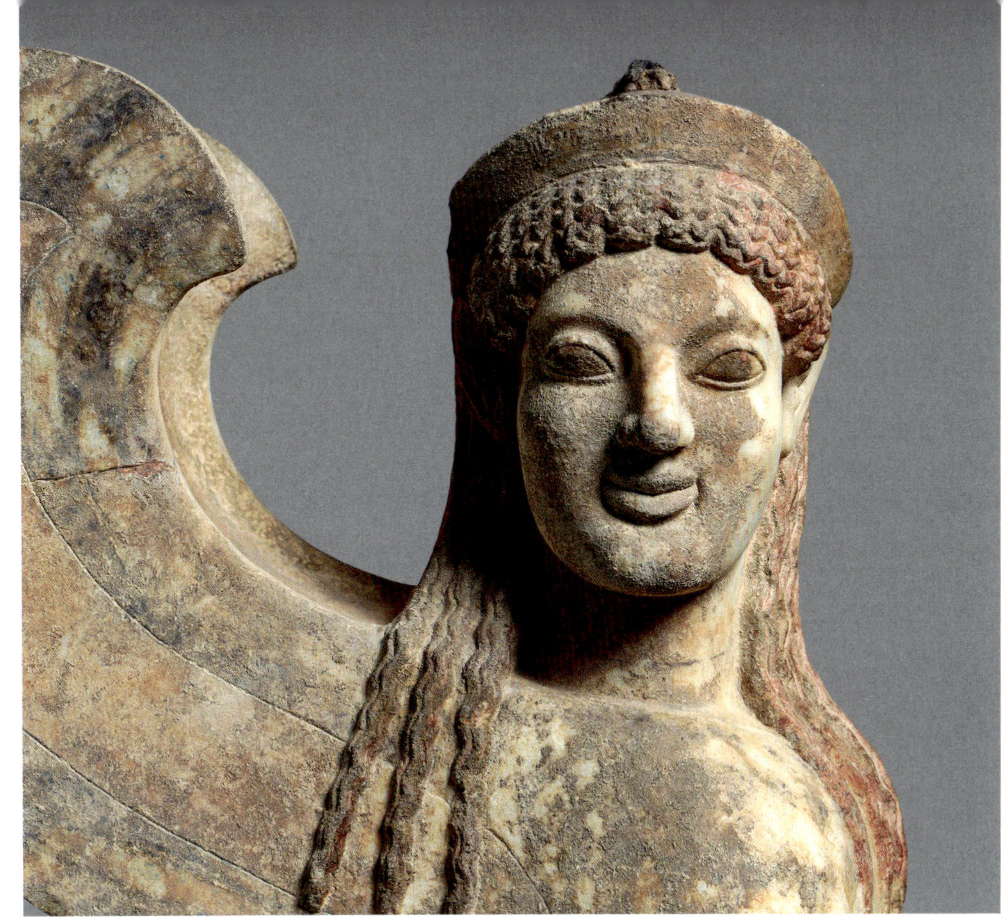

Fig. 9. Detail of a finial in the form of a Sphinx, with extensive remains of polychromy. Greek, Attic, Archaic period, ca. 530 B.C. Marble. Munsey Funds, 1936, 1938 (11.185d, x)

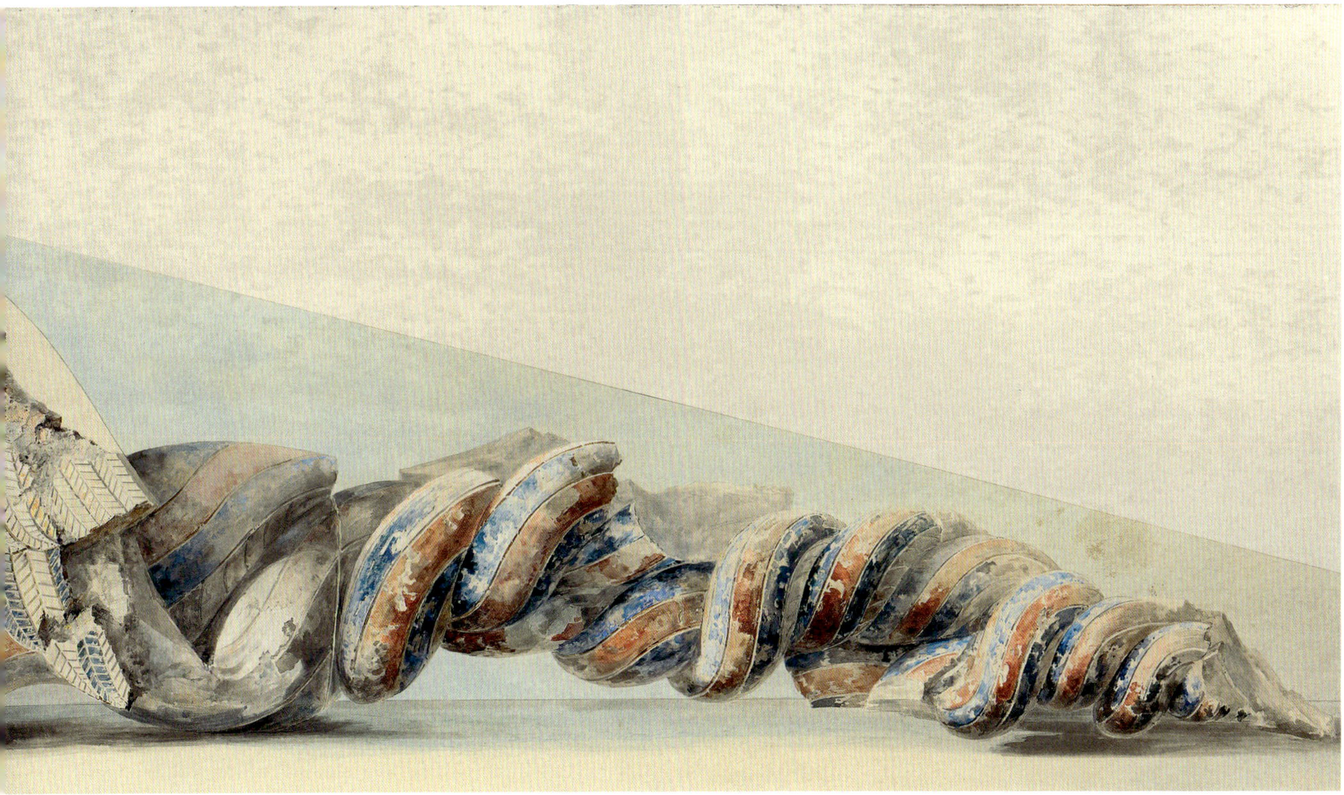

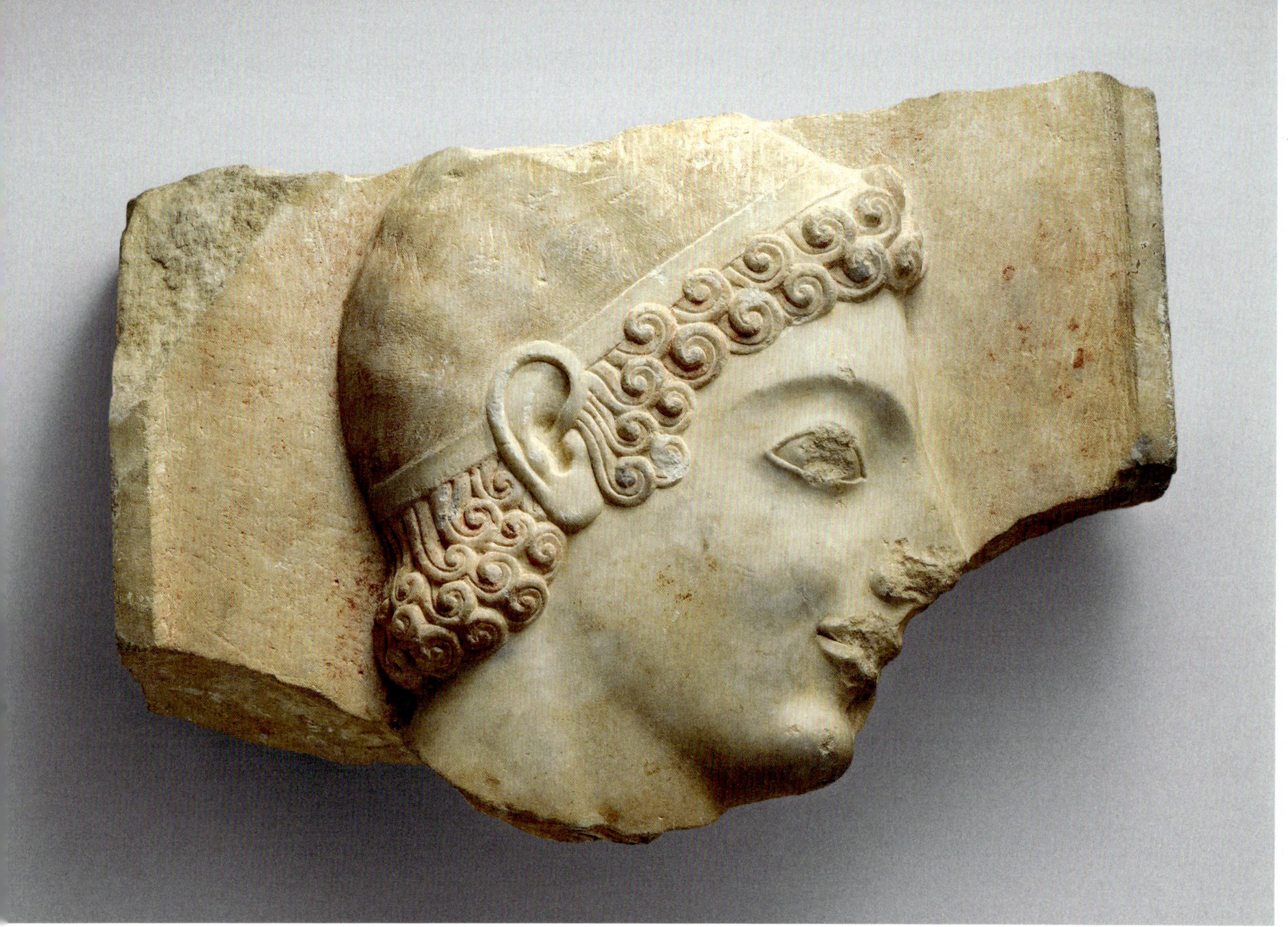

Fig. 10. Head of a youth from a stele (grave marker). Greek, Attic, Archaic period, ca. 525 B.C. Marble, H. 10¼ in. (26 cm). Rogers Fund, 1942 (42.11.36)

better-preserved examples (no. 9, for instance) reveal that the relief was part of a grave stele for a youth who died before his time; the damages to his eye, nose, and mouth contrast markedly with the preserved surface elsewhere and are indicative of intentional desecration. Equally distinctive of The Met collection, however, are the outstanding complete works representing each major period (nos. 1, 5–9, 12, 15, and 32) that enable us to appreciate the entire sculptural form, even if the coloration of the bronze has changed or the paint on the marble has faded.

Greek sculpture was made in a wide variety of materials and took many shapes. Clay, which was malleable and widely available, was a popular medium for freestanding works, sculptural embellishments on vases, and architectural elements. The particularly rich variety of sculptural vases in the Archaic period is well represented in The Met collection (figs. 6 and 11a–f). There are carefully observed

Opposite: Figs. 11a–f. Aryballoi (perfume vases) in various forms

a. Monkey. Greek, Rhodian, Archaic period, ca. 600–575 B.C. Terracotta, H. 3 11/16 in. (9.3 cm). Purchase, Sandra Brue Gift, 1992 (1992.11.2)

b. Helmeted head. East Greek, Archaic period, ca. 600–575 B.C. Terracotta, H. 2¾ in. (7 cm). Rogers Fund, 1941 (41.162.74)

c. Phallus. Greek, Archaic period, ca. 550–500 B.C. Terracotta, H. 4½ in. (11.4 cm). Classical Purchase Fund, 1999 (1999.78)

d. Eagle's head. Greek, Rhodian, Archaic period, ca. late 7th–early 6th century B.C. Terracotta, L. 4⅜ in. (11.1 cm). Purchase, Anonymous Gift, in memory of Sleiman and Souad Aboutaam, 2006 (2006.267)

e. Sandaled right foot. Greek, Rhodian, Archaic period, ca. 550 B.C. Terracotta, H. 2 15/16 in. (7.5 cm). Fletcher Fund, 1924 (24.97.4)

f. Hedgehog. Greek, Rhodian, Archaic period, ca. 550 B.C. Terracotta, L. 2¾ in. (7 cm). Purchase, Winslow Carlton Gift, 1969 (69.11.3)

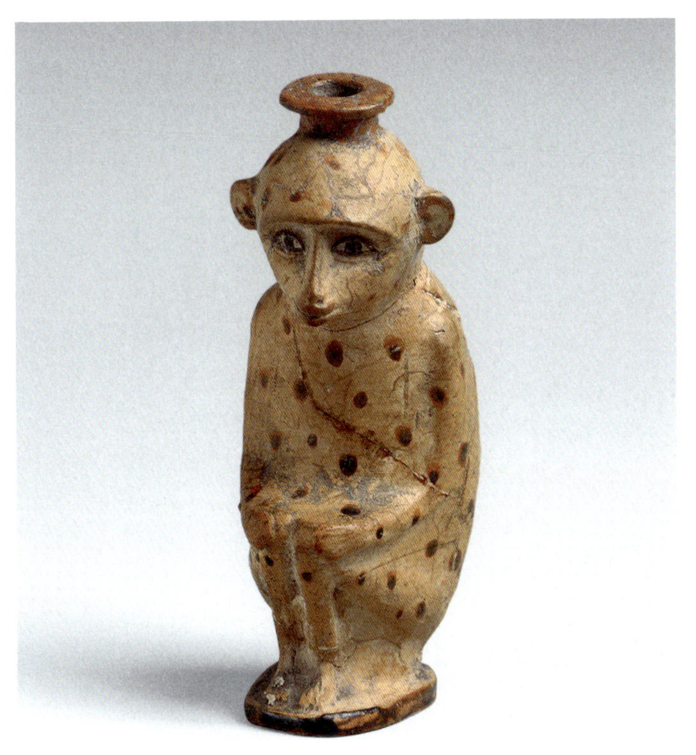

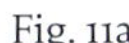
Fig. 11a

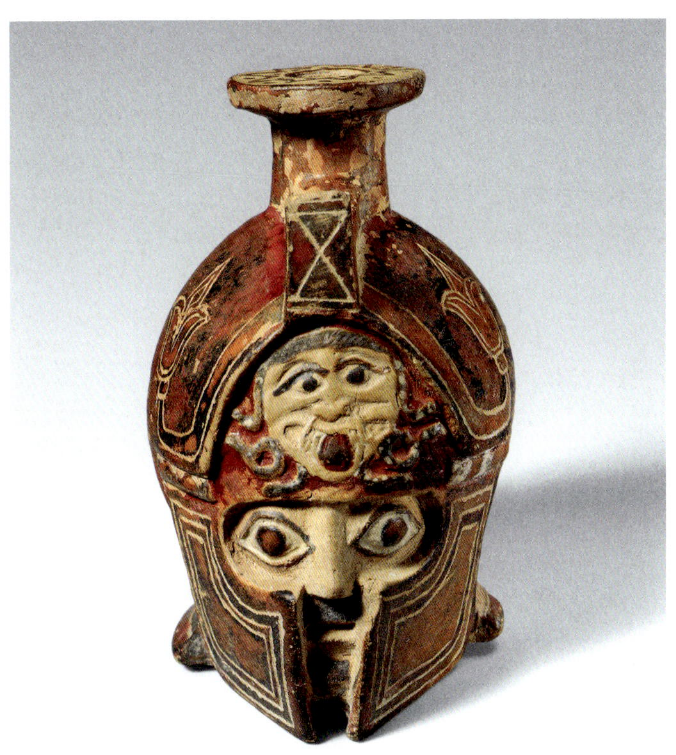

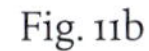
Fig. 11b

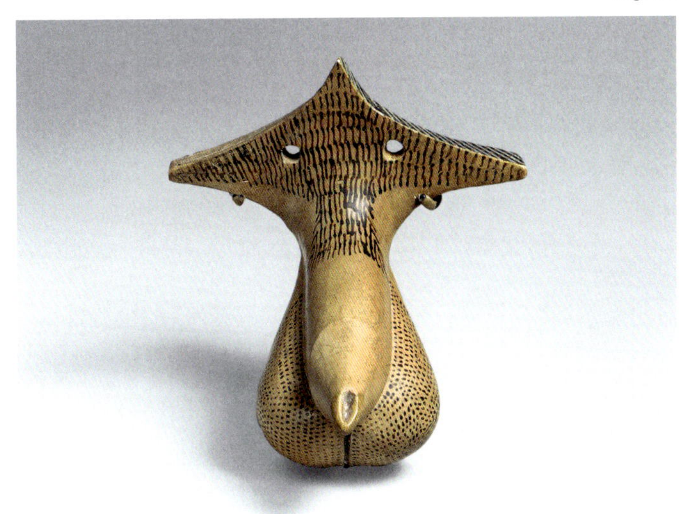

Fig. 11c

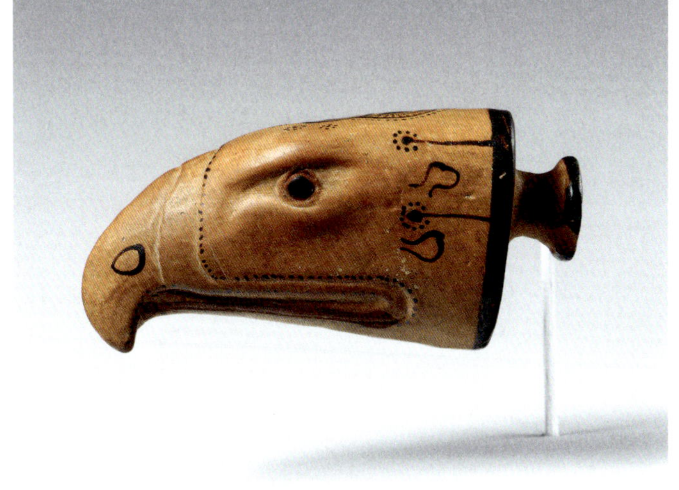

Fig. 11d

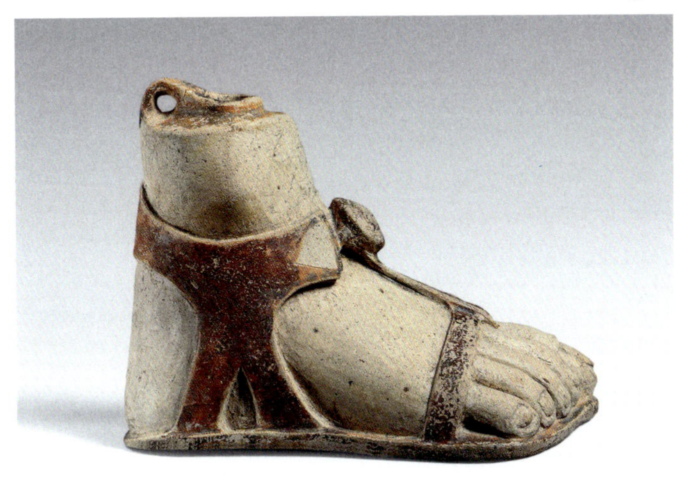

Fig. 11e

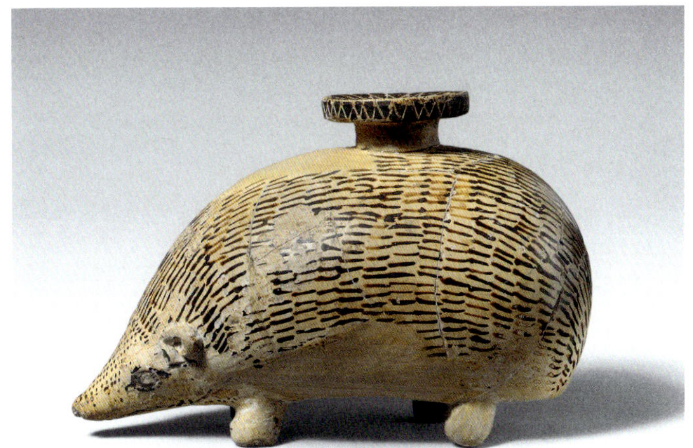

Fig. 11f

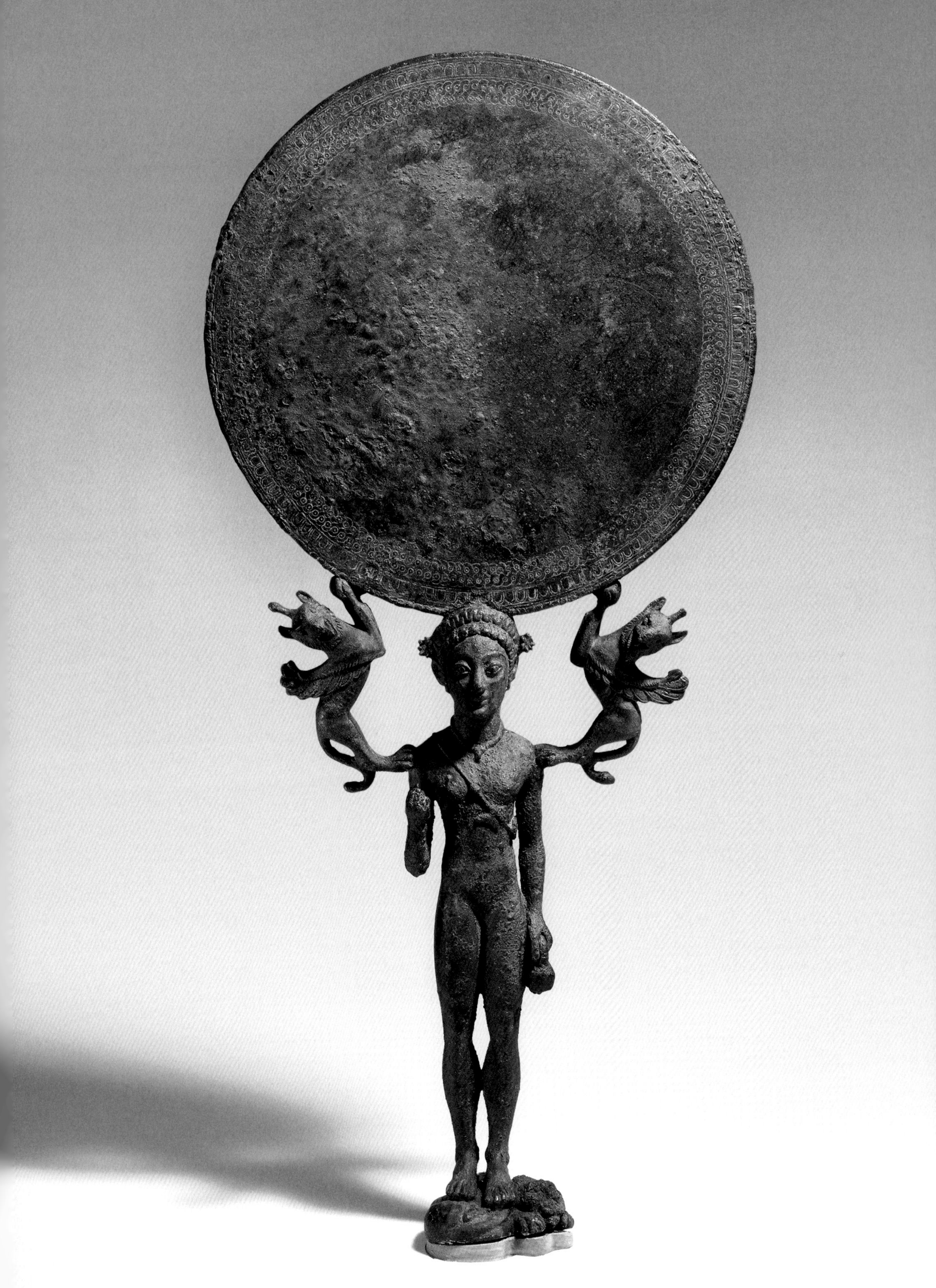

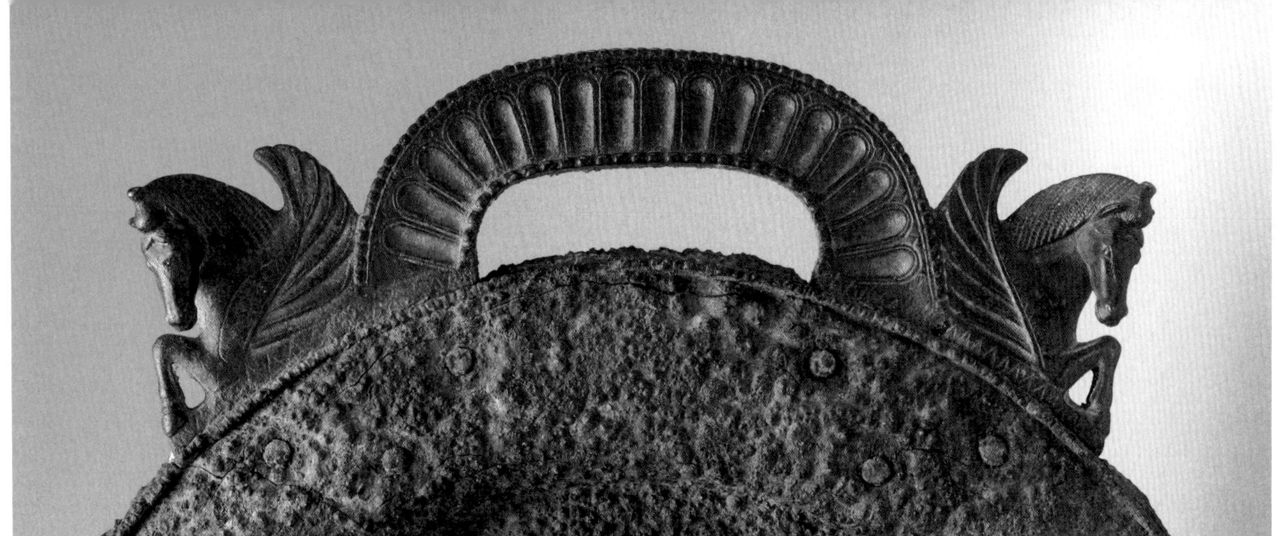

animals, such as monkeys and birds, as well as mythical creatures, including Sirens and the Minotaur. The human form is presented whole (no. 7) or in part, from the feet to the head and everything in between. These small-scale sculptural vases, manufactured in molds and embellished with painted details, often exhibit undercurrents of humor that are a significant aspect of Greek art and not usually seen in monumental sculptures, which are typically imbued with religious significance.

During the Archaic period, artistic styles and preferences varied greatly among regions. Even the Greek language exhibits significant differences from region to region as to the form of the letters of the alphabet, the spelling of words, and their pronunciation. For Greek sculpture, the variation can be seen not only in stylistic trends but also in iconographic choices. A fine bronze mirror with a handle in the form of a nude young woman presents a powerful image of the feminine (fig. 12). The young girl, who may be a devotee of Aphrodite or Artemis, stands on a lion as griffins spring from her shoulders. Grasping a pomegranate by its stem, she wears two flowers in her hair, a necklace with an amulet, and a band across her chest from which hang a crescent pendant and a ring. An Athenian artist would not have represented a young woman nude, but this was clearly not an issue in Laconia, where the mirror was made: the Spartans allowed women to compete in athletic events, and women trained like men.

Finally, before turning to the Classical period, we should take note of a trend in Greek sculptural decoration that has its roots in early Greek art. While the skillful incorporation of sculptural elements into furniture, vessels, and utensils had already begun in the Geometric period, the technique was mastered in the Archaic period. Consider the prancing horses of a bronze rod tripod stand (no. 5) or, in a different way, a marble lamp (no. 8), whose complex shallow relief carving must have come to flickering life when its oiled wick was lit. A particularly fine example is a bronze plate with handles supported by winged horses representing the famous Pegasos (fig. 13). In this balanced and lively design, the horses appear to emerge on either side of the handle, their wings spread as if bearing the plate into the air.

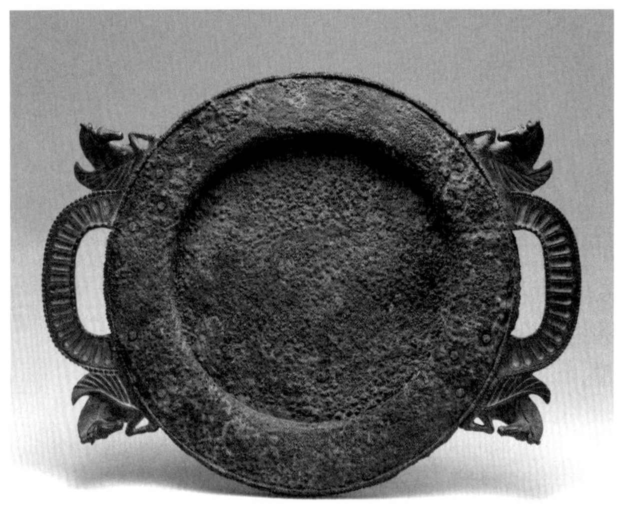

Fig. 13. Plate, with detail of handles. Greek, Archaic period, ca. 550–500 B.C. Bronze, H. $11\frac{1}{4}$ in. (28.6 cm). Gift of Norbert Schimmel, 1986 (1986.322.2)

Fig. 12. Mirror with a support in the form of a nude girl. Greek, Laconian, Archaic period, ca. 550–500 B.C. Bronze, H. $13\frac{5}{16}$ in. (33.8 cm). Said to be from southern Italy. Fletcher Fund, 1938 (38.11.3)

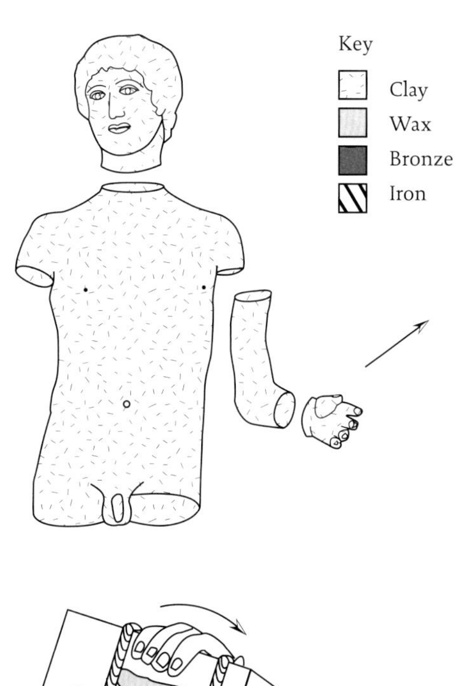


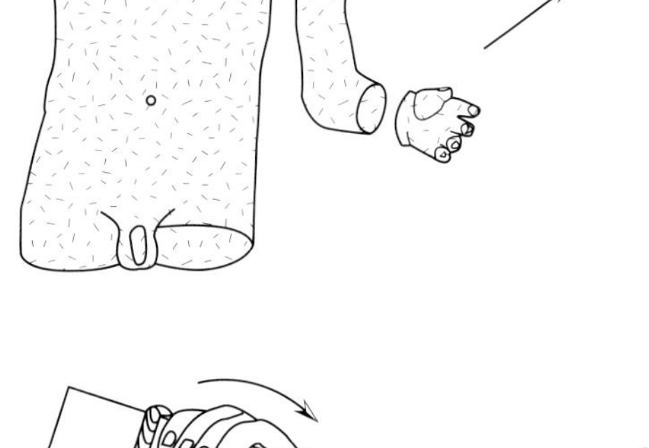

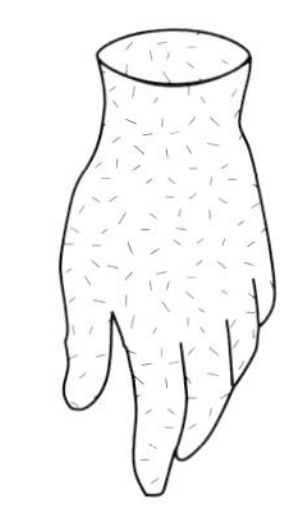

1. Original clay model.

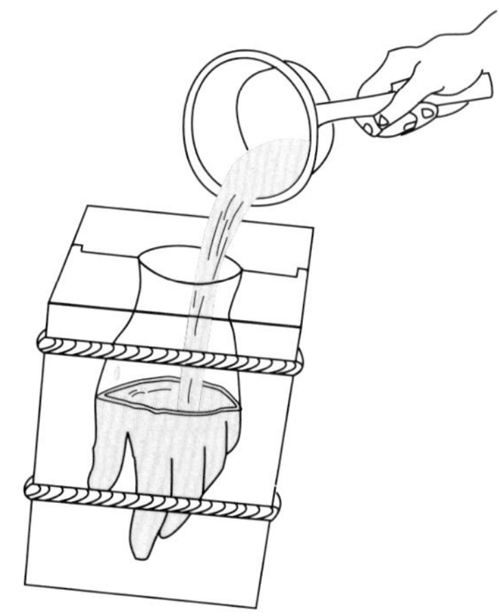

3. Hot wax is poured into the master molds, agitated, and brushed over the inner surface.

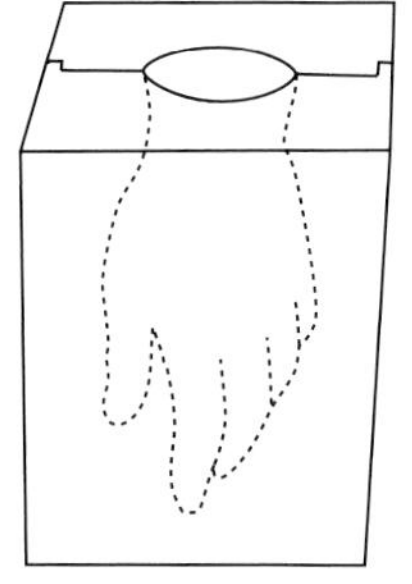

2. Master molds taken from clay model.

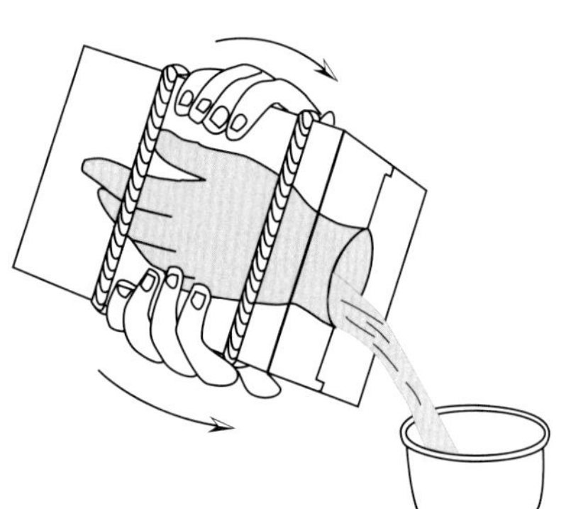

4. Excess wax is poured out, leaving a thin coating except, in this case, for solid fingers.

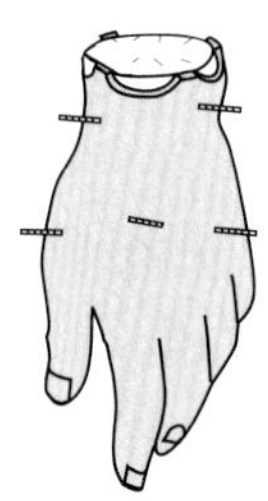

5. Finished wax-working model with fingernails marked, clay core poured inside, and metal chaplets stuck through wax into core.

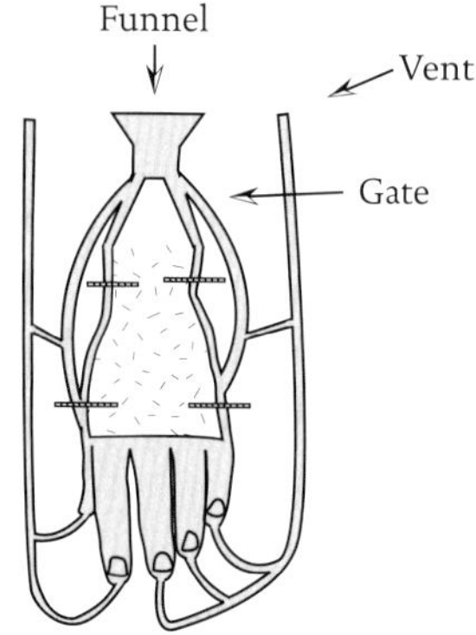


6. Cross section of wax-working model with wax funnel, gates, and vents attached.

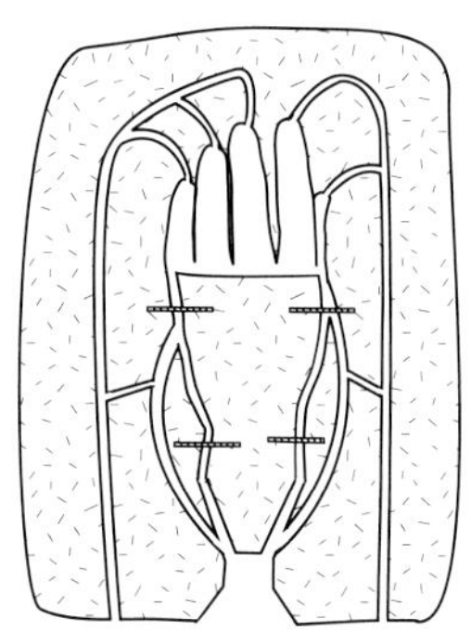

7. Cross section of investment mold inverted for baking, with hollow tubes where wax-working model and gate system have been burned out.

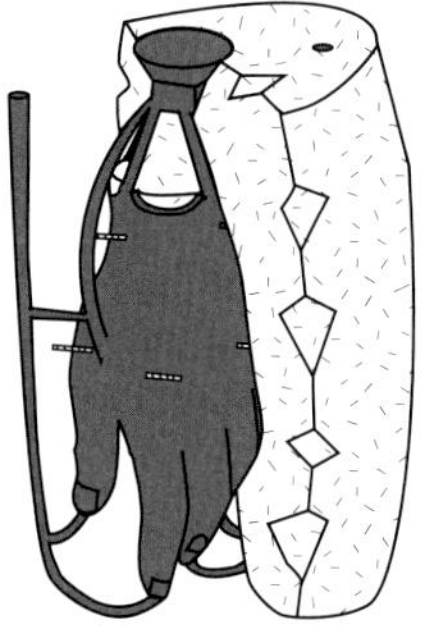

8. Bronze has been poured, investment mold partially broken away.

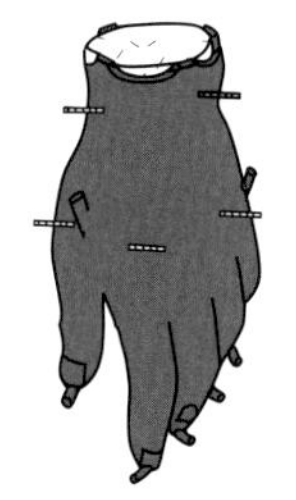

9. Cast-bronze hand with core, chaplets, and clipped gate system.

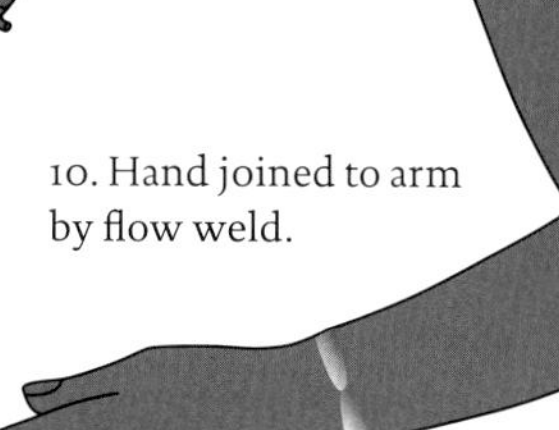

10. Hand joined to arm by flow weld.

Fig. 14. Hollow lost wax casting: the indirect method. Drawing by Seán Hemingway

## CLASSICAL PERIOD

The Classical style emerged after major conflicts between the Greeks and Persians, beginning with the Ionian revolts of the early fifth century B.C., when powerful Greek city-states on the coast of Asia Minor rose up against Persian rule and were beaten back into submission. The Persian king then sought to expand his empire into mainland Greece, invading and plundering Greek centers, even destroying the Athenian Acropolis. He ultimately suffered a resounding defeat, first at sea in the decisive naval battle at Salamis in 480 B.C. and finally on land at the battle of Plataea in 479 B.C. Athens's crucial involvement in the victory led both to its hegemony in the fifth century B.C. and, for a time, to a sense of Greek unity that had never been achieved previously.

Technological advances also contributed to the development of sculpture in the Classical period (480–323 B.C.). By the end of the sixth century B.C., Greek sculptors had perfected sophisticated methods for casting bronze statues in sections and joining the pieces together seamlessly (fig. 14). Bronze, an alloy of approximately ninety percent copper and ten percent tin, became the preferred medium for statuary. It was valued for its tensile strength and ability to render the human body in a wide variety of poses that moved far beyond the traditional sculptural types favored in the Archaic period.

Sculptors continued to show great interest in the human form and its perfection, especially with regard to the male body. This phenomenon is well represented in The Met sculpture collection by images of Greek athletes, who typically exercised in the nude. While Archaic sculpture emphasized symmetry to the point of abstraction, with the transition to the Classical style Greek sculptors began to explore asymmetries evident in fundamental shifts of body weight or position, such as the turn of a head. Perhaps the best example is the introduction of contrapposto (counterpoise), in which a human figure stands with most of his or her weight on one leg, freeing the other leg, which is bent at the knee (no. 19). An Early Classical bronze statuette of a discus thrower presents a Greek athlete with a finely tuned physique in the initial stages of a throw (fig. 15). His right foot extended forward, he raises the discus in his left hand to build momentum

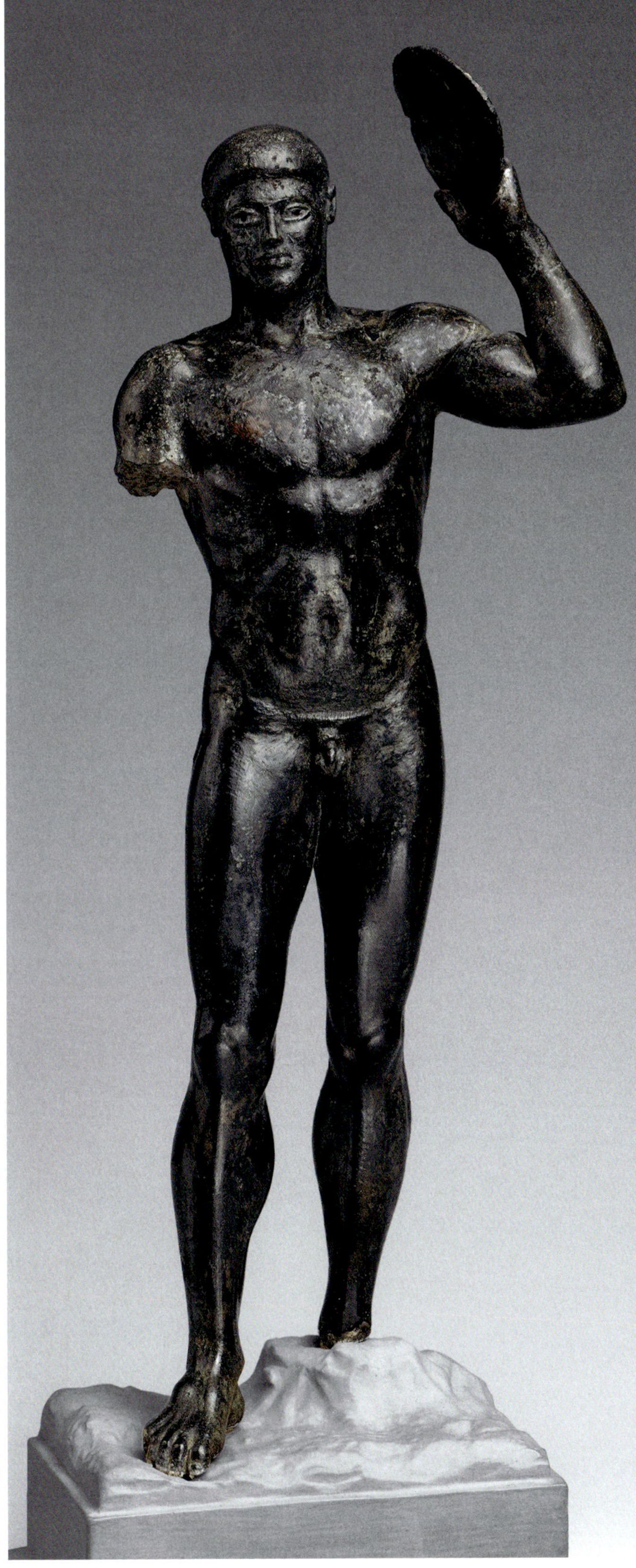

Fig. 15. Statuette of a discus thrower. Greek, Early Classical period, ca. 470 B.C. Bronze, H. 9 11/16 in. (24.5 cm). Said to be from the Peloponnese. Rogers Fund, 1907 (07.286.87)

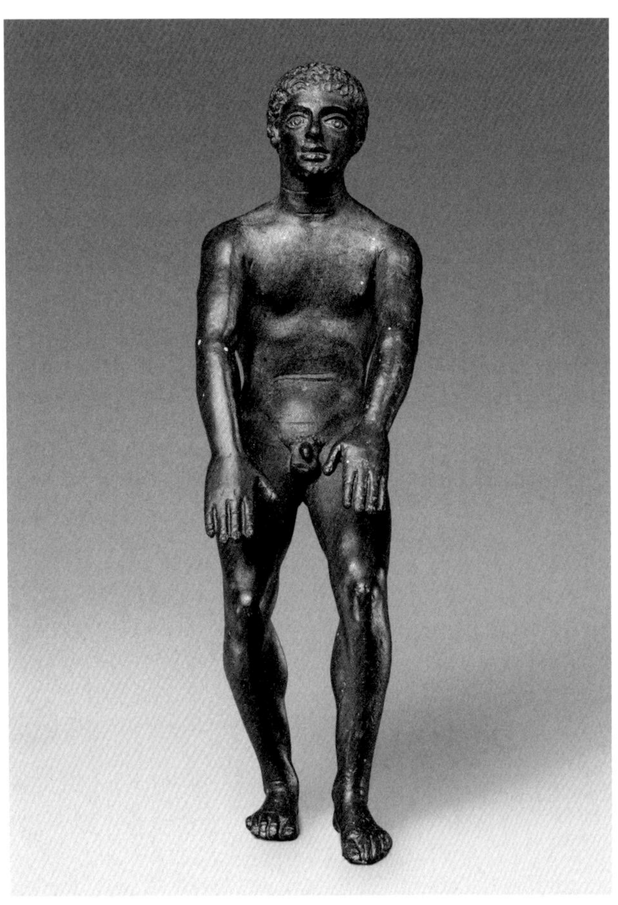

Fig. 16. Statuette of an athlete. Greek, Classical period, ca. 450 B.C. Bronze, H. 8⅜ in. (21.3 cm). Rogers Fund, 1908 (08.258.11)

before transferring it to his right hand and sending it far into the field. His intense gaze suggests not only his singular focus on the throw but also a self-awareness not previously seen in Archaic Greek sculpture. Another bronze statuette, made some twenty years later, represents an athlete with his legs bent at the knees and both arms placed out in front of him (fig. 16). He may be a runner about to start a race or more likely, given that his carefully balanced weight rests on the back of his feet, an athlete who has just completed a long jump.

Although bronze became the preferred medium for making large-scale statuary, precious few such statues survive because of the physical properties of the material, including its ability to be melted and reused. The study of Classical Greek statuary is thus often made through the lens of Roman copies. This is true also for the lost cult statues, known as chryselephantine (gold and ivory), that were the greatest achievements of famous Classical sculptors such as Pheidias (no. 18), an Athenian skilled in many media. The most important work by Pheidias, the master sculptor for the Parthenon temple on the Acropolis of Athens, was a chryselephantine statue of Zeus at Olympia, considered one of the Seven Wonders of the Ancient World. These monumental cult statues were truly the finest works of sculpture created in fifth-century-B.C. Greece, but practically nothing survives of them.

The ancient Romans had a deep appreciation for Greek culture and its arts, especially the sculptures of the Classical Age. Since they had only a limited number of original Greek works, they supported a thriving industry of copies and adaptations in the Classical style. They used the sculptures they created for their own purposes, which were often quite different from the contexts of the Greek models. Certainly, Roman copies offer an imperfect means for understanding Classical sculpture, especially since Roman sculptors often made adaptations and variants of the earlier Greek works. Nevertheless, very close copies were also produced (nos. 17 and 20) and were apparently valued as such by the ancient Roman patricians who commissioned them.

Among the Classical sculptors who wrote about their works and theories was Polykleitos of Argos, whose treatise on sculpture, called the *Canon*, is now lost except for two or three fragments. Various sculptures, known only from later copies, have been attributed to him (nos. 19 and 39). One of the most securely attributed of these is the Diadoumenos (Fillet-Binder). Commemorating an athlete's victory in the Panhellenic games, it represented the athlete in a contrapposto stance tying a ribbon around his head with both hands. Fragments of a marble copy carved in the late first century give a good sense of the basic appearance of the original bronze statue (fig. 17). These fragments were later joined with a plaster cast of another marble copy from the early first century B.C.

Fig. 17. Fragments of a statue of the Diadoumenos (Fillet-Binder). Roman, Flavian period, ca. A.D. 69–96. Copy of a bronze statue of ca. 430 B.C. by Polykleitos. Marble, H. 73 in. (185.4 cm). Fletcher Fund, 1925 (25.78.56)

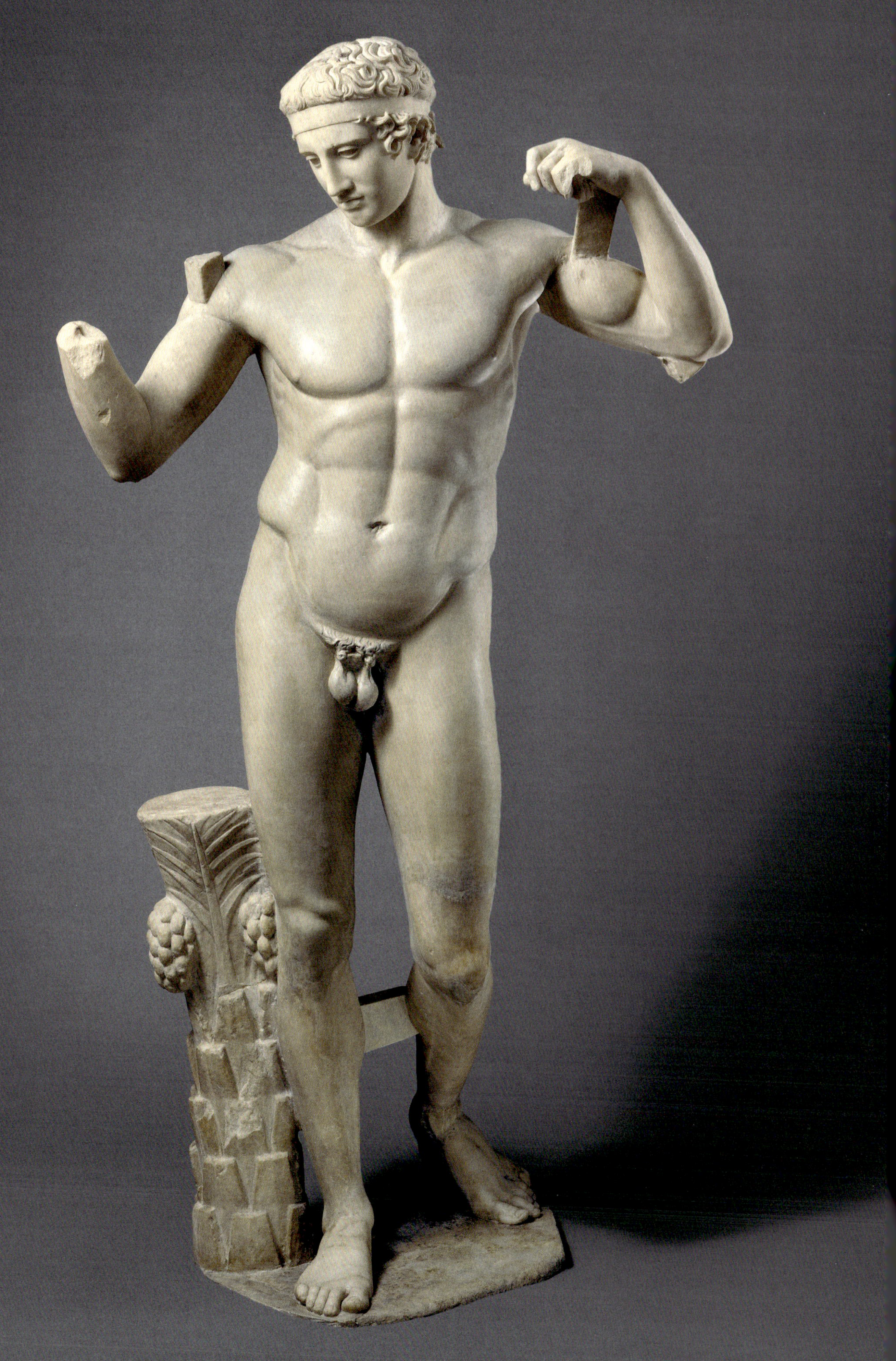

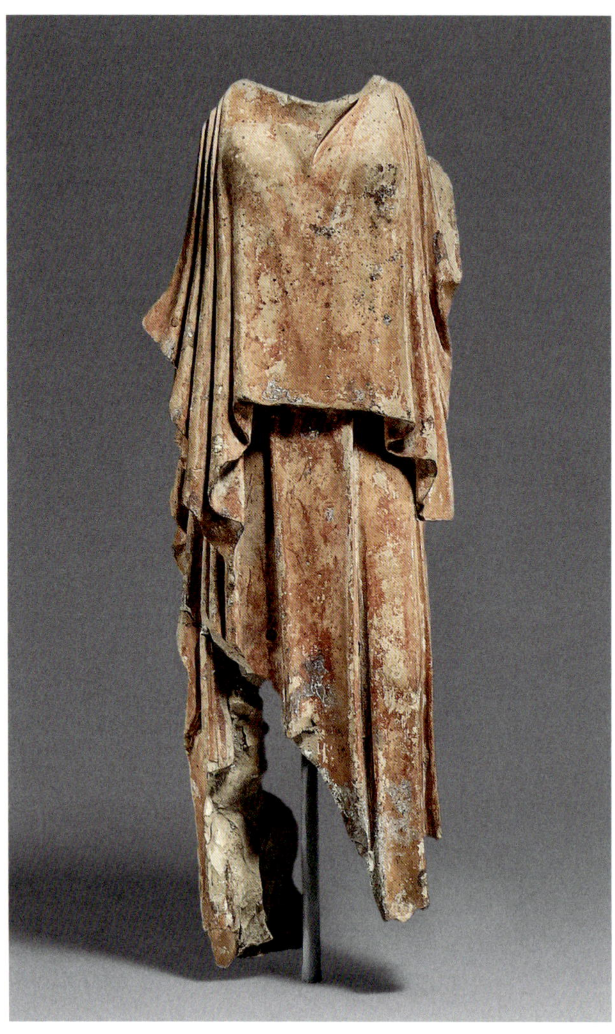

Fig. 18. Large statuette of a woman wearing a peplos. Greek, Classical period, ca. 450 B.C. Terracotta, H. 17 11/16 in. (45 cm). Rogers Fund, 1906 (06.1151)

excavated on the island of Delos. Even though the replica from Delos is some two centuries older than the fragments, the scales are identical and the forms correspond closely, indicating the ability of the copyists to make very accurate replicas.

The major technique used by ancient Greek craftsmen to make bronze sculpture was lost wax casting. Indirect lost wax casting was particularly well suited for this purpose (see fig. 14 for the basic steps). Typically, statues were cast in several pieces, such as head, torso, arms, and legs (no. 34). Fundamental to the indirect lost wax process was the creation of a master model from which impressions were taken to form molds for casting. Although such models rarely survive, one likely example is a fragmentary terracotta standing draped female figure (fig. 18). The great benefit of this technique is that the master model was not lost in the casting process, which happened in direct lost wax casting (see no. 40), and could be reused to recast sections of the statue or make a series of castings.

In the Classical period, Greek temples continued to be important places for sculptural display. The Panhellenic sanctuaries were filled with sculptural dedications, especially statuary of bronze, and lavished with monumental temples that exhibited outstanding Classical architectural sculpture, best seen today at Olympia and Delphi. The building program of the Athenian statesman Perikles on the Acropolis, centered around the Parthenon, was the most ambitious and dazzling of the fifth century B.C., involving large numbers of masons and sculptors (no. 16). The Athenian Acropolis became both a shining sculptural monument for religious devotion and a symbol of civic pride.

Classical sculpture often presents an ideal beauty that has a timeless quality, balanced and pure in equal measure (nos. 14–16). In the last quarter of the fifth century B.C., a new, impressionistic style developed that featured mannered calligraphic effects conveyed by carefully modeled, windswept drapery. This can be seen both in reliefs (no. 21) and in sculpture in the round, such as the Venus Genetrix, a statue type known from numerous Roman copies. One such statue in The Met collection, found in the Tiber, exhibits the reddish patina characteristic of works that were buried at the bottom of that river for centuries. While worn, the statue conveys a vivid sense of drama. This is especially true from the side view: you can see how diaphanous the chiton is from the front, revealing the figure's sensuous body, and how it contrasts with the heavier himation draped over her bent left arm and falling behind her in columnar folds to the ground (fig. 19).

Fig. 19. Back view of a statue of Aphrodite, the so-called Venus Genetrix. Roman, Imperial period, 1st–2nd century A.D. Copy of a Greek bronze statue of the late fifth century B.C. attributed to Kallimachos. Marble, H. 59½ in. (151.1 cm). Purchase, 1932 (32.11.3)

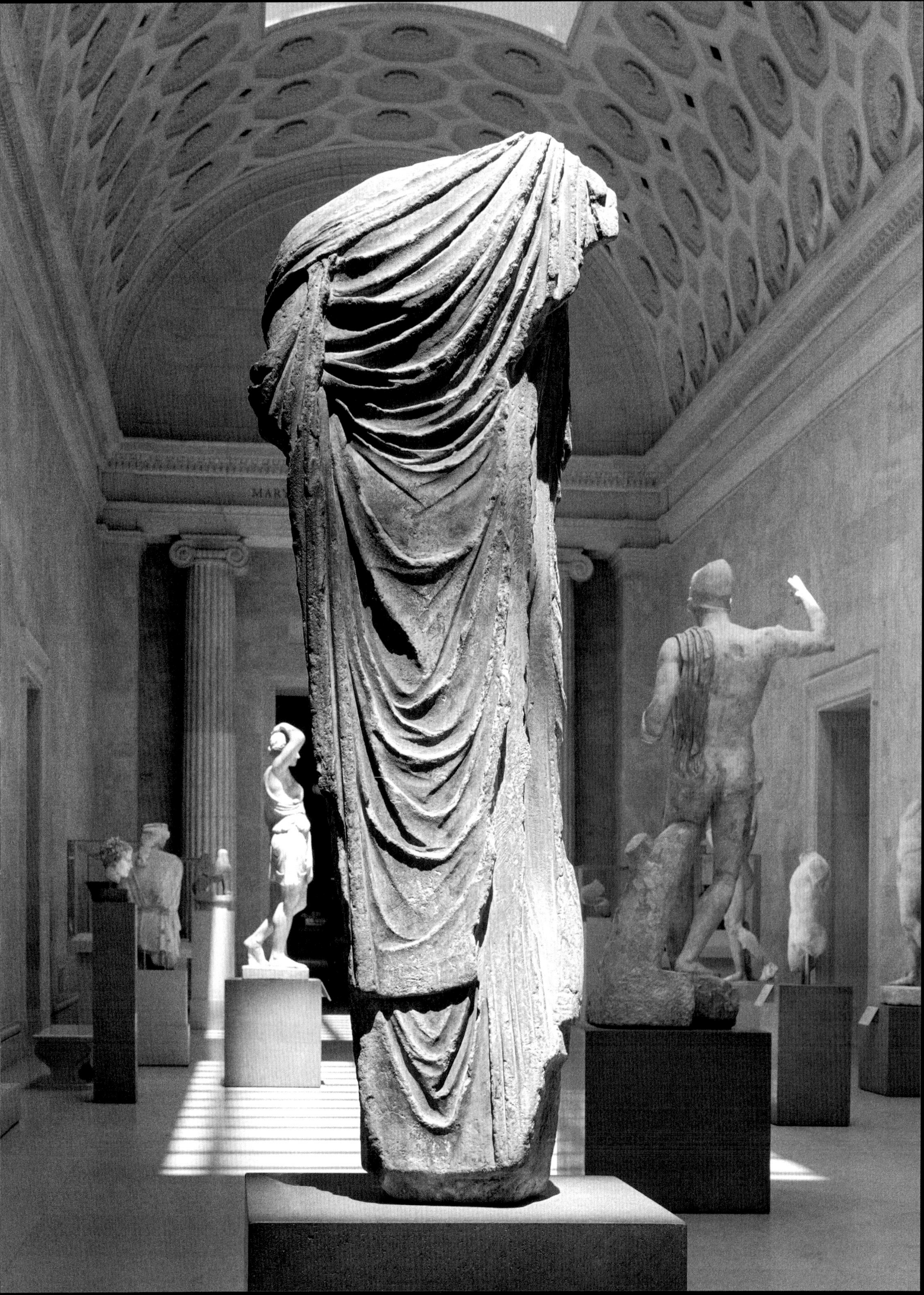

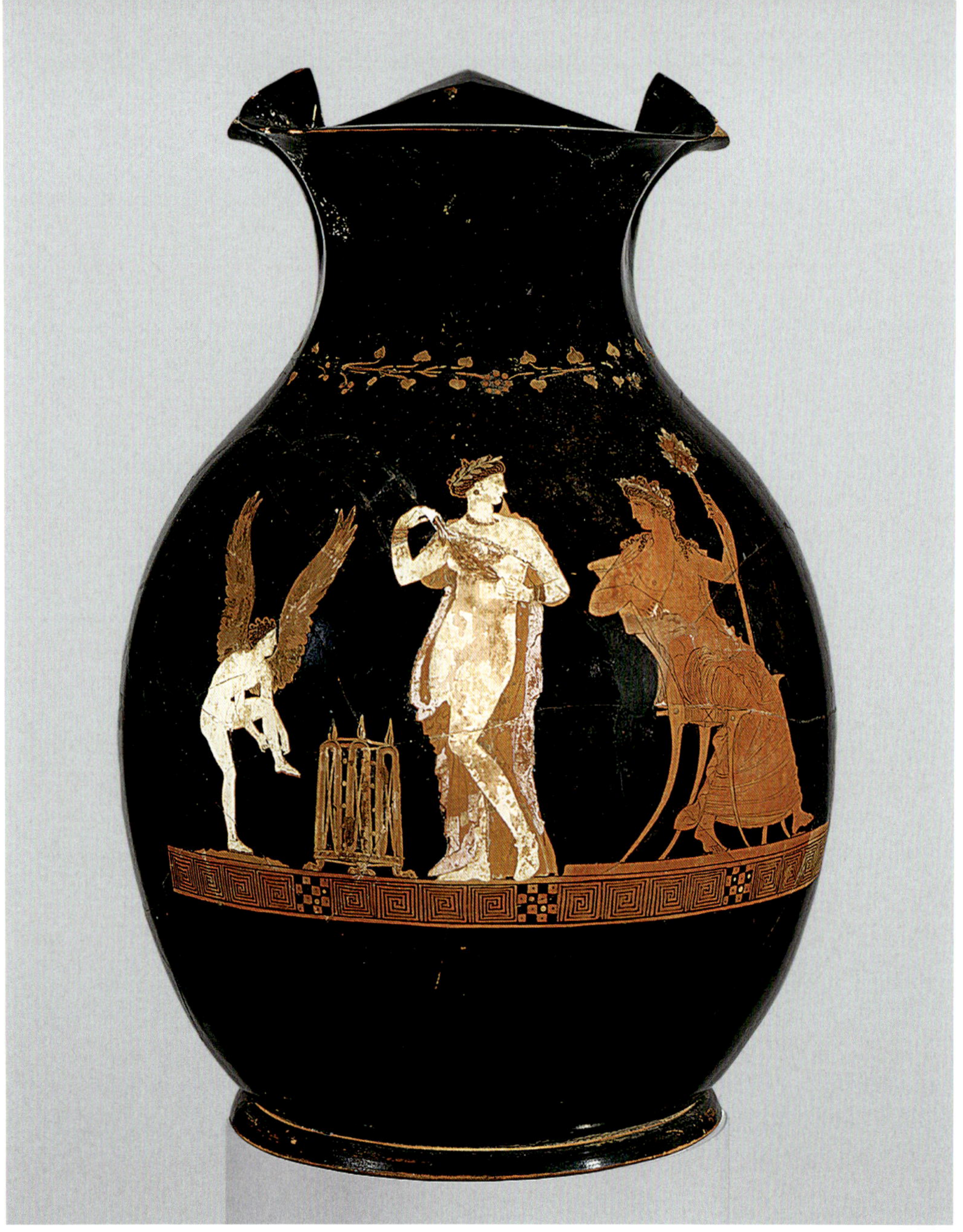

Fig. 20. Oinochoe (jug). Greek, Attic, Late Classical period, ca. 350 B.C. Terracotta, red-figure, H. 9¼ in. (23.5 cm). Rogers Fund, 1925 (25.190)

Funerary monuments, especially from the region around Athens, are a major strength of the Late Classical sculpture collection at The Met (nos. 23–26). Naturally enough, such monuments tended to be conservative, often evoking the fifth-century-B.C. High Classical style exemplified in the Parthenon (nos. 24 and 25). Yet Greek sculptors of the period were also innovators, working on a more international scale than their predecessors. Skopas of Paros traveled throughout the eastern Mediterranean to carry out various commissions, including multiartisan works like the Mausoleum at Halikarnassos, another Greek sculptural monument considered to be one of the Seven Wonders.

Praxiteles of Athens created one of the most celebrated statues in antiquity—the first fully nude sculpture of the goddess Aphrodite—for a sanctuary at the site of

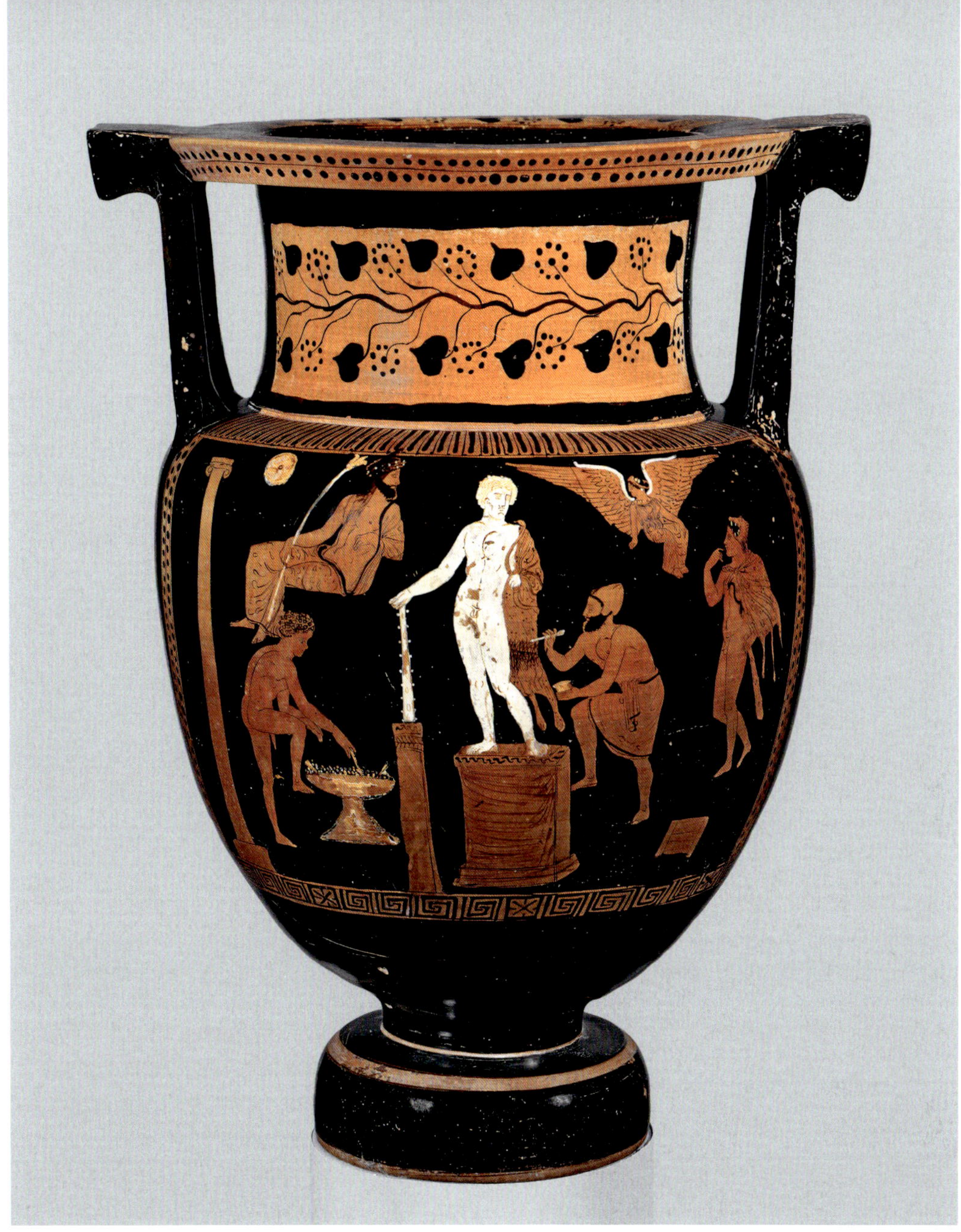

Fig. 21. Column-krater (bowl for mixing wine and water). Greek, South Italian, Apulian, Late Classical period, ca. 360–350 B.C. Attributed to the Group of Boston 00.348. Terracotta, red-figure, H. 20¼ in. (51.4 cm). Rogers Fund, 1950 (50.11.4)

Knidos on the coast of modern-day Turkey. Over the succeeding centuries, this statue spawned a host of nude female figures in a variety of poses (no. 36). An Athenian vase in The Met collection shows how quickly the influence of Praxiteles's statue spread (fig. 20). Dated to the middle of the fourth century B.C., it represents a rare scene: Pompe, the female personification of a procession, standing between Eros and Dionysos. The sensuous figure of Pompe, whose mantle only accentuates her nudity, was clearly inspired by sculptures of Aphrodite such as the Venus Genetrix (see fig. 19) and especially the Knidian Aphrodite by Praxiteles.

An Apulian vase in The Met collection provides a rare representation of a Greek artist painting a statue of the hero Herakles (fig. 21). Using a technique known as encaustic, the artist employs a spatula to apply a mixture of pigment and wax to the hero's lion skin. A young assistant tends the brazier used to heat the tools for mixing pigments and applying the tinted wax. In a charming twist, Herakles himself approaches to admire the statue, while Zeus, greatest of the Olympian gods and father of Herakles, and Nike, personification of victory, watch from above. The vase reminds us that Classical sculpture, like its Archaic predecessors, was typically colorful although often only traces of the inlays (no. 13) or pigments survive on sculptures today.

The most important artist of the fourth century B.C. was probably Lysippos of Sicyon, the court sculptor to Alexander the Great. The Roman author Pliny the Elder wrote that Lysippos, who worked exclusively in bronze and was incredibly prolific, created some fifteen hundred statues, and his career is thought to have spanned more than fifty years. Yet not a single signed original work by his hand is preserved today. His portrait of Herakles contemplating the completion of his labors, the so-called Weary Herakles, glimpsed through a host of later copies, must have been sublime. The range of commissions attributed to Lysippos suggest an artist of great ingenuity and talent. His works, notably portraits of Alexander, and those they influenced mark the culmination of Classical Greek sculpture—a synthesis of naturalism and illusionism—and inaugurate the new Hellenistic era.

## HELLENISTIC PERIOD

The Hellenistic period (323–31 B.C.) begins with the death of Alexander the Great, whose conquests changed the face of the ancient world forever. It ends with the battle of Actium, by which Octavian's defeat of Mark Antony and Cleopatra VII cemented the dominance of the Roman Empire in the Mediterranean region. Alexander fostered contacts between cultures far and wide that had a significant impact on the future of Greek sculpture. After his death, his generals, known as the Successors, divided his empire among themselves into dynastic kingdoms—the Ptolemies in Egypt, the Seleucids in Asia Minor and the Near East, and the Antigonids in Macedonia and Greece.

Sculpture in the Hellenistic Age could be truly monumental. The Colossus of Rhodes, a bronze statue of the sun god Helios that stood by the city's harbor, was comparable in size and stature to New York's Statue of Liberty. Religious architecture, which continued to incorporate sculpture, reached new levels of grandeur (no. 28), such as in the reconceived Temple of Artemis at Ephesos. This structure was destroyed by fire in 356 B.C. and was still in ruins when Alexander saw it in 334 B.C. When rebuilt in the Early Hellenistic period, with a forest of columns decorated with sculptural reliefs, it came to be considered another Wonder of the Ancient World. Also notable for its splendor is the Great Altar from the city of Pergamon in Turkey, a shining example of Hellenistic royal patronage. Its magnificent frieze depicting the epic battle between the Giants and the Olympian gods at the gates of Mount Olympus, today painstakingly reconstructed in the Pergamon Museum in Berlin, is the greatest surviving masterpiece of ancient Greek baroque sculpture.

Greek sculptors could also be masterful miniaturists, working in a variety of precious materials. A pair of gold earrings with the eagle of Zeus bearing the young Ganymede up to Mount Olympus to be the cupbearer of the gods is a particularly outstanding example of the Early Hellenistic period (fig. 22). The goldsmith has created a figural group, less than one and a half inches high, that is remarkable in its detail and poignancy. Said to have been found in a tomb near Thessaloniki in northern Greece, the earrings are part of a parure, or matched set, that included four gold fibulae (clasps), two rock crystal bracelets with gold ram's-head finials, a gold necklace, and an emerald ring set in a gold bezel. The style of wearing two identical bracelets follows Persian fashion, introduced to Greece through Alexander the Great's melding of cultural customs after his conquest of Persia. The subject of Ganymede and the Eagle is purely Greek, the composition undoubtedly a free adaptation of a famous statue group from a generation earlier by the Athenian sculptor Leochares. The overt eroticism of the naked youth and the tender way he is held by the eagle would not have been features of Leochares's original bronze group but are daring reinterpretations fitting for women's jewelry.

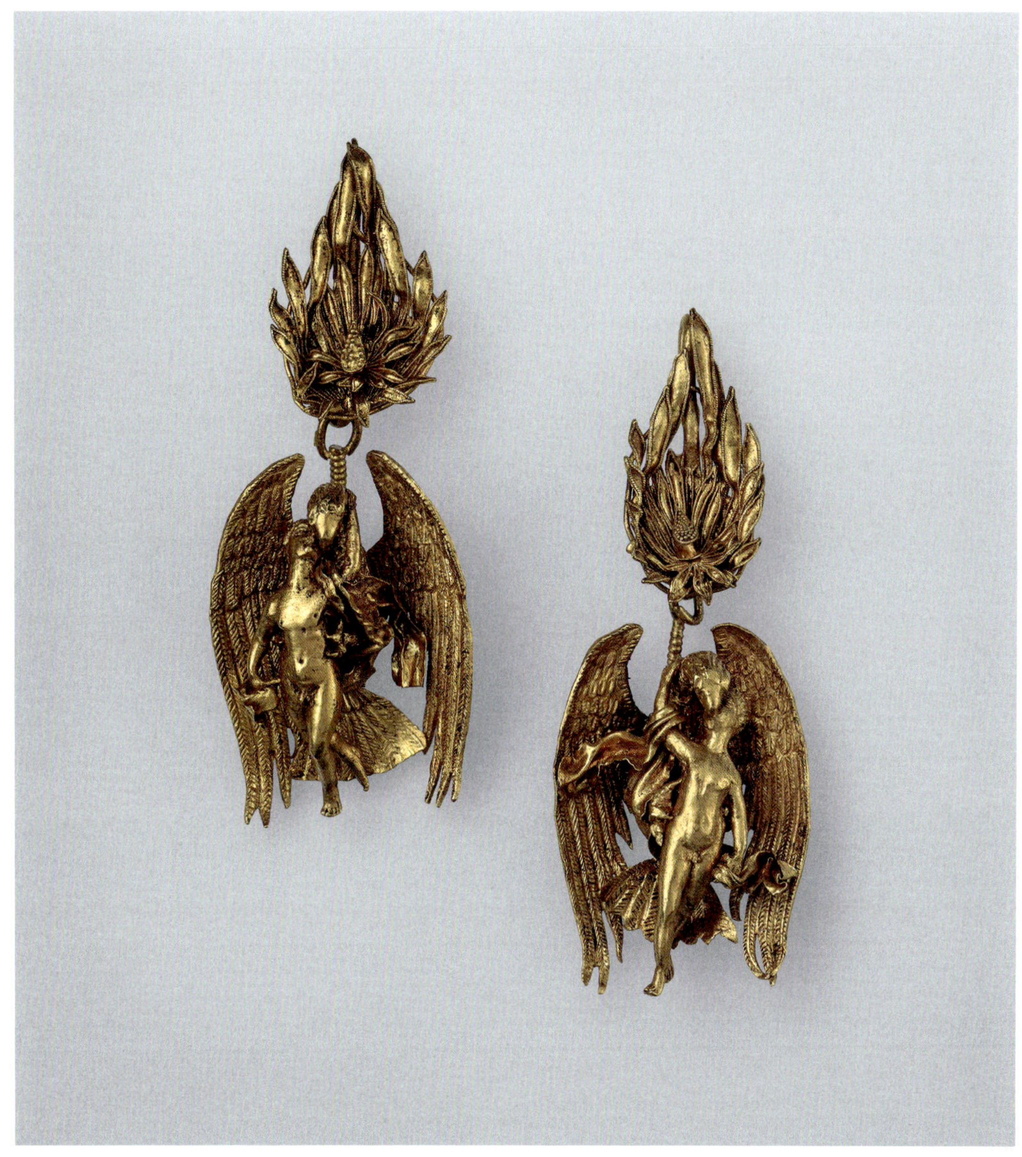

Fig. 22. Pair of earrings with Ganymede and the Eagle. Greek, Thessaloniki, Hellenistic period, ca. 325–300 B.C. Gold, overall H. 2⅜ in. (6 cm). Harris Brisbane Dick Fund, 1937 (37.11.9, .10)

Freestanding small-scale sculptures were produced in a variety of media during the period. Following Alexander's example, portraiture became an important vehicle for the presentation and commemoration of Hellenistic royalty (nos. 30 and 31). Gem engravers, who also carved the dies for striking coins (see figs. 52–54), produced sensitive renditions of royalty such as the chalcedony gem with a portrait of a woman most likely representing Queen Laodice, wife of King Mithridates IV of Pontus (fig. 23).

That Hellenistic sculpture did not follow one dominant stylistic trend, as earlier Greek examples had, is a reflection of the greatly expanded Hellenic world. The

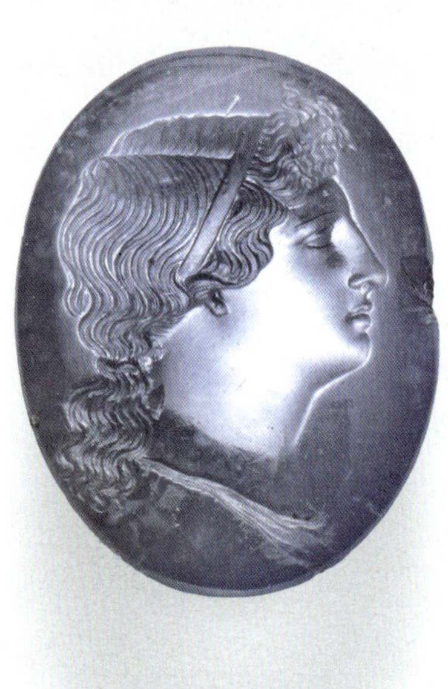

Fig. 23. Gem with female portrait head. Greek, Hellenistic period, 2nd century B.C. Chalcedony, H. ¾ in. (1.9 cm). Said to be from Amisos (modern Samsun) in the Pontic region of Turkey. Purchase, Joseph Pulitzer Bequest, 1942 (42.11.26)

many different styles used concurrently and the lack of securely dated sculptural monuments make a close dating of Hellenistic sculpture difficult. There was a much wider range of subject matter than before, especially in small-scale sculpture. A statuette of a dog gnawing a bone, for example, presents a reflection on a moment of everyday life with tender sympathy (fig. 24). Sculptors created images of youth (no. 34) and old age (no. 37) with heightened realism. Physical states of being were explored, from sleep (no. 34) and death to medical conditions and psychological states, including impressions of the mind at work (no. 38). Sculptors took a greater interest in ethnic types and the diverse physiognomies of people at various levels of society. A statuette of an acrobat in midperformance presents a professional entertainer with strongly developed muscles who appears nimble and athletic despite his stunted legs and the pronounced curvature of his spine, realistic details that add to the impression of a real-life figure (fig. 25).

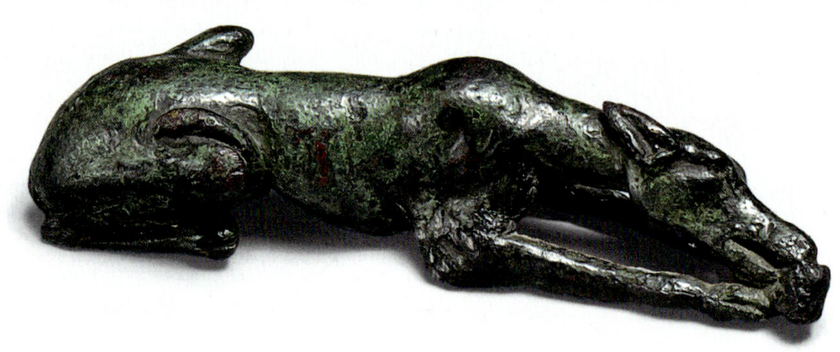

Fig. 24. Statuette of a hound. Greek, Hellenistic period, 3rd–2nd century B.C. Bronze, L. 3 in. (7.6 cm). Fletcher Fund, 1936 (36.11.12)

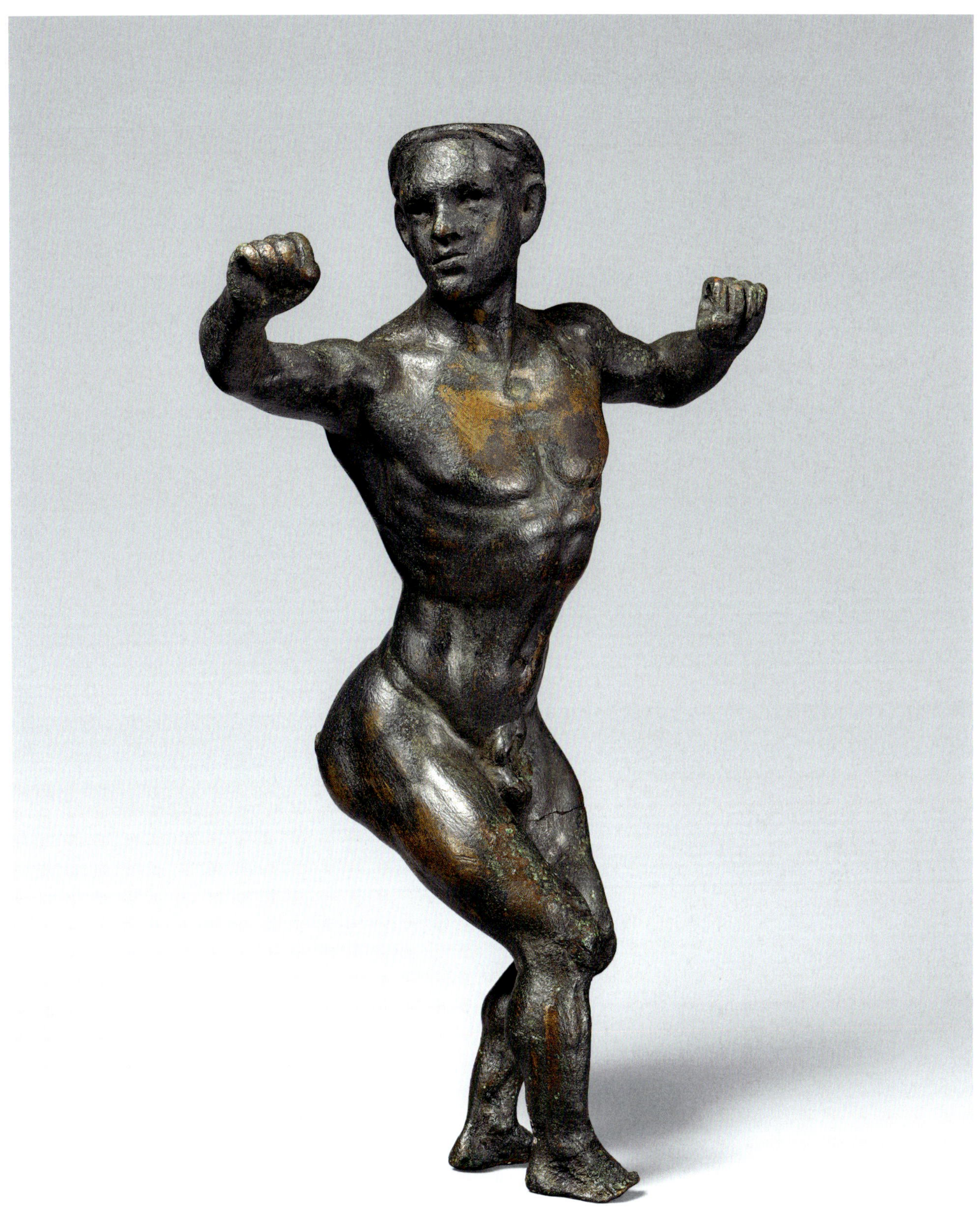

Fig. 25. Statuette of an acrobat. Greek, Hellenistic period, 3rd–2nd century B.C. Bronze, H. 8⅝ in. (21.9 cm). Rogers Fund, 1952 (52.11.7)

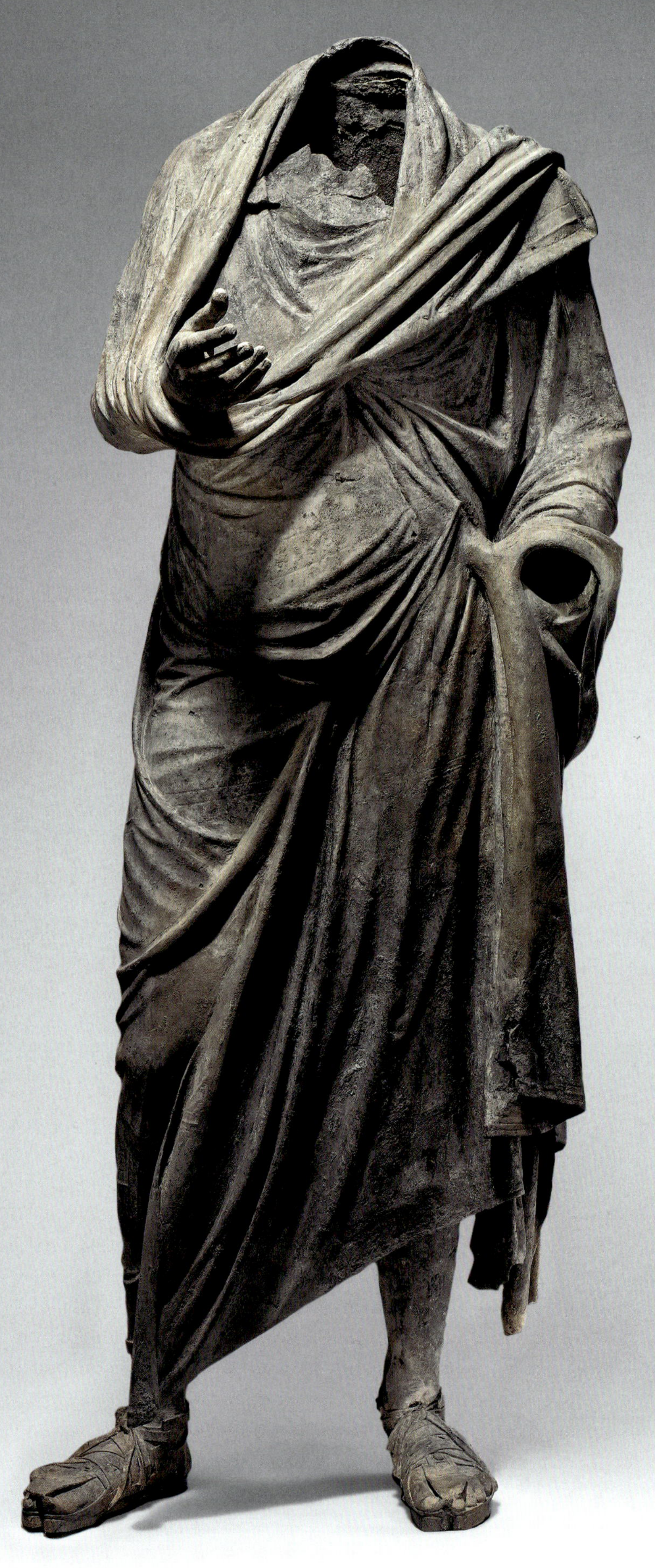

Honorific bronze statues were set up in civic spaces all over the Hellenistic world. Serving to acknowledge important benefactions, these were among the highest honors that a city-state could bestow upon an individual. A powerful example of the Late Hellenistic period in The Met collection represents a man draped in a fine cloak and wearing sandals who stands with his weight on his left leg (fig. 26). His pose is that of an orator: right hand extended before him with fingers curled from his open palm and left arm positioned carefully at his side. Characteristically for a Greek portrait, this well-dressed man of words is portrayed as much through the figure as it would have been through the portrait head, which is unfortunately now missing. The base on which the statue stood would have identified the individual and given the reasons for his commemoration.

Although the indirect lost wax process made the serial replication of bronze sculptures feasible, so few ancient Greek bronze statues survive that such series rarely exist today. However, in the Hellenistic period, large quantities of terracotta statuettes were produced, of which many still remain (no. 39). Some of these apparently represent contemporary women. These statuettes of elegant young females fashionably dressed, often wearing hats and holding fans, are known as Tanagra figurines after a site in Boeotia that was a major center of production. They were arguably first produced in Athens in the last quarter of the fourth century B.C. and eventually came to be made in many parts of the Hellenistic world. Variants of the same type in The Met collection indicate how sculptors experimented with the theme, making small changes from the turn of the head to the fall of the drapery to the placement of the woman's hands. The statuettes also show how brightly colored the figures often were, especially in details of their clothing (fig. 27).

Hellenistic sculptors not only made copies of famous Classical works (no. 39), they also adapted the earlier styles of the Archaic and Classical periods for new creations (no. 40). Despite Pliny the Elder's statement that Greek art ended after the sculpture of the Classical period (*Natural History* 34.19), many Romans clearly admired

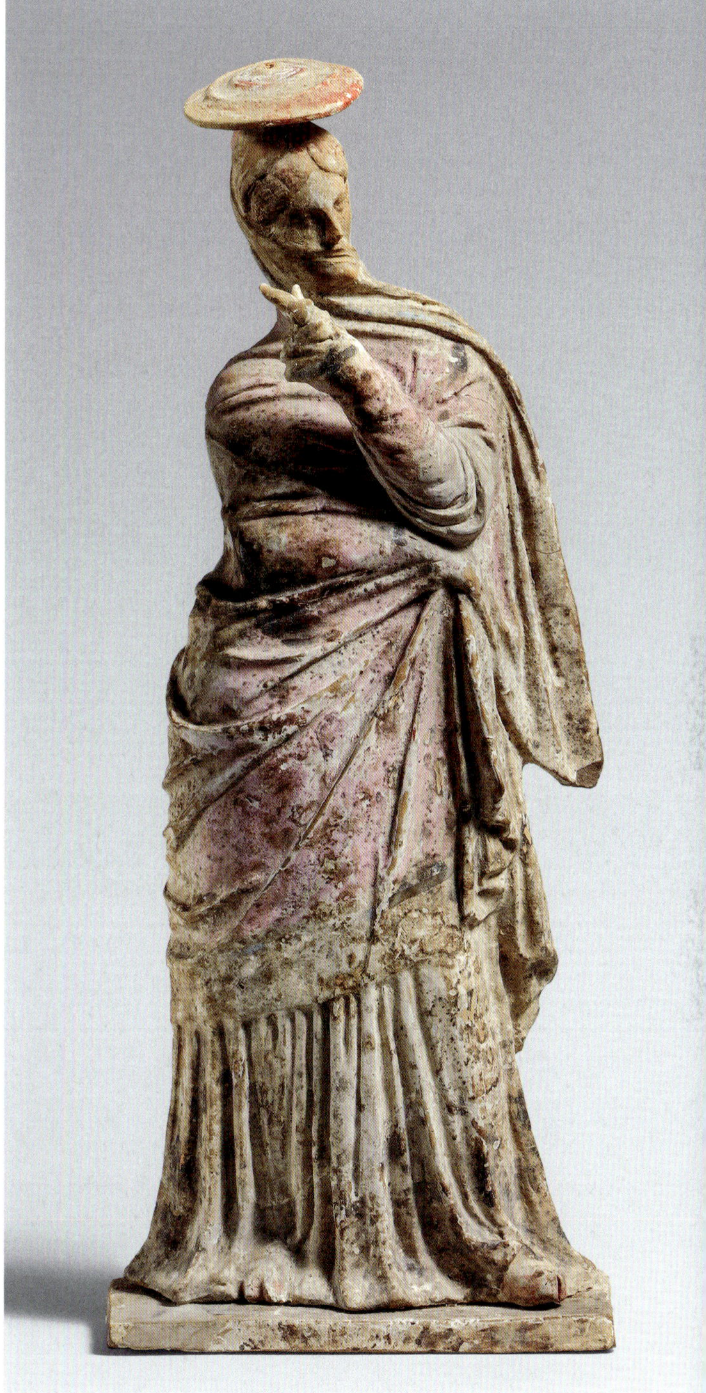

Fig. 27. Statuette of a woman. Greek, perhaps from Asia Minor, Hellenistic period, 2nd century B.C. Terracotta, H. 11¾ in. (29.8 cm). Gift of Mrs. Saidie Adler May, 1930 (30.117)

Fig. 26. Statue of an orator. Greek, Late Hellenistic period, ca. 50–30 B.C. Bronze, H. 73 in. (185.4 cm). Gift of Renée E. and Robert A. Belfer, 2001 (2001.443)

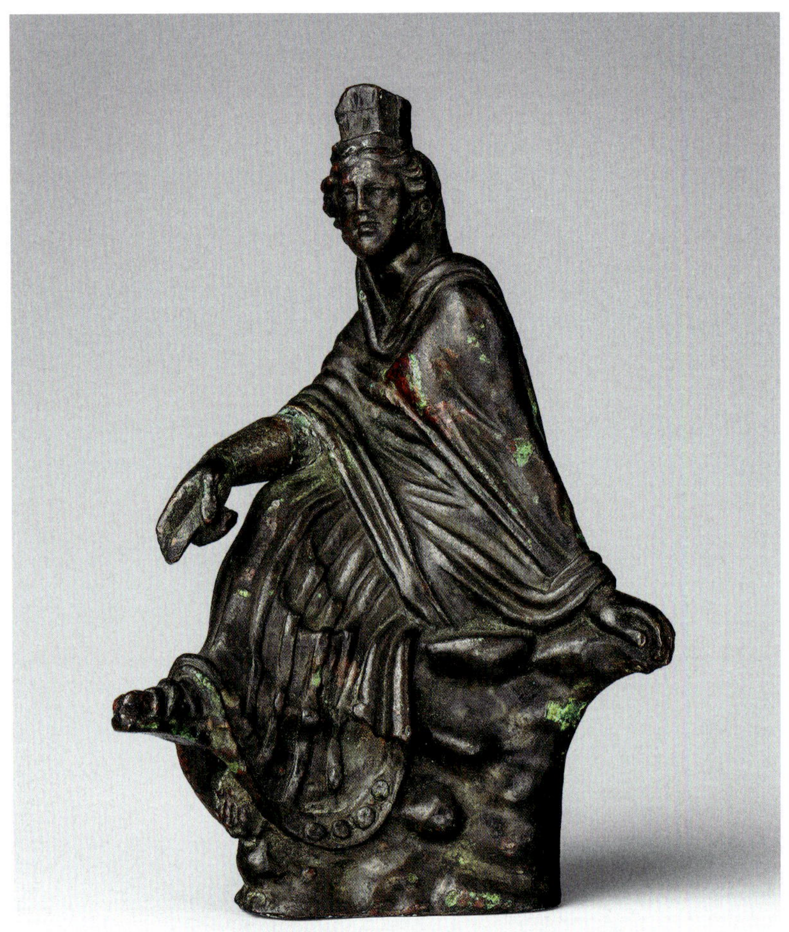

Fig. 28. Statuette of Tyche (Fortune). Roman, Early Imperial period, 1st century A.D. Reduced version of a bronze statue of ca. 300 B.C. by Eutykides. Bronze, H. 4 in. (10.2 cm). Rogers Fund, 1913 (13.227.8)

Fig. 29. Statue of the Three Graces. Roman, Imperial period, 2nd century A.D. Copy of a Greek work of the 2nd century B.C. Marble, 48 7/16 × 39 3/8 in. (123 × 100 cm). Purchase, Philodoroi, Lila Acheson Wallace, Mary and Michael Jaharis, Annette and Oscar de la Renta, Leon Levy Foundation, The Robert A. and Renée E. Belfer Family Foundation, Mr. and Mrs. John A. Moran, Jeannette and Jonathan Rosen, Malcolm Hewitt Wiener Foundation and Nicholas S. Zoullas Gifts, 2010 (2010.260)

Hellenistic sculpture. Images of illustrious Greeks (no. 35) and Hellenistic rulers were especially esteemed, although a variety of other works were copied and adapted (nos. 29 and 37). A famous Hellenistic statue of the goddess Tyche (Fortune) made for the city of Antioch on the Orontes River by the sculptor Eutykides of Sicyon, a pupil of Lysippos, is known both from images on Roman coins minted in Antioch and from Roman copies and adaptations (fig. 28).

As much as possible, this book has emphasized original Greek works, but the student of Greek sculpture must also be able to sift through the evidence provided by Roman copies. For the Hellenistic period, that evidence is often even more difficult to parse because of the complexity of coexisting styles, the vast geographic range involved, and the lack of well-documented, dated originals. A useful example is the Statue of the Three Graces, a type known from a series of Roman marble statues, reliefs, and images in various other media (fig. 29). The concept was hugely successful and worked well for both sculpture and painting. With so little information preserved about the nature of the original, we cannot be certain if it was even a three-dimensional sculpture, although its conception in the second century B.C. by a Greek artist seems assured.

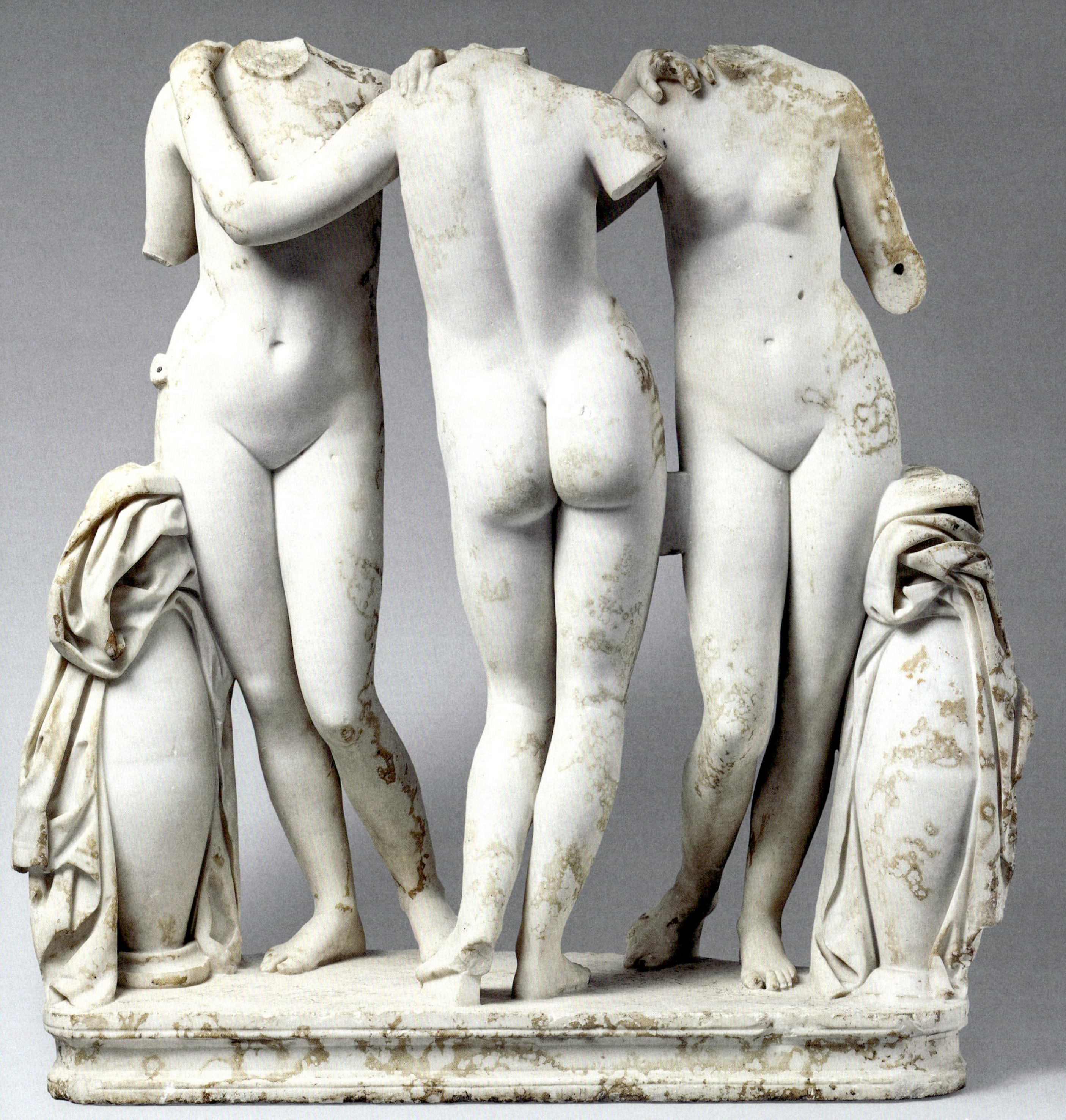

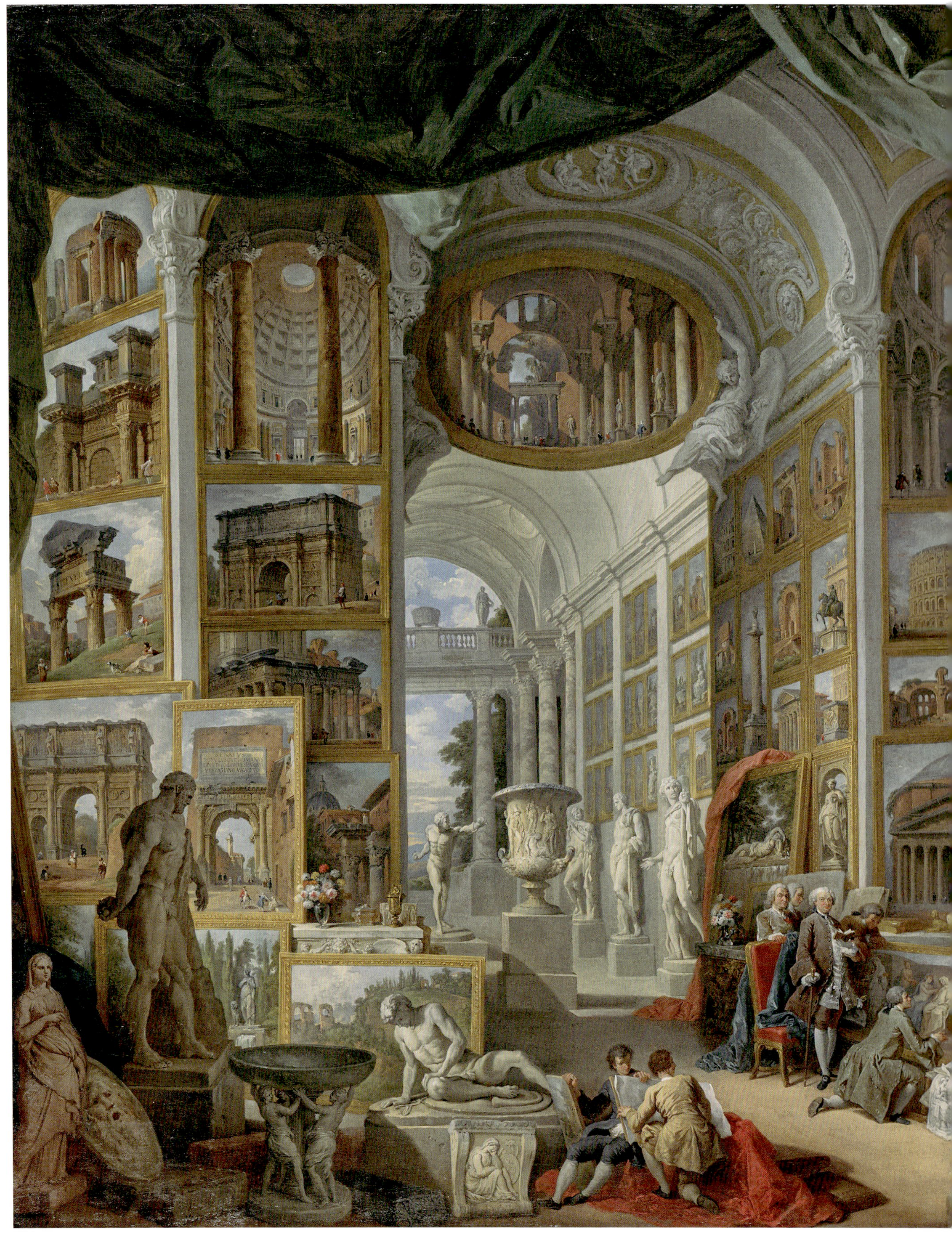

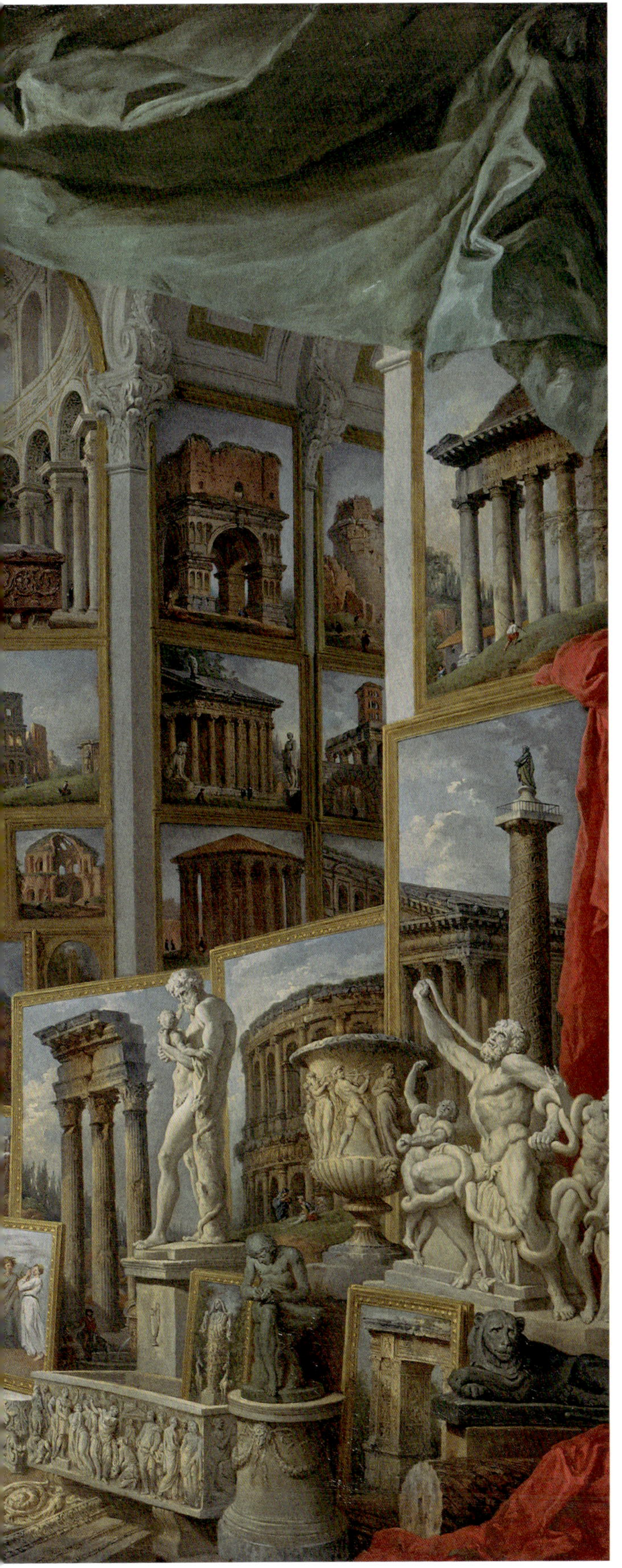

## A NOTE ON PROVENANCE

The archaeological contexts of ancient Greek sculpture provide valuable information about their history. Only rarely, though, is a sculpture found in its initial context of use, such as on the building for which it was made or in its original location as a funerary monument. More often, a statue has been damaged and appears in a context of reuse (no. 37), such as built into a medieval wall. Many of the extant Greek bronze statues have been discovered in the sea, often as cargo on ancient ships that have foundered en route to their destination or as chance finds in fishermen's nets. Thousands of Greek statues were brought to Rome in antiquity, frequently as war booty plundered from Greek cities and sanctuaries (no. 23). The ancient Romans sometimes rededicated the statues in their own sanctuaries or set up them up in private villas, houses, and gardens for personal reflection and enjoyment. A painting by Giovanni Panini illustrates some of the most famous statues that were displayed in Rome during the Renaissance and into the eighteenth century as the riches of the Classical world were rediscovered and entered into papal and aristocratic private collections (fig. 30).

Nearly every one of the Greek sculptures in The Met collection was acquired on the art market and thus lacks its archaeological provenance. In some cases, the sculpture has a long ownership history in distinguished European and American art collections (nos. 14, 16, 17, and 31), but more often nothing is known about its original findspot. Occasionally, the work itself reveals something of its long history (nos. 34 and 37). When a Greek sculpture lacks an archaeological provenance, fundamental questions need to be raised. Is the sculpture ancient? Has it been restored or altered in any way? Does it raise any legal or ethical issues? For further elucidation of these matters, there is more information available on the Museum's website, www.metmuseum.org, including The Met's current rigorous guidelines for the acquisition of antiquities as well as the provenance and ownership histories of the works discussed in this book.

Fig. 30. Giovanni Paolo Panini (1691–1765). *Ancient Rome*, 1757. Oil on canvas, 67 13/16 × 90 1/2 in. (172.2 × 229.9 cm). Gwynne Andrews Fund, 1952 (52.63.1)

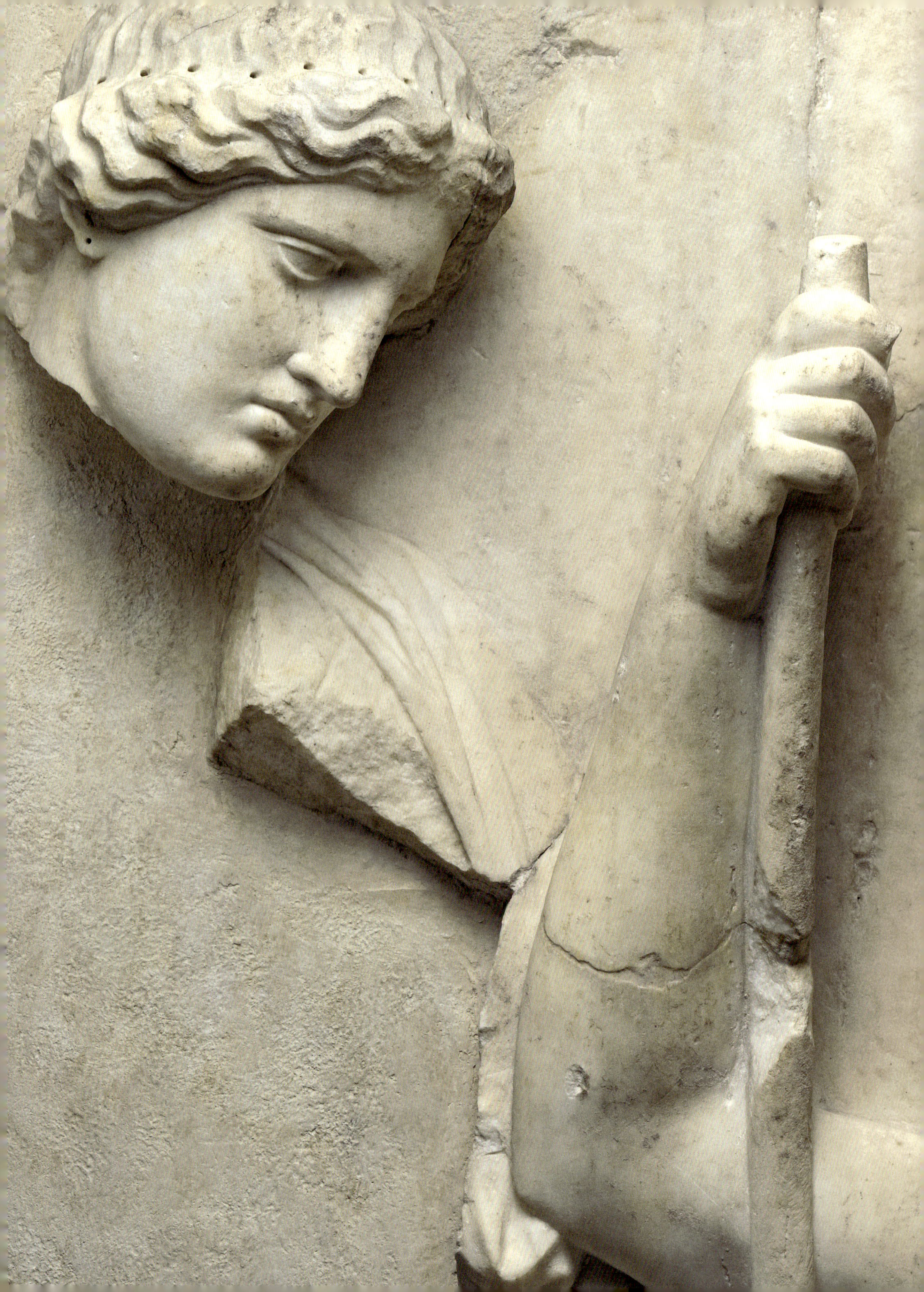

# The Sculptures

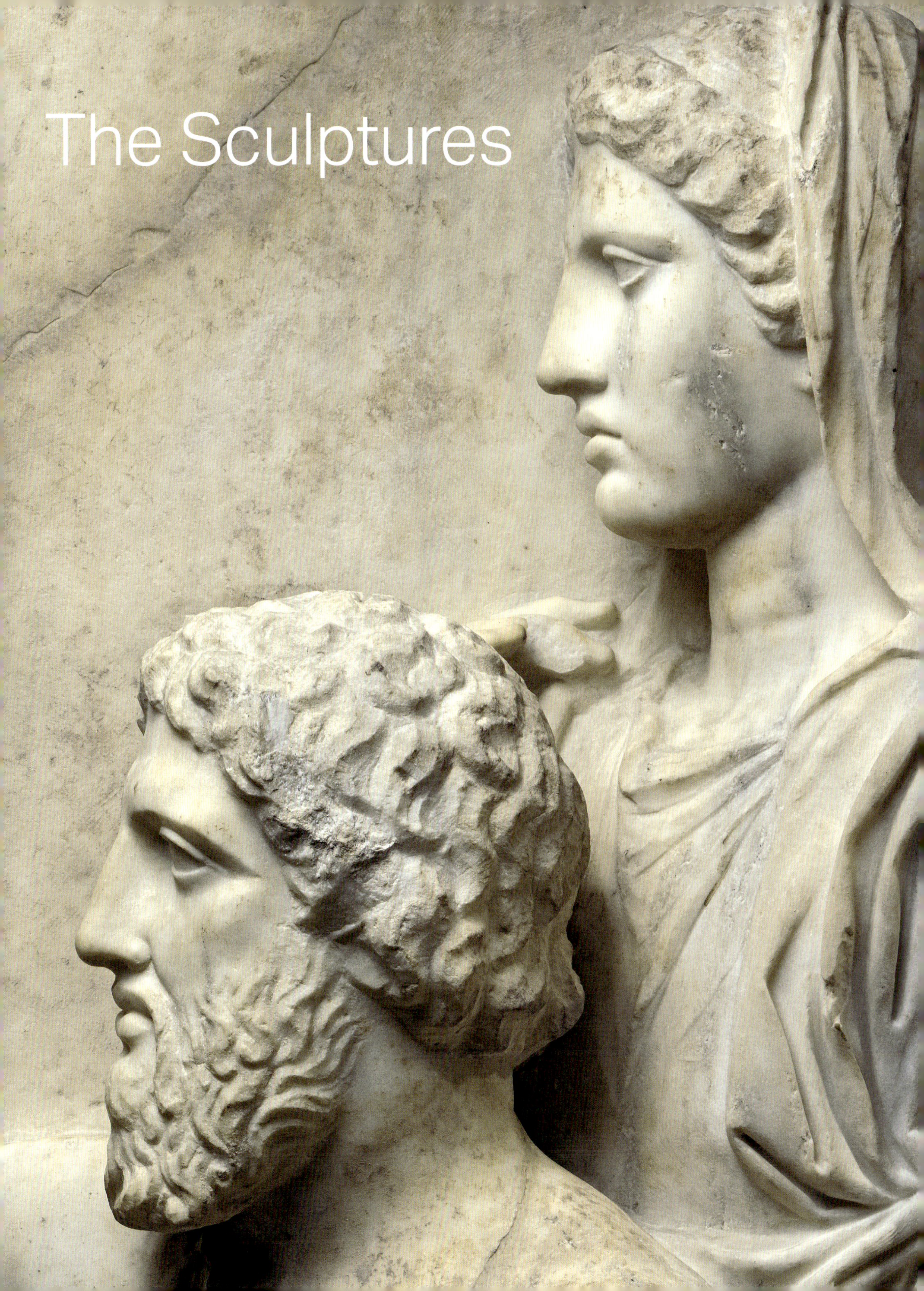

1

# Statuette of a horse

Greek, Corinthian, Geometric period, 8th century B.C.
Bronze, H. 5¼ in. (13.3 cm), L. 6 15/16 in. (17.6 cm)
Rogers Fund, 1921 (21.88.24)

Among the most distinctive works of art produced in the Geometric period, bronze statuettes of horses have been found in many parts of the Greek world, especially at sanctuaries, where they were offered to the gods as votive dedications. This statuette, a large and particularly fine example, has been attributed to a Corinthian workshop. It was solid cast by means of the direct lost wax process; the original model for the horse and its intricately decorated base would have been destroyed during the casting process, making it essentially a unique work.

The horse stands at attention with its ears pricked forward. Each element of the animal's anatomy has been reduced to its essence. The sculptor has emphasized the powerful hind legs, taut, elegant body, and fine, thin legs. The knees of the front legs are depicted in an inverted position to balance symmetrically with those of the hind legs, while the penis sheath makes clear that a stallion is represented. A thick, strong neck with an arched mane seamlessly transitions to a carefully delineated head, which emphasizes the long jawline and prominent muzzle. The extension of the tail all the way to the base adds stability to the sculpture. This design, characteristic of such depictions of horses, would have facilitated the flow of bronze during the casting process.

Since horses were first introduced into Greece, probably from the Eurasian steppes through the northern Balkans sometime in the Bronze Age (3000–1600 B.C.), they held a special place in ancient Greek art and society. They constitute one of the primary pictorial symbols of the Geometric period. Throughout the Greek mainland and on Crete, workshops manufactured solid-cast bronze horse statuettes that achieved an extraordinary elegance and clarity of form. Individual male horses like this one were especially popular. Groups, such as pairs of horses or a mare and foal (see fig. 4), are also known but are much less common.

In most Greek city-states, ownership of horses was a defining characteristic of the upper class. Cavalry was a prominent feature of the military, playing a decisive role in the outcome of some of the first historic battles, such as the Lelantine War (ca. 710–650 B.C.). Horse and chariot races were the most prestigious events of the Panhellenic games held at Olympia, Delphi, Nemea, and Isthmia, which were first established according to tradition in the first quarter of the eighth century B.C. As one of the finest stylized renderings of a horse preserved from ancient Greece, this statuette epitomizes Greek Geometric art at its most accomplished.

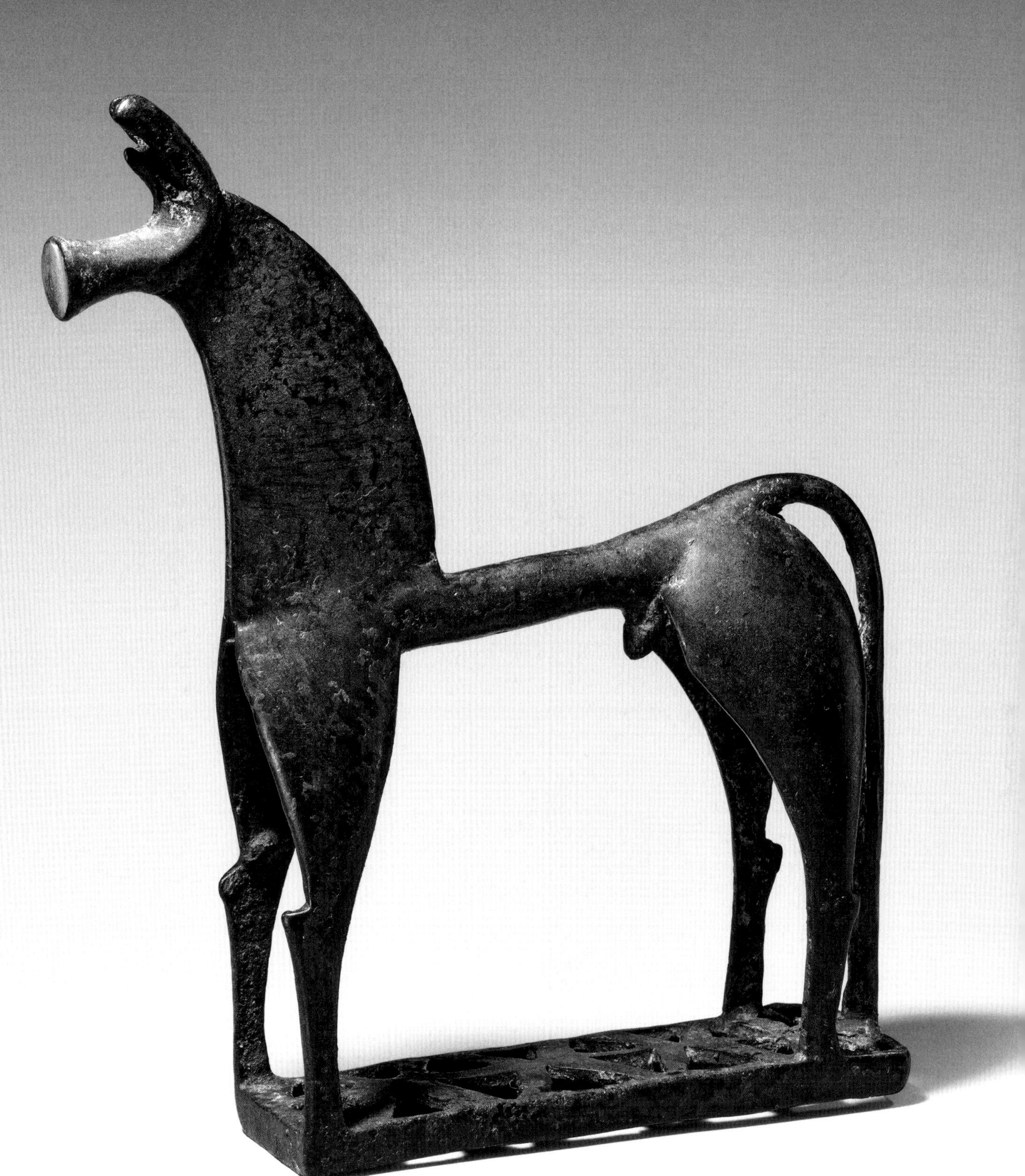

2

# Statuette of a man fighting a centaur

Greek, Peloponnesian, Late Geometric period, ca. 750 B.C.
Bronze, with silver and iron inlays, H. of man 4⅜ in. (11.1 cm),
H. of centaur 3 15/16 in. (9.9 cm), L. 5⅝ in. (14.3 cm)
Gift of J. Pierpont Morgan, 1917 (17.190.2072)

The simplified style of this powerful figural group belies the tense action of the scene and imbues the statuette with a static, almost monumental quality. The man stands upright, naked except for a broad belt and a tall conical helmet. Both legs firmly planted on the ground, he towers over the centaur, with whom he is locked in combat. It is likely that the centaur held the branch of a tree or another weapon in his right hand. With his left hand, the centaur grasps the man's right arm, which held a weapon, either a spear or more likely a sword, the remains of which protrude from the centaur's side. The centaur is represented with the body of a man attached to the hindquarters of a horse, a characteristic way to depict this hybrid creature in early Greek art.

Close inspection reveals interesting, finely wrought details. The centaur wears a conical helmet similar to that of his antagonist. A line of hair, represented as a herringbone pattern, delineates his equine spine all the way to the tail. The general characteristics of man and centaur—the proportions of the bodies, the large rounded heads with small pointed beards and pronounced ears—are similar, but the man is distinguished by his towering stature. His deep-set eyes were originally inlaid with silver, traces of which remain. Recent scientific analysis of the centaur has shown that his large round eyes are also inlaid but with an iron-rich metal that would have given them a wild, reddish hue contrasting markedly with those of the man. The man's superior height and the centaur's mortal wound indicate the outcome of the combat.

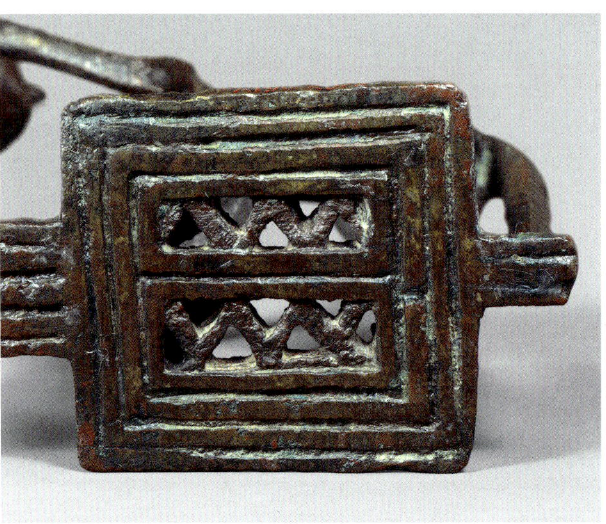

Figural groups are rare in Geometric art, and this statuette is among the finest. Said to have come from Olympia, it may be associated with a Laconian or other Peloponnesian workshop. The lack of attributes and of close parallels for the scene at this early date makes it difficult to identify the figures with any certainty, although a mythological scene is surely represented. Scholars have suggested a wide variety of identifications, including Zeus battling the monster Typhon; Zeus battling a Titan; Zeus battling Kronos, his father and king of the Titans; or a Lapith combating a centaur. More likely, the scene depicts Herakles fighting the centaur Nessos, who had abducted the hero's wife while they were crossing the river Euenos in Aitolia (central Greece). The ornamentation on the base, with its central repeated zigzag pattern (see detail), may well reference the moving waters of the river. The moment when Herakles slays Nessos was a pivotal one in his life: this act of chivalry would ultimately be the cause of his death. On a generic level, the scene represents the battle between civilized man and wild beast, the conflict between order and chaos that is a central tenet of ancient Greek philosophical thought.

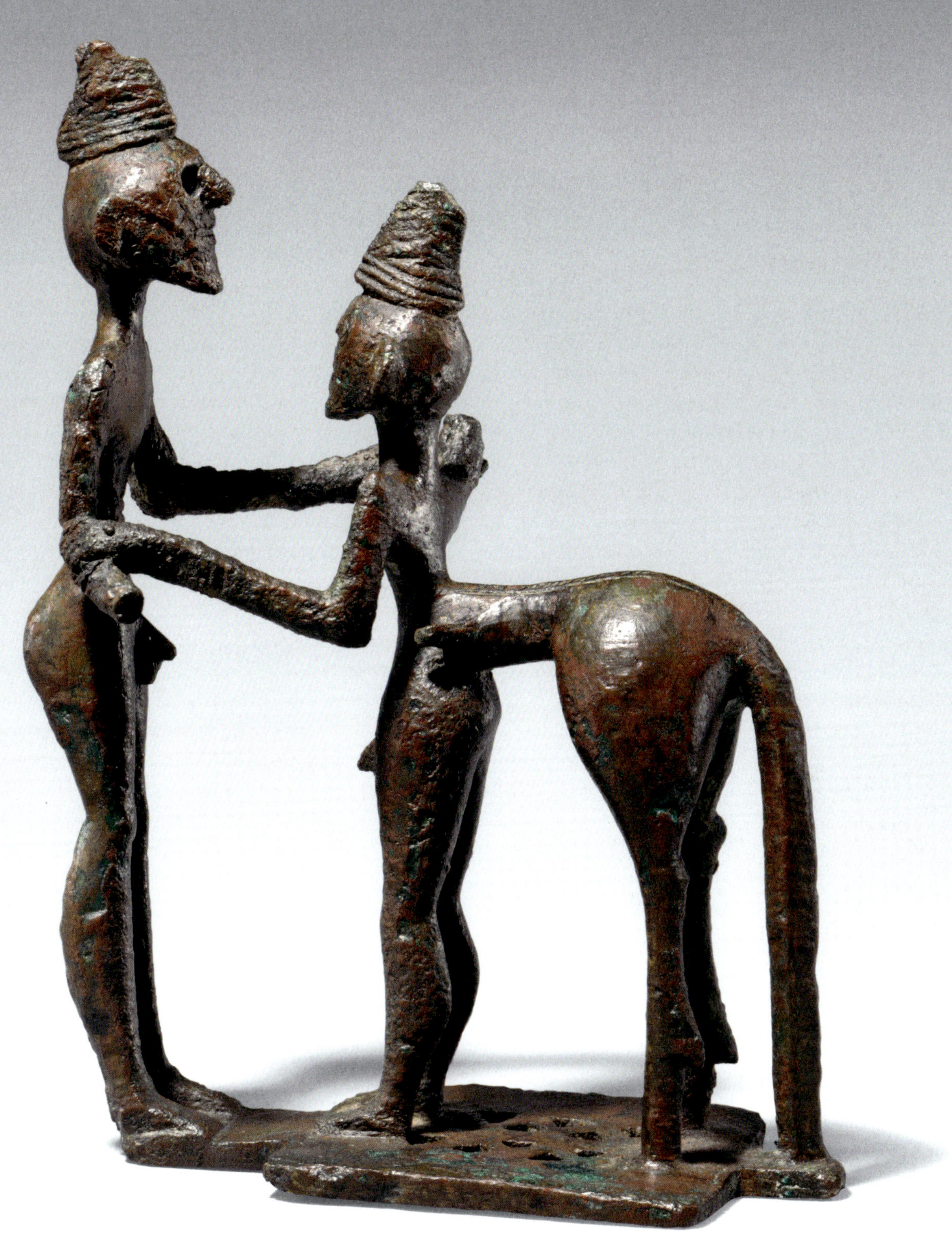

3

# Plaque with two women

Greek, possibly Cretan, Archaic period, ca. 650–625 B.C.
Ivory, H. 5⅜ in. (13.7 cm), W. 2¾ in. (7 cm), Thickness ⅝ in. (1.6 cm)
Gift of J. Pierpont Morgan, 1917 (17.190.73)

The two female figures standing side by side are carved from a single tusk of elephant ivory, an exotic material that had to be imported into Greece. Flat at the back, with two holes for attachment, the relief was an appliqué. While the carefully finished edges indicate that the plaque is an independent group, the way the women's feet are rendered in profile and the slight turn of the head of the woman on the right in the same direction as the feet reveal that the figures were part of a larger scene composed of one or more additional plaques decorating a large wooden box or chest. A likely precursor of such a chest would be the famous one owned by Kypselos, a seventh-century-B.C. Corinthian tyrant. When the Roman travel writer Pausanias saw the chest of Kypselos many centuries later in the temple of Hera at Olympia, he described it as made of cedar and ornamented in relief with figures of ivory, gold, and wood.

Although one head and parts of the women's arms are missing, enough is preserved to read the dramatic scene. The headless figure grasps the two ends of her belt and is undoing it, while one side of her garment has slipped from her shoulder and hangs down over her arm, exposing her right breast. The other figure wears a himation, loosely draped over her shoulders, and holds up one edge of the cloak as though she has just pulled it from her body, revealing her breasts and pubis. Representing an elaborately woven textile, the himation is richly decorated with an interlocking pattern of meanders bordered by a row of dots on its upper edge and a wave pattern on the lower fringe. No traces of color are preserved, but the original effect would have featured polychromy comparable to that found on the approximately contemporary Cretan limestone statue of a woman from Auxerre in the Louvre or the brightly painted Archaic korai of the Athenian Acropolis. Prominent snail curls frame the woman's forehead, and her hair flows behind her heavy-jawed face in rows of thick braids. The large almond-shaped eyes, distinctive hairstyle, heavy proportions, athletic build, and long legs align the plaque with the Daedalic style prevalent in Crete in the seventh century B.C.

One suggestion for the mythological scene represented is that the figures are Peitho, the personification of persuasion, and Aphrodite, the goddess of love. It is more likely that they are part of an early myth about the advent of the god Dionysos in Greece and represent the daughters of King Proitos of Argos, who were driven mad by the god when they refused to acknowledge his divinity. In retribution, Dionysos caused them to commit violent and unseemly acts, like the undressing occurring here, until they were healed by the seer Melampos. Such cautionary stories reminded the ancient Greeks of the need for piety and the dangers of disrespecting the gods.

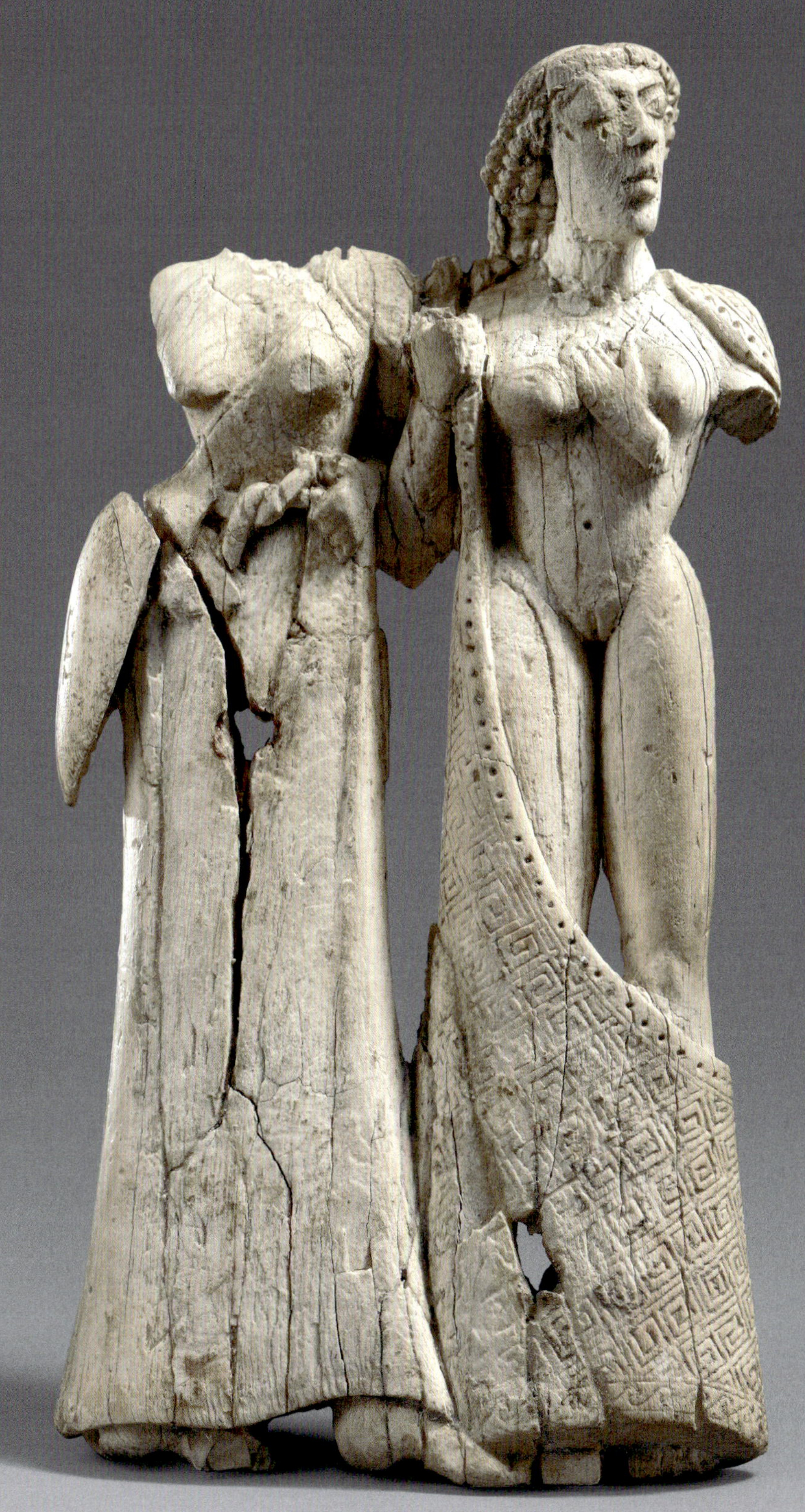

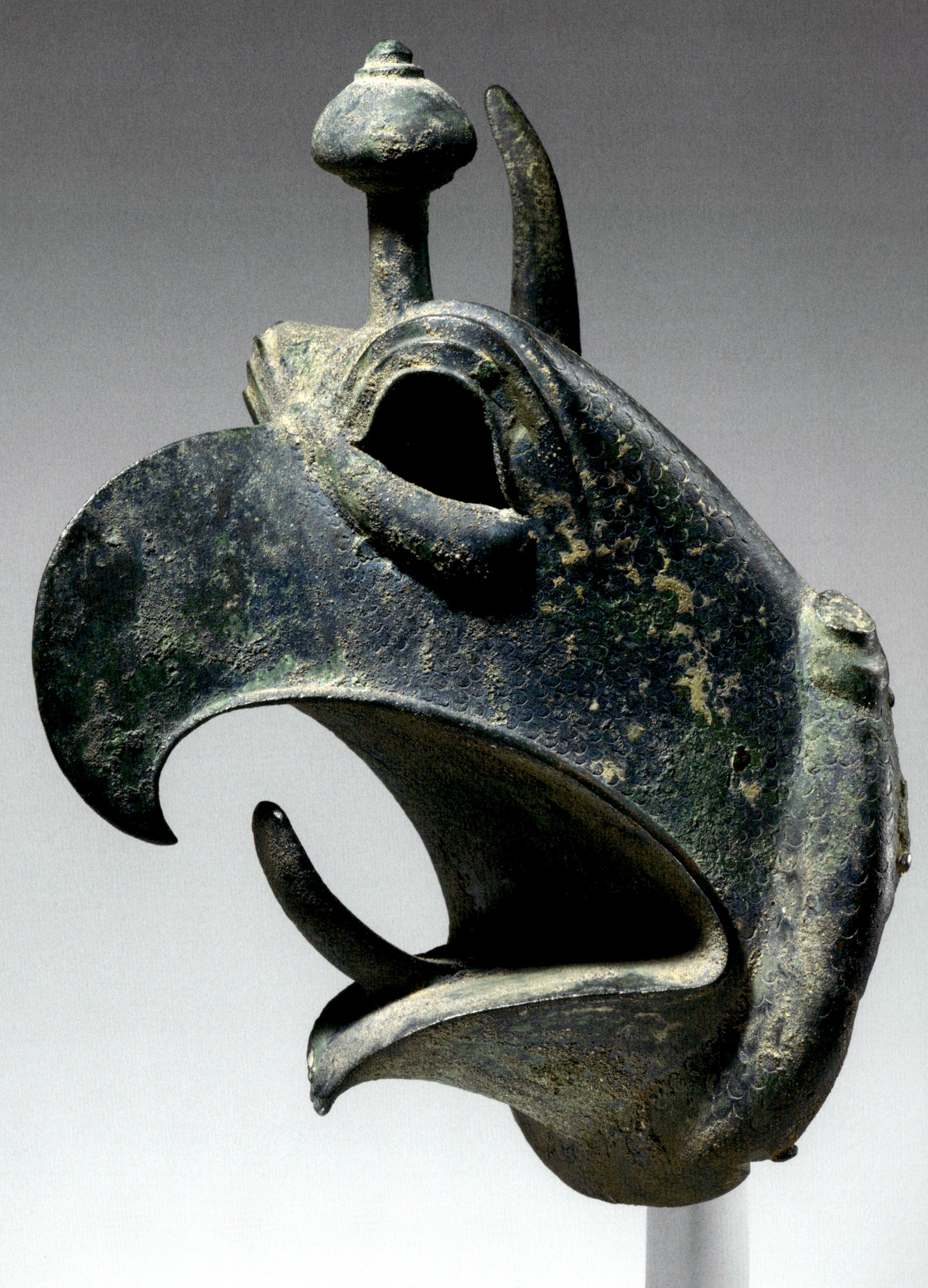

4

# Head of a griffin

Greek, Archaic period, third quarter of the 7th century B.C.
Bronze and copper, H. 10 3/16 in. (25.8 cm)
Bequest of Walter C. Baker, 1971 (1972.118.54)

The griffin is a powerful mythical beast with the head and wings of an eagle and the body of a lion. Although the creature appears in Bronze Age Aegean art, its origins lie in the Ancient Near East, and its reemergence in Greek art in the seventh century B.C. is due to the strong connections with the East at the time.

This griffin stares straight ahead with heavy brows and beak agape, its tongue extending upward. Its eyes, now hollow, would originally have been inset, giving the head a lifelike appearance. One of its long straight ears is missing. A tall decorative pommel graces the center of its head. Behind the beak and above the eyes, rows of scales that extend all around the head have been carefully added with a punch—cold-working that was done after the head was cast in one piece. A narrow band of hammered copper decorated with a bead-and-reel design originally encircled the back of the head and was attached with copper nails, six of which remain. With its brighter color, this band securing the neck would have stood out from the bronze.

The head was made to serve as a protome, an adornment for the rim of a large bronze cauldron (fig. 31). Hundreds of Archaic Greek bronze griffin protomes are known today, with especially large numbers having been discovered at the sanctuaries at Olympia and Samos. Massive cauldrons with animal-shaped attachments were among the most spectacular dedications made at sanctuaries in ancient Greece in the Archaic period. The Greek historian Herodotus described seeing truly monumental specimens, including one commissioned by King Croesus of Lydia that could hold 2,700 gallons and another with griffin protomes set up on a group of three kneeling over-lifesize bronze figures at the sanctuary of Hera on the island of Samos.

This example, one of the largest of its type to have survived from antiquity, was found in 1914 in the bed of the Kladeos River, near the gymnasium at ancient Olympia. It is one of three that have been associated because of their similar size and technique, the others being in the National Archaeological Museum, Athens, and the Archaeological Museum of Olympia. All three griffin heads are thought to have been part of a single votive dedication—a cauldron featuring multiple projecting griffin protomes—that is estimated to have stood more than ten feet high. Peering out with their strong, sharp beaks open wide, the griffins served as protectors that would have instilled awe and respect in the viewer.

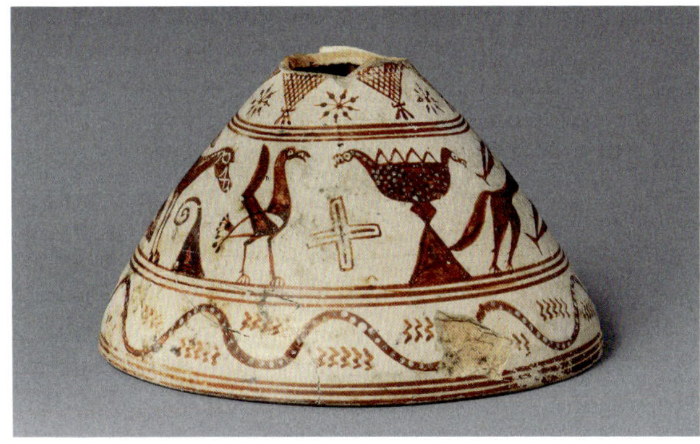

Fig. 31. Conical lekythos (oil flask) illustrating a bronze cauldron with protomes on a conical stand. Greek, Corinthian, Archaic period, ca. 700 B.C. Terracotta, H. 3 5/8 in. (9.2 cm), Diam. 6 7/16 in. (16.4 cm). Rogers Fund, 1923 (23.160.18)

5

# Rod tripod stand

Greek, Archaic period, late 7th century B.C.
Bronze, H. 29⅝ in. (75.2 cm)
Gift of Mr. and Mrs. Klaus G. Perls, 1997 (1997.145.1)

This impressive tripod stand demonstrates how successfully ancient Greek metalsmiths incorporated flowers and animals, both mythical and real, into their vessels and utensils. Rising from feline-paw feet, the central rod of each leg is capped with a palmette and, above this, on the upper ring, with a couchant Sphinx. Above the inverted U-shaped intermediate rods, large horse protomes, each including the forelegs as well as the head turned out to its right, decorate the upper rim. A lotus blossom appears below each horse protome.

Methodical and ornate, the disparate elements seen in this stand were popular motifs in Archaic Greek art. The

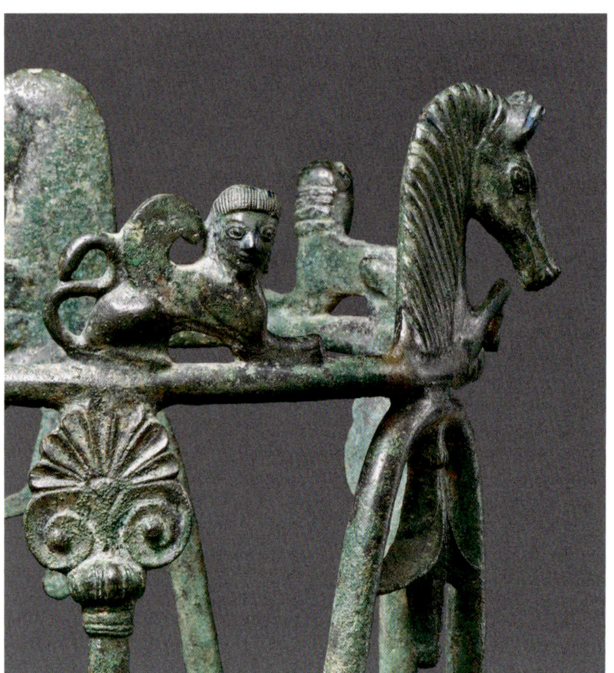

Sphinxes, feline feet, and lotus blossoms look to Near Eastern iconography at a time when greatly expanded trade contacts with the cultures of Mesopotamia, the Levant, Asia Minor, and Egypt were reflected in Greek art. The prominent, lively rampant horses attest to the continued importance of that powerful and graceful animal for the ancient Greeks in the late seventh century B.C. Palmettes became one of the most favored decorative motifs in Greek bronze vessels and utensils, where they appeared especially in connective areas. Such floral motifs contributed an element of natural life to the design.

Rod tripod stands have a long history in the eastern Mediterranean. The earliest examples appeared on Cyprus in the thirteenth century B.C., and the type continued to be produced there and elsewhere in the succeeding centuries. The widely distributed Cypriot version has been found on Cyprus, Crete, and the Cyclades as well as in mainland Greece, Sardinia, and Italy. This stand is an early example of a later, ornate type of Greek manufacture. Cast in several pieces and then soldered and jointed together, it is a highly accomplished piece of metalwork and would have supported a bronze vessel, most likely a cauldron. Two other well-preserved specimens of this type are known, one from Trebenishte in North Macedonia and the other from Metapontum in southern Italy; both are later in date, belonging to the sixth century B.C., and have been attributed to Laconian workshops. Close parallels for the Sphinxes, horses, and palmettes support the suggestion that this stand was made on the island of Samos, home of the great sanctuary of the goddess Hera and known as an important center of Early Archaic bronze production.

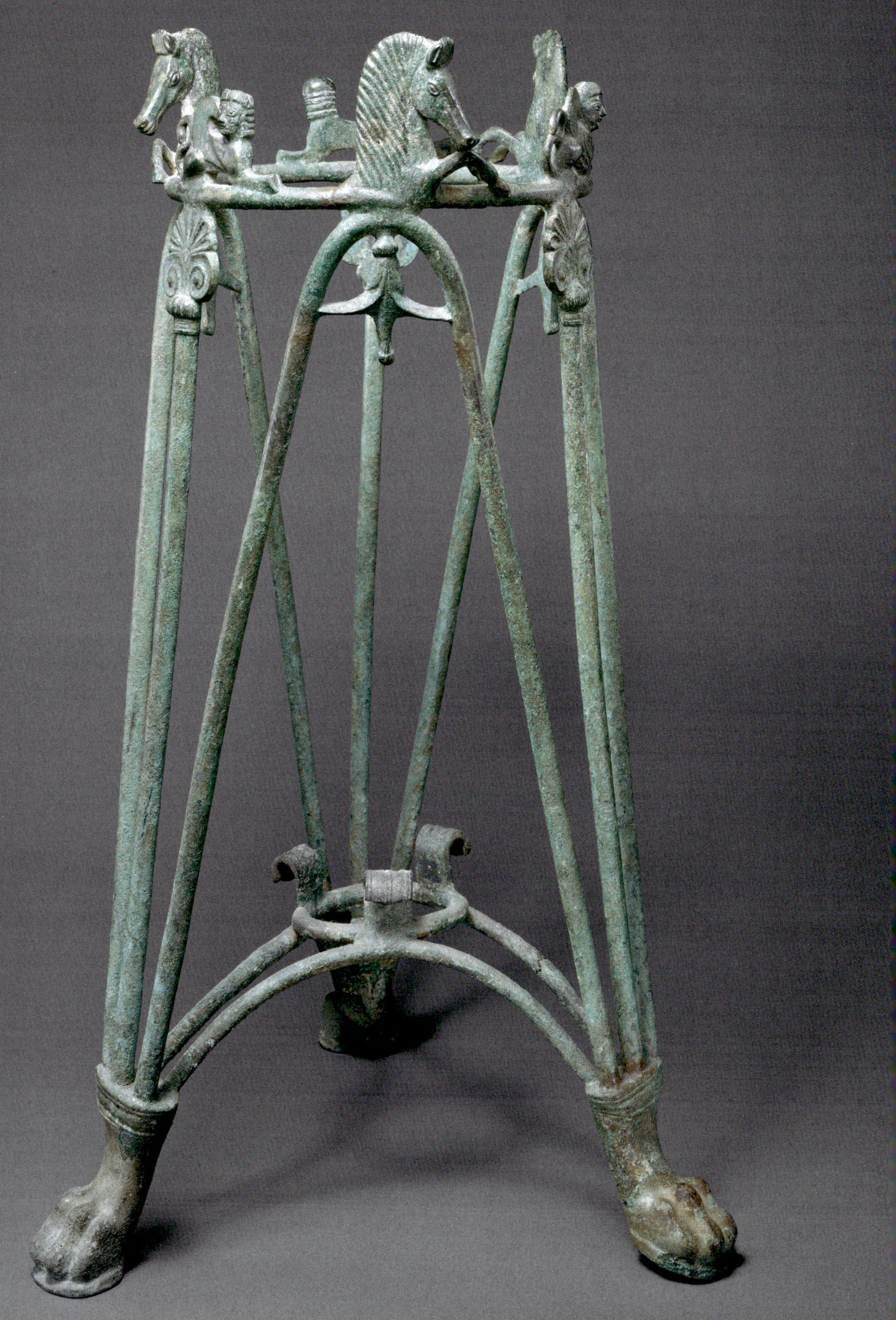

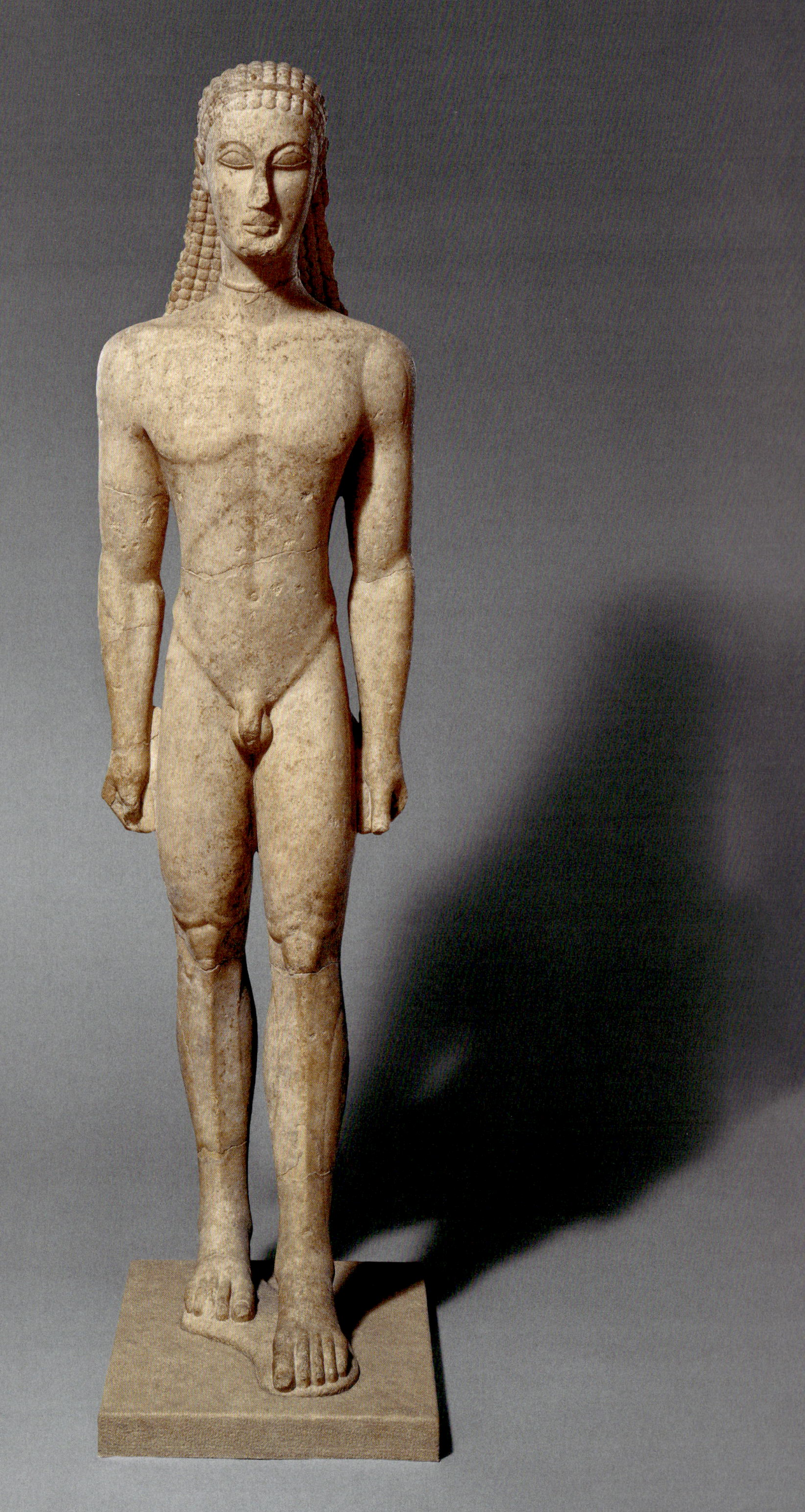

6

# Statue of a *kouros* (youth)

Greek, Attic, Archaic period, ca. 590–580 B.C.
Marble, H. without plinth 76⅝ in. (194.6 cm)
Fletcher Fund, 1932 (32.11.1)

The most characteristic type of male sculpture made in Greece during the Archaic period is the kouros, or statue of a nude youth. The New York Kouros, as the present work is known, is among the earliest surviving examples of the type from Attica, the region around Athens. The type would endure for more than a hundred years. The ancient Greeks learned how to carve monumental stone sculpture from Egypt, where there was a long history of the practice. This statue is remarkable in that it makes a direct link with its Egyptian predecessors by using an Egyptian canon of proportions. When carving reliefs or sculpture in the round, Egyptian artists used a grid that allowed them to conform the proportions of figures to their notion of the ideal human form. Nevertheless, the Greek sculptor has made the composition his own, daring to free the figure from attachment to a stone support at the back, which was a characteristic feature of the Egyptian examples for centuries (see fig. 55).

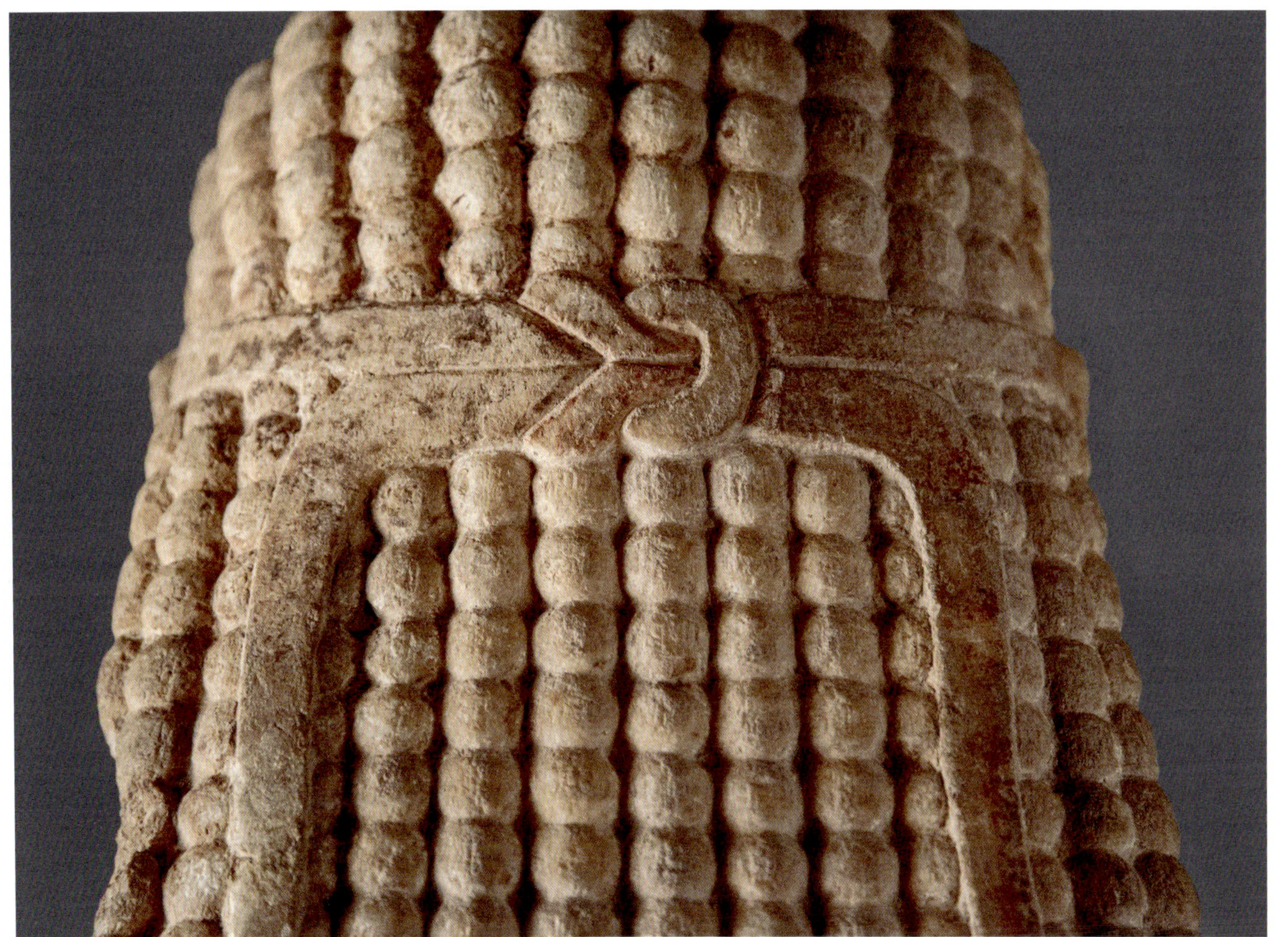

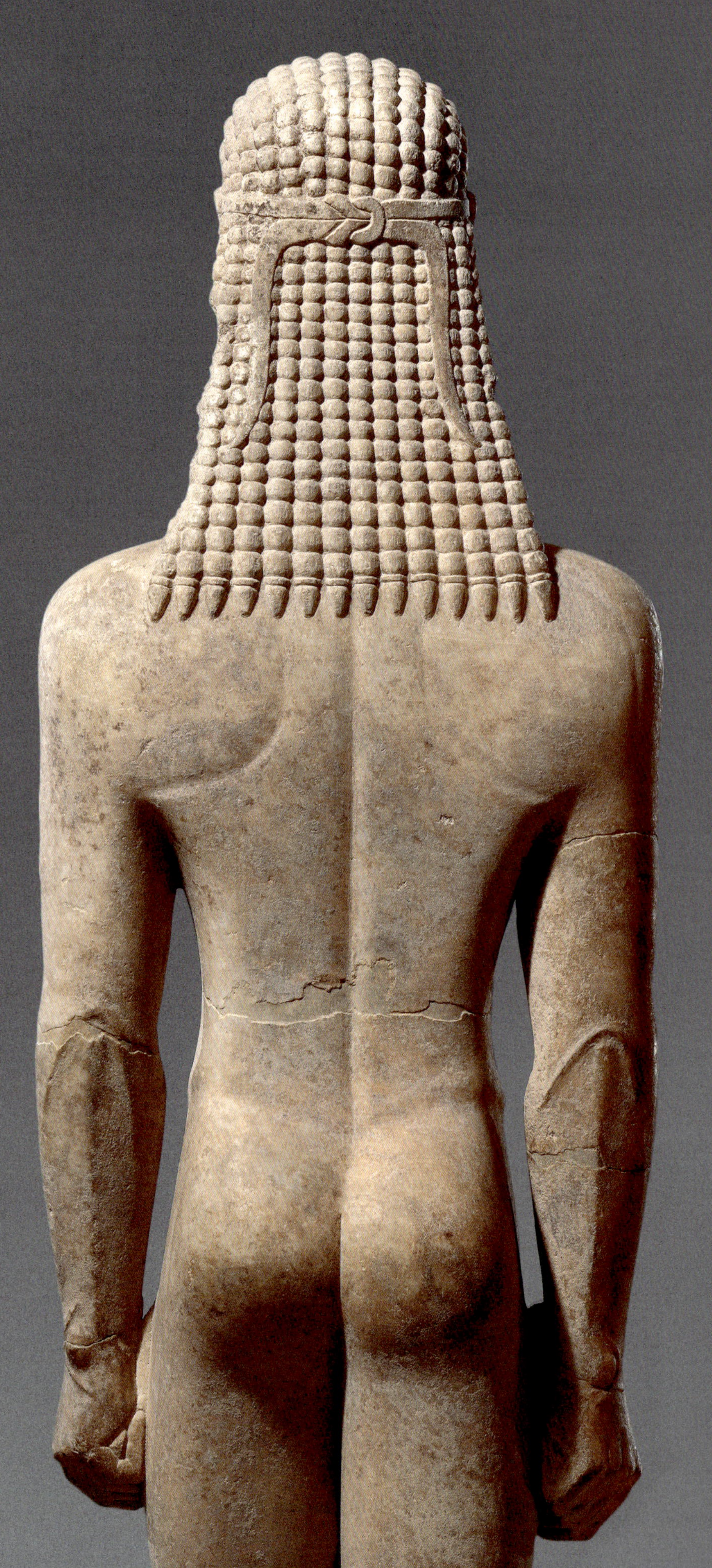

Although today we call the period in which the statue was made Archaic, which generally means ancient or old-fashioned, this statue would have seemed incredibly new and lifelike to those who saw it at the time that it was made, in the early sixth century B.C. The figure stands on his own two feet with his arms at his side, and the left foot is placed forward to indicate motion. His long hair, hanging down to his shoulders and adorned with a fillet, is carefully coiffed. Extensive polychromy remains on the figure, including traces on the eyes, the hair, and the fillet, the band around his neck, his nipples, and the area of his pubic hair, all of which would have added to the realistic impression. The idealized and heroized nudity celebrates the human male form at the height of its physical beauty.

Looking at the sculpture from each side, one can imagine the piece of marble from which it was carved, and indeed it retains a blocklike quality. Details of the anatomy, such as the pectorals, rib cage, calf muscles, and shoulder blades, are carefully delineated with a geometric precision that is rooted in the art of the preceding age. The way in which features like the tendons around the wrists and elbows are applied to the surface in an abstract way, rather than being subsumed beneath the skin, is typical of Early Attic marble sculpture from the first half of the sixth century B.C. Also characteristic are the symmetry of the figure, the almond-shaped eyes, and the "Archaic smile," an enigmatic trait that appears on most sculptures of the period and adds to their vitality.

Used as dedications at sanctuaries and as grave markers, statues of *kouroi* (youths) have been found in many parts of the ancient Greek world. This example probably served to mark the grave of a young aristocratic Athenian. Excavations in the Kerameikos cemetery of Athens have yielded a very similar marble head that also would have marked the grave of an Athenian youth. It was likely carved in the same workshop or even by the same sculptor.

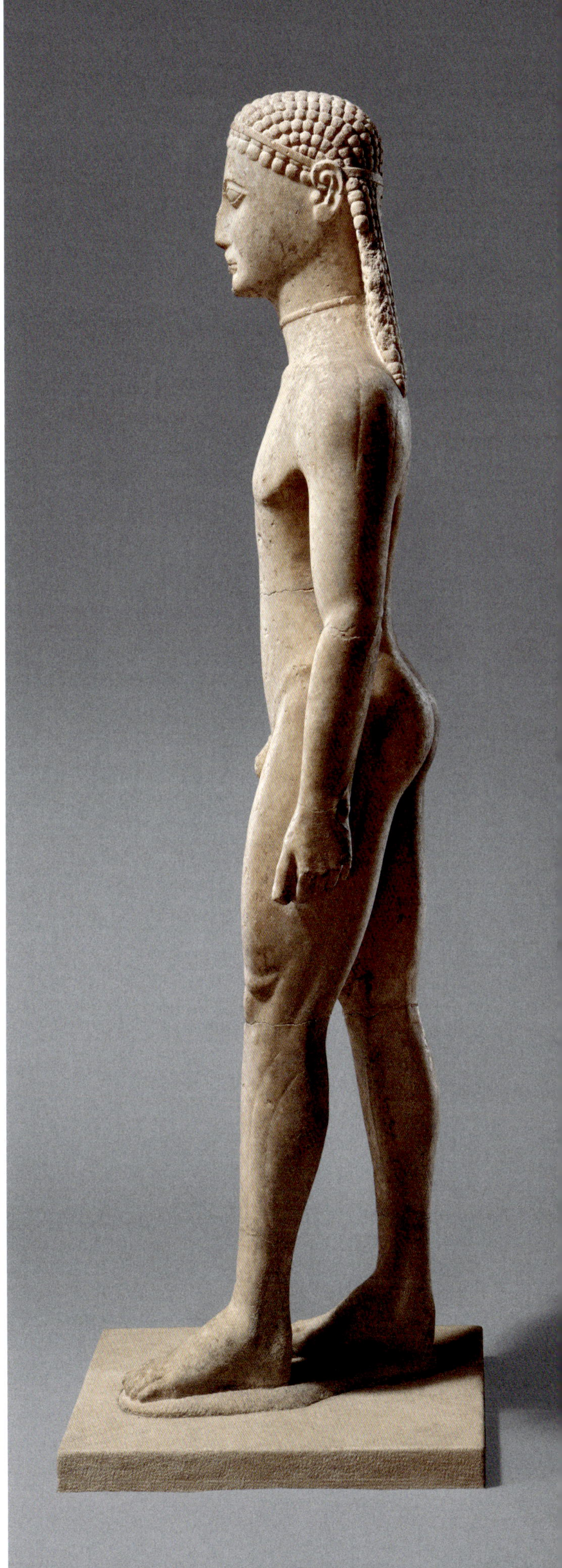

7

# Alabastron in the form of two women back-to-back

Greek, Rhodian, Archaic period, ca. 540 B.C.
Terracotta, H. 10⅝ in. (27 cm)
Fletcher Fund, 1930 (30.11.6)

During the sixth century B.C., sculptural vases in many forms were popular throughout the Greek world. Each side of this vase, meant to contain scented oil, represents a *kore* (maiden) holding a bird. The wide lip on the top served for the dispensation of a small amount of precious oil that the owner could dab her fingers into and apply as needed. Such a scene appears on a remarkable Etruscan amber bow fibula of the late sixth century B.C. showing a woman reclining on a couch with a man and extracting oil from an alabastron (fig. 32).

Although wearing identical garments and assuming essentially the same pose, the two women are represented slightly differently. One holds her right hand at her side, while the other clasps the bird with both hands. Paint enlivens the figures, but only traces of the polychromy are preserved. In their stance, the garments they wear, and the way they hold the birds, the figures recall the korai, large-scale marble statues of young women that served as dedications at sanctuaries, particularly in the Dodecanese Islands and the Greek settlements along the western coast of Asia Minor. While most likely made on the island of Rhodes, this piece is said to have been found in western Sicily and illustrates the wide circulation that sculptural vases had in the Archaic period.

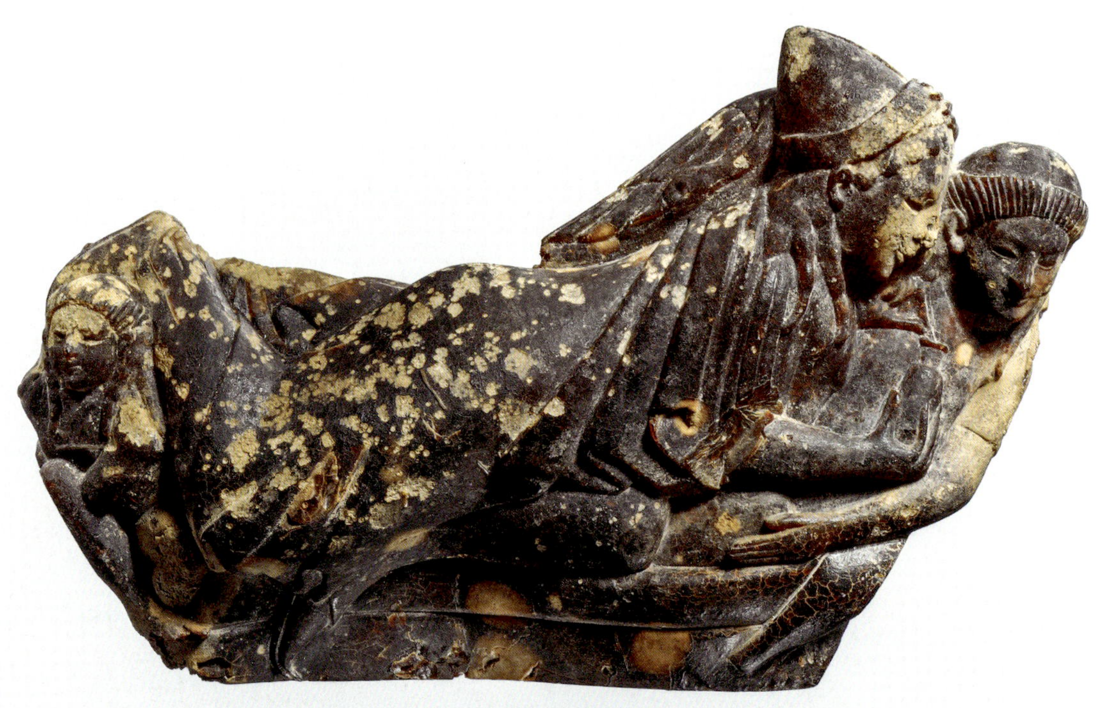

Fig. 32. Bow from a fibula (clasp) with a man and woman reclining on a couch. Etruscan, Archaic period, ca. 500 B.C. Amber, H. 3 5/16 in. (8.4 cm). Gift of J. Pierpont Morgan, 1917 (17.190.2067)

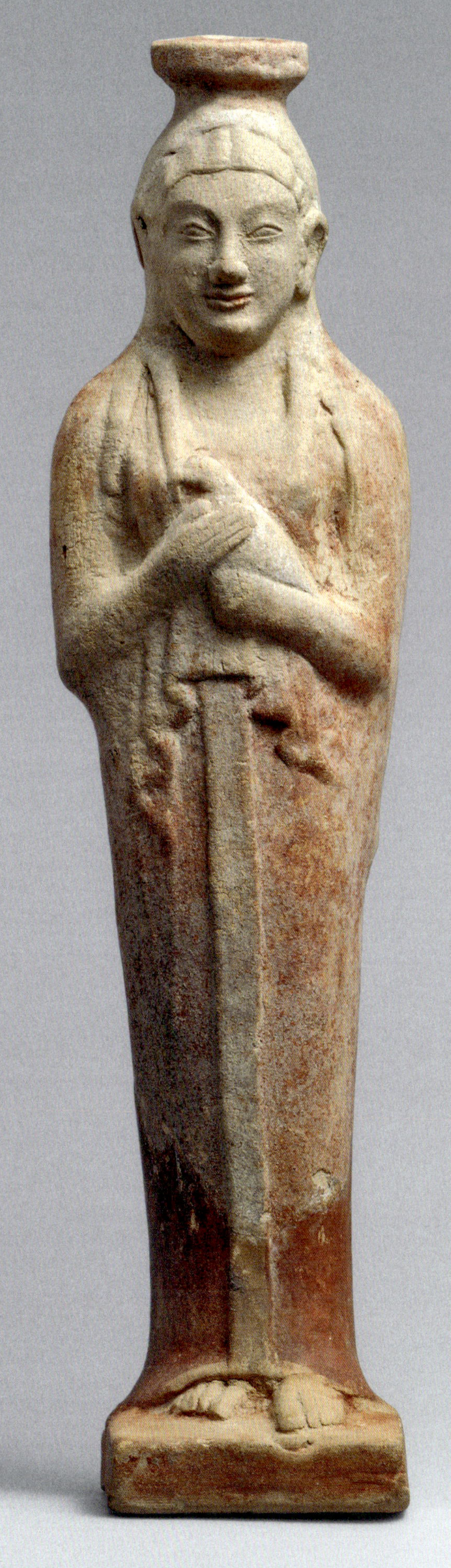

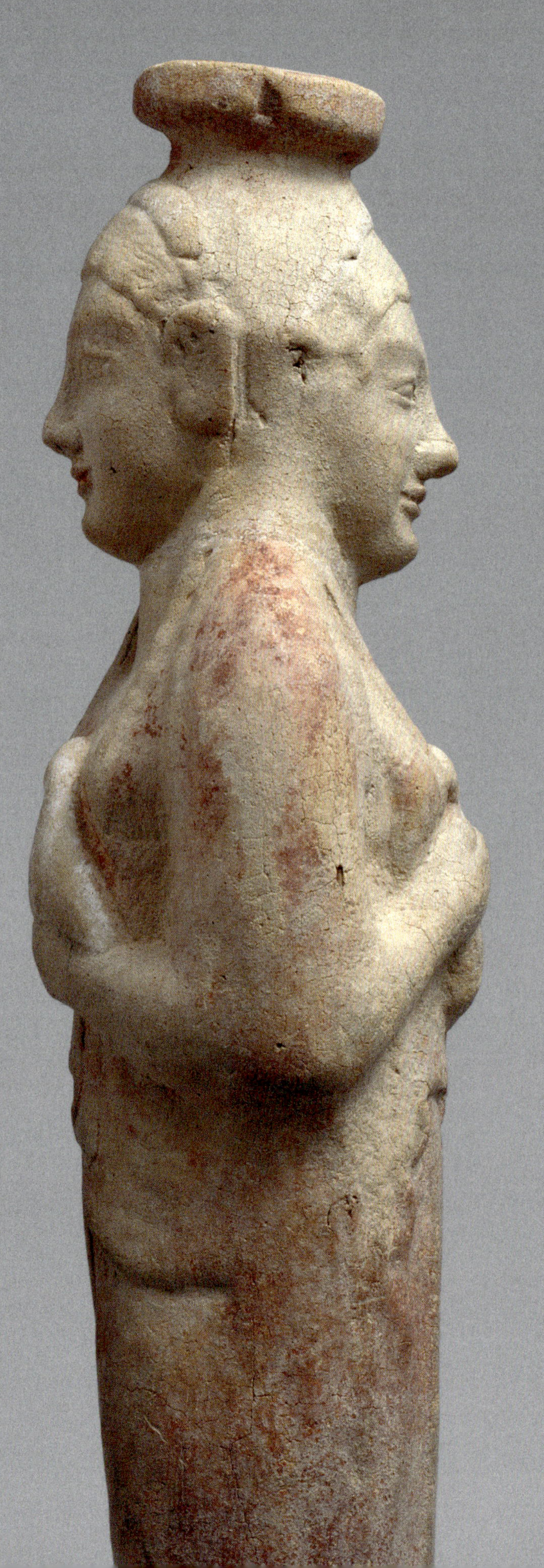

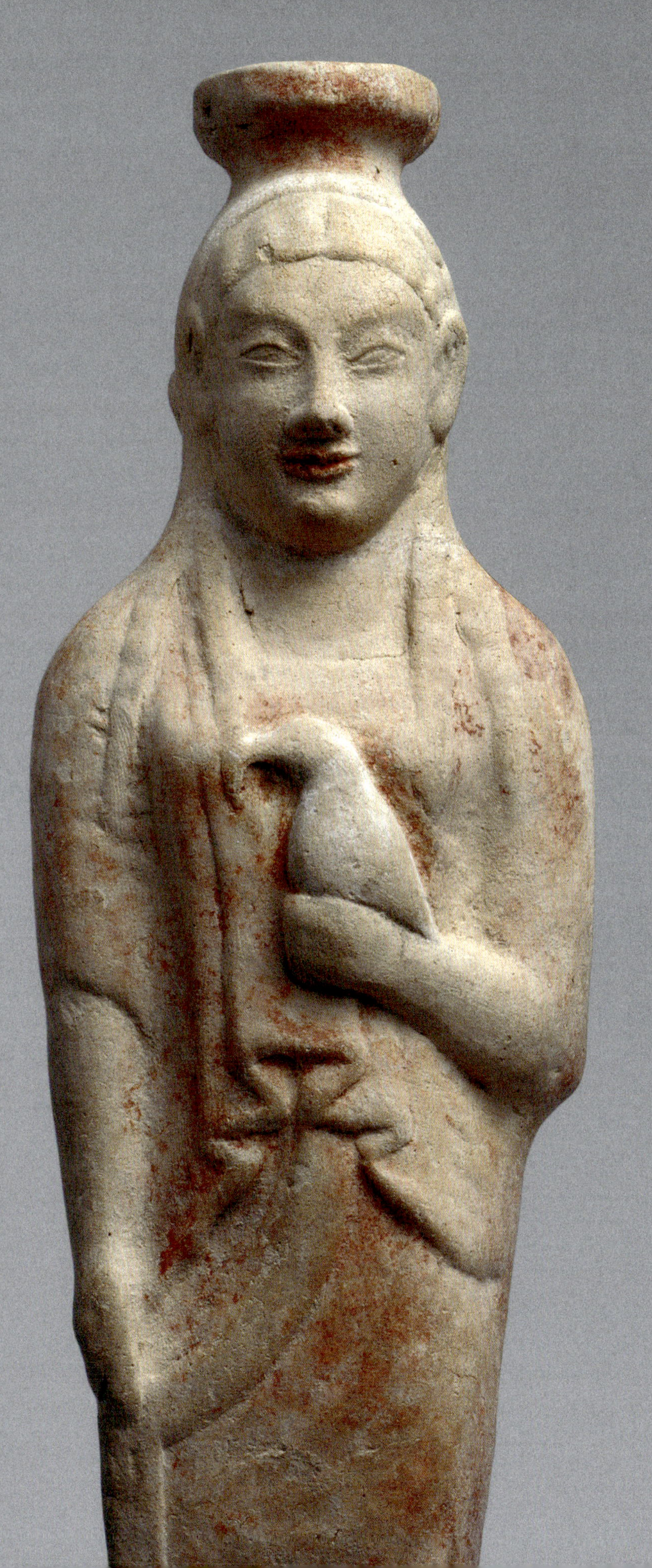

8

# Oil lamp

Greek, Archaic period, third quarter of the 6th century B.C.
Marble, H. 2½ in. (6.4 cm), Diam. 6½ in. (16.5 cm)
Rogers Fund, 1906 (06.1072), and Lent by the Museum of Fine Arts, Boston (L.1974.44)

A prominent feature of ancient Greek life, oil lamps were made in a variety of media, including terracotta, stone, bronze, gold, and even glass. This circular example has three nozzles that project symmetrically from its sides. Each nozzle contained a wick that drew oil from the central well and, when lit, radiated light from a flame just above the top of the marble. Of the two grooves that encircle the top, one continues around each of the nozzles to form a lip. At the center of the base is a hole for an iron spike that was used to raise the lamp above the ground. Part of the spike is still lodged inside the hole.

The lamp is richly carved in shallow relief over much of its surface, while the bold, carefully articulated elements of its form are embellished with architectural ornament. Vertical bead-and-reel moldings frame the main panels of each of the sides, which are capped with an overhanging horizontal ovolo (egg-shaped) molding. Each panel is decorated with a pair of different mythical creatures facing each other: Sirens, griffins, and Sphinxes. Carved into the nozzles in shallow relief are more pairings, each different and drawn from the natural world: rams' heads, rampant and confronted roaring lions, and birds of prey perched on lotus flowers growing out of palmettes. The soft light that flickered from the nozzles would have lit up the lively, richly detailed animals, an effect further enhanced by the translucency of the marble.

The lamp in The Met collection is said to have been found at Thebes in Boeotia. Currently joined to it is a fragment comprising the nozzle decorated with rams' heads and part of the griffin panel that has been lent by the Museum of Fine Arts, Boston. This fragment was once in the collection of the art historian Adolf Furtwängler, who believed that it was found in Attica between Athens and Eleusis. The different alleged provenances for the lamp fragments have made both of them uncertain and are a reminder that such undocumented provenances cannot necessarily be relied on.

In the late seventh and sixth centuries B.C., Greek sculptors created a variety of marble oil lamps with one to three nozzles and occasionally featuring carved relief decoration. Some have central holes for spikes, like this lamp; others are pierced around their rims and were suspended by rope or chains. Such lamps have been found in tombs and at a number of sanctuaries around the Greek world, including the Athenian Acropolis, the island of Samos, and the Greek colony of Selinus in Sicily, where they were votive objects that probably served to provide light for nighttime rituals. The present lamp is one of the best preserved and most ornate examples of its type—a fine example of the excellent work that Greek marble sculptors achieved in the Archaic period and the attention they lavished on small-scale utilitarian artifacts.

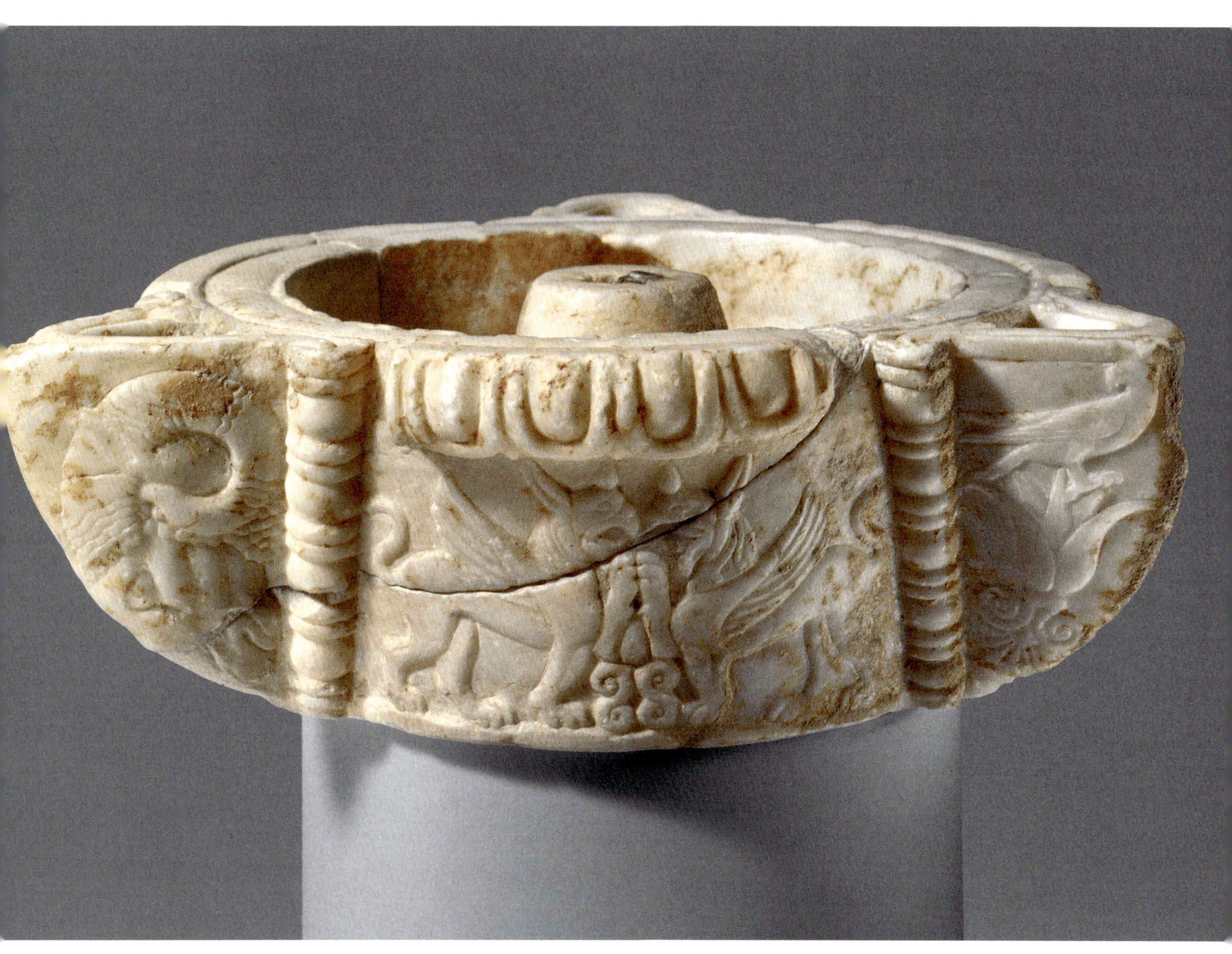

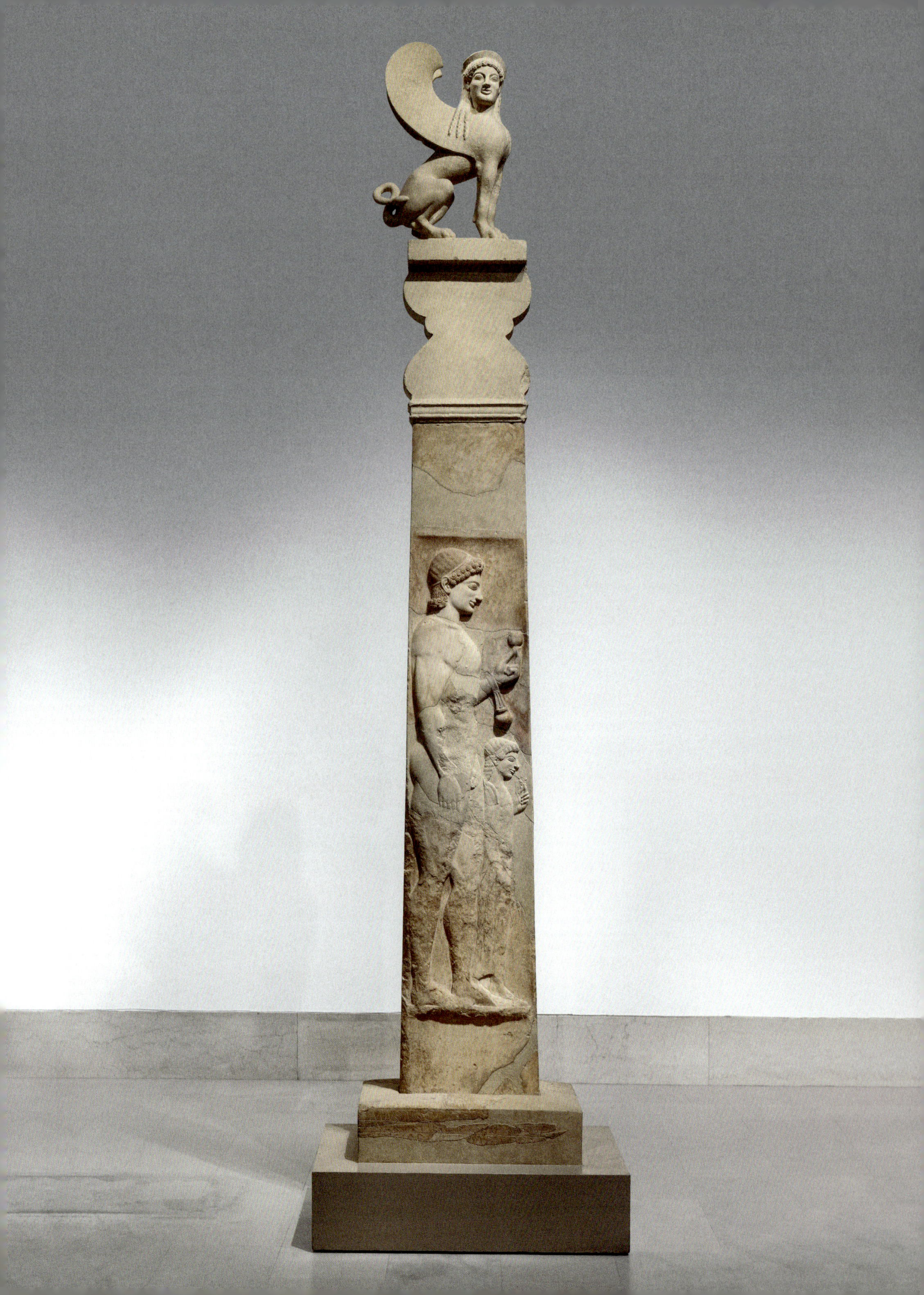

9

# Stele of a youth and a little girl

Greek, Attic, Archaic period, ca. 530 B.C.
Marble and lead, H. overall 13 feet 10 11/16 in. (423.4 cm)
Frederick C. Hewitt Fund, 1911; Rogers Fund, 1921; Munsey Funds, 1936, 1938; and Anonymous Gift, 1951 (11.185a–d, f, g, x)

Inscribed on base: To the dead Philo and Me[. . .] the father erected (this) monument, and together the dear mother . . .

This imposing, exquisitely detailed tomb marker is one of the most impressive Archaic Greek grave monuments to survive. It is made up of four sections that have been recomposed from fragments: a base with an inscription, a shaft with a relief scene of a youth and a little girl, a capital, and a Sphinx. The inscription carved into the base is not completely preserved, but enough remains to indicate that the monument was erected by both parents of the deceased. It is said to be from Kataphygi in Attica, southeast of Hymettos.

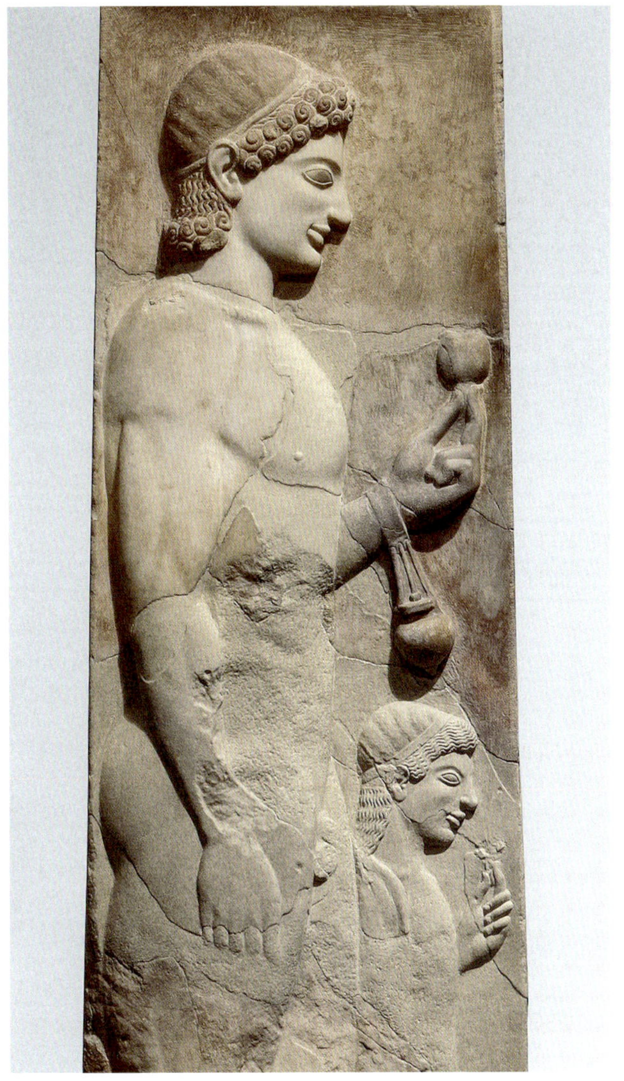

The youth and small child probably represent the deceased and his younger sister. The youth is shown as an athlete, naked with an aryballos (oil flask) around his wrist and holding in his left hand a pomegranate, a symbol of death and rebirth. The little girl standing next to him holds a flower bud in her hand. She is represented with the long hair of a maiden and the features of a miniature adult, as was typically done in Greek sculpture before the Hellenistic period. Her small scale indicates that she is a child and much younger than the youth. The top of the monument is crowned with a Sphinx, a mythical beast with the body of a lion, the wings of an eagle, and the head of a beautiful woman. She wears upon her head an ornate crown decorated with a fine painted meander pattern. Other details, such as her necklace, the feathers on her wings, and the ornate floral decoration of the capital, can be traced through remains of the original paint. Some painted details become quite visible under ultraviolet light, including the spirals that are bound together to form

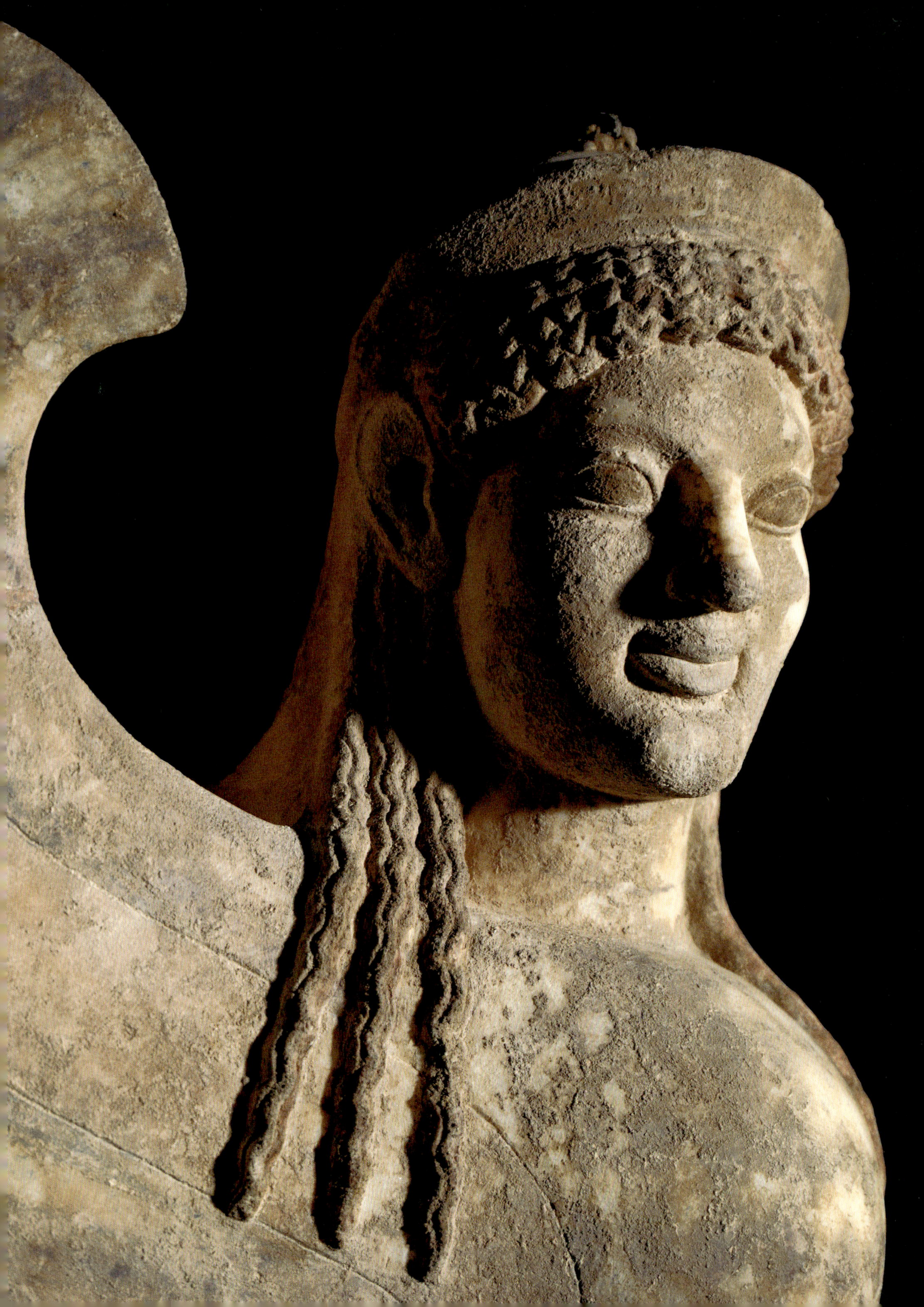

the double volute capital, which is decorated at its base with a large painted central palmette (fig. 33). Although the painted decoration is faded today, enough traces remain to make us realize how ornate it originally was.

It is useful to compare the rendering of the youth's musculature to that of the New York Kouros, which is dated some fifty to sixty years earlier (no. 6). Although the stance is essentially the same in each, the sculptor presents a much more naturalistic representation here. The physiognomic details are no longer applied to the surface but have been subsumed within the flesh. The Sphinx also gives a remarkably lifelike impression. Notice the spirited quality of her tail, like that of a feline predator who has noticed something nearby. Standing on her haunches as though ready to pounce, she served as a guardian of the tomb, helping ensure that no one would rob the grave and desecrate the memory of the deceased. The tallest such monument preserved today, this stele must have been visible from a great distance as one approached the cemetery.

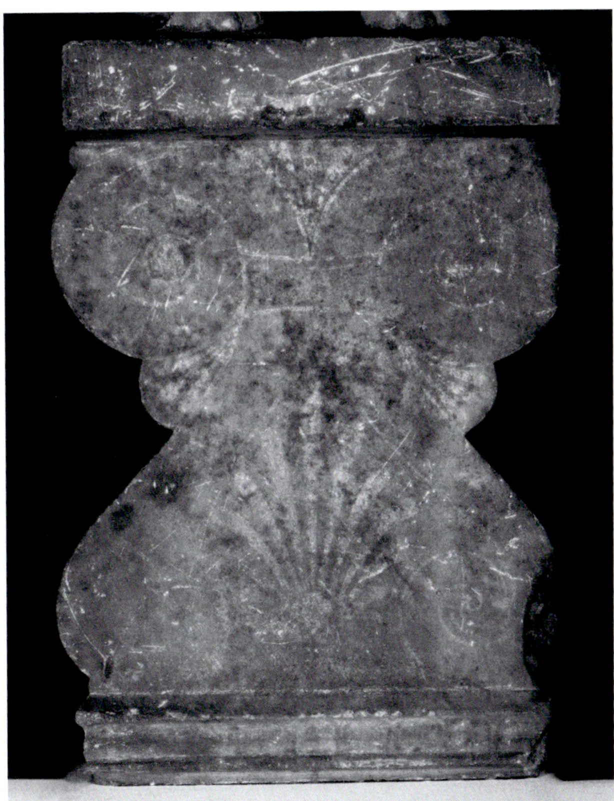

Fig. 33. Enhanced Ultraviolet Light (UVL) image of the capital revealing traces of the original painted decoration

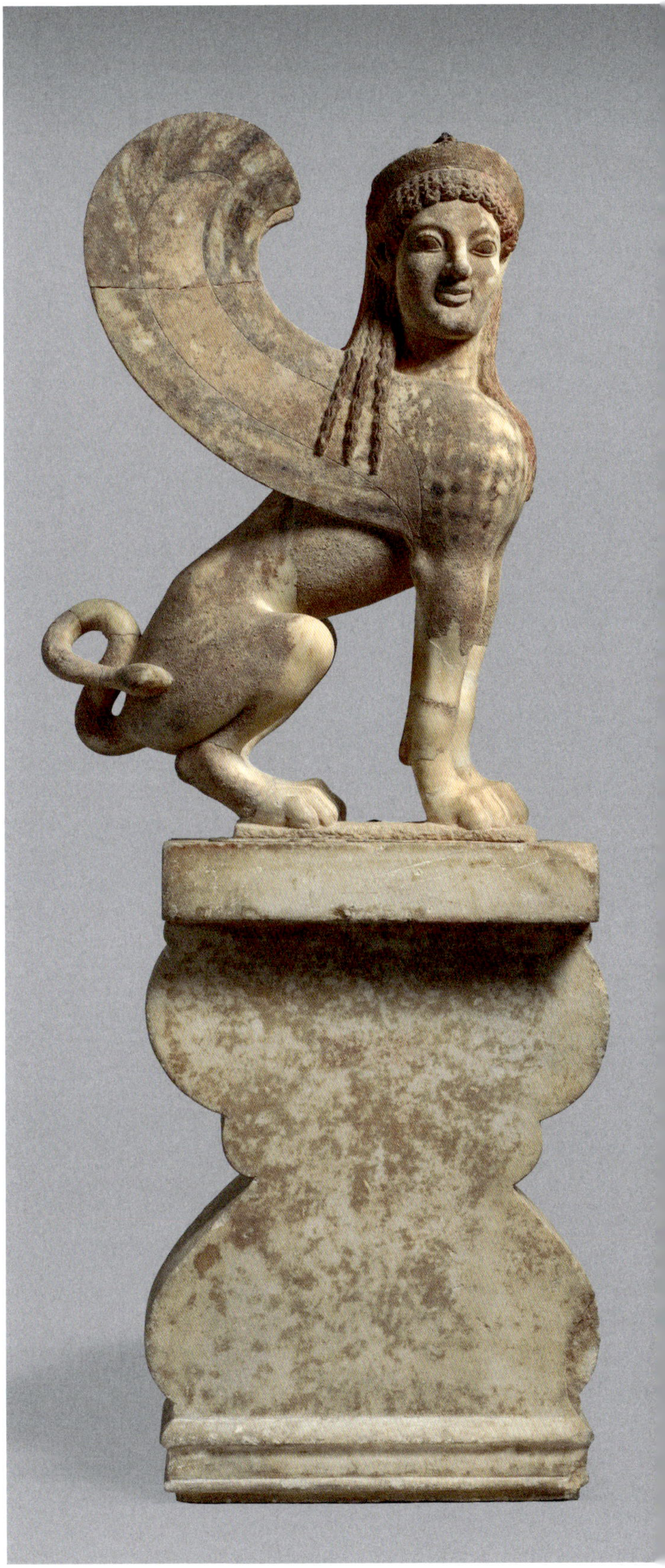

10

# Fragment of a stele of a hoplite

Greek, Attic, Archaic period, ca. 525–515 B.C.
Hymettian marble, 55 15/16 × 20 1/8 in. (142.1 × 51.1 cm)
Fletcher Fund, 1938 (38.11.13)

Representing the legs and feet of a hoplite (foot soldier) standing in profile, this fragment of a grave marker is notable for its fine carving and the significant traces of polychromy preserved on its surface. Hoplites were the regular heavily armed infantry of the Greek city-states. Citizens who had sufficient means to arm themselves but could not afford to maintain horses were required to serve as hoplites. The standard kit of these soldiers included a helmet, cuirass, and greaves of bronze. As seen on the stele, the latter safeguarded the shins and calves as well as the especially sensitive kneecaps, which could be protected with additional apotropaic designs intended to ward off evil (fig. 34).

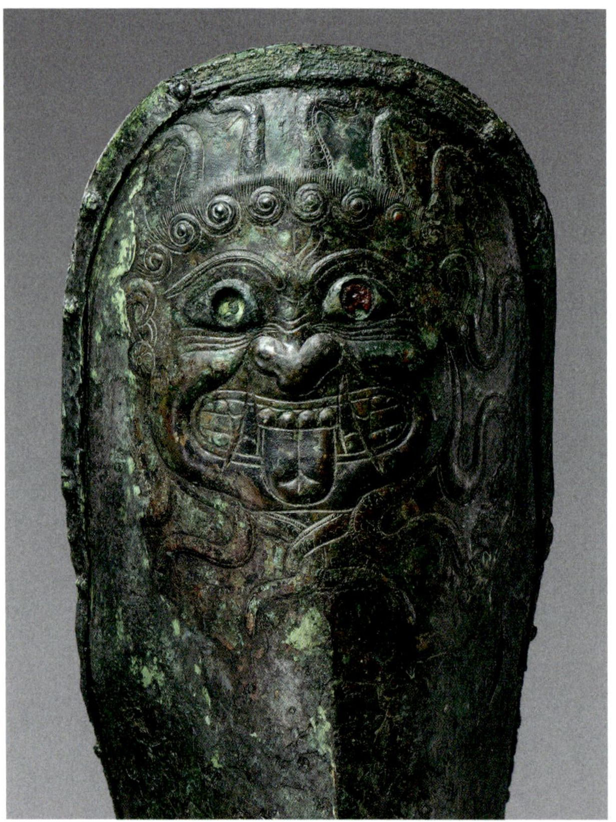

Fig. 34. Greave with the head of Medusa on the kneecap. Greek, South Italian, Archaic period, ca. 550–500 B.C. Bronze, 19 13/16 × 4 3/16 in. (50.4 × 10.7 cm). Private collection, New York

Hoplites typically carried a shield, sword, and spear, the lower shaft of which is also shown here. The deep plinth on which the soldier stands allowed the sculptor ample space to render the feet: placing them one behind the other, with the spear planted at the back and the toes of the right foot just slightly curling over the plinth, he successfully created a natural impression of depth. The principal relief is framed on the vertical sides with a guilloche pattern, whose intricate weave is highlighted by alternating strands of blue, green, and red.

Below the relief is an incised panel showing a warrior mounting a four-horse chariot reined by a charioteer. The warrior wears the full armor of a hoplite, including a crested Corinthian helmet. Small details of the charioteer, such as the edges of his garment at the neck and arms, are not delineated with carving and must have been indicated by paint. The black background of the scene and the primarily red horses and figures have led scholars to draw parallels with red-figure vase painting, which was just being introduced at this time. The details of the chariot and the horses are masterfully rendered. Each pair of horses awaits the arrival of the warrior and appears ready to launch forward, their black hooves raised in anticipation.

There are two main theories about the scene shown in the relief. It may represent the deceased engaging in an *apobates* race, an armed equestrian event that was part of the Panathenaic games held in Athens in honor of the goddess Athena. Alternatively, it may refer to the epic past described in Homer's *Iliad*, when chariots were used in warfare, thus lending a heroic aura to the deceased or alluding to his noble lineage.

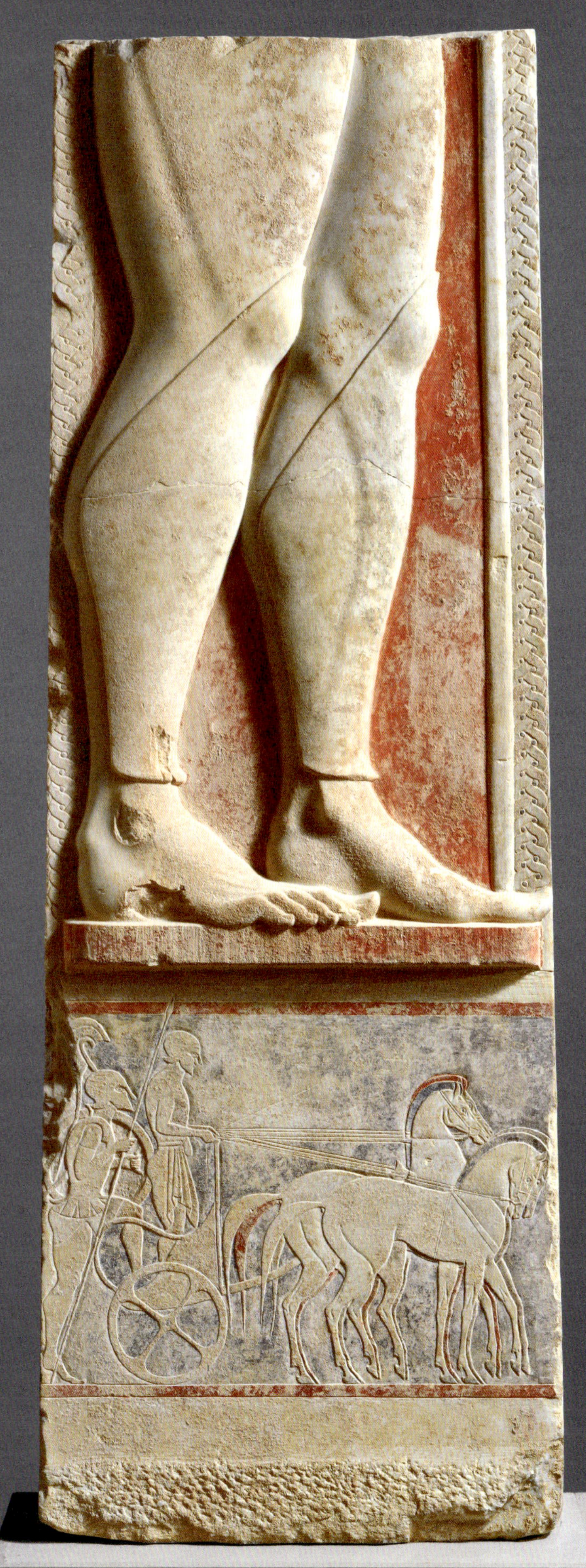

11

# Pediment fragment with a lion felling a bull

Greek, Archaic period, ca. 525–500 B.C.
Marble, 25 3/16 × 28 5/16 × 7 in. (64 × 72 × 17.8 cm)
Rogers Fund, 1942 (42.11.35)

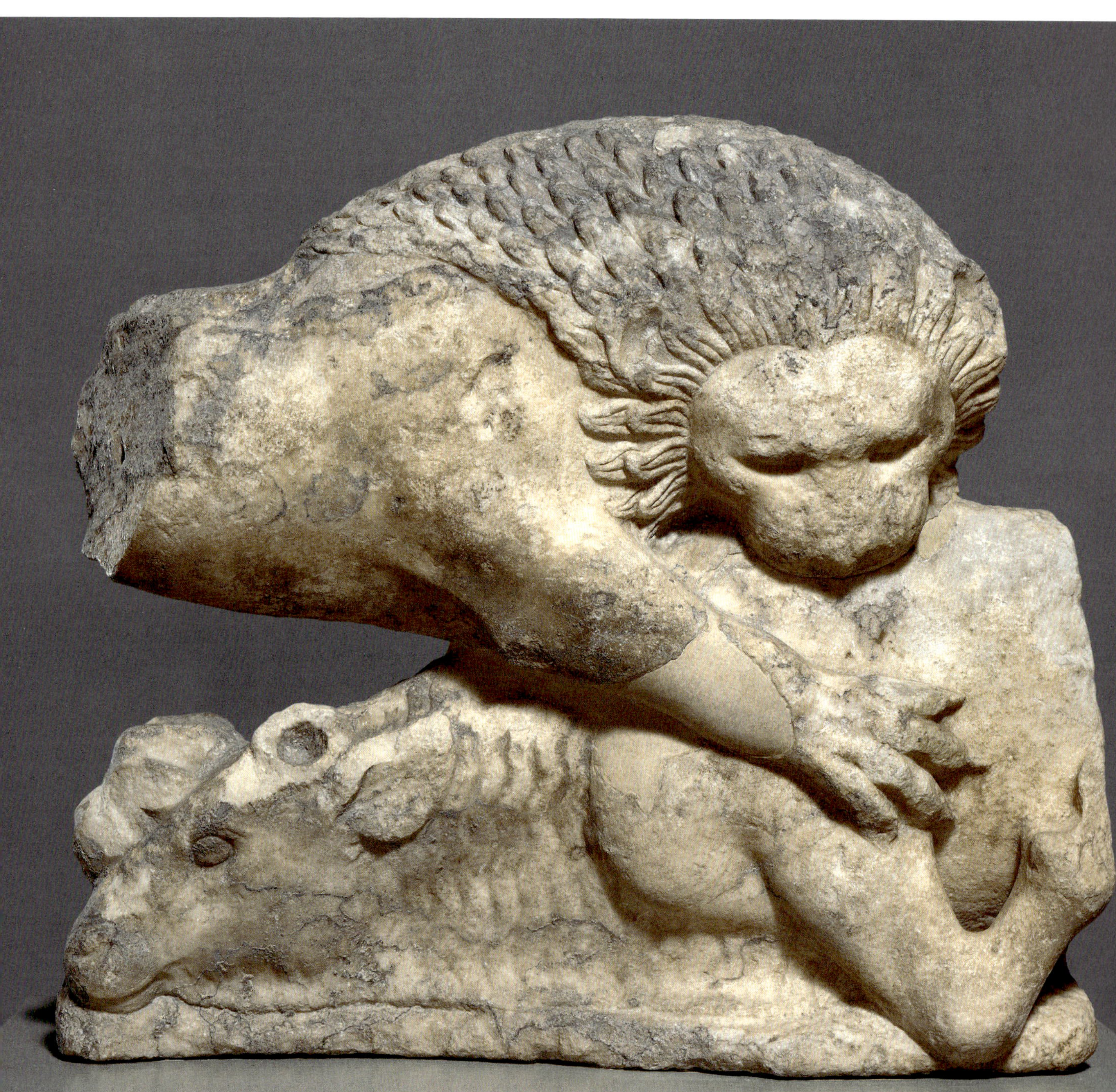

Even in its fragmentary state, this depiction of a lion dominating a felled bull has a palpable emotive power. The bull lies stretched out with its head and body flat on the ground, while the weight of the lion, biting into its back, is evident from the unnatural position of the bull's front fetlock. Holding the bull's body with the long claws of its right foreleg, the lion braces its hind foot against the bull's head. The lion's thick mane recedes rhythmically from its head and flows back with rows of flamelike curls. As its heavy jaw tears into the animal's flesh, its deep-set eyes are focused down on the bull. Although the relief now bears few traces of polychromy, it was originally brightly painted, which would have added to the power of the scene and helped to bring out details seen from a distance.

The fragment joins up with another, discovered in 1863 near the monumental temple known as the Olympieion in Athens, now in the National Archaeological Museum, Athens. Together the pieces formed a triangular shape representing two lions attacking a bull that would have decorated the pediment of a small building, such as a treasury or modest temple. Typically, pedimental sculpture was used for columned temples with superstructures of stone and gabled roofs executed in the Doric style, the predominant architectural mode in mainland Greece. However, after the construction of the Panhellenic sanctuary at Delphi, where Ionic and Doric architecture coexisted, pedimental sculpture sometimes adorned smaller Ionic buildings such as the Treasury of the Siphnians, which was built slightly before this sculpture was carved. Given the interest of Athenian architects in experimenting with both the Doric and Ionic orders, we cannot know for certain what the rest of the building with the lion and bull pediment looked like. Nonetheless, the pediment would have been a primary focus of the decorative program.

The scene chosen here, a popular composition for architectural sculpture in the sixth century B.C., was a clever symmetrical solution for filling the triangular space beneath a gabled roof at the ends of the building. Similar imagery occurs in Homeric poetry and appears in a variety of other media, including small-scale works such as engraved gems (fig. 35). The interest in portraying violence is notable and stands at the beginning of a long tradition in ancient Greek art. The king of the beasts, at the top of the natural order of animals, displays his dominance over another powerful animal. As a symbol of power, centrally displayed with a frontality that added to its apotropaic quality, the image would have resonated strongly for the ancient Greeks, even as it does today.

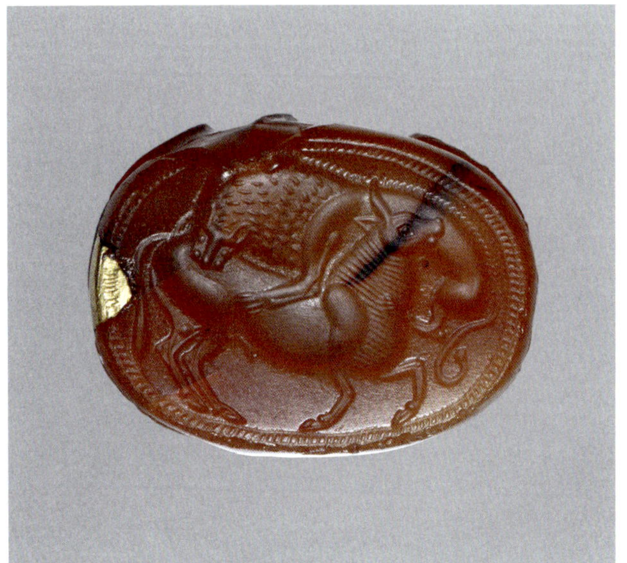

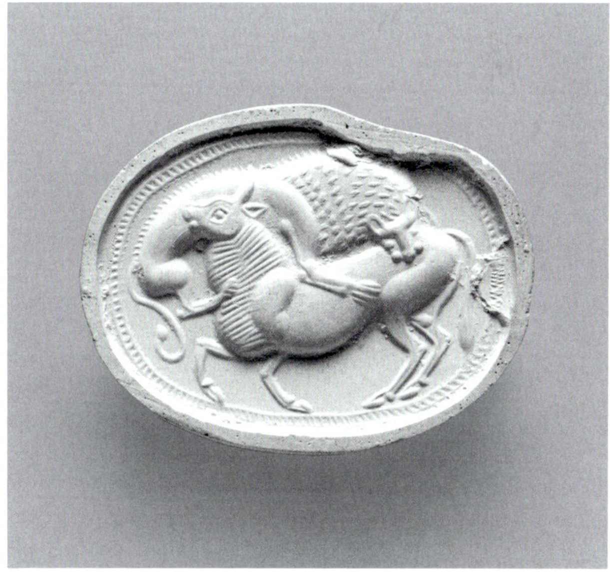

Fig. 35. *Left*: Scarab with a lion attacking a bull; *right*: impression of scarab. Greek, Archaic period, late 7th–early 6th century B.C. Carnelian, 1 × 1 11/16 in. (2.5 × 4.2 cm). Purchase, Joseph Pulitzer Bequest, 1942 (42.11.15)

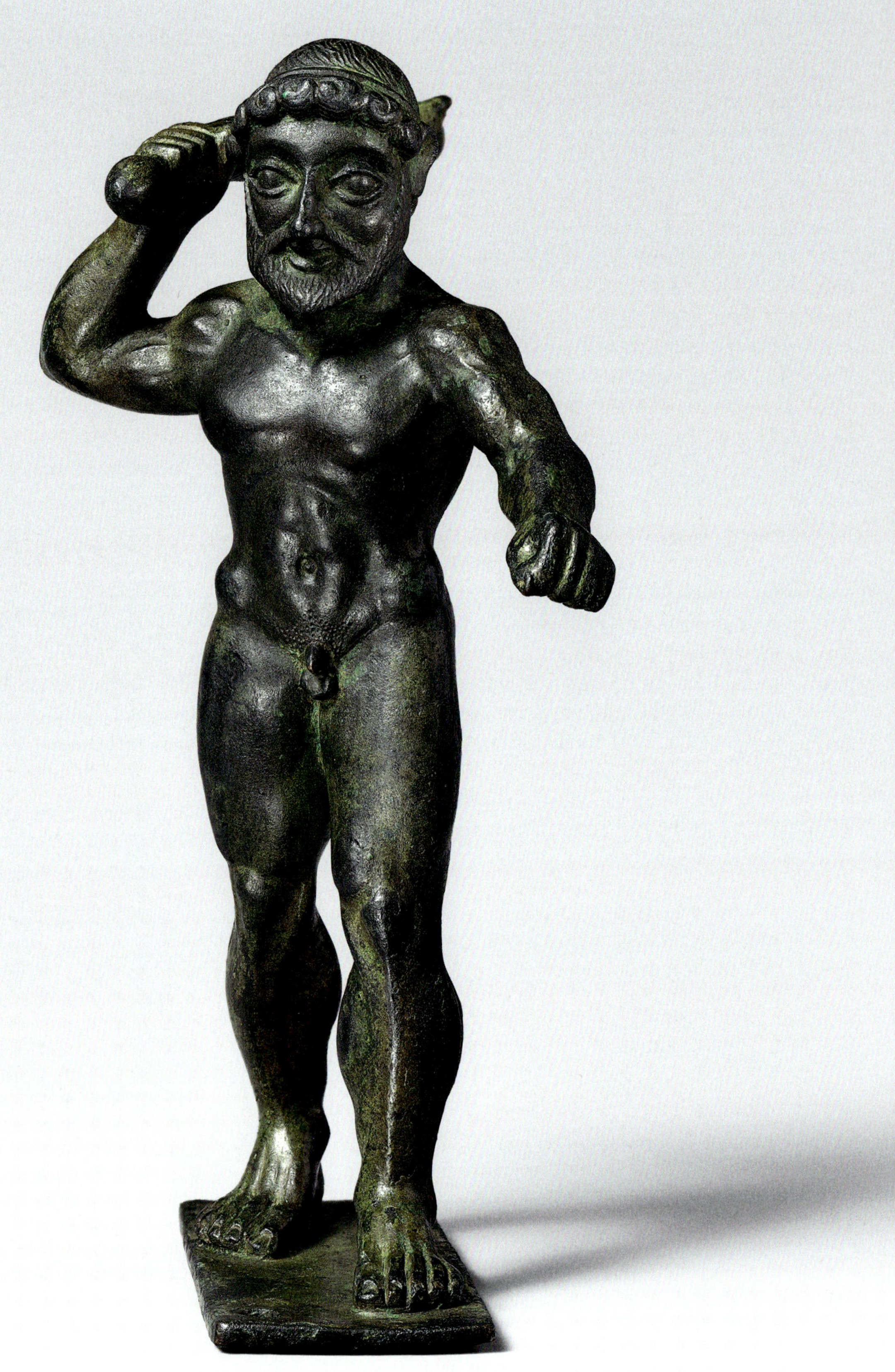

12

# Statuette of Herakles

Greek, Archaic period, last quarter of the 6th century B.C.
Bronze, H. 5 1/16 in. (12.8 cm)
Fletcher Fund, 1928 (28.77)

Although small in scale, this powerful bronze statuette conveys with great clarity the mighty strength of the most popular and best-known hero from ancient Greece. Wielding his club in a smiting position, Herakles stands with both feet planted squarely on the ground. His left arm and leg are stretched out in front of him and balance carefully with the right side of his body, which is ready to spring into action. His nudity enables the viewer to appreciate his sculpted physique, from his huge calves to the taut muscles of his arms and his washboard abdomen.

Characteristically for the Archaic period, the hero is represented as a mature man, with a carefully coiffed beard and hair bound with a fillet. Even his pubic hair is rendered precisely with punched dots. Several features,

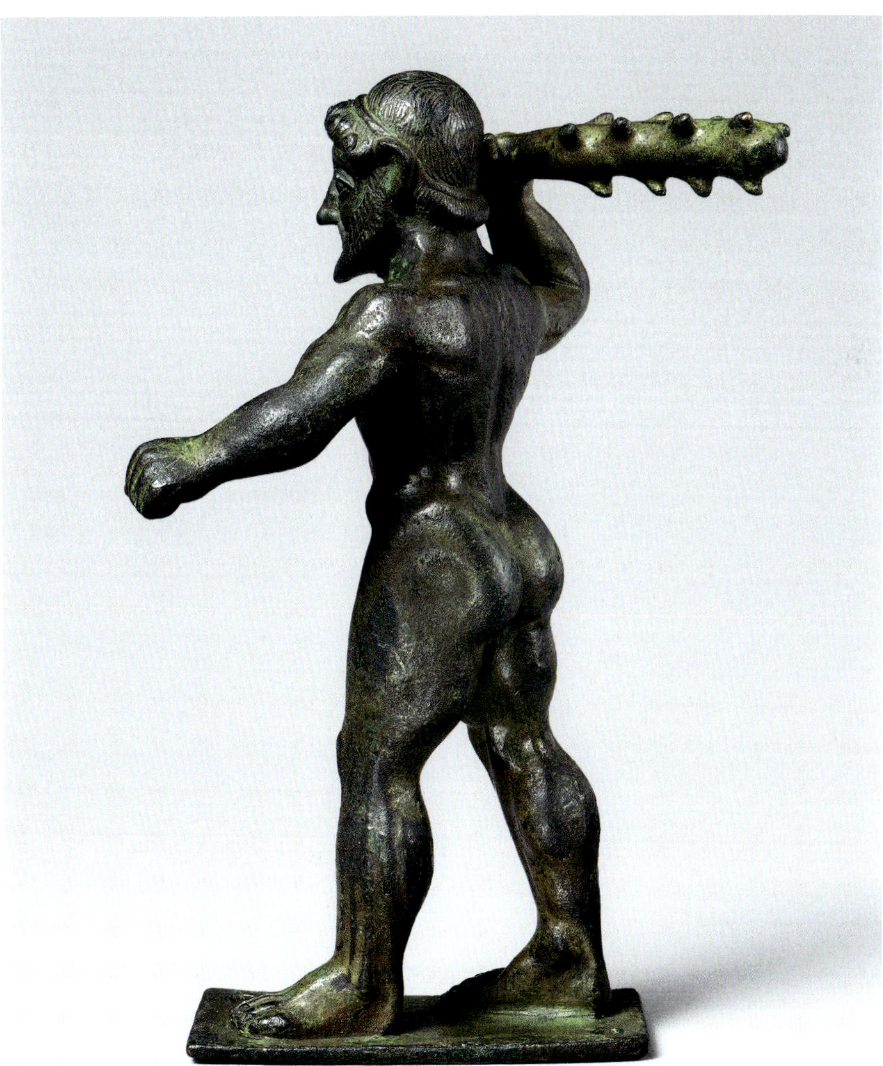

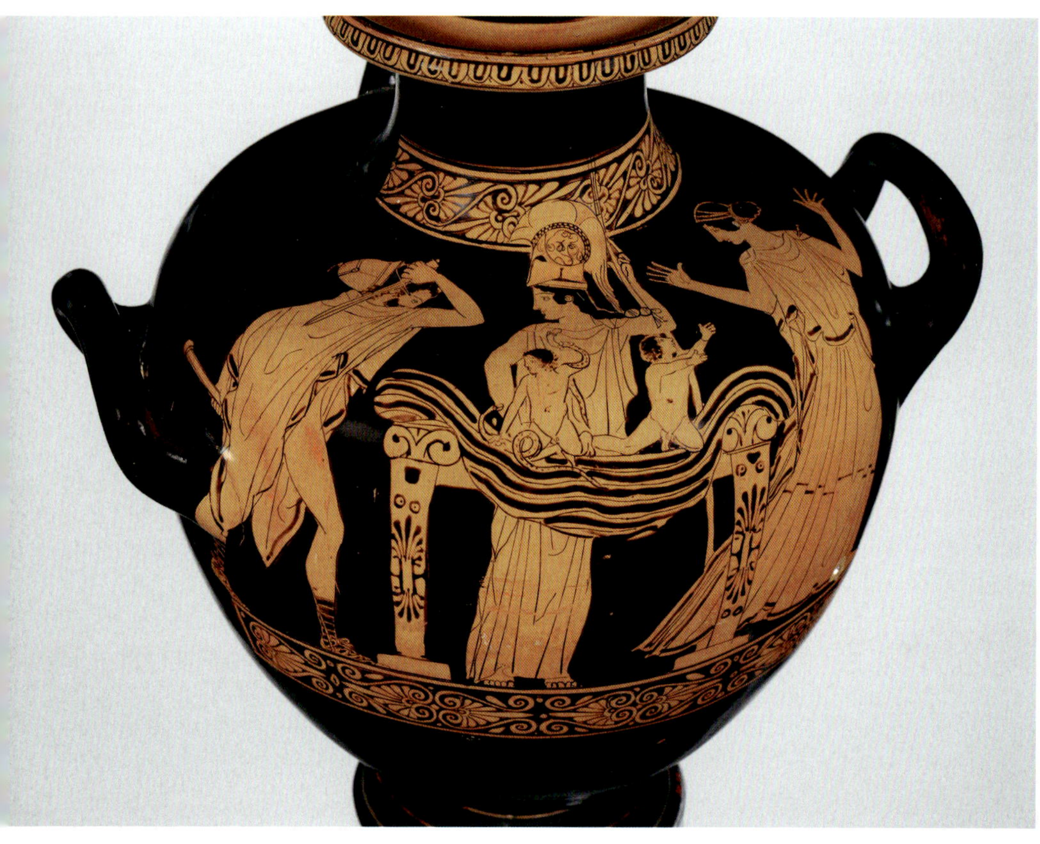

Fig. 36. Hydria (water jar) with the infant Herakles strangling snakes sent by Hera. Greek, Classical period, ca. 460–450 B.C. Attributed to the Nausicaä Painter. Terracotta, H. 14½ in. (36.8 cm). Fletcher Fund, 1925 (25.28)

including the large almond-shaped eyes, the smile, the snail curls running across his forehead, and the ordered balance of the composition, are typical of the Archaic style of Greek sculpture. The greenish tinge of the bronze is a patina that has formed over thousands of years; the original surface was most likely a coppery brown to indicate the color of tanned skin.

Herakles's strength was legendary even from his birth. A myth sometimes represented in ancient Greek art relates that when he was born Hera, queen of the gods and wife of Zeus, sent poisonous snakes to kill him, but the baby vanquished the serpents (fig. 36). Herakles was best known for his labors, of which twelve undertaken for King Eurystheus of Argos became canonical. While many of the labors occur in the Peloponnese, some take the hero to the very ends of the known world. Among these are retrieving the Apples of the Hesperides and stealing the cattle of Geryon, a triple-bodied monster who lived on the far western shore of the Mediterranean Sea. Herakles's most common attributes are his club and the skin of the Nemean lion, another of his conquests.

This statuette, said to have been found in Mantinea in the Peloponnese, was most likely a freestanding sculpture, as suggested by the rectangular shape of the base with its lack of attachments. Statuettes of this scale were popular votives at sanctuaries, where they were deposited as dedications to a deity, typically as thank offerings in return for some answered prayer. Herakles, the son of Zeus and the mortal Alkmene, was primarily considered a hero, but he was eventually welcomed into the pantheon of the Greek gods. His hero cults were set up throughout the ancient Greek world.

13

# Pair of eyes

Greek, Early Classical period, 5th century B.C. or later
Bronze, frit, marble, quartz, and obsidian, W. of left eye 2 5/16 in. (5.8 cm), of right eye 2 3/8 in. (6 cm)
Purchase, Mr. and Mrs. Lewis B. Cullman Gift and Norbert Schimmel Bequest, 1991 (1991.11.3a, b)

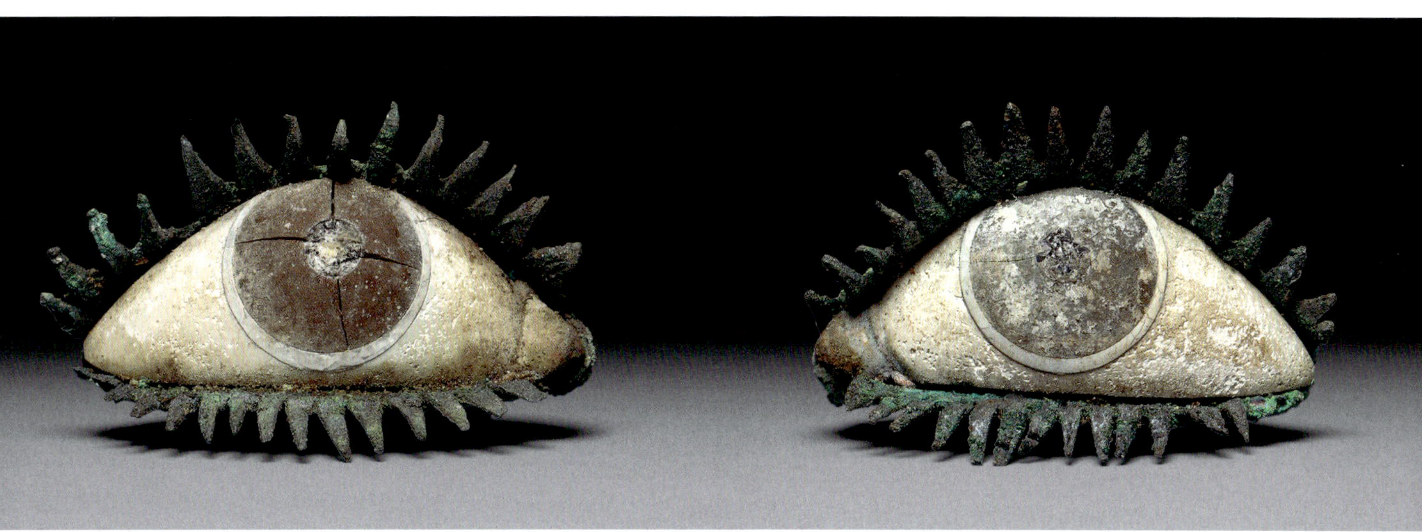

In the early fifth century B.C., bronze became the preferred medium for monumental freestanding statuary, being valued both for its tensile strength and for its ability to produce dynamic compositions. The stylistic trend at this time was toward naturalism. The Early Classical Greek sculptor Myron, for example, was famous for his lifelike compositions, which included a lowing bronze cow that was erected in Athens and stirred great emotion in many of those who saw it.

Part of the success of Classical Greek bronze sculpture stemmed from the use of inlays to create colorful realistic impressions. Lips and nipples were frequently inlaid with copper, and teeth with silver, but more than any other part of the body the eyes were so decorated. It is they that show life, and the gods were even sometimes known by epithets that referred to these features. Athena, the goddess of wisdom, was known as gray-eyed or bright-eyed, and Hera was identified as cow-eyed, a reference to her large brown eyes. To capture the subtle nuances of the eye, the ancient Greeks created dramatic new renderings of the feature for their sculptures.

This pair of eyes would have been set into a monumental, over-lifesize statue. The variety of the materials here reflects the complexity, and even the anatomy, of the eye. Forming a casing for the rest, the eyelashes are cut from two sheets of bronze. The whites are made from frit, a kind of glass paste; the cornea and iris are framed with marble and made from colored quartz; and the pupils, although damaged, were perfect circular disks of black obsidian, a volcanic glass. Both eyes exhibit the characteristic care lavished on the finest Greek statuary, and they would have added significantly to the expense of the commission. They give a strong sense of the lifelike impression that ancient sculpture could convey.

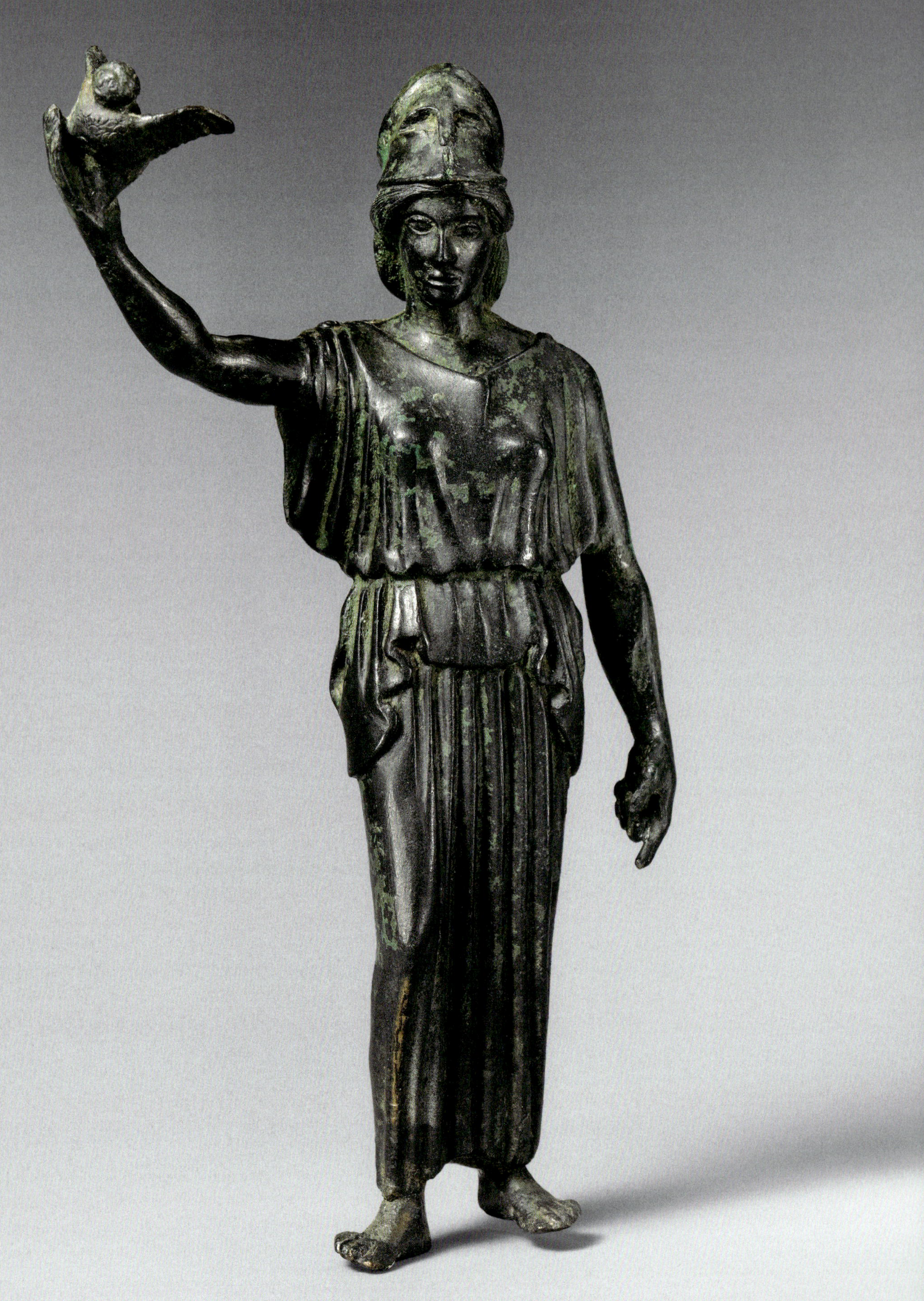

14

# Statuette of Athena flying her owl

Greek, Attic, Classical period, ca. 460 B.C.
Bronze, H. 5 15/16 in. (15 cm)
Harris Brisbane Dick Fund, 1950 (50.11.1)

Athena, goddess of wisdom and patron deity of the ancient Greek city-state of Athens, stands with her right hand raised to fly her owl. She wears a peplos, a traditional heavy woolen garment belted at the waist with an overfold. The Corinthian helmet pulled back on her head has its crest broken off, and her left hand once held a shaft, most likely a spear—attributes of the goddess that indicate her warlike nature and her role as protectress. Athena does not wear her other characteristic protective attribute, a snaky goatskin known as the aegis. The figure's serenity and idealized beauty are also typical of Classical Greek sculpture. Solid cast using the lost wax method, the statuette reflects the great care the artist has taken in the finishing. Despite its small scale, he has painstakingly chased the face and hair as well as chasing and punching the feathers of the bird.

This statuette with a monumental quality may reflect a lost Classical bronze statue of Athena, of which there were many set up in Athens, especially in her sanctuary on the Acropolis. A contemporary Athenian red-figure

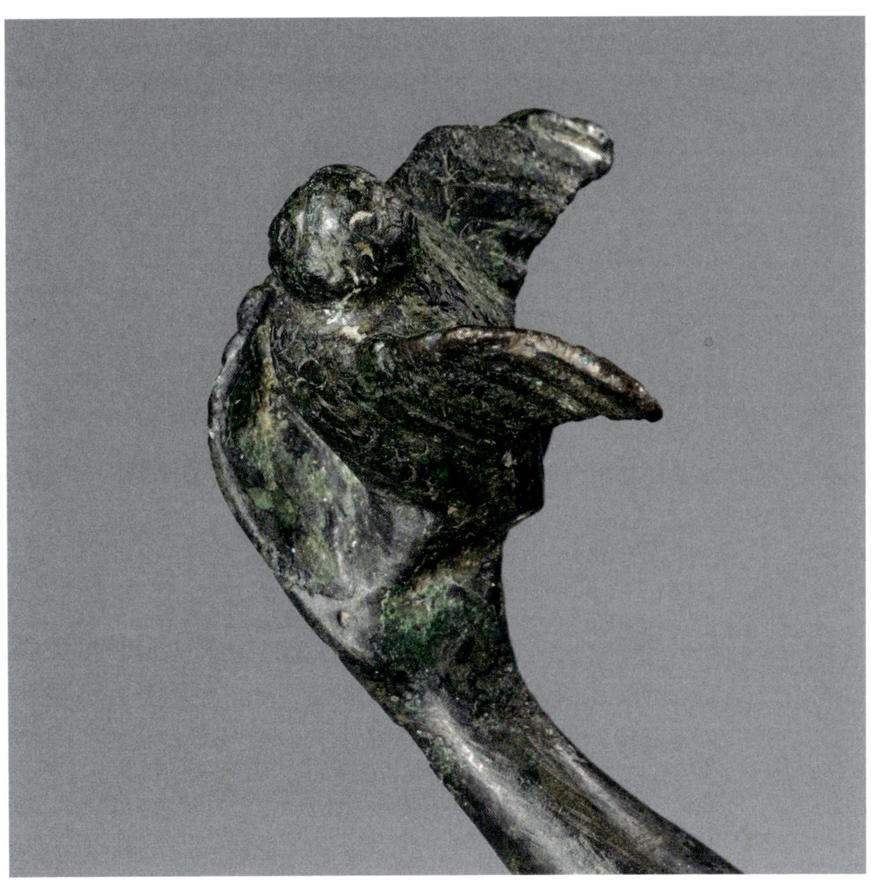

vase in The Met collection shows a citizen gazing at such a statue set up on a column (fig. 37). In that image, she also holds a spear and wears a Corinthian helmet, complete with crest, and has the aegis not included here.

Owls were sacred to Athena and featured prominently on the principal coinage of Athens; the bird was shown on the reverse of a coin bearing a portrait head of the goddess on the obverse. Small owls can still be seen flying around the Athenian Acropolis. The subspecies particularly associated with the goddess is *Athene noctua*, or the Little Owl, which is distinguished by its rounded head without tufts or prominent feathers, as seen here. Athena may be sending a message with the bird, which is about to take flight. Zeus is also sometimes shown flying his eagle in ancient Greek art.

This fine bronze statuette was once part of the collection of Lord Elgin and probably comes from Attica. It did not pass with the Parthenon marbles to the British Museum in 1816 but remained with the family at least into the twentieth century before it was acquired by The Met in 1950.

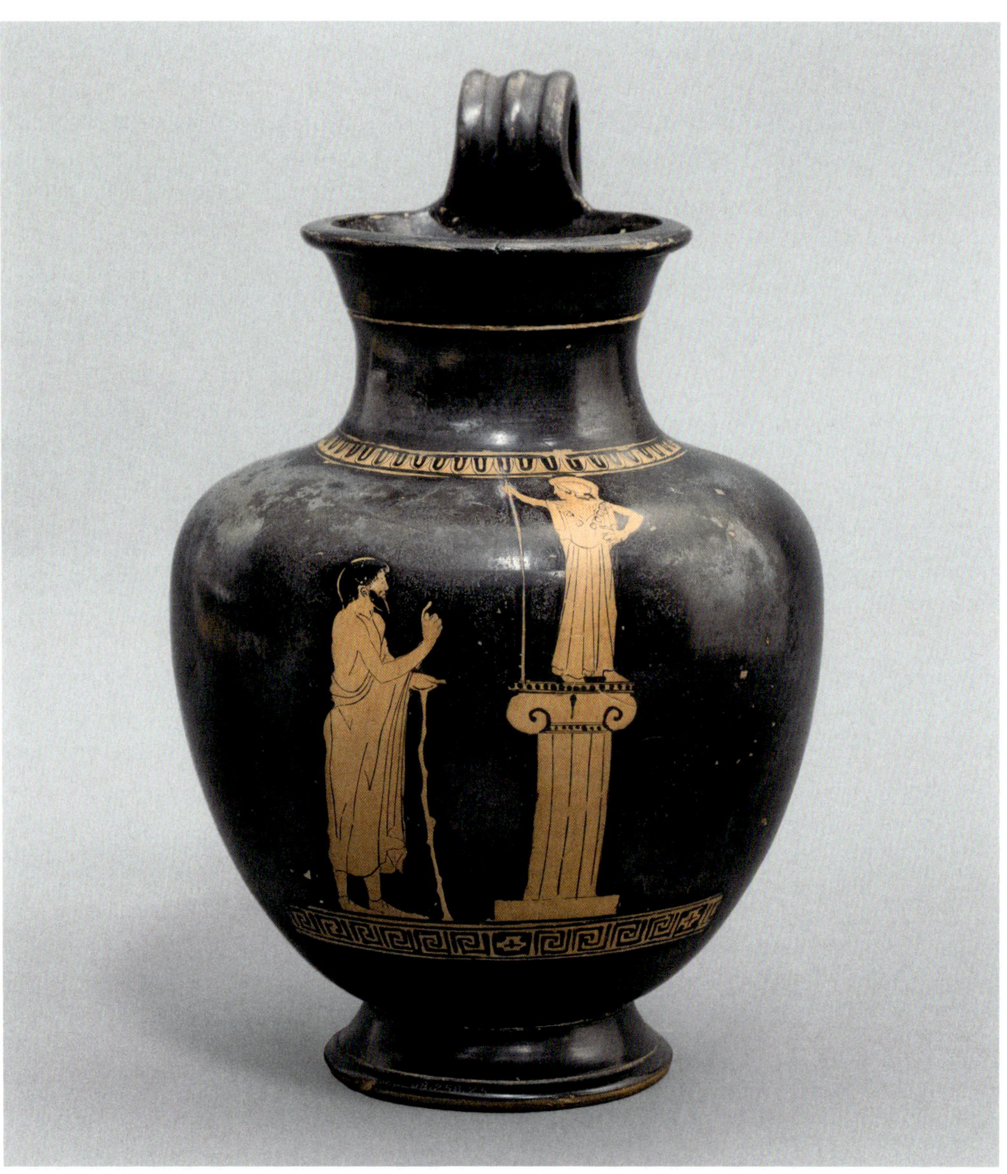

Fig. 37. Oinochoe: olpe (jug). Greek, Attic, ca. 470–460 B.C. Attributed to the Group of Berlin 2415. Terracotta, red-figure, H. 8 in. (20.3 cm), Diam. 5 7/16 in. (13.8 cm). Rogers Fund, 1908 (08.258.25)

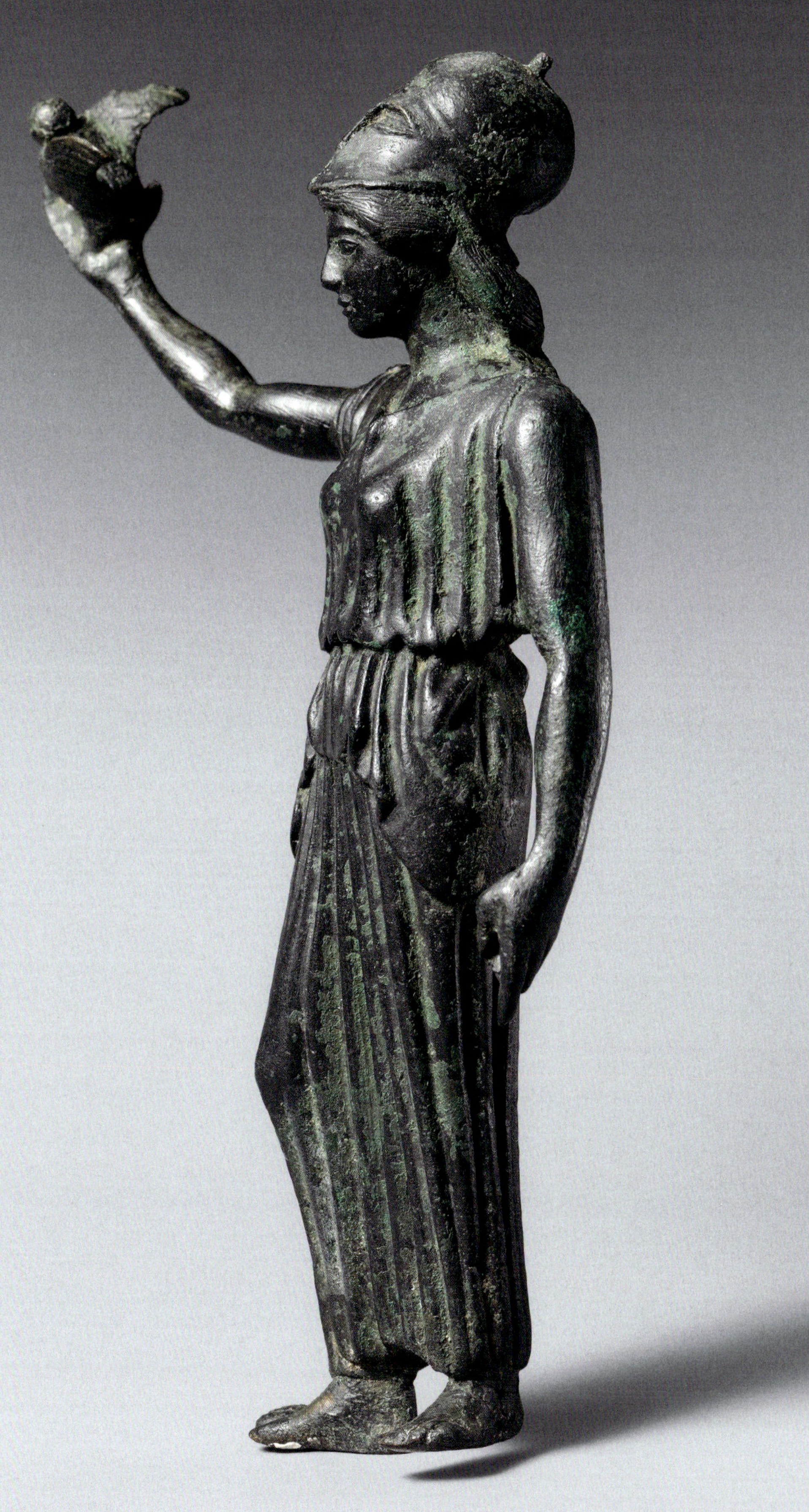

15

# Caryatid mirror

Greek, Argive, Classical period, mid-5th century B.C.
Bronze, H. 15 15/16 in. (40.4 cm), Weight 2 lb. (0.9 kg)
Bequest of Walter C. Baker, 1971 (1972.118.78)

The ancient Greek bronze caryatid mirror is one of the most distinctive and elegant artistic creations known from Classical antiquity. The original source of inspiration probably came from Egypt, where there was a long history stretching back into the Bronze Age of mirrors with supports in the form of human figures (fig. 38). The Greek examples have three main elements: a disk, a handle in the form of a female figure, and a base. Frequently, they are elaborately decorated with subsidiary ornamentation.

During the Archaic period, there was considerable variation in the types of mirrors with human figural supports. In the Greek colonies of southern Italy and Sicily, for instance, supports in the form of male figures were also popular and could become quite elaborate, as seen in a handle in The Met collection that features a man with the forepart of a horse on each shoulder and the upper part of a female figure on his head (fig. 39). By the second quarter of the fifth century B.C., caryatid mirrors became much more homogeneous and are thought to have been produced by a relatively small group of workshops in the Peloponnese, where they continued to be made through the end of the century. The present mirror is a particularly fine and well-preserved specimen that allows us to appreciate the form as a complete work of art, much as it looked in antiquity, in contrast to so many ancient Greek sculptures in existence today.

A variety of elements—human, animal, and mythical—animate the mirror. The domed circular base rests on three lion's paws that grow organically into architectural supports recalling the form of Ionic capitals with tendrils. A tall female figure wearing a peplos stands gracefully holding a dove in her outstretched right hand. She most likely represents heavenly Aphrodite, goddess of love.

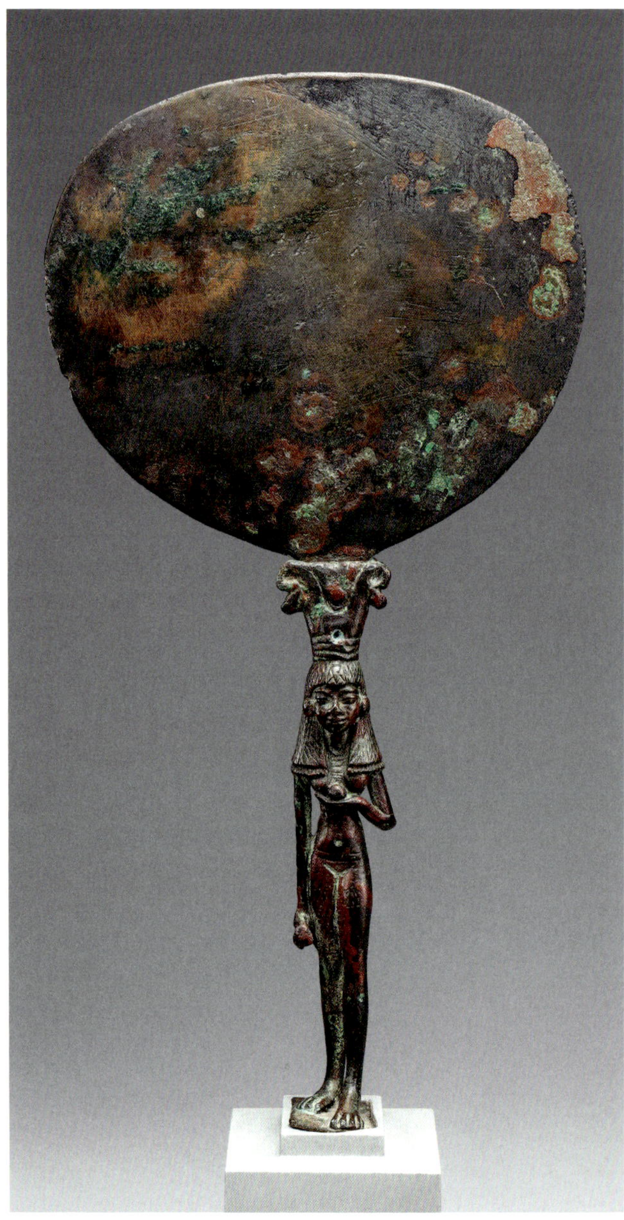

Fig. 38. Caryatid mirror representing a young girl. Egyptian, New Kingdom, Ramesside period, ca. 1295–1070 B.C. Leaded bronze, H. 10 1/16 in. (25.5 cm). Purchase, Lila Acheson Wallace Gift and Gift of Diane Carol Brandt Fund, in memory of her husband, Martin Lewis, 2019 (2019.25)

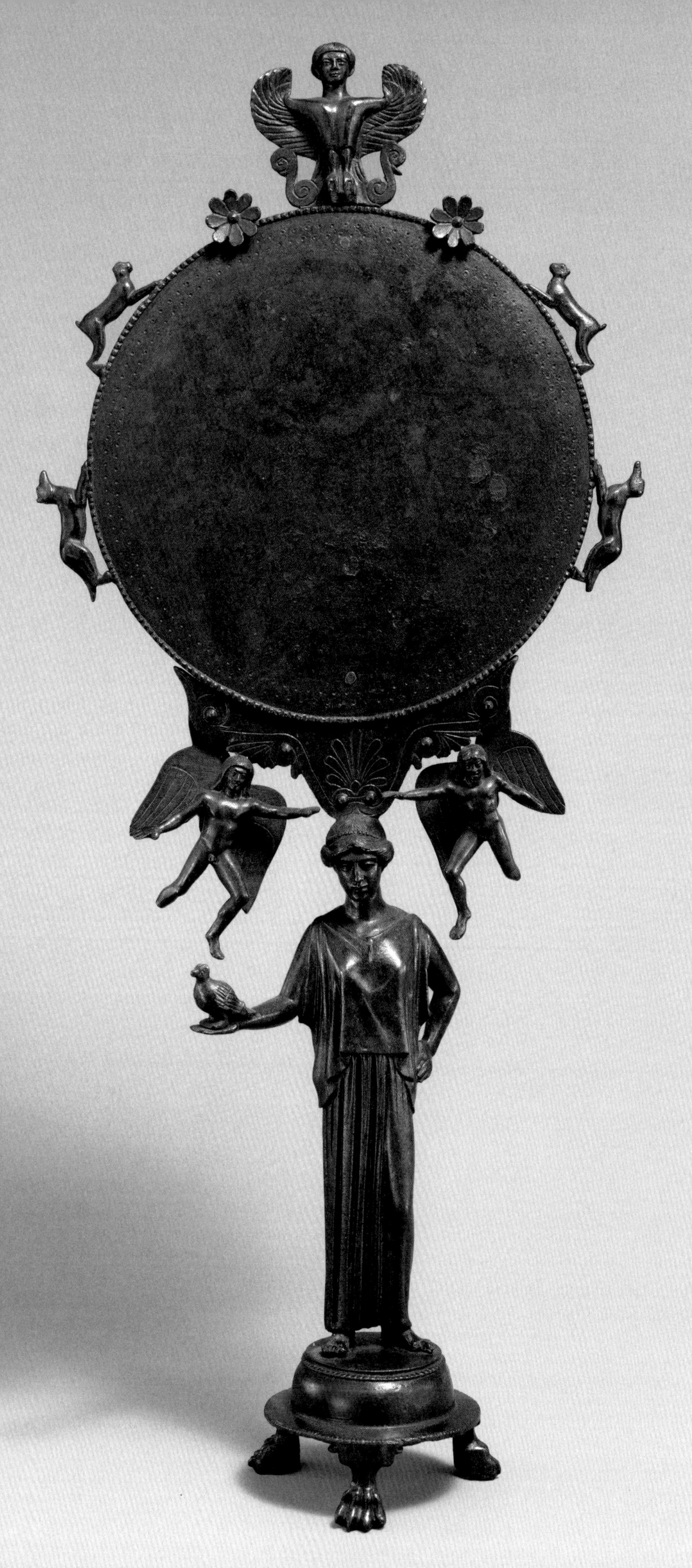

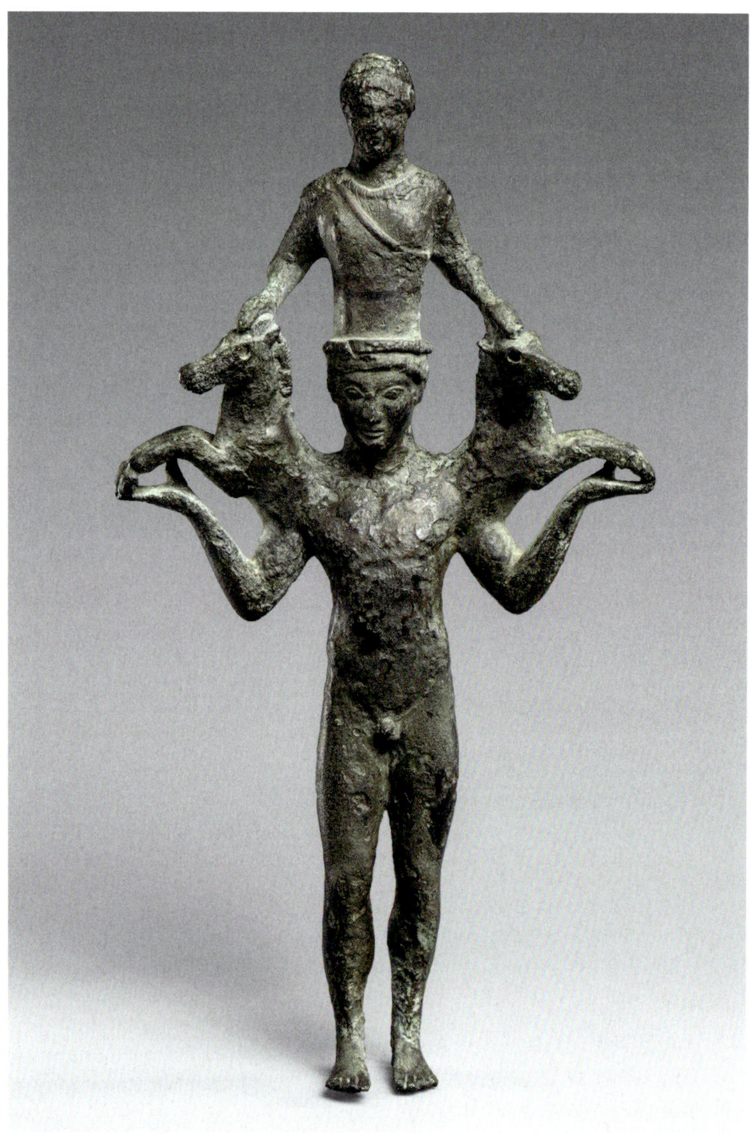

Fig. 39. Mirror support in the form of a man. Greek, South Italian, Archaic period, early 5th century B.C. Bronze, H. 8⅝ in. (21.9 cm). Rogers Fund, 1920 (20.203)

Hovering around her head are two winged erotes. This phenomenon, which appears on many Classical caryatid mirrors, is the earliest doubling of the young god of love in Greek art; in the Hellenistic period, Eros is multiplied many times, as if to express an abundance of love. A hound chasing a hare up either side of the disk is likely a metaphor for amorous pursuit, and perched at the top is a Siren, part bird, part woman, a powerful and dangerous mythical creature.

One is immediately struck by the artist's attention to the entire object and his ability to integrate complex imagery into a unified, balanced composition. The mirror is carefully worked on both front and back, and decoration has been lavished upon every area, from top to bottom. The ornamentation is not excessive but arranged with the almost mathematical precision characteristic of the finest Classical Greek art. In this respect, it reflects the interest in order first manifested in the Geometric period.

16

# Stele of a little girl

Greek, Cycladic, Classical period, ca. 450–440 B.C.
Parian marble, H. 31¾ in. (80.6 cm)
Fletcher Fund, 1927 (27.45)

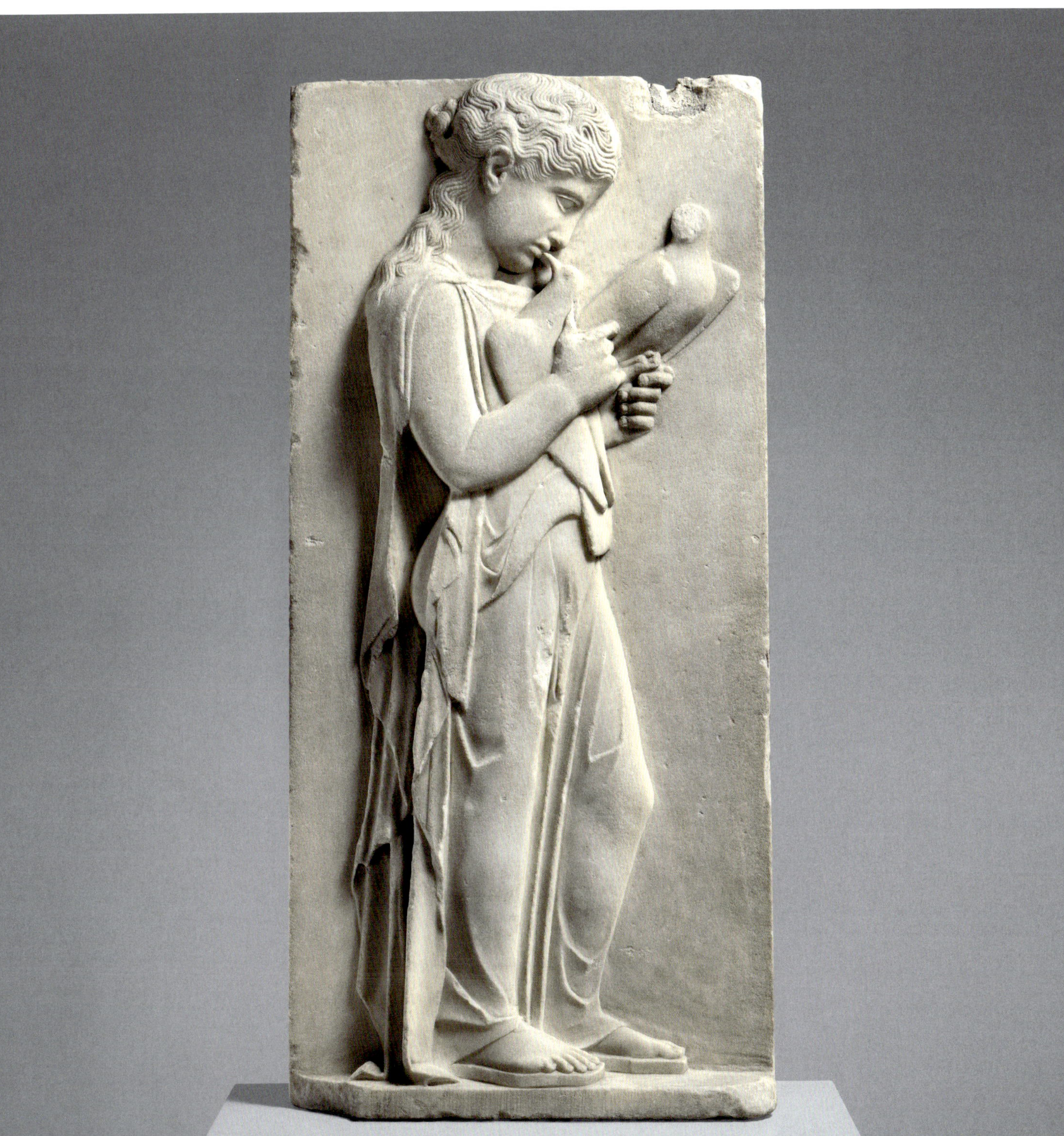

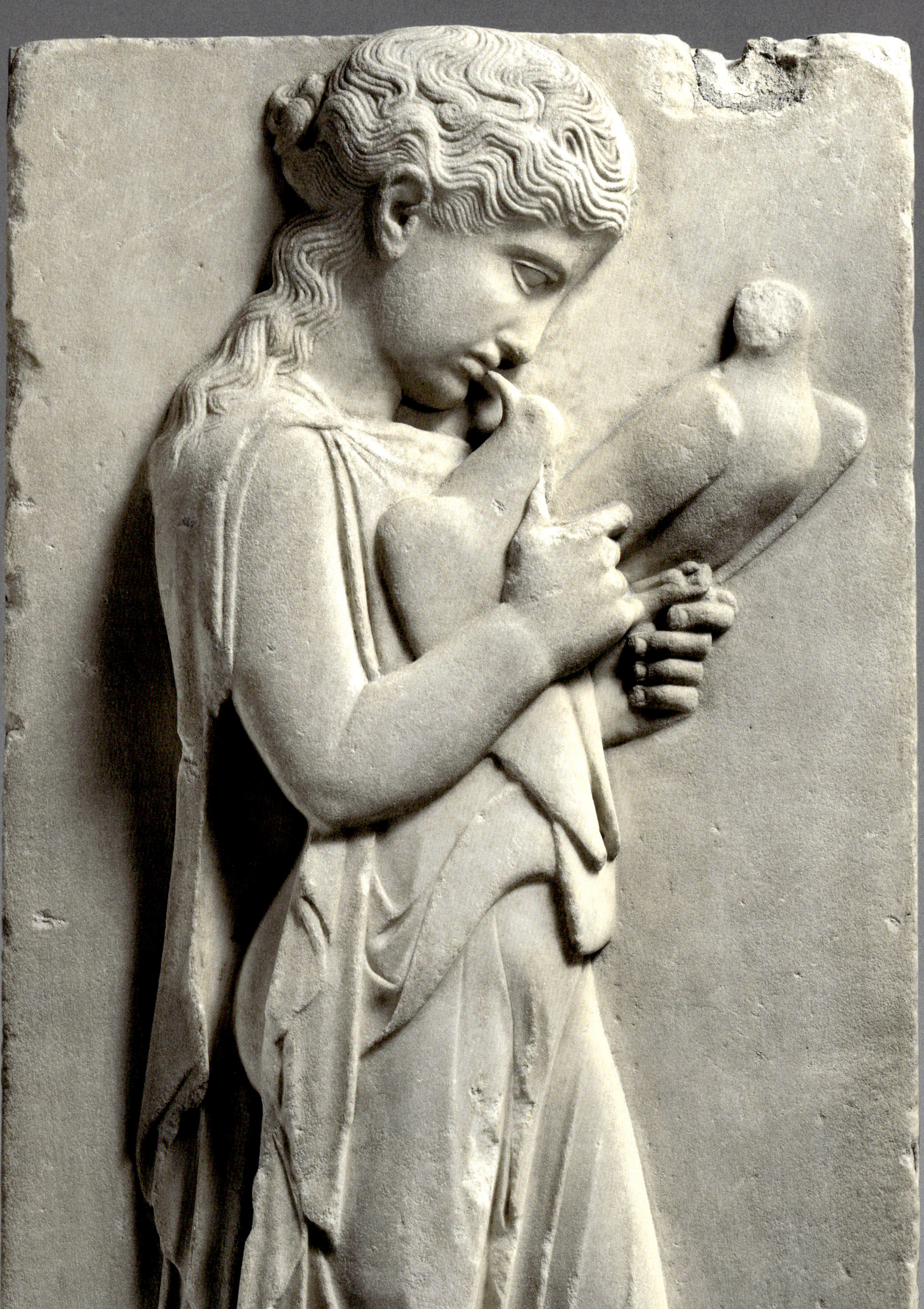

This superb relief marked the grave of a girl much too young to die. For the ancient Greeks, it was a particular tragedy for a woman to die before marriage and childbirth, which was considered the natural way to perpetuate one's memory. Therefore, if the parents could afford it, it was especially important to create a prominent marker at the child's tomb, where they could come to remember the deceased and where his or her name was recorded for all to see.

As is typical of Classical Greek sculpture, the girl is represented as a young adult with idealized features. The artist, nonetheless, uses other means to make clear that a very young girl is represented. The innocence of youth is portrayed in the way she wears her chiton, unbelted and exposing the line of her buttocks; an adult woman would not be shown this way on her tombstone. Also indicating her youth are the long tresses hanging down her back in rhythmic patterns, so beautifully sculpted in shallow relief. The intimacy between her and her pet doves reflects the familiarity and harmony that often exist between young children and animals. One bird perches on her left hand, clinging to her fingers with its feet, as the beak of the other nearly touches her lips. She looks down contemplatively, expressing the gravity of her situation in a timeless, eloquent way. Although no traces of polychromy are preserved on the relief, the straps of her sandals must have been rendered with paint, since only the soles are indicated by carving; other features would likely have been painted as well.

The stele was found on Paros in 1785 and was presumably set up at a tomb on the island. It was probably originally crowned with a floral finial similar to that on the slightly earlier Stele Giustiniani in the Antikensammlung, Berlin (fig. 40). At the time that both were made, in the mid-fifth century B.C., such elaborate tomb markers were not being erected in Athens, as a measure of austerity in remembrance of the Persian desecration of the Acropolis in 480 B.C., and the practice was probably not overturned until the start of the Peloponnesian War (about 430 B.C.). This relief bears a strong stylistic resemblance to the sculptures of the Parthenon, especially those on the frieze that framed the entablature of the temple. It is quite possible that the artist who made it was among those who came to Athens to help create the Parthenon, which was built between 447 and 432 B.C. Among these were Cycladic sculptors, who had ready access to local marble, the finest in the world, and were known to have traveled to undertake commissions.

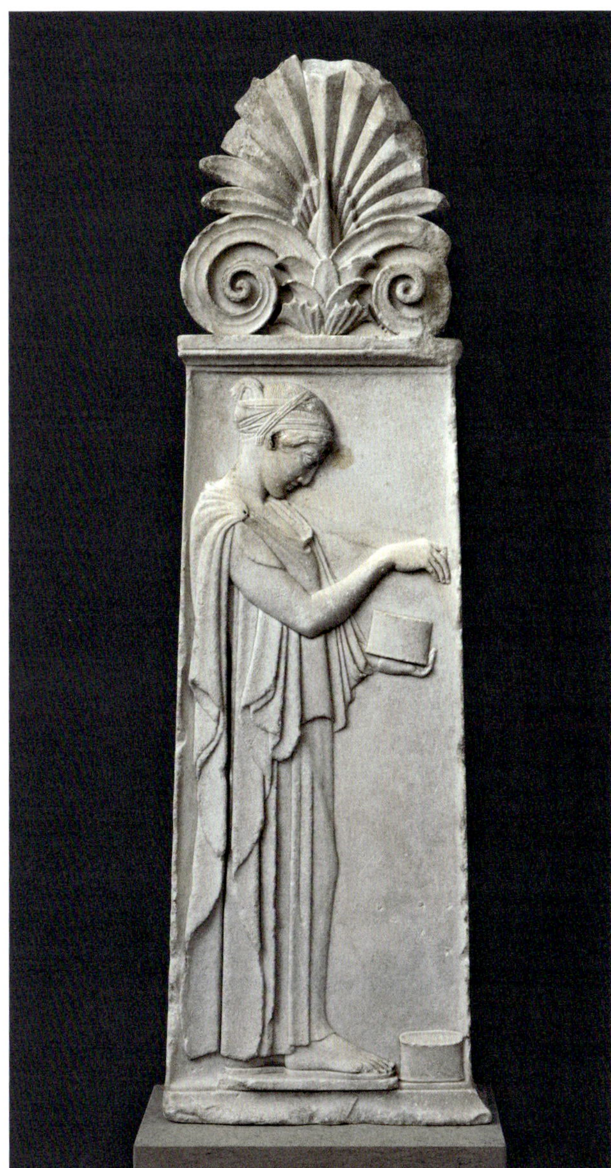

Fig. 40. Stele of a young girl, the so-called Stele Giustiniani. Greek, Classical period, ca. 460–450 B.C. Parian marble, H. 56 5/16 in. (143 cm). Staatliche Museen zu Berlin, Antikensammlung

17

# Statue of a wounded Amazon

Roman, Claudian period, A.D. 41–54
Copy of a Greek bronze statue of ca. 450–425 B.C.
Marble, H. 80¼ in. (203.8 cm)
Gift of John D. Rockefeller Jr., 1932 (32.11.4)

The Amazons were a mythical race of warrior women from the fringes of the known world. The ancient Greeks had many legends about them, and they often appear in Greek art, especially in combat with Greeks. This statue representing an Amazon wounded in battle is among the most accomplished of some nineteen Roman replicas of a Greek bronze statue made in the third quarter of the fifth century B.C. The Roman writer Pliny the Elder mentions that there was a contest between five Classical Greek sculptors, including Polykleitos, Pheidias, and Kresilas, to create statues of Amazons, which were set up in the sanctuary of Artemis at Ephesos. This statue type is generally associated with that contest. Two other replica series of Classical bronze statues of Amazons have been identified as representing other statues from the same famous contest.

The Amazon is bleeding: a wound from just behind her right breast drips blood, which is vividly rendered by the sculptor with raised drops and would have been represented on the original bronze with inlaid copper droplets gushing from her side. Her right arm is held over her head

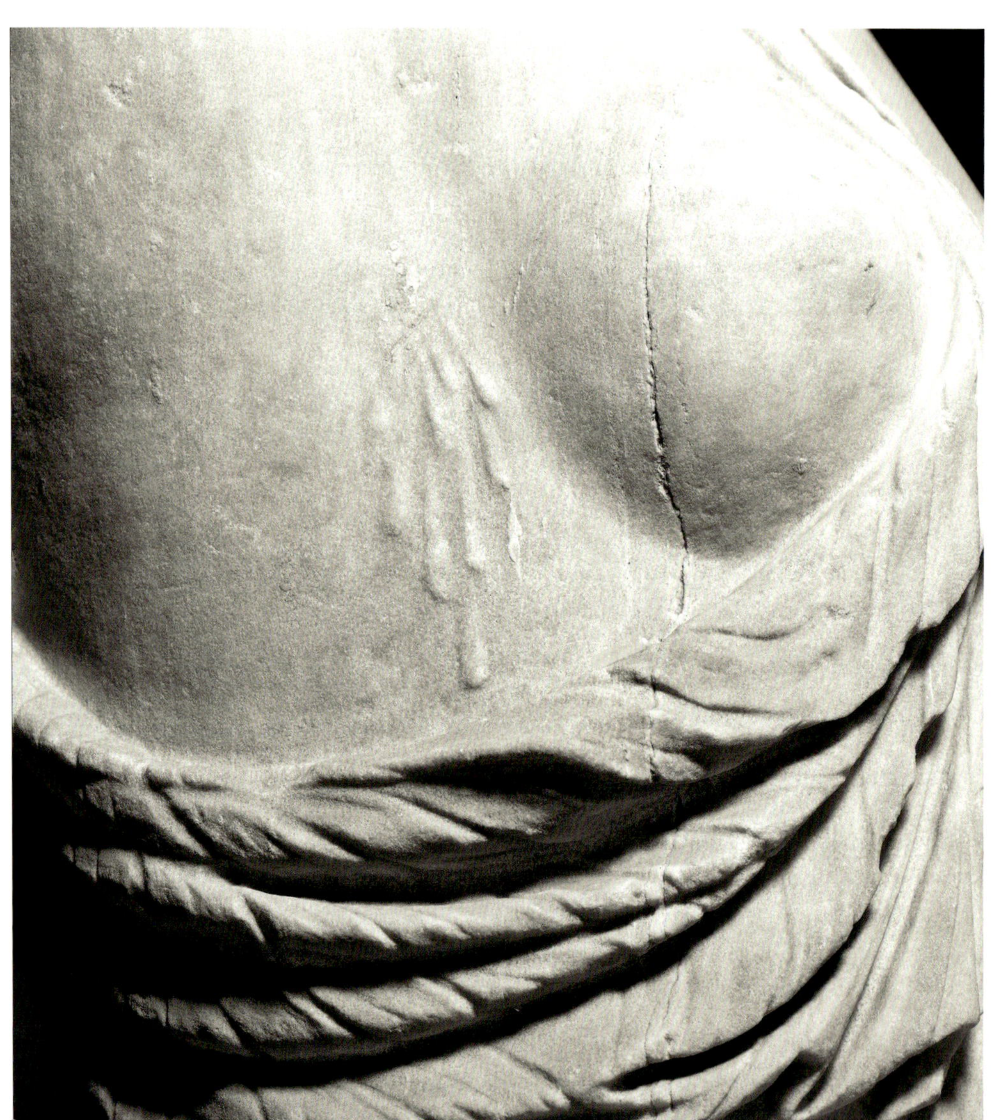

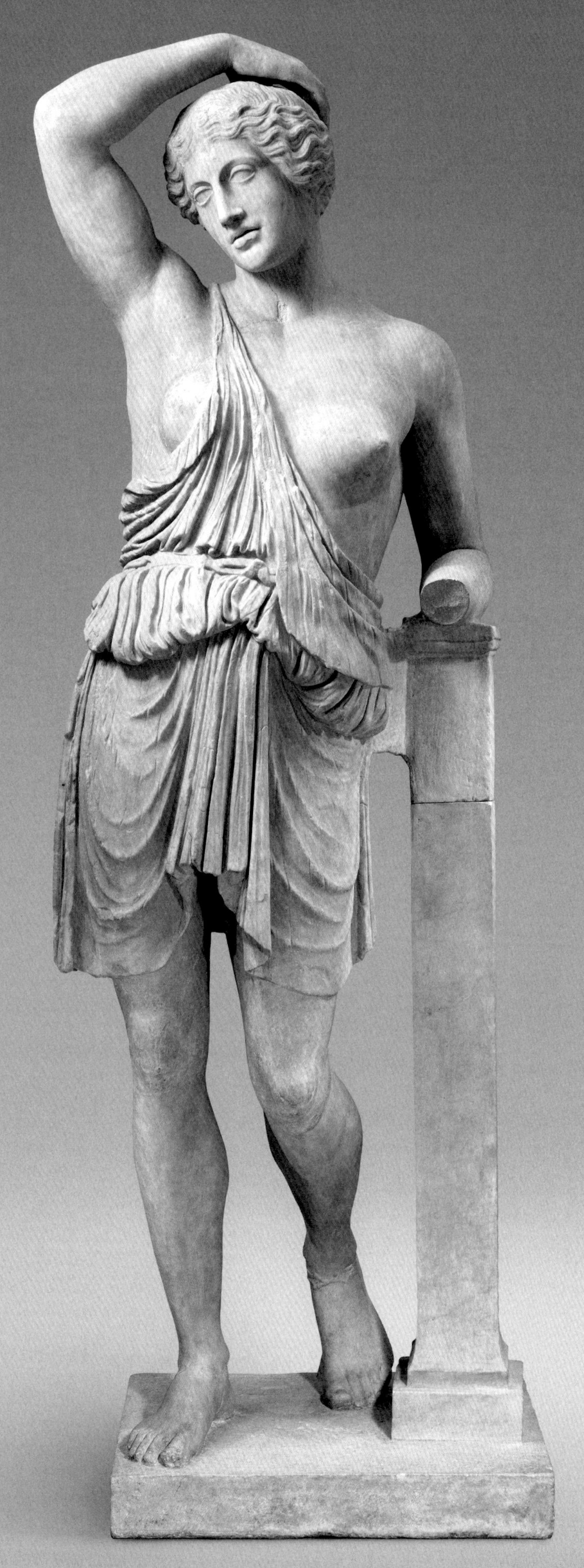

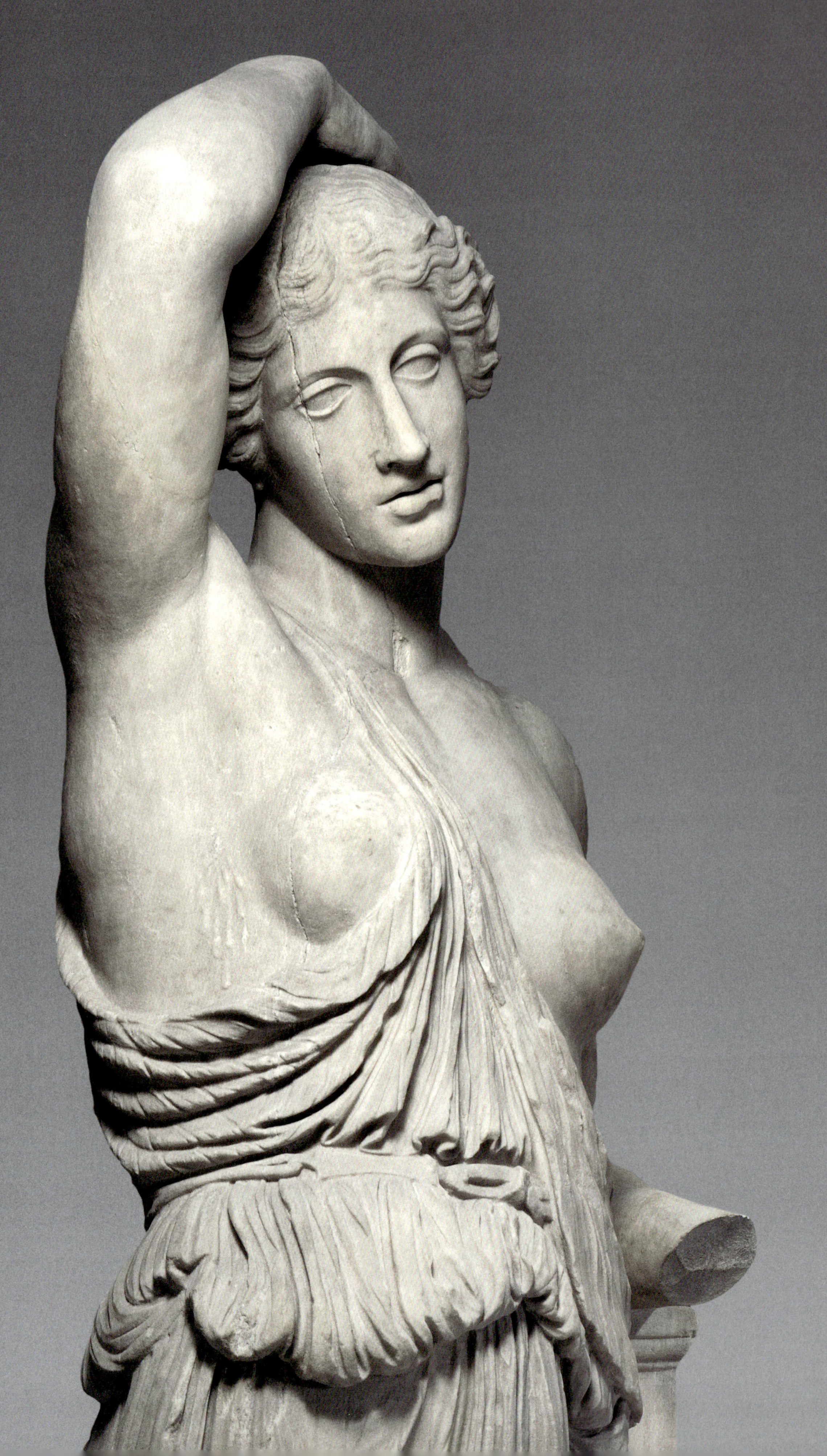

in a gesture that typically connotes sleep or death and indicates here that she is dying. She leans on a pillar with her left arm, another indication of her exhaustion.

The woman's dress, a short chiton, is disheveled and unfastened at one shoulder, exposing her left breast. As seen in the detail opposite, the chiton is drawn up over a belt to form an overhanging pouch, or *kolpos*, and is then belted again. The second belt has been identified as part of the harness and reins of her horse. This telling detail, it has been suggested, indicates that her horse is dead, and that she herself has been ungirdled and probably raped. In characteristic Classical style, the Amazon's noble, beautiful face gives no indication of the pain and suffering she is experiencing. In fact, the statue generally adheres closely to what we know as the Classical Greek style. However, certain elements such as her slightly slender, elongated proportions and the archaizing pattern of folds of the drapery against her thighs were most likely introduced by the Roman copyist.

The statue belonged to the Marquess of Lansdowne, England, who acquired it in Rome in the 1770s, and it was restored at that time. Most of the right arm, the lower part of the plinth, and the base are eighteenth-century marble restorations. The lower legs and feet were restored in the twentieth century with plaster casts taken from Roman copies of the same type in Berlin and Copenhagen.

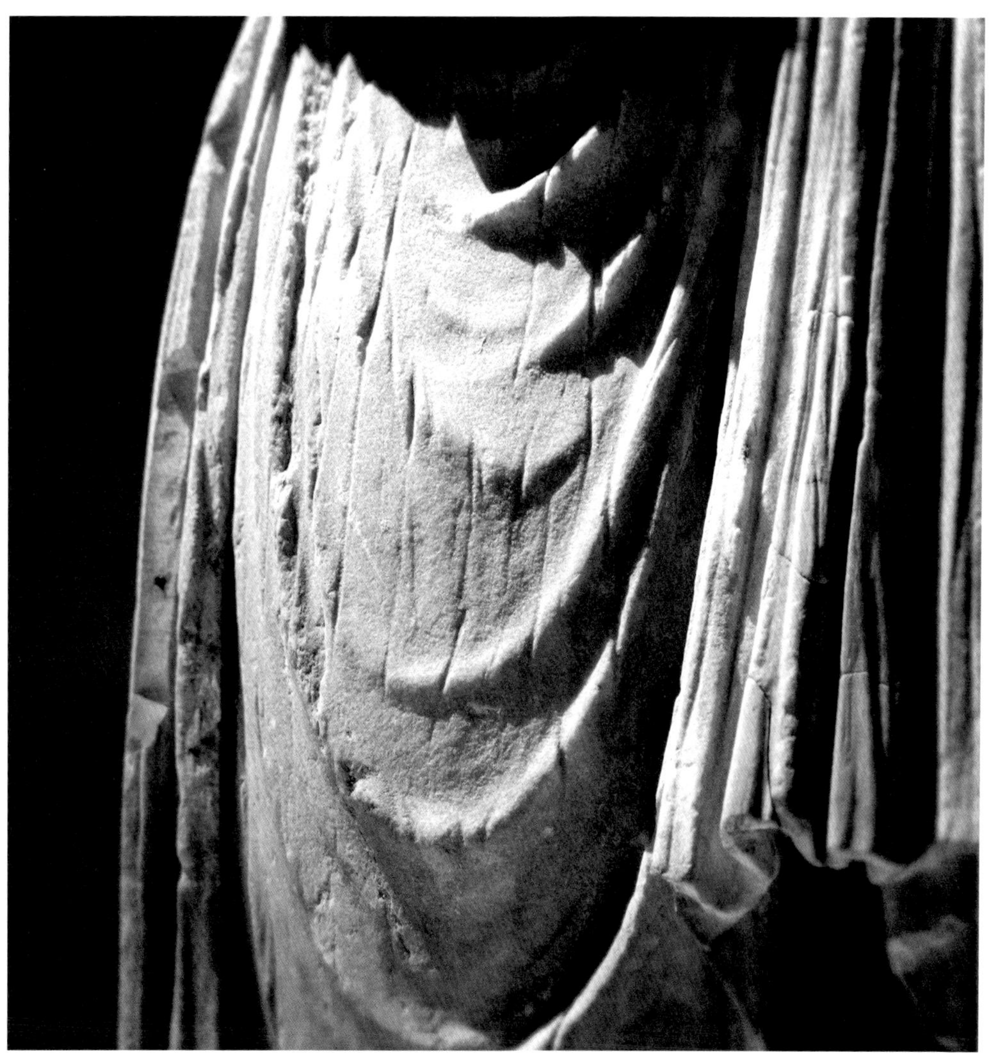

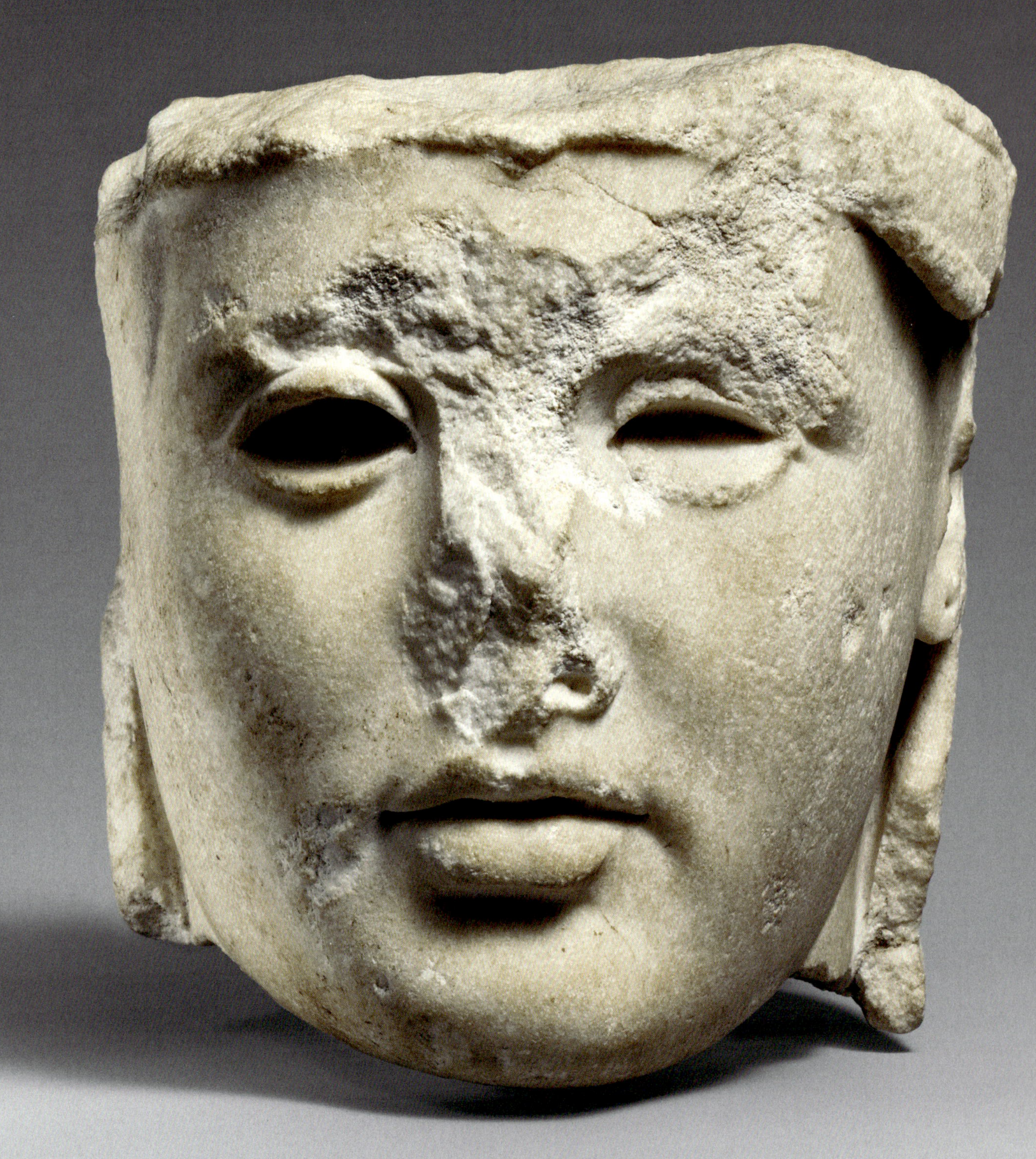

# Head of Athena

Roman, Imperial period, ca. A.D. 138–192
Copy of a Greek statue of ca. 430 B.C. attributed to Pheidias
Marble, H. 7⅞ in. (20 cm)
Rogers Fund, 2007 (2007.293)

At first glance, this head appears rather battered and fragmentary, although a well-lit frontal view captures some of its original majestic power. Remnants of an Attic helmet found on the head—a part of the frontlet that protected the forehead and a neck guard—are clearly identifiable features of a helmet typically worn by Athenian soldiers in the Classical period. Further study revealed that the head is one of some thirty Roman copies of a famous Classical Greek statue, while comparison with those other copies indicated that the goddess Athena is represented. The type is known as the Athena Medici after a marble standing draped figure of the goddess in the collection of the Louvre.

Although only the marble survives, the head in The Met collection was originally an acrolithic statue, one made from many materials and intended to imitate a special class of Classical Greek sculpture, known as chryselephantine, that was fashioned from gold and ivory and typically used for cult statues. The fine white marble imitates ivory to give the impression of silky flesh, the hollow eye sockets would have contained lifelike inset eyes probably made from colored marble, and the small hole in the left ear would have been fitted with a metal earring. Of particular interest is the treatment of the top and back of the head, which are carved in two flat planes with smooth surfaces that have been worked with shallow point marks. A single narrow vertical channel is cut into the center of each plane, like a dovetail groove in woodworking. This channel would have secured the wooden upper parts of the helmet's dome and crest, which were gilded to appear like solid gold. Gilded wood would also have been used for elements of her drapery, and marble for her limbs.

The original over-lifesize chryselephantine statue of Athena has been attributed to Pheidias, the most celebrated artist of the Classical period, and is presumed to have been located in Athens. Pheidias was famous for creating the gold-and-ivory cult statue of Athena Parthenos on the Athenian Acropolis and the seated cult statue of Zeus at Olympia, considered one of the Seven Wonders of the Ancient World. An Athenian by birth, Pheidias worked in many materials and was best known for his images of deities, in contrast to his contemporary Polykeitos, who excelled in bronze statues of athletes. Although none of Pheidias's original sculptures survive, ancient literary sources reveal that he could conceive of the divine with the imagination of a brilliant artist and, through his extraordinary skills, create sculptures that were considered equal to the majesty of the gods he portrayed. The surviving physical copies and adaptations of Pheidian sculpture, like this head, were made many centuries later and are only pale reflections of the originals.

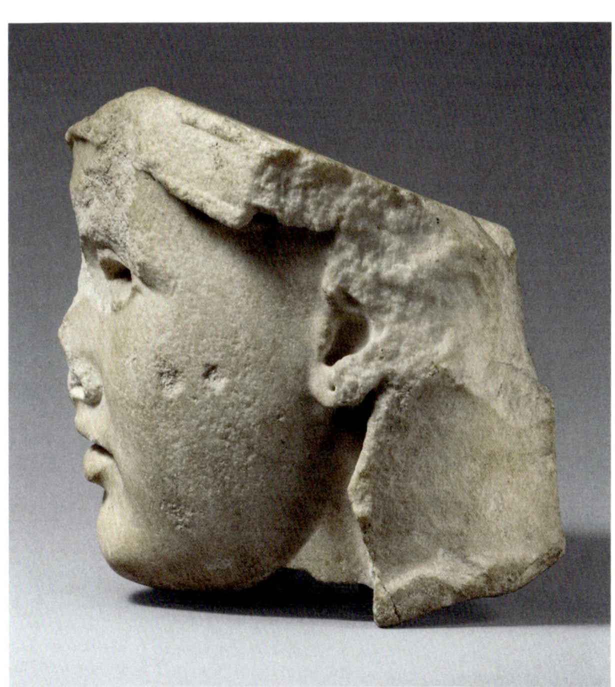

19

# Statuette of a youth

Greek, Classical period, late 5th century B.C.
Bronze, H. 6¼ in. (15.9 cm)
The Cesnola Collection, Purchased by subscription, 1874–76 (74.51.5679)

This statuette, which has great presence, reflects the high standard of craftsmanship characteristic of the finest Classical Greek bronzes. In the carefully balanced proportions of the limbs and perfectly formed abdomen, we see the ideal male form through the eyes of a Classical Greek sculptor. The youth stands with his weight on his left leg. His physique and especially the shift in the weight of his body suggest features thought to have been among the major achievements of Polykleitos of Argos, one of the most influential and famous bronze sculptors of the fifth century B.C.

Celebrated by later writers—Cicero thought that his sculpture was perfection itself—Polykleitos was among the first artists to write about his work, in a treatise entitled the *Canon*. He also embodied his ideas in a particular statue, which most scholars believe was his Doryphoros (Spear-Bearer), as well as establishing a highly influential system of proportions. Although only a few fragments of his treatise survive, a significant number of later copies and adaptations of his statuary allow us to have a reasonable understanding of his work.

This small statuette, said to have been found on the island of Cyprus, is part of the Cesnola Collection at The Met, the first major group of antiquities to enter the Museum. Entirely Greek in style, it was surely an import to the island. In fact, such small-scale statuettes are probably one way that Polykleitos's innovations spread throughout the Greek world beginning as early as the fifth century B.C. Noteworthy as well is the artist's attention to the whole figure, which can be appreciated from every angle. The specific identity of this figure is ambiguous, like that of Polykleitos's Doryphoros, which could be either an athlete or a military figure. He originally held something in his left hand, which is now lost.

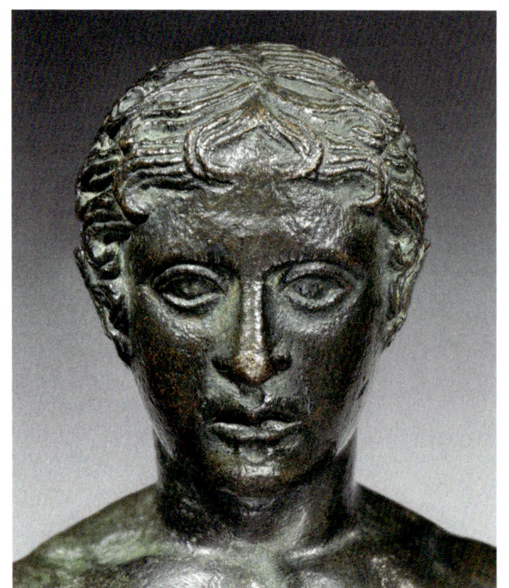

Detail of no. 19

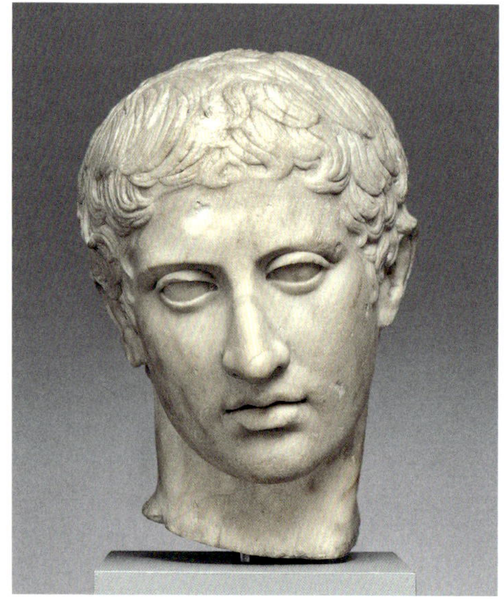

Fig. 41. Head of a youth. Roman, probably Claudian period, ca. A.D. 41–54. Copy of a Greek bronze statue of ca. 450 B.C. attributed to Polykleitos. Marble, H. 11¼ in. (28.6 cm). Rogers Fund, 1907 (07.286.116)

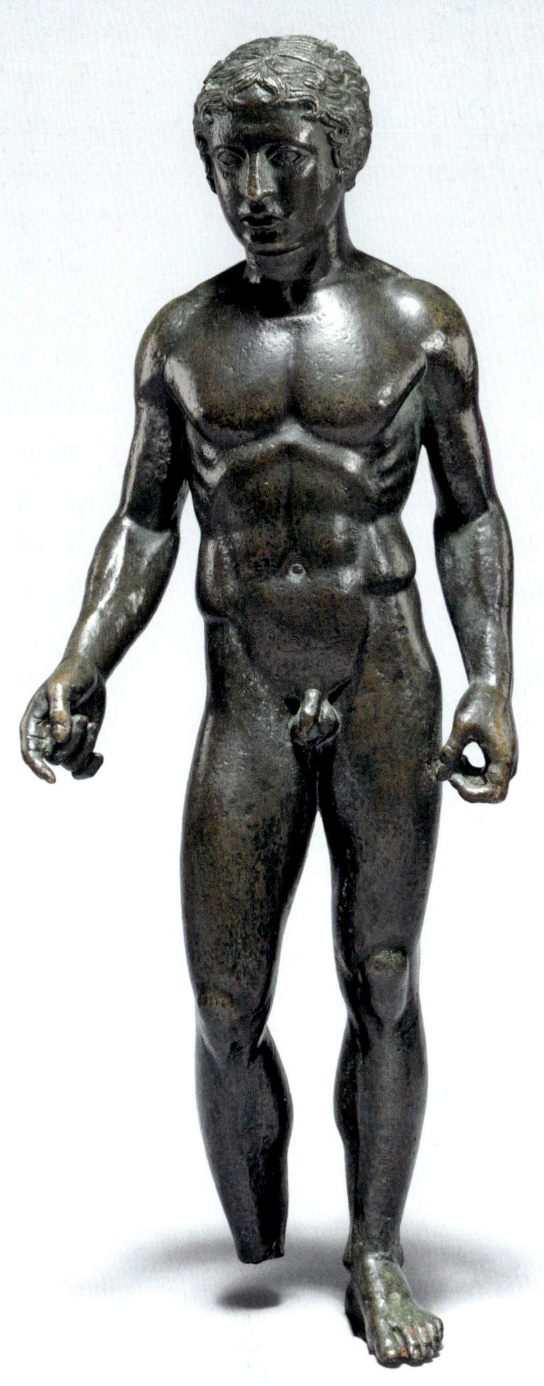

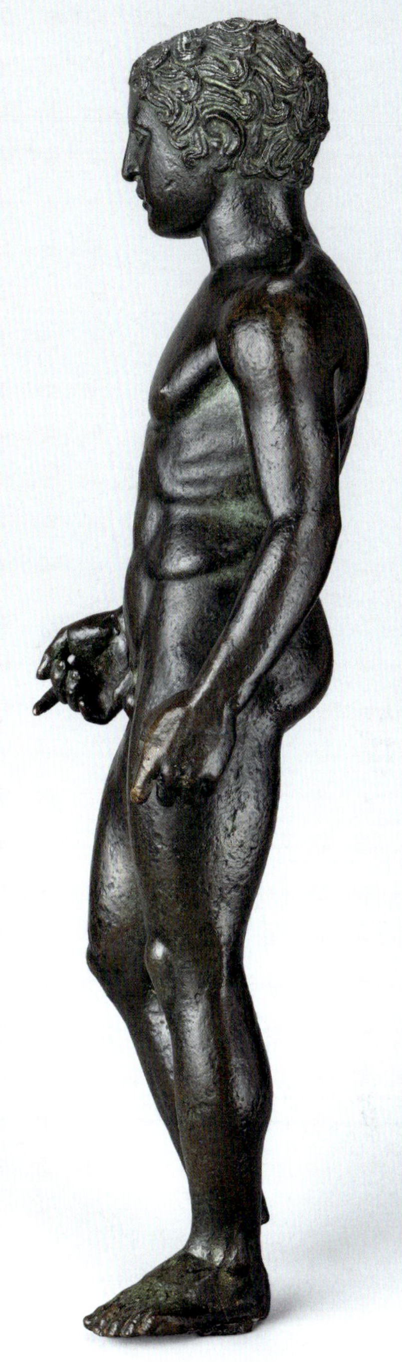

It is instructive to compare the treatment of the hair with that seen in a Polykleitan marble head in The Met collection (see detail and fig. 41). Notice the same rhythmic approach and the fundamentally similar coiffures, especially evident in the pairs of concentric comma-shaped curls framing the forehead. Both works, although removed in time by centuries and made in different media at dramatically different scales, nonetheless appear to derive from the same prototype, which was most likely a bronze statue by Polykleitos.

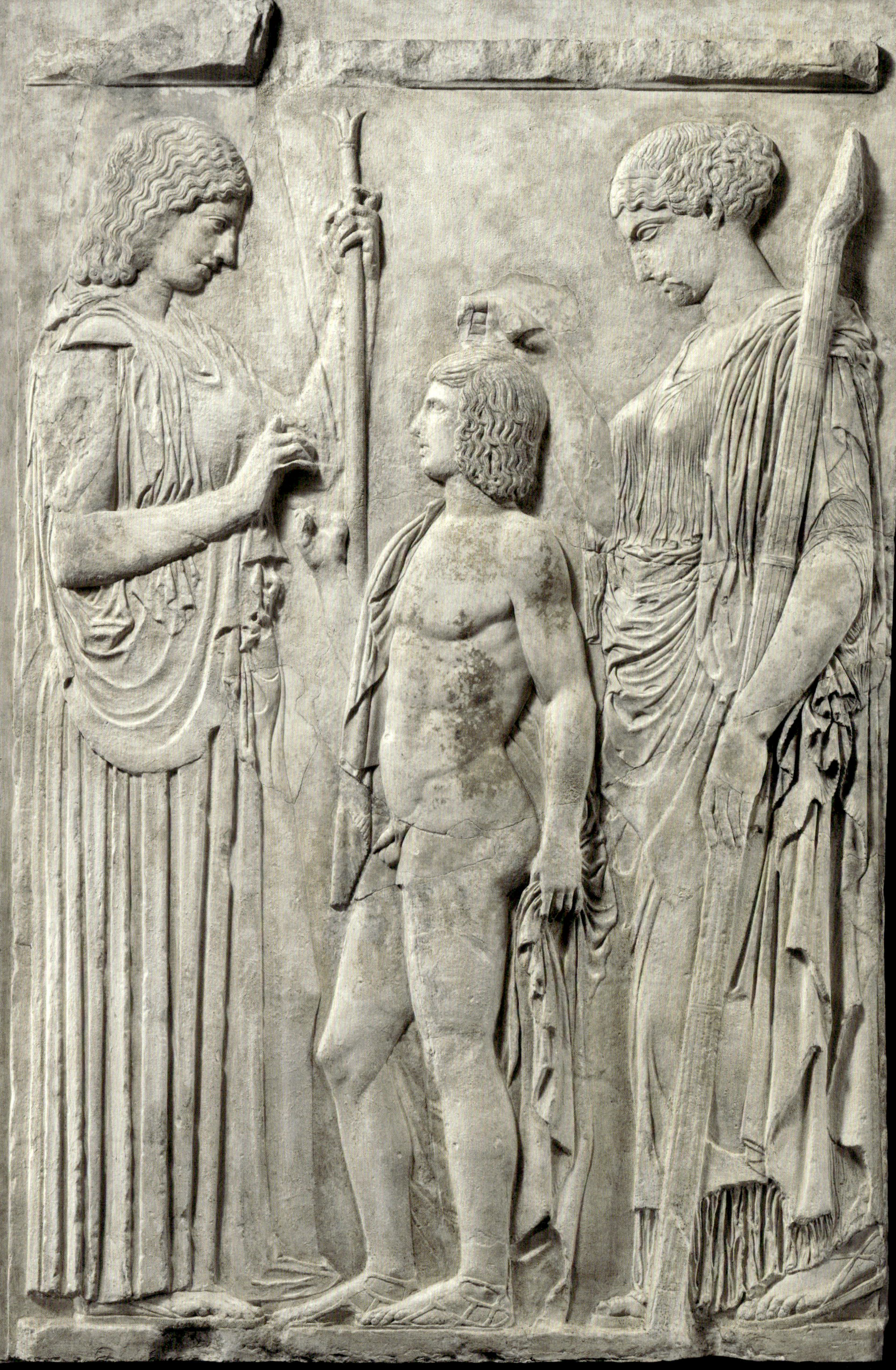

20

# Ten fragments of the Great Eleusinian Relief

Roman, Augustan period, ca. 27 B.C.–A.D. 14
Copy of a Greek marble relief of ca. 450–425 B.C.
Marble, H. (restored) 89⅜ in. (227 cm)
Rogers Fund, 1914 (14.130.9)

This impressive relief is arguably the most important Roman copy of an ancient Greek sculpture in The Met collection. Known as the Great Eleusinian Relief, it is a monumental cult image from the sanctuary of Demeter at Eleusis, the site of one of the major mystery cults of antiquity. Demeter, goddess of agricultural abundance, is shown on the left, wearing a peplos and himation and holding a scepter. On the right is her daughter Persephone, who wears a chiton and himation. Between them is a nude young man to whom they extend their right hands. The youth is best identified as Triptolemos, the legendary first initiate of the Eleusinian mystery cult, who was sent by Demeter to teach mankind to cultivate grain, a myth that also appears in Classical Greek vase painting (fig. 42).

The original marble relief was carved in the third quarter of the fifth century B.C. and set up in the sanctuary of Demeter, where it was discovered intact. It now resides in the National Archaeological Museum in Athens. Plaster casts from the original have been used to restore the ten fragments at The Met, which were carved at the same scale and join quite seamlessly. A comparison between the details from the two reliefs shows that The Met copy, which comes from Augustan Rome, is remarkably close to the original. All the locks of Demeter's hair, for example, have been faithfully rendered, although those on the Roman copy are sharper and in shallower relief. Not every part of the relief is an exact copy. Some drapery folds of Persephone's chiton are different. On the whole, however, the relief indicates how careful Roman copyists could be.

Ancient sculptors achieved this copying precision by means of what is called a pointing machine. Molds of the original relief would have been taken in Eleusis and brought to Rome, where a plaster cast was made from them to serve as a master model for the sculptor. By taking many measurements from the model and transferring them in precisely corresponding positions to a rough-hewn marble block, the sculptor could remove the excess stone until the correct depth of the point was reached. Such work required careful measurements as well as skill.

Roman copies of Greek sculpture are often not as exact as this one. The artist made alterations to the original for a host of reasons, including to suit the stylistic preferences of his own era or to appeal perhaps to the desires of his clients. In some cases, working in a Classical idiom, Roman sculptors adapted freely from ancient Greek sculptures to fashion their own quite different creations. Consequently, when an original Greek sculpture is not preserved to compare with the copy, it is impossible to know how close a likeness a Roman sculpture actually is. The Great Eleusinian Relief in The Met is therefore important since it is a rare case in which we can compare a copy with the original.

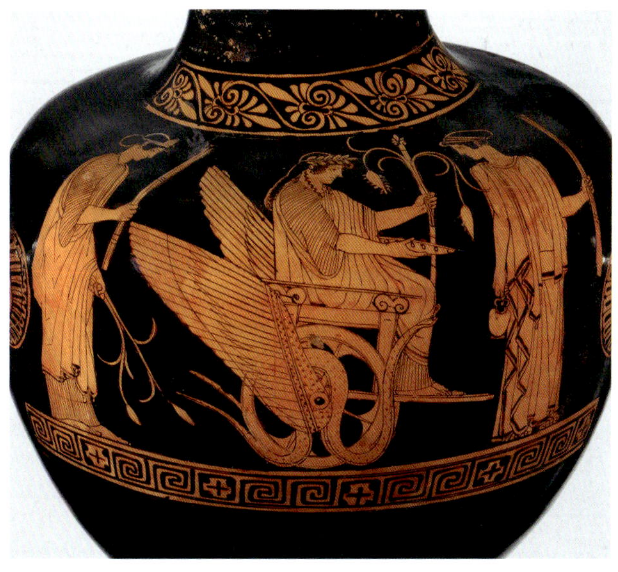

Fig. 42. Hydria: kalpis (water jar). Triptolemos between Demeter and Persephone. Greek, Attic, ca. 460–450 B.C. Attributed to the Niobid Painter. Terracotta, red-figure, H. 10 15/16 in. (27.7 cm). Rogers Fund, 1941 (41.162.98)

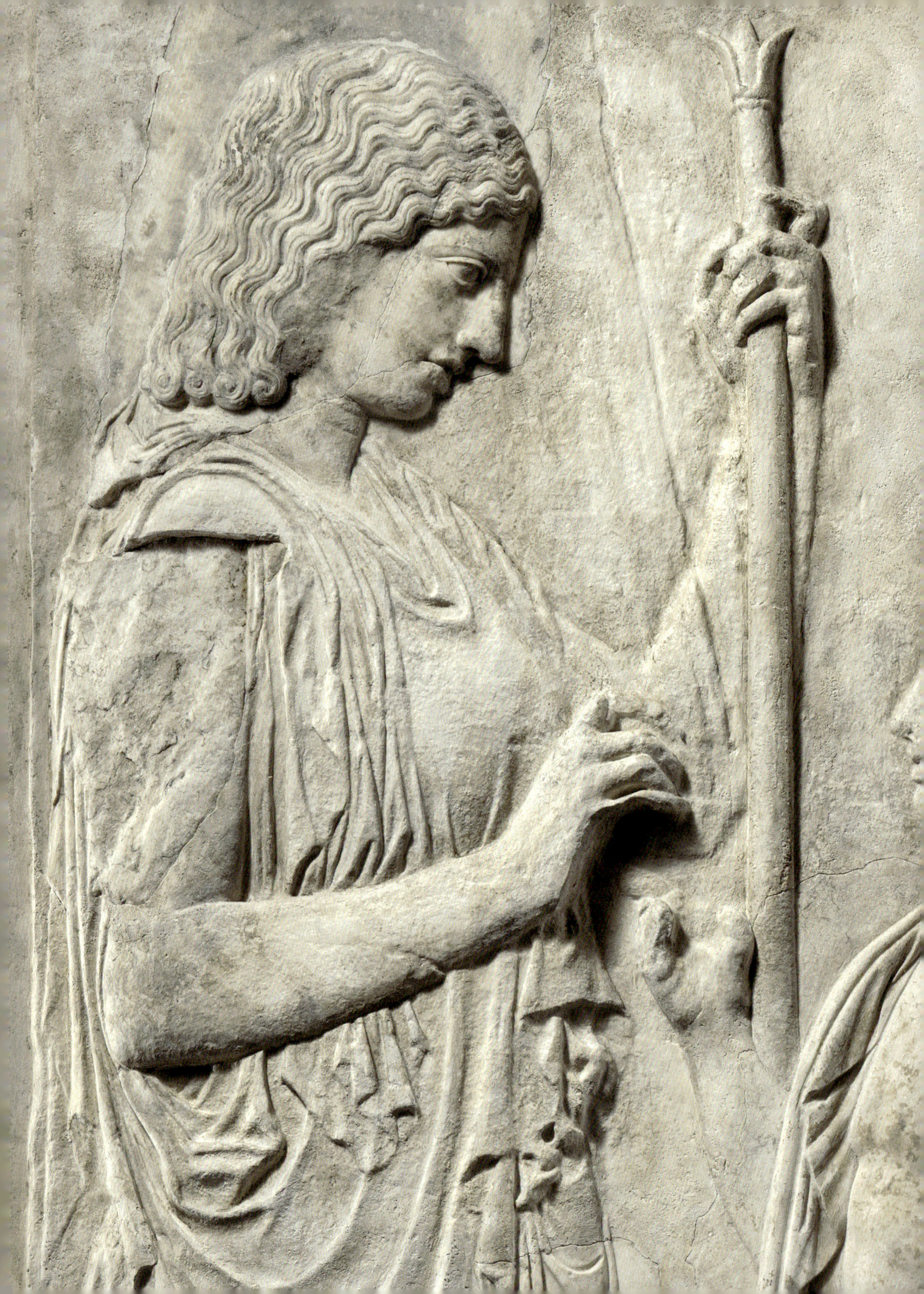

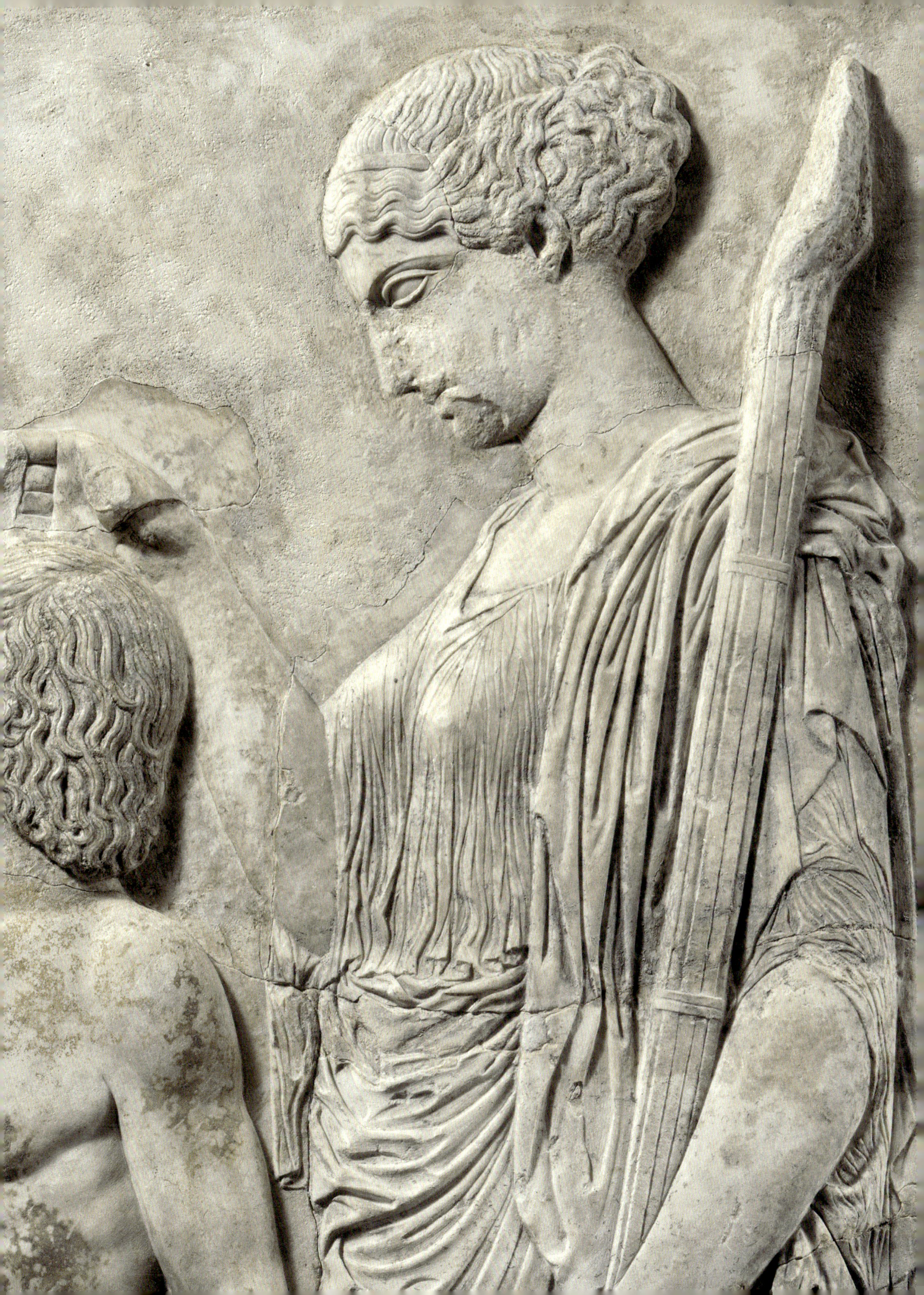

# Relief with a dancing maenad

Roman, Augustan, ca. 27 B.C.–A.D. 14
Copy of a figure from a Greek relief of ca. 425–400 B.C. attributed to Kallimachos
Marble, H. 56 5/16 in. (143 cm)
Fletcher Fund, 1935 (35.11.3)

The figure carved on this relief is a maenad, one of the mythological female followers of Dionysos, the god of wine. Rhythmically swaying to music and gazing downward as if in a trance, she holds a thrysos, a tall stick of fennel decorated with ivy, berries, and a ribbon. In her hair is a wreath of ivy. Her long, billowing chiton, diaphanous in places, reveals the shapely form of her body. The swooping folds of her drapery seem to take on a life of their own, as though filled with the sound of music, accentuating the line of her long legs and revealing her delicate ankles. The soles beneath her feet come from sandals whose straps would have been depicted with paint. The proportions of her body, the rendering of her long hair, and the windswept drapery reflect the prevalent style employed by Greek sculptors during the late fifth century B.C.

This graceful figure is thought to have been adapted from a famous Greek relief featuring some six to nine dancing maenads that may have adorned the base of a cult statue of Dionysos or a sacrificial altar erected in Athens. The original relief has been attributed to Kallimachos, a sculptor and architect who is known to have worked in Athens in the late fifth century B.C. and who is said to have invented the Corinthian capital. Ancient writers record that Kallimachos carried his attention to detail to excess, and Pliny mentions that he carved dancers. The windblown style of the present relief would have suited the sculptor's taste, but this is not enough to allow for a secure attribution or to provide a true sense of his work.

The stylistic elements seen here were popular in the late fifth century B.C. and occur in a variety of media, including small-scale engravings such as a silver ring with an ecstatic maenad in The Met collection (fig. 43). Maenad reliefs, which appear in a wide variety of Roman works of art, from architectural reliefs like this one to relief-decorated marble kraters and candelabra, spanned more than three centuries, from the Late Republican period through the middle of the Imperial Age. They were among the most widely copied and adapted Greek sculptures in the ancient Roman world.

In Greek mythology, maenads celebrate Dionysos in song, music, and dance, roaming through the mountains in an ecstatic state brought on by the god. Accompanying Dionysos on his triumphant journey to the East, where he spread his cult far and wide, they are often represented cavorting with their male Dionysian counterparts, the Satyrs and silenoi. The Classical Greek playwright Euripides celebrates their primeval power in his play *The Bacchae*. Another possible source for the original relief featuring the dancing maenads is a monument sculpted by Kallimachos in 406–405 B.C. that was set up in Athens as a votive offering in commemoration of a performance of Euripides's play.

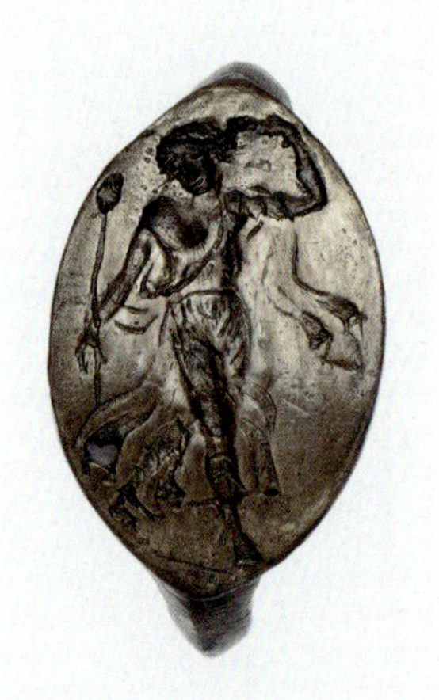

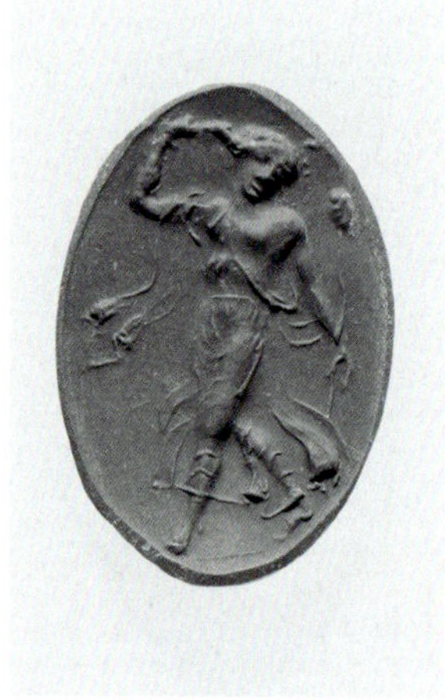

Fig. 43. *Left*: Ring with an ecstatic maenad; *right*: impression of ring. Greek, Classical period, ca. late 5th century B.C. Silver, L. 7/8 in. (2.2 cm). Fletcher Fund, 1925 (25.78.101)

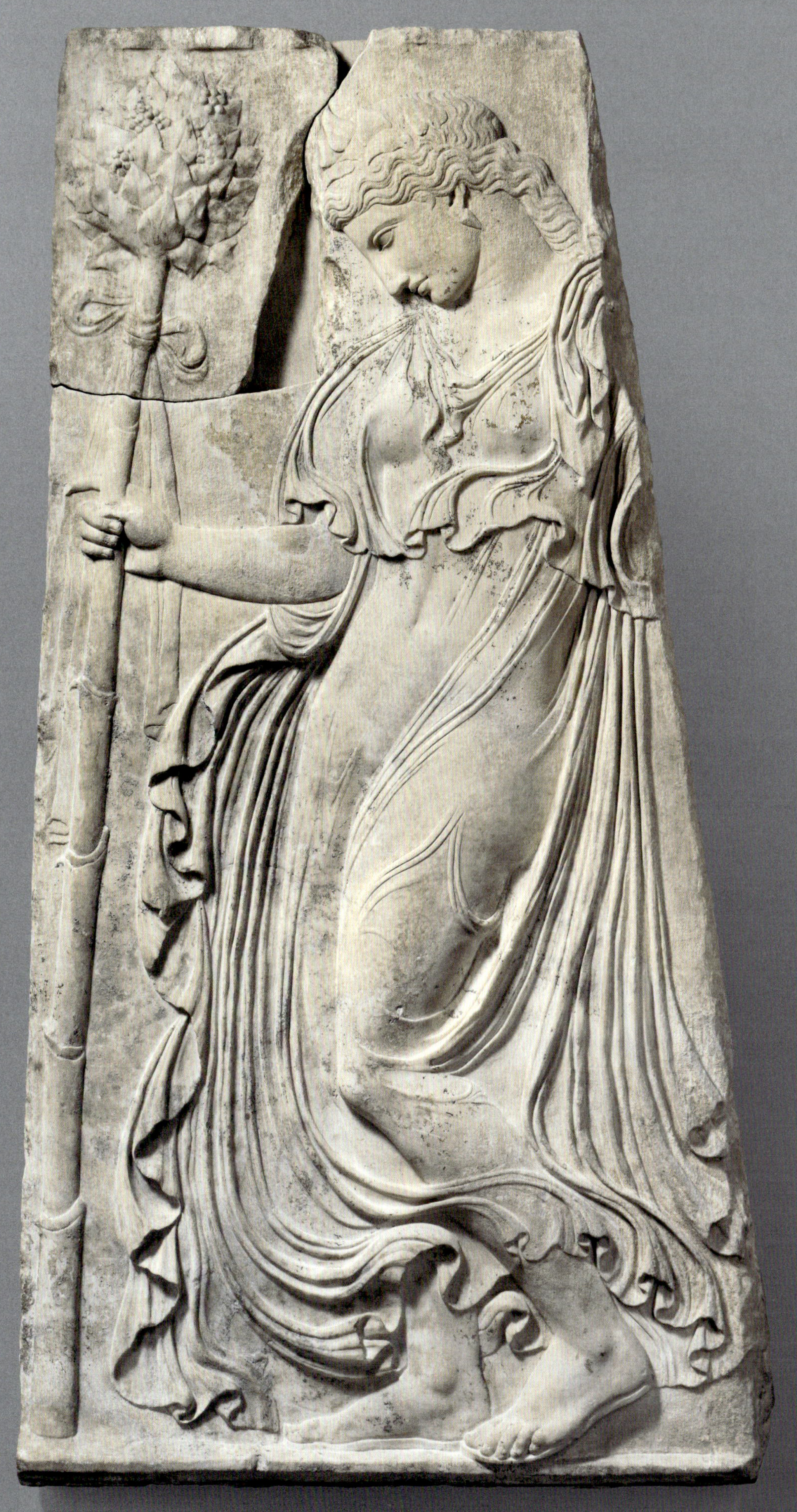

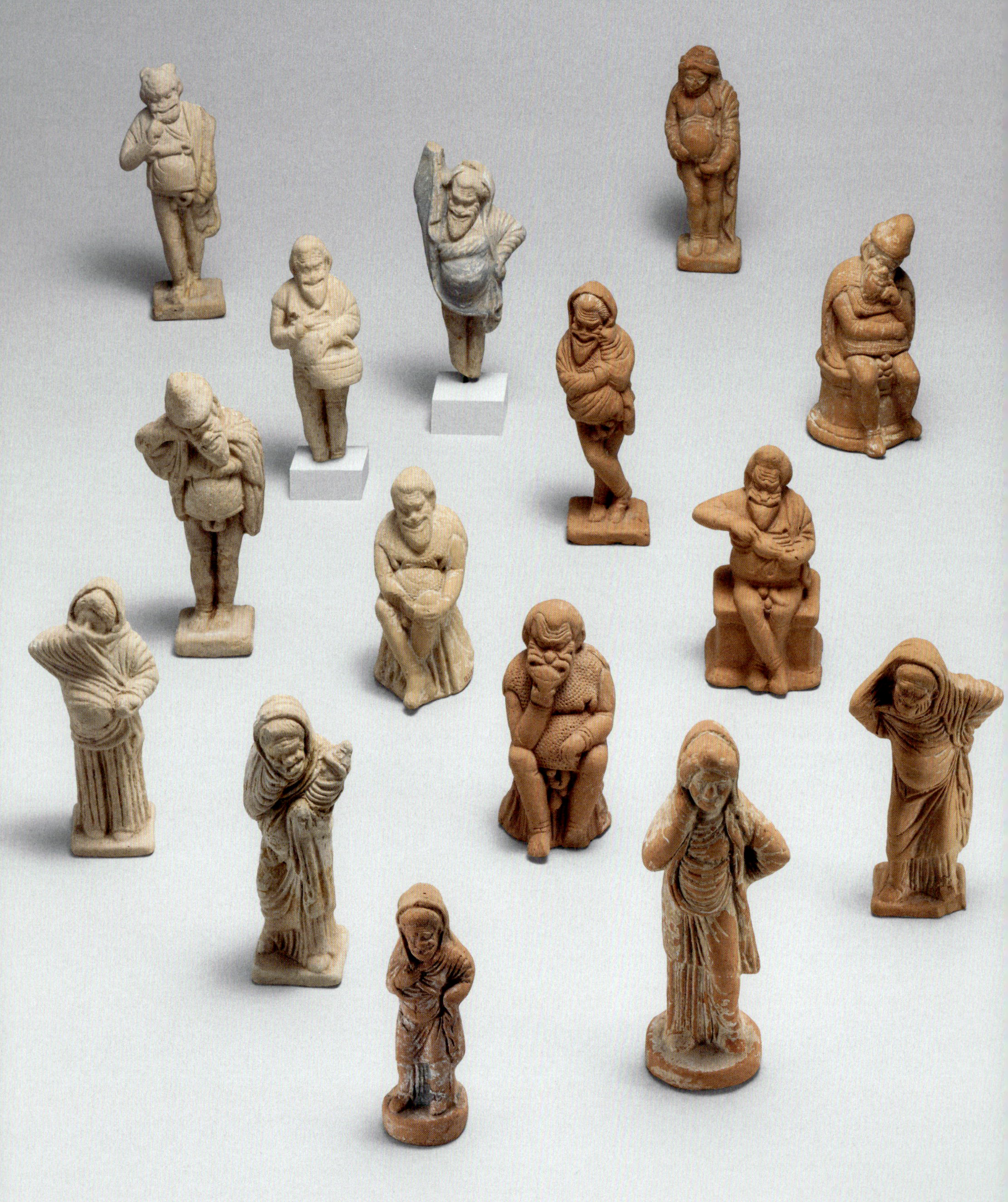

22

# Statuettes of actors

Greek, Classical period, late 5th–early 4th century B.C.
Terracotta, H. of tallest 4¾ in. (12.1 cm)
Rogers Fund, 1913 (13.225.13, .14, .16–.28)

Fourteen of these terracotta statuettes are said to have been found together in a tomb in Attica. They are among the earliest surviving sculptures of comic actors from ancient Greece. Documenting the beginning of standardized characters and masks, the figures represent stock characters from comedy, types that were used again and again in the theater. Only men performed in the ancient Greek theater, and masks were employed to portray both male and female characters. The masks have exaggerated features that could be seen from a distance by the audience. Among the remarkable range of figures represented here are the hero Herakles with his club and the skin of the Nemean lion; a nurse carrying a baby in swaddling clothes; and a bearded old man wearing the conical hat of a traveler and daubing his eye with the edge of his cloak. Many of the figures resemble characters in the comic plays written in the late fifth century B.C. by the Greek dramatist Aristophanes.

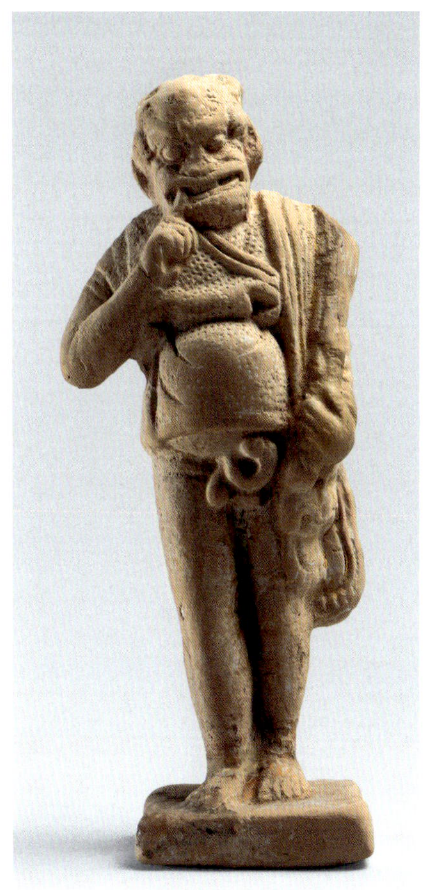

Herakles

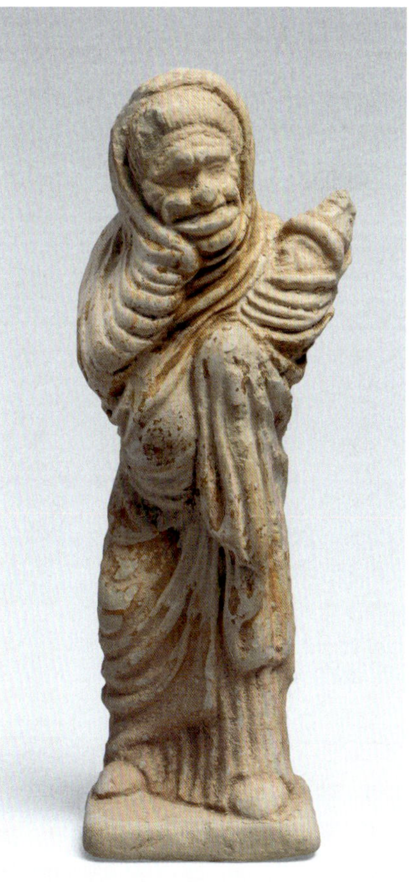

The Old Nurse

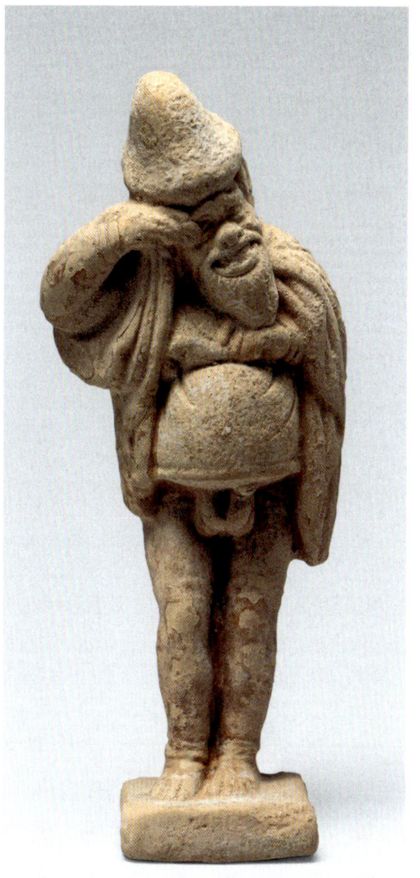

The Old Man

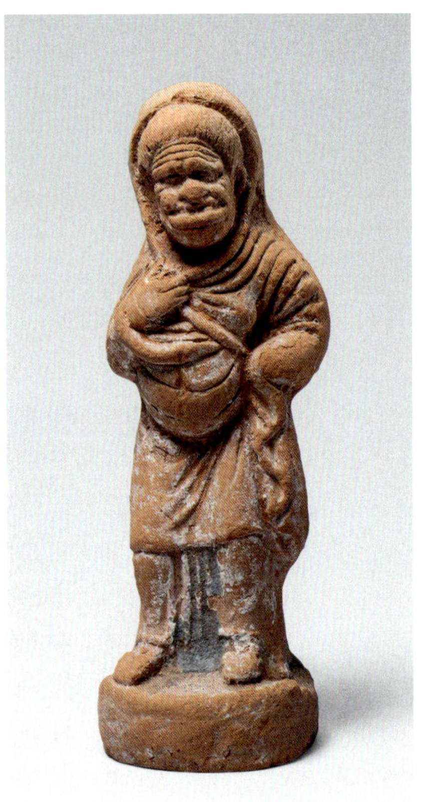

The Hag

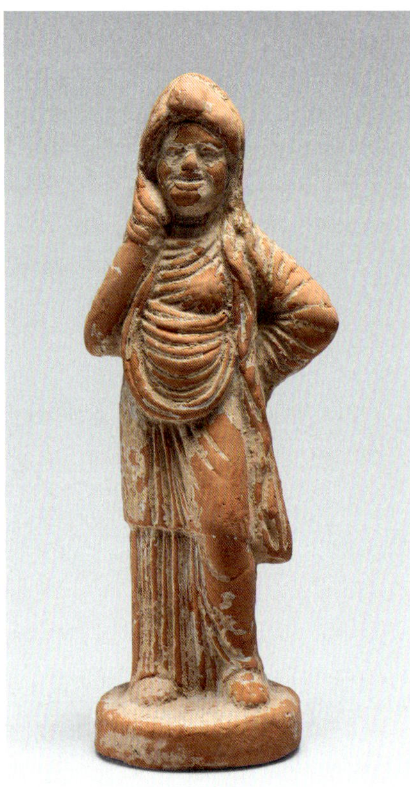

The Courtesan

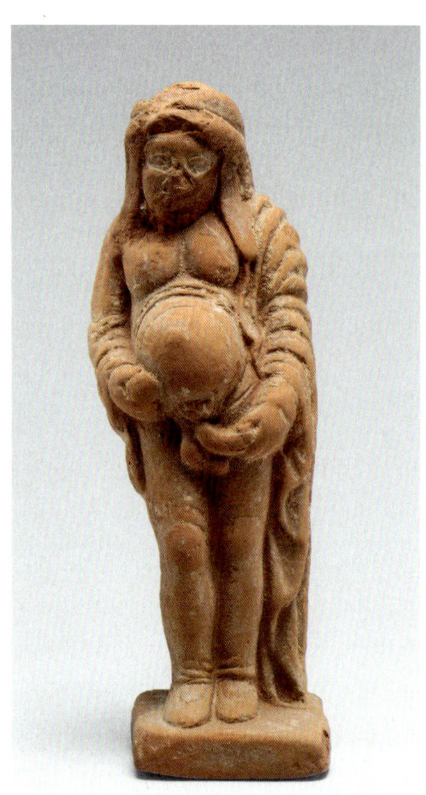

Youth touching himself

The old man and the old woman, along with caricatures of enslaved persons, became well-known characters in Greek comedy, instantly recognizable by their costumes and masks. Sexual jokes, such as those represented by the elderly courtesan here, were popular in both comedies and farces. A feature of many of the male characters is a large phallus, which is typically rolled up and used only for certain scenes to indicate that it is part of the costume. One of these figures has his phallus out and is touching it. A similar character appears in a Greek vase from southern Italy: pirouetting with his phallus out, he and his accomplice attempt to steal a goose from an old woman (fig. 44).

These statuettes of actors may have been produced by Greek theater companies as mementos of their performances. The figures were made in molds and would have been easily reproduced. Some of them bear traces of paint, including red, yellow, and blue, and originally all would have been brightly colored. Such statuettes circulated throughout the ancient Greek world and came to be produced in many different regions.

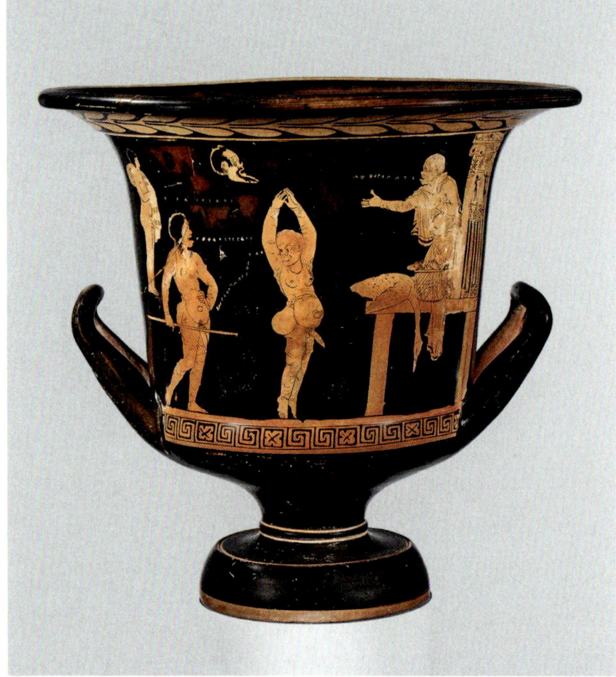

Fig. 44. Calyx-krater (mixing bowl) with scene from Greek comedy. Greek, South Italian, ca. 400–390 B.C. Attributed to the Dolon Painter. Terracotta, red-figure, H. 12 1/16 in. (30.6 cm). Fletcher Fund, 1924 (24.97.104)

23

# Statue of a lion

Greek, Late Classical period, ca. 400–390 B.C.
Parian marble, H. 31¼ in. (79.4 cm), L. 63½ in. (161.3 cm)
Purchase, Rogers Fund, and James Loeb and Anonymous Gifts, 1909 (09.221.3)

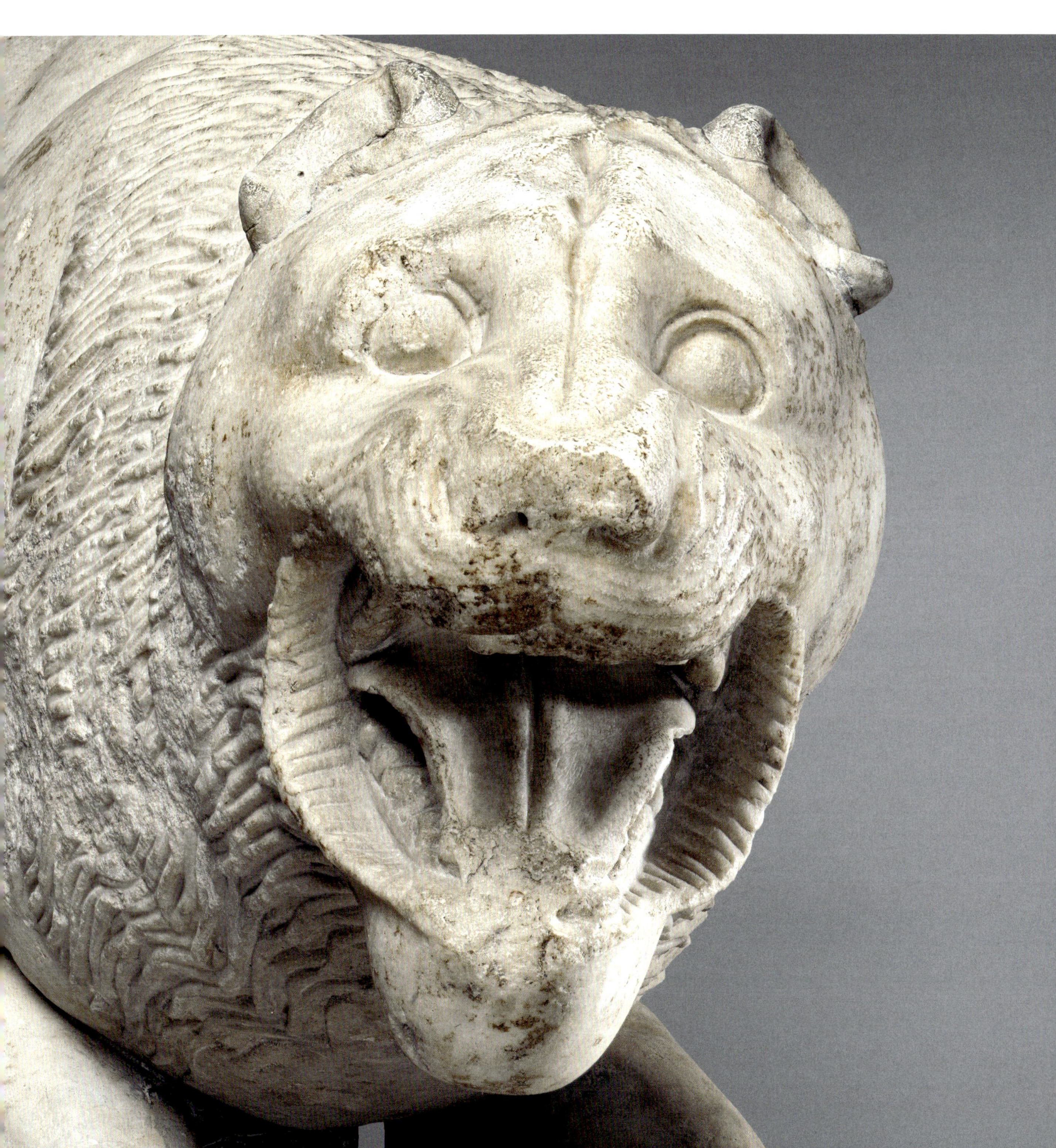

Crouching down on its front paws, the lion seems ready to attack. Its mouth gapes open ferociously, and its ears are set back to indicate aggression. The head is turned slightly to the right, while the long hairs of the full mane are rendered in shallow relief. The primary view is from the right profile and, to a much lesser extent, from the front.

By the Classical period, lions no longer roamed the Greek countryside, and the sculptor who carved this beast would not have seen one in the flesh. He would have looked to other representations of the animal, including those on gems (see fig. 35) and earlier monumental sculptures popular in the Archaic period (see discussion under no. 11). In its physiognomy, notably the treatment of the hindquarters, rib cage, and narrow body, the statue draws upon other prototypes for inspiration, such as dogs and domesticated cats.

This lion was probably one of a confronting pair that guarded the ends of a family plot in a Classical Greek cemetery located outside city walls. It would have served as a symbolic protector of the grave, much like the Archaic

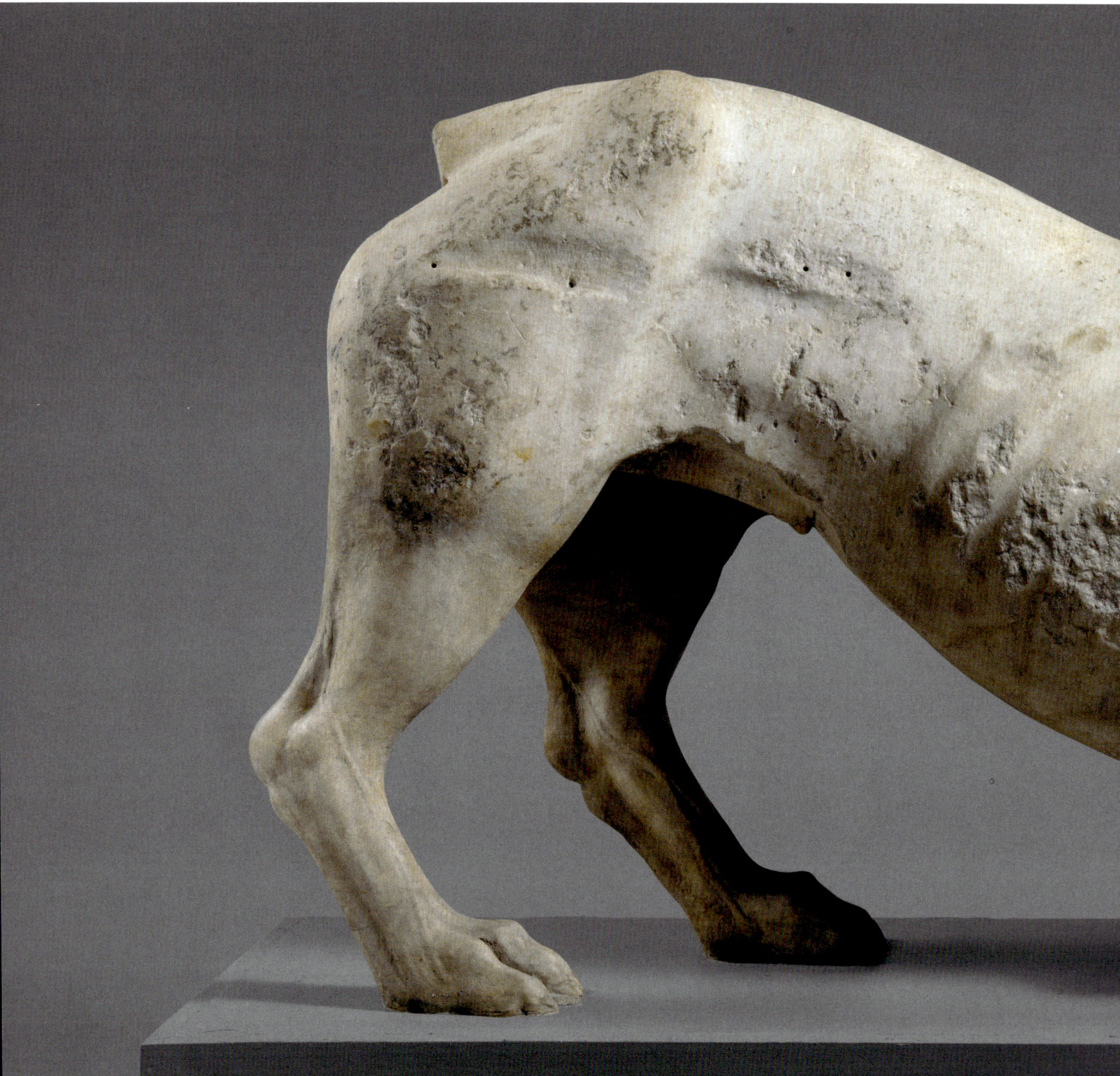

Sphinx on the stele with a youth and young girl discussed earlier (see no. 9). It would also have functioned as a display of the family's wealth and power. In Athens, the extent of these lavish displays led to a law passed in 317 B.C. that banned ostentatious tomb markers.

During the fourth century B.C., marble statues of lions were also used to mark individual tombs and even monumental mass graves from significant battles, such as the one at Chaeronea in 338 B.C. In those instances, the beast was not only a symbolic protector but also a representative of the bravery and might of the deceased. The power of lions is mentioned multiple times in connection with battle in Homer's *Iliad*. The present statue was unearthed in Rome and is believed to have been brought there in antiquity. Its context of use there would have been quite different. The ancient Romans valued Greek statuary, collected it, and often displayed it for decorative purposes in their homes and gardens.

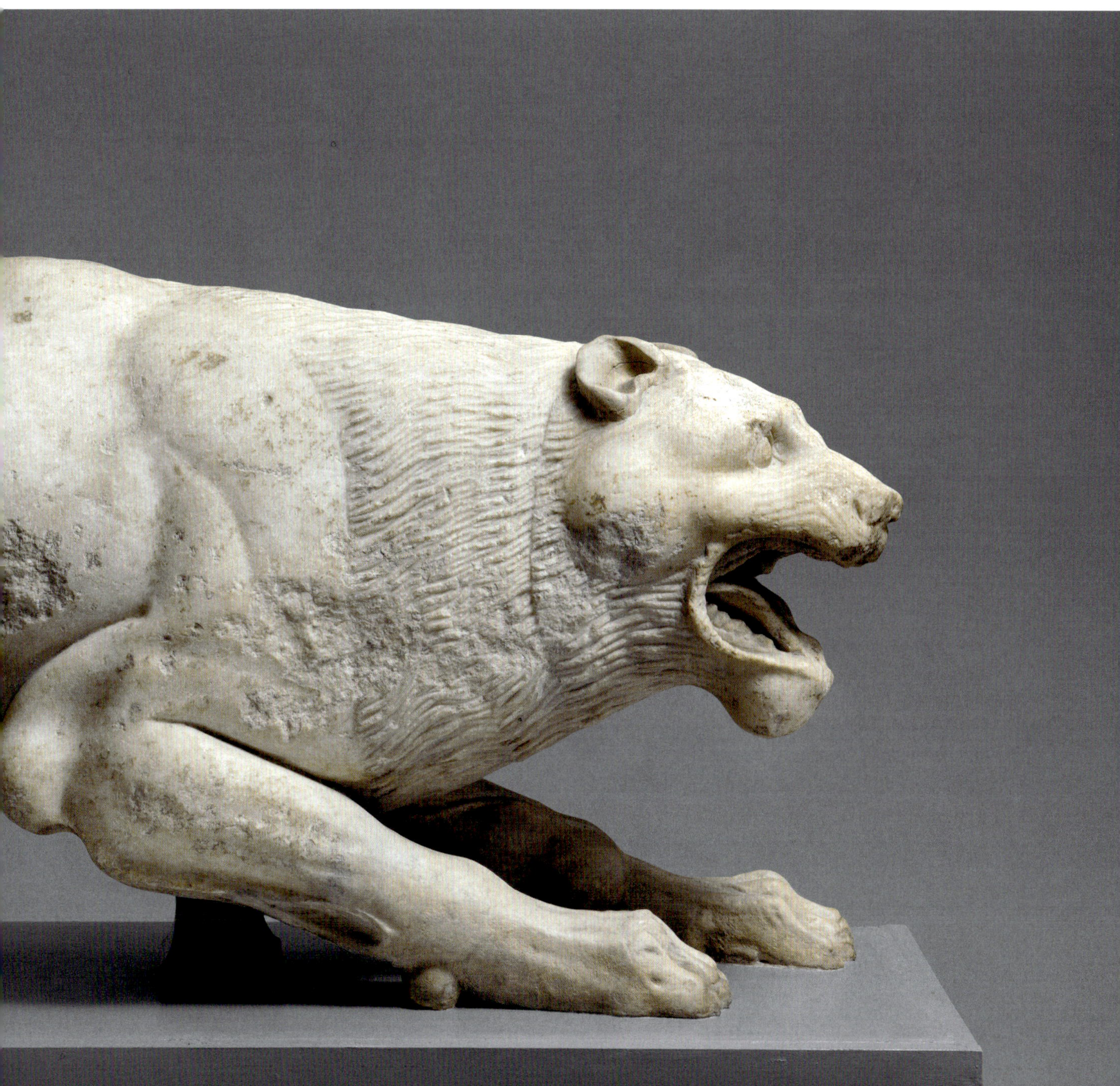

24

# Funerary lekythos of Kallisthenes

Greek, Attic, Classical period, ca. 410–390 B.C.
Marble, H. 62 in. (157.5 cm)
Rogers Fund, 1947 (47.11.2)

Toward the end of the fifth century B.C., Greek sculptors working in Attica began to sculpt large marble lekythoi (oil flasks) as memorials to the dead. The shape was appropriate as it monumentalized a form of terracotta vessel that had specific funerary connotations and played an important role in funerary ritual in the fifth and fourth centuries B.C. Sometimes deposited with the dead, terracotta lekythoi were also left as offerings at the tomb, which was occasionally represented on the receptacles themselves (fig. 45). The marble lekythoi were treated in a variety of ways: they could be plain, painted, or decorated in relief, as in this well-preserved example.

On the body of the vase, carved in low relief, is a funerary scene of farewell. The standing figure on the left represents Kallisthenes, the deceased, whose name is inscribed in Greek letters on either side of his head. The only identified figure, he is a young man, as his lack of a beard indicates. Wearing a half-draped himation, Kallisthenes clasps the hand of the seated older man, who most likely represents his father. The lower part of this man's face has losses, but he would originally have been bearded. He sits on a finely made klismos (armchair) with a backrest and elegant outward-curving legs. The two men appear to be looking directly at each other; the older

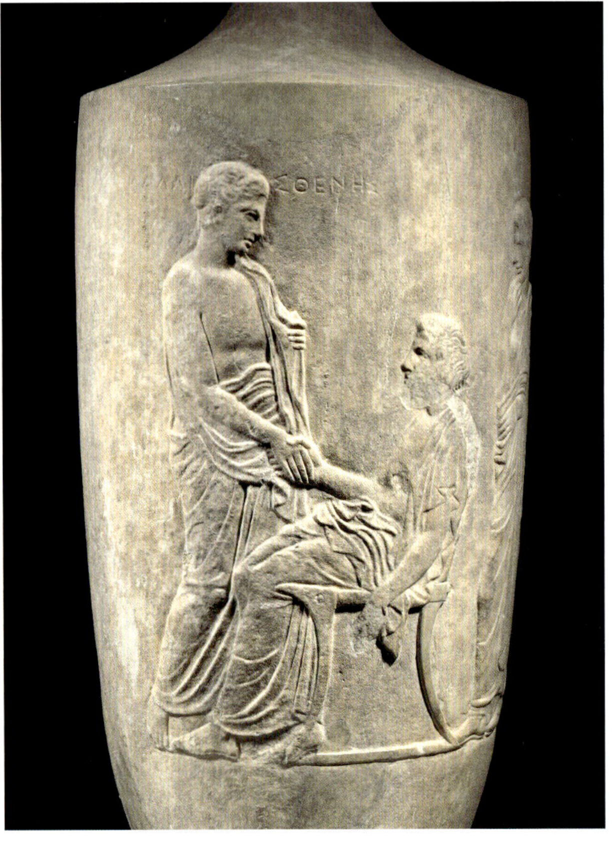

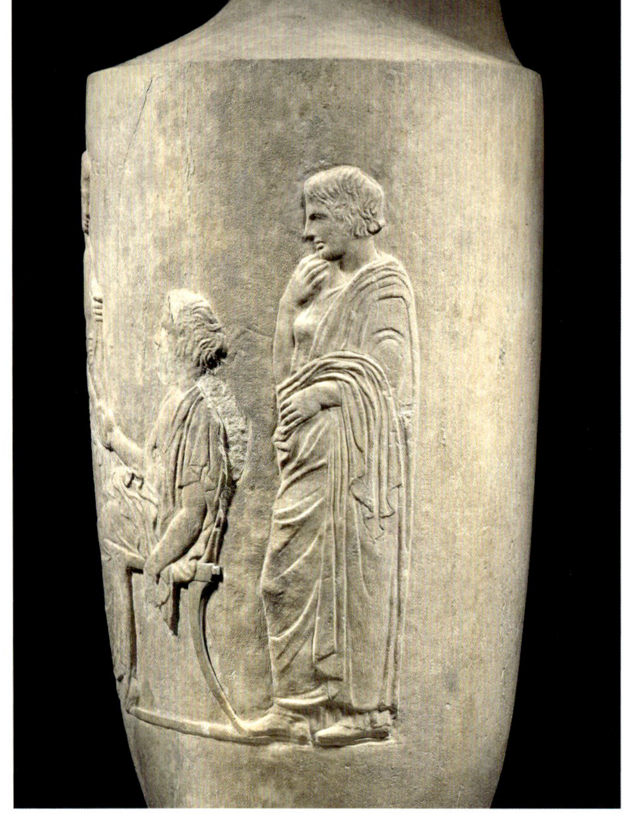

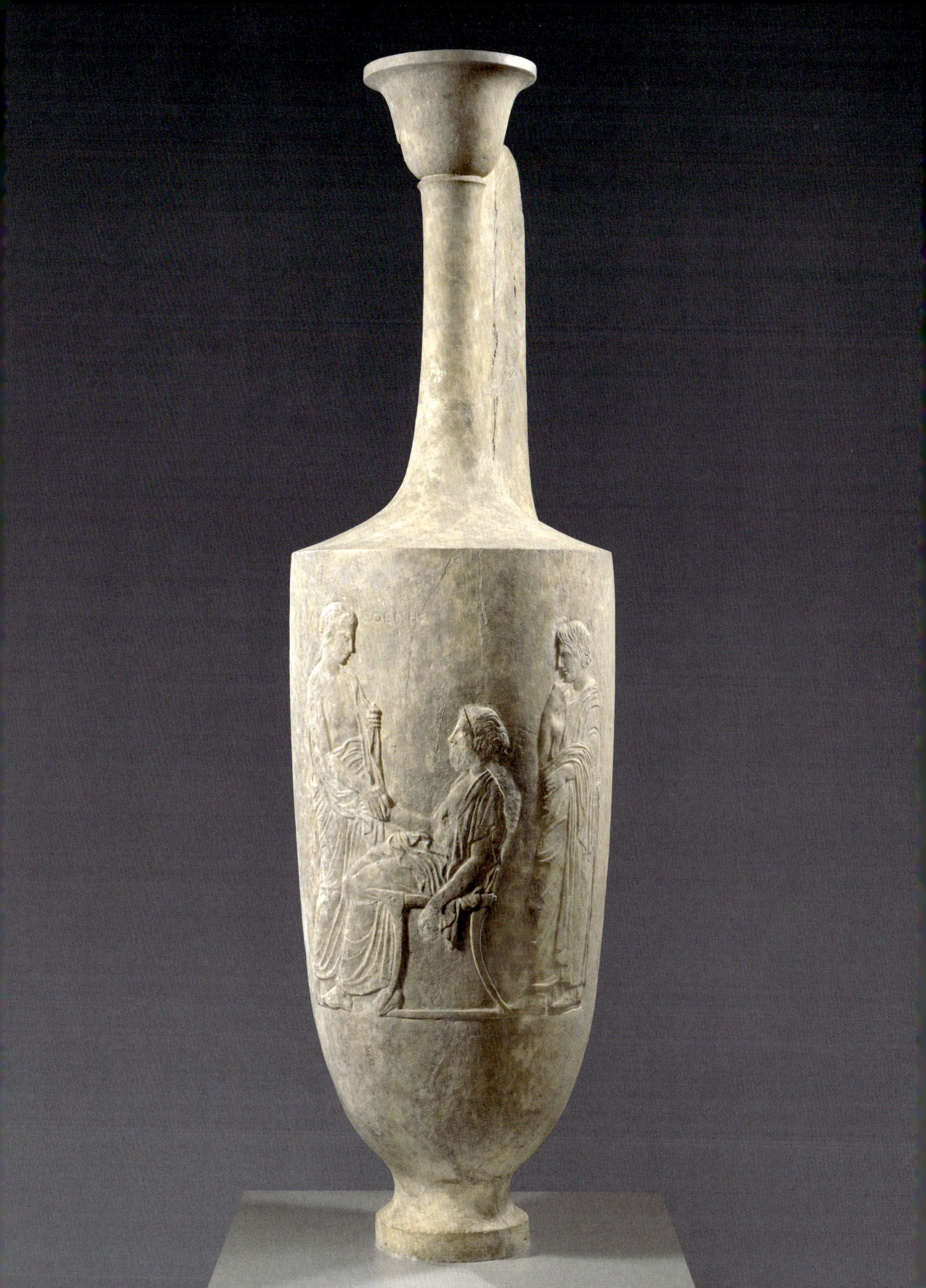

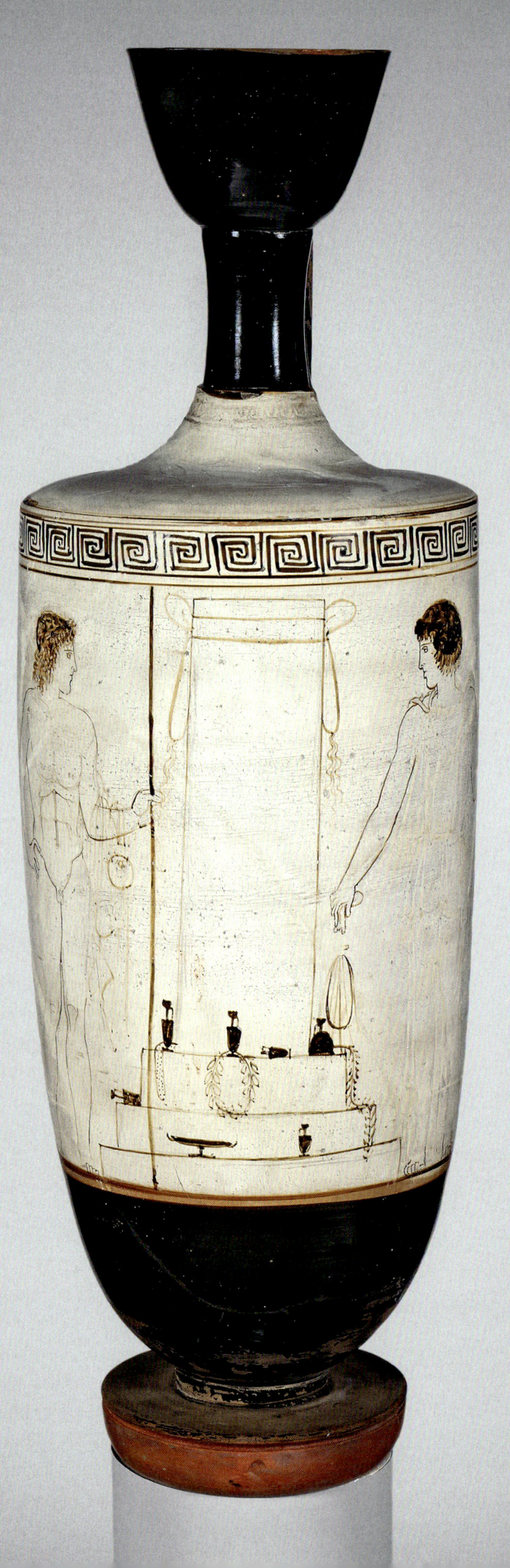

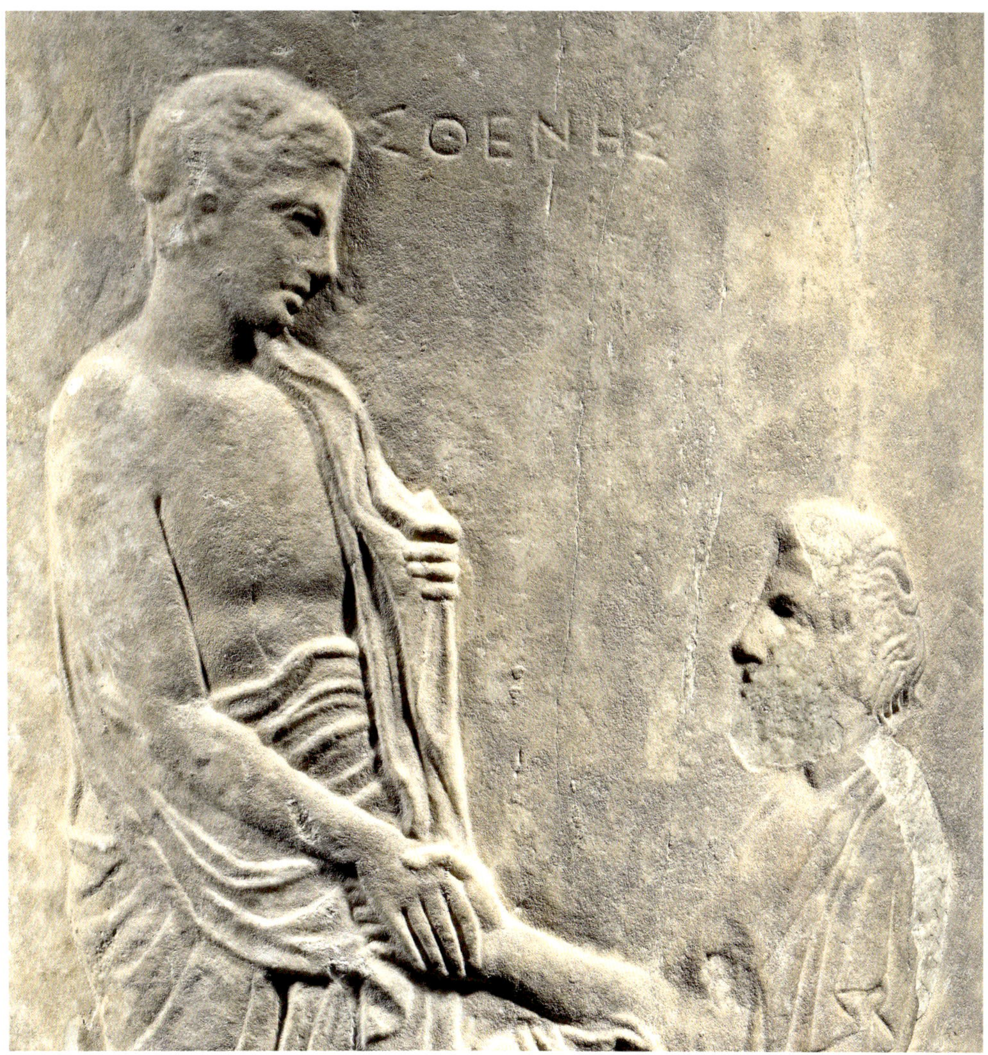

man, his left arm hanging limply, slumps in his chair as though distraught.

Behind the seated man and looking at Kallisthenes, a woman draped in a himation holds her hand up to her chin in a customary gesture of concern or grief. Most likely the mother or sister of the deceased, she wears her hair cut short to indicate she is in mourning. The soles appearing beneath the figures' feet indicate that the rest of their sandals were painted. Many other parts of the scene and even the vessel itself would have been as well, judging from other examples with better-preserved paint. It has been observed that the austerely simple style of the three figures recalls that of the Parthenon, which was carved some forty years earlier. Funerary monuments tended to be conservative by nature, and the Parthenon, an icon from the golden age of Athens, was frequently emulated in later sculptures.

The gesture of clasping hands between the deceased and the living is one of the most common on Classical grave reliefs. Not simply a token of farewell, it also emphasizes the importance of making a connection between the living and the dead. The notion of maintaining this connection long after the burial was a fundamental aspect of ancient Greek funerary practice. The tombs of ancestors and relatives were visited regularly to preserve their memory and honor their spirits through the performance of periodic rituals.

Fig. 45. Lekythos (oil flask). Greek, Attic, Classical period, ca. 440–430 B.C. Attributed to the Bosanquet Painter. Terracotta, white ground technique, H. 15¼ in. (38.7 cm). Rogers Fund, 1923 (23.160.38)

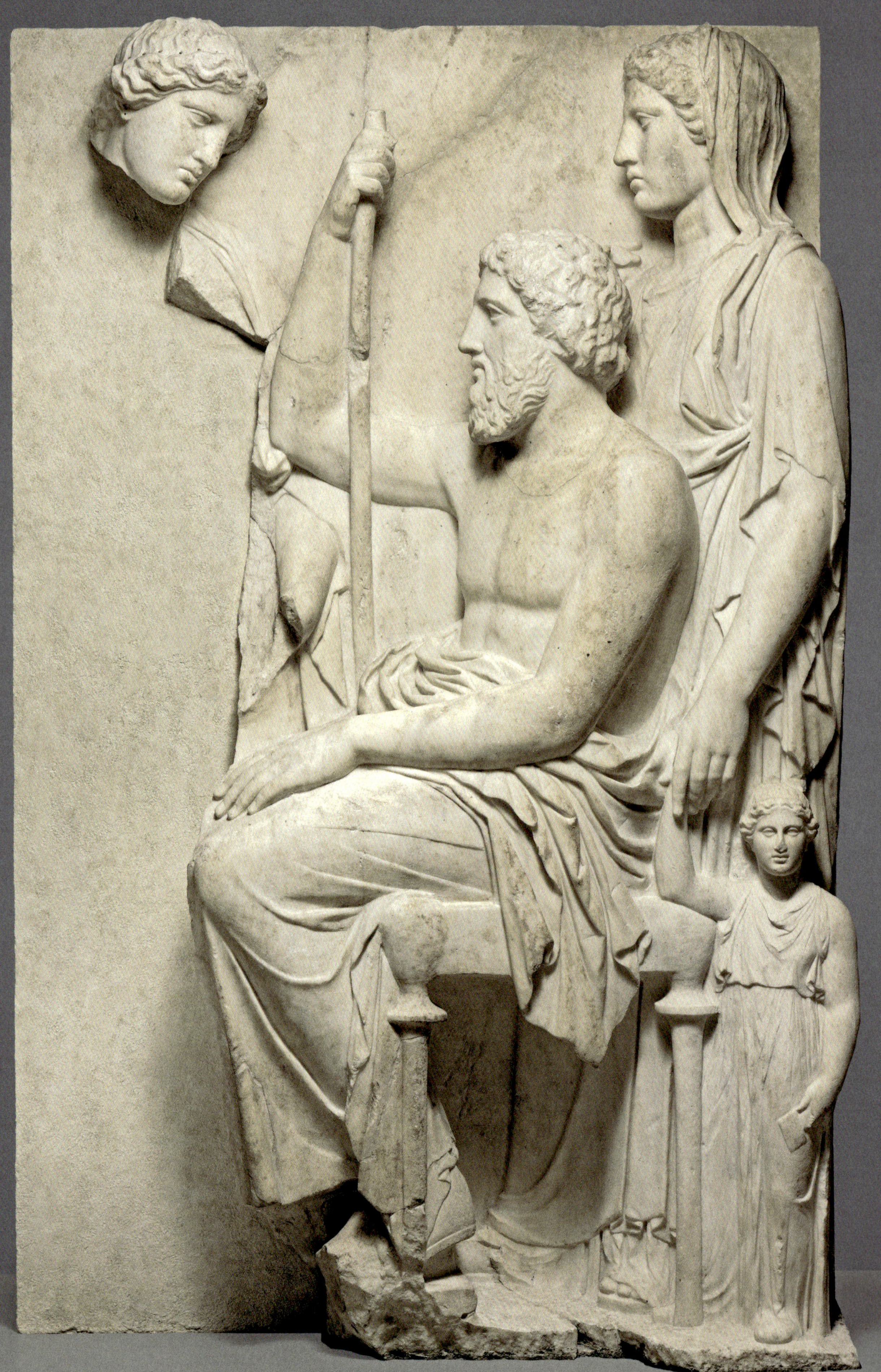

25

# Stele of a family group

Greek, Attic, Late Classical period, ca. 360 B.C.
Marble, H. 67⅜ in. (171.1 cm)
Rogers Fund, 1911 (11.100.2)

Sculpted funerary monuments became larger and more elaborate in the fourth century B.C. Although fragmentary, this grave stele of a family group is impressive for its scale and the quality of its carving. Originally, the slab would have been set up within an architectural setting to resemble a small three-sided roofed shrine (*naiskos*). Since the scene is not complete and the inscriptions identifying the deceased are not preserved, it is difficult to read the monument with certainty. As such, it allows us to recognize how interpretations can vary dramatically when crucial pieces of information are missing, which unfortunately is often the case with ancient Greek sculpture.

A young woman, whose lower body is missing, stands to the left. She originally clasped her hands (now lost) as she looks down at the bearded older man, who wears a himation draped around his waist. Seated on a backless chair, he holds a tall staff in his right hand, while his left arm rests on his thigh and his feet on a small stool. Behind the man stands a draped woman with a veil, which indicates she is married, either the man's wife or his daughter. She holds the hand of her small child, who looks straight out toward the viewer. Although rendered as a miniature adult, the child is shown in small scale and holds a rattle, both of which indicate her young age. The seated man and veiled woman stare straight out in front of them—are they the deceased, or do they mourn the young woman opposite them? There are holes drilled into the head of the young woman that would have accommodated a crown of another material, most likely metal. These may signify that she is the deceased, but the funerary crown could also have been added later. In addition to the losses in the body of the young woman, the rest of the left side of the scene is missing and could have included another figure.

Compositionally, the focal figure is the seated man. He is represented Zeus-like (fig. 46), with a serene, idealized face and strong physical presence, to emphasize his role as a model father figure in life. It is most likely that he is the deceased. Although ambiguity remains concerning how to read the scene, and none of the figures' gazes meet, the relief exhibits an enduring sense of family unity rendered with the restraint characteristic of Classical Greek sculpture. Like the scene represented on the marble lekythos previously discussed (no. 24), it skillfully echoes Classical sculpture of the previous century.

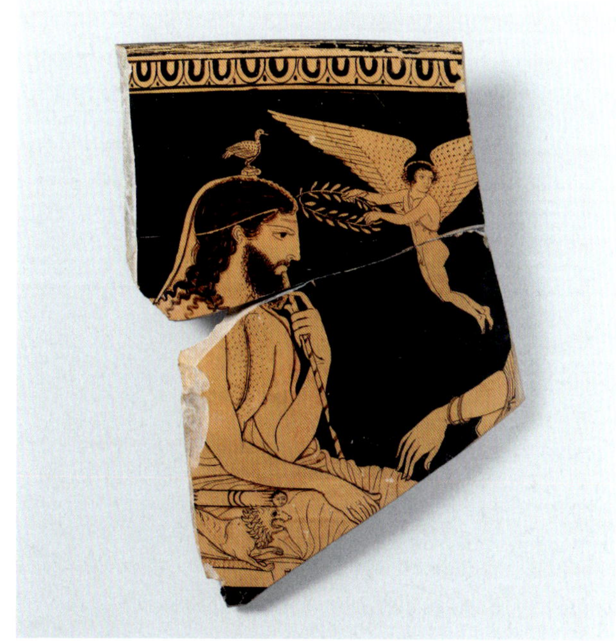

Fig. 46. Fragment of a terracotta skyphos (deep drinking cup). Greek, South Italian, Lucanian, Classical period, ca. 430–400 B.C. Attributed to the Palermo Painter. Terracotta, red-figure, 8 × 5¼ in. (20.3 × 13.3 cm). Rogers Fund, 1911 (11.212.12)

26

# Akroterion

Greek, Attic, Late Classical period, ca. 350–325 B.C.
Marble, 41¼ × 28¾ × 10¾ in. (104.8 × 73 × 27.3 cm)
Rogers Fund, 1920 (20.198)

Ancient Greek sculptors frequently looked to nature when embellishing architectural forms. In this ornate sculpture, which once crowned a tall stele marking the grave of a prominent citizen, the primary decoration takes the form of a double palmette whose fluted stems rise from lush acanthus leaves. While the ornament evokes the regenerative powers of nature, teeming with life, it is also very carefully modeled with attention to balance and symmetry in accordance with the norms of Classical Greek architecture. Tendrils curl upon themselves, creating little volutes that mirror each other. The flower crowning the top once had a painted stem, traces of which remain. Indeed, the entire sculpture may have been painted, adding a colorful aspect now missing. The deeply carved surfaces would have stood out strongly under the bright Mediterranean sun and cast lively shadows from the elaborately carved elements. The back, which features analogous decoration, was left unfinished.

The akroterion is displayed on a tall shaft in The Met to give a sense of its original placement (fig. 47). The stele on which it stood would have had an inscription that identified the deceased. Many similar examples of these markers, some reaching twelve feet in height, have been found in the cemeteries around Athens and the surrounding territory of Attica.

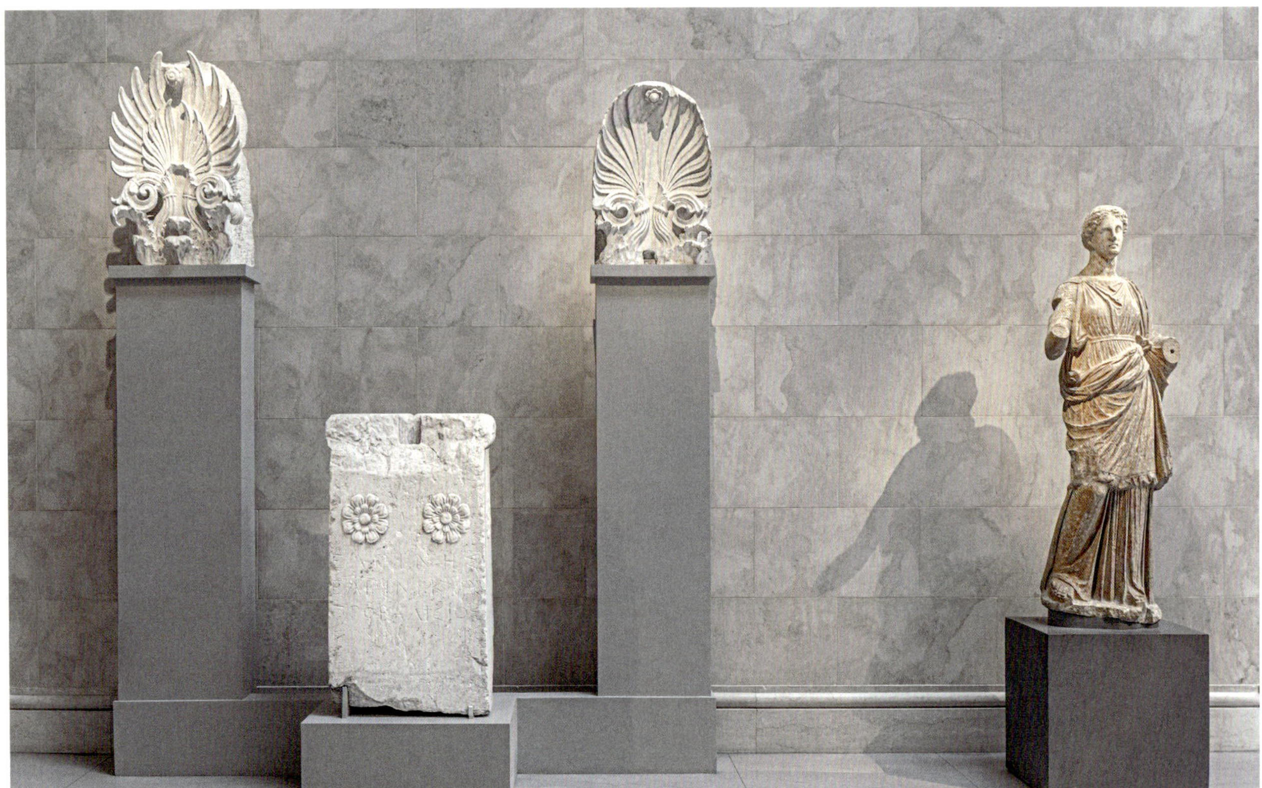

Fig. 47. The akroterion on display in the Mary and Michael Jaharis Gallery for Greek Art at The Metropolitan Museum of Art

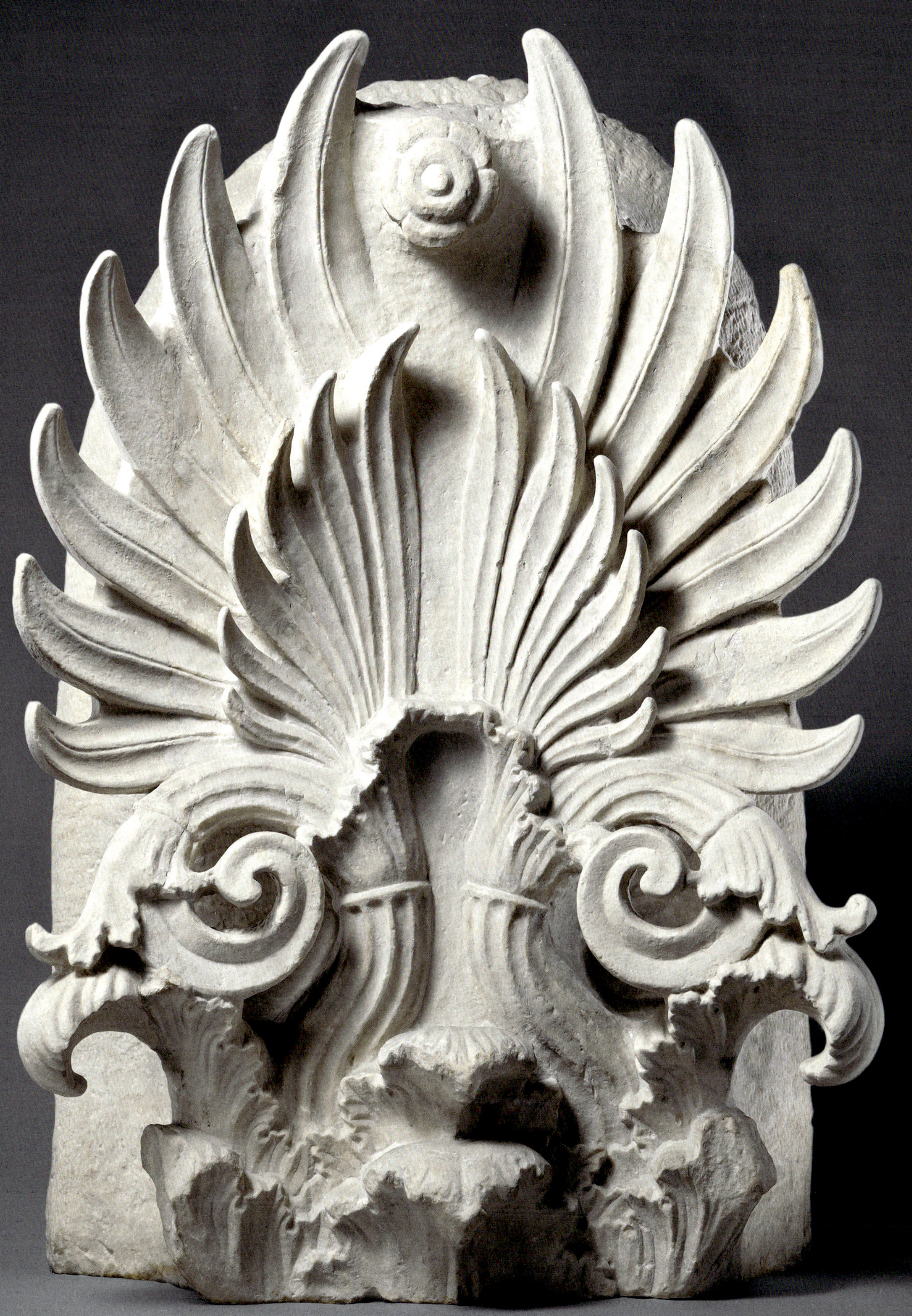

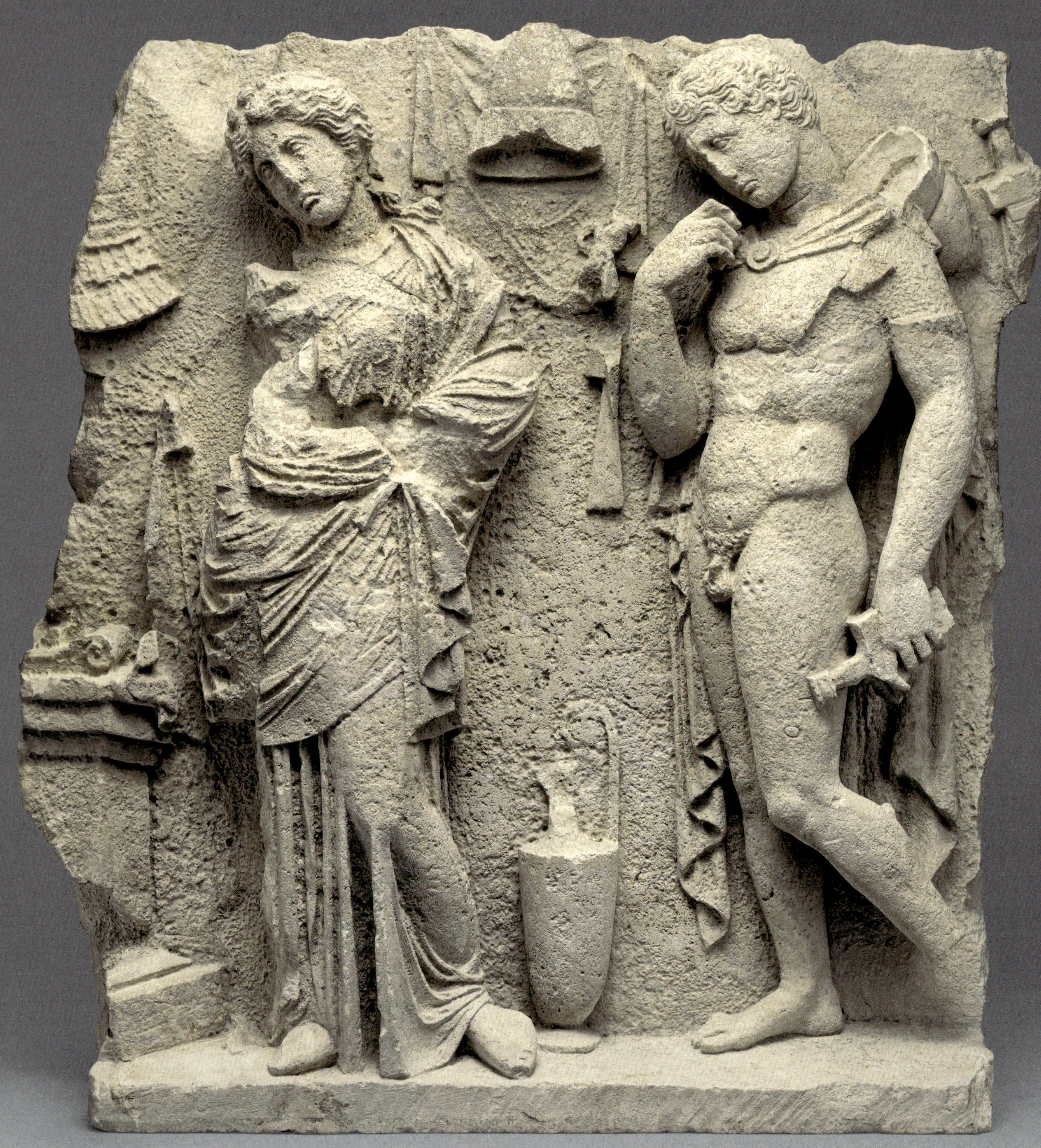

27

# Fragment of a funerary relief

Greek, South Italian, Tarantine, Early Hellenistic period, ca. 323–300 B.C.
Limestone, 23 1/16 × 21 1/16 in. (58.5 × 53.6 cm)
Fletcher Fund, 1929 (29.54)

From the second half of the fifth through most of the fourth century B.C., the Spartan colony Taras (Tarentum) was the leading Greek city-state in southern Italy. Its wealth relied in large part on its choice location in the instep of the boot of Italy along the major trade routes between Greece and Italy. Unlike the Greek islands and parts of central Greece, southern Italy and Sicily did not have good native sources of marble. Consequently, Greek sculptors active there developed traditions of working in other materials such as limestone and terracotta. This striking relief, carved from a local limestone, originally adorned the entablature of a grave monument, most likely in a necropolis near Taras. The small templelike sepulcher it decorated was a popular form of Greek funerary architecture in the fourth century B.C.

The fragment depicts a young man and a young woman standing by an altar. Between them is a tall-handled vase used for pouring libations. The youth is shown in

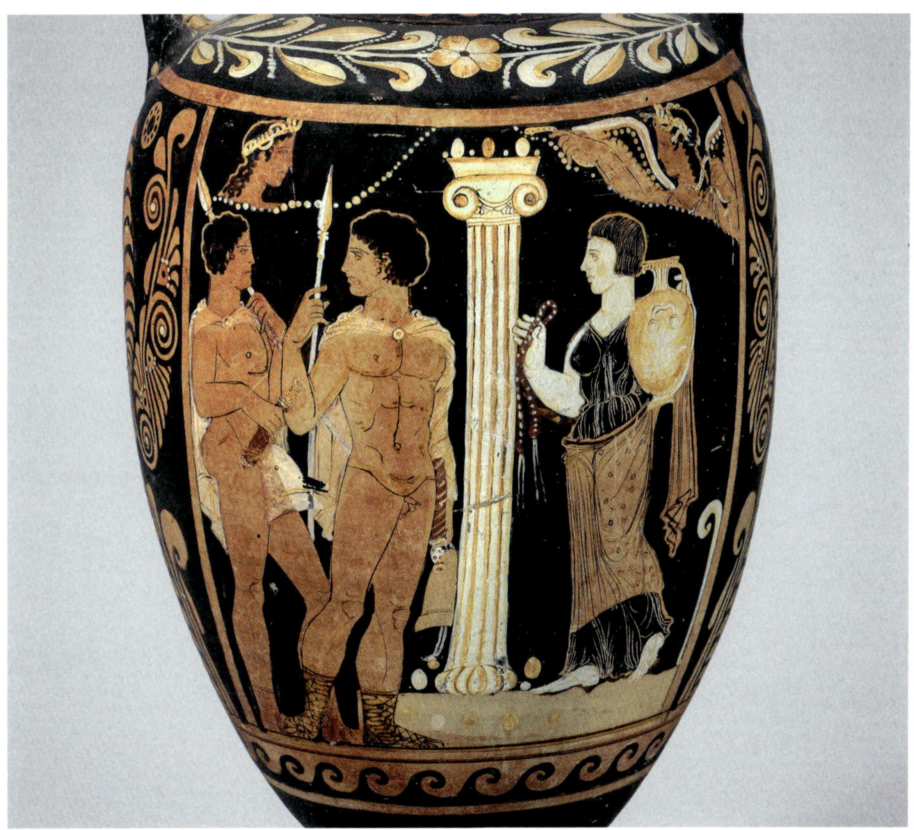

Fig. 48. Amphora with twisted handles. Orestes and Elektra at the Tomb of Agamemnon. Greek, South Italian, Paestan, Classical or Hellenistic period, ca. 335–320 B.C. Name vase of the Boston Orestes Painter. Terracotta, red-figure, H. 20 3/16 in. (51.3 cm). Museum of Fine Arts, Boston, Henry Lillie Pierce Fund (99.540)

heroic nudity, wearing only a chlamys (cloak) secured with a pendant at the center of his chest. Holding a sword in his left hand, he has a conical helmet that hangs behind his back as though from a strap around his neck; the strap would have been painted on. The young woman wears a chiton with a himation draped around her left arm and across her waist. The cuirass, helmet, and sword on the wall in the background are presumably the armor of the deceased warrior whom the figures mourn with intense downward gazes and furrowed brows.

It has been suggested that the figures represent Elektra and Orestes at the tomb of their father, Agamemnon. Scenes of Greek tragedy were popular in the funerary arts of the Greeks in southern Italy during the fifth and fourth centuries B.C. The legendary house of Atreus and its tales of power and woe resonated with many ancient Greeks, who valued their own strong family ties and understood the complexities they can bring. A popular trilogy of plays centered around the murder of Agamemnon, king of Mycenae, upon his return from the Trojan War by his wife, Clytemnestra, and her lover, Aegisthus, and the consequent revenge taken by Orestes. Written by the great Athenian tragedian Aeschylus, the plays were first performed together in 458 B.C. in Athens during the City Dionysia, a festival that was held in honor of Dionysos, patron deity of theater.

The first scene of the second play in the trilogy, *The Libation Bearers*, opens with Orestes and Elektra meeting at Agamemnon's tomb. Variations of this scene have been identified in contemporary South Italian vase paintings. A particularly good example is found in the collection of the Museum of Fine Arts, Boston, and its painter has been named by scholars the Boston Orestes Painter after this vase (fig. 48). The painting on the vase is also instructive for its vibrant use of color, such as in Orestes's yellow cloak and Elektra's spotted himation and black chiton, the latter an indication of mourning. Brightly painted details enlivened the present relief as well.

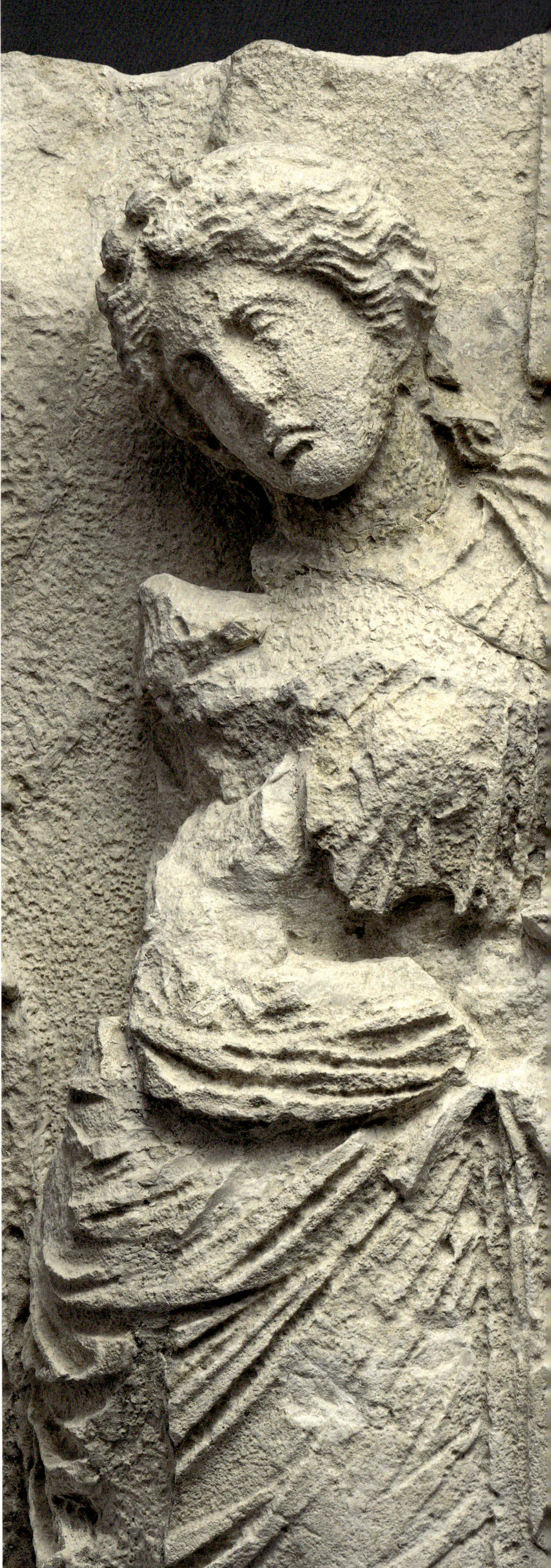

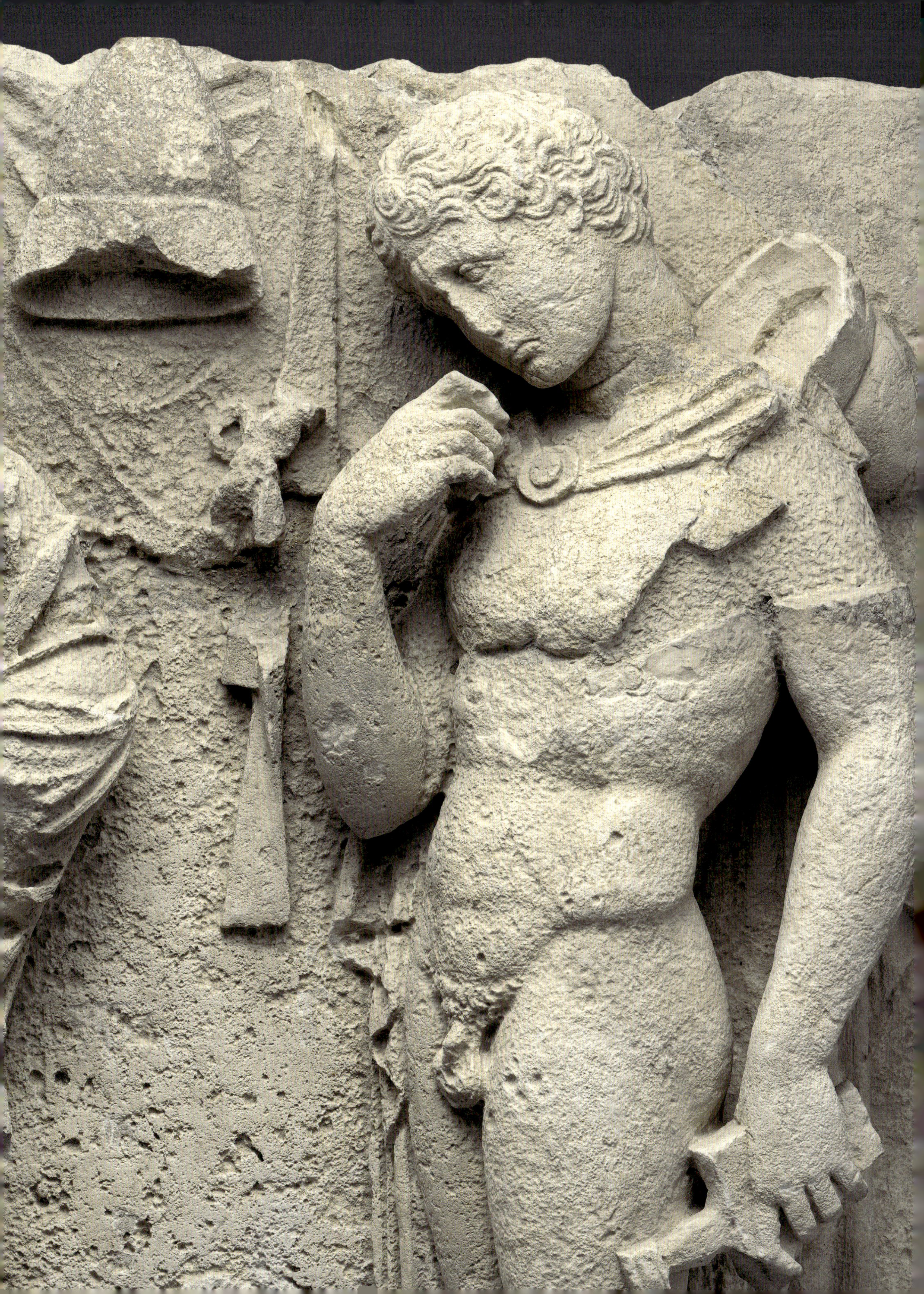

# Column from the Temple of Artemis at Sardis

Greek, Hellenistic period, ca. 300 B.C.
Marble, H. 11 ft. 10⅛ in. (361 cm)
Gift of the American Society for the Excavation of Sardis, 1926 (26.59.1)

The Ionic column to which these sections belonged originally stood nearly sixty feet high. It comes from one of the largest ancient Greek temples ever conceived, that of Artemis at Sardis, the ancient capital of Lydia in western Turkey. The fluted drums that constituted its middle section are missing. What we see is the ornate base with its torus exhibiting a vegetal, scalelike pattern supported by a series of three double moldings stacked one upon the other at intervals. Above is the capital, which is one of the finest examples of the Ionic order preserved today and the most ornate among the extant capitals from the temple.

The column was not found in situ but among the ruins of the temple during excavations conducted by archaeologists between 1910 and 1914. That the original column would have been slightly smaller than others found at the site indicates that it comes from an area other than the outer colonnade. It would most likely have been placed as one of a pair in the east or west porch (fig. 49). Another possible location was the cella (inner room) or the inner opisthodomos (back porch), although these parts of the temple were remodeled in Roman times and very little of the original architecture is preserved from these areas.

The delicate carving of the capital provides an excellent example of how ancient Greek architects embellished their creations with ornate details that would have come alive not only in the light of the sun but also in moonlight or by torches at night. The volutes at either end of the capital swirl toward their centers, and additional carved decoration appears on their long ends. The area between the volutes is embellished with richly carved moldings: a bead-and-reel pattern surmounted by an egg-and-dart design, which is topped on the main side at the center by a flower. These various vegetal motifs add an organic character to the architectural form. Such ornamentation on Greek temples would typically have been painted, but no traces of paint survive today.

The Temple of Artemis dates to the early third century B.C., when Sardis was part of the kingdom of the Seleucids, who ruled much of Asia Minor after the death of Alexander the Great in 323 B.C. It had a long construction history stretching into the second century A.D. and was never completed. This column, as well as capital fragments from engaged pilasters of the entranceways and a series of marble roof tiles, are among the few existing architectural elements of the superstructure preserved from the original Hellenistic edifice.

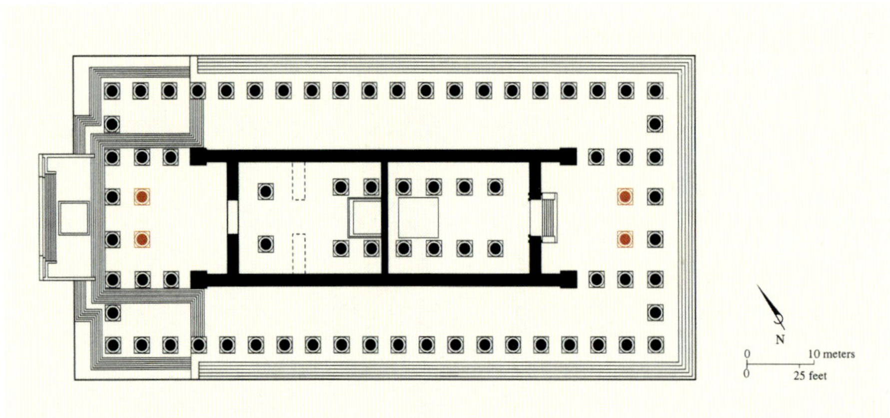


Fig. 49. Restored plan of the Temple of Artemis at Sardis in the 2nd century A.D. Red indicates possible locations for no. 28

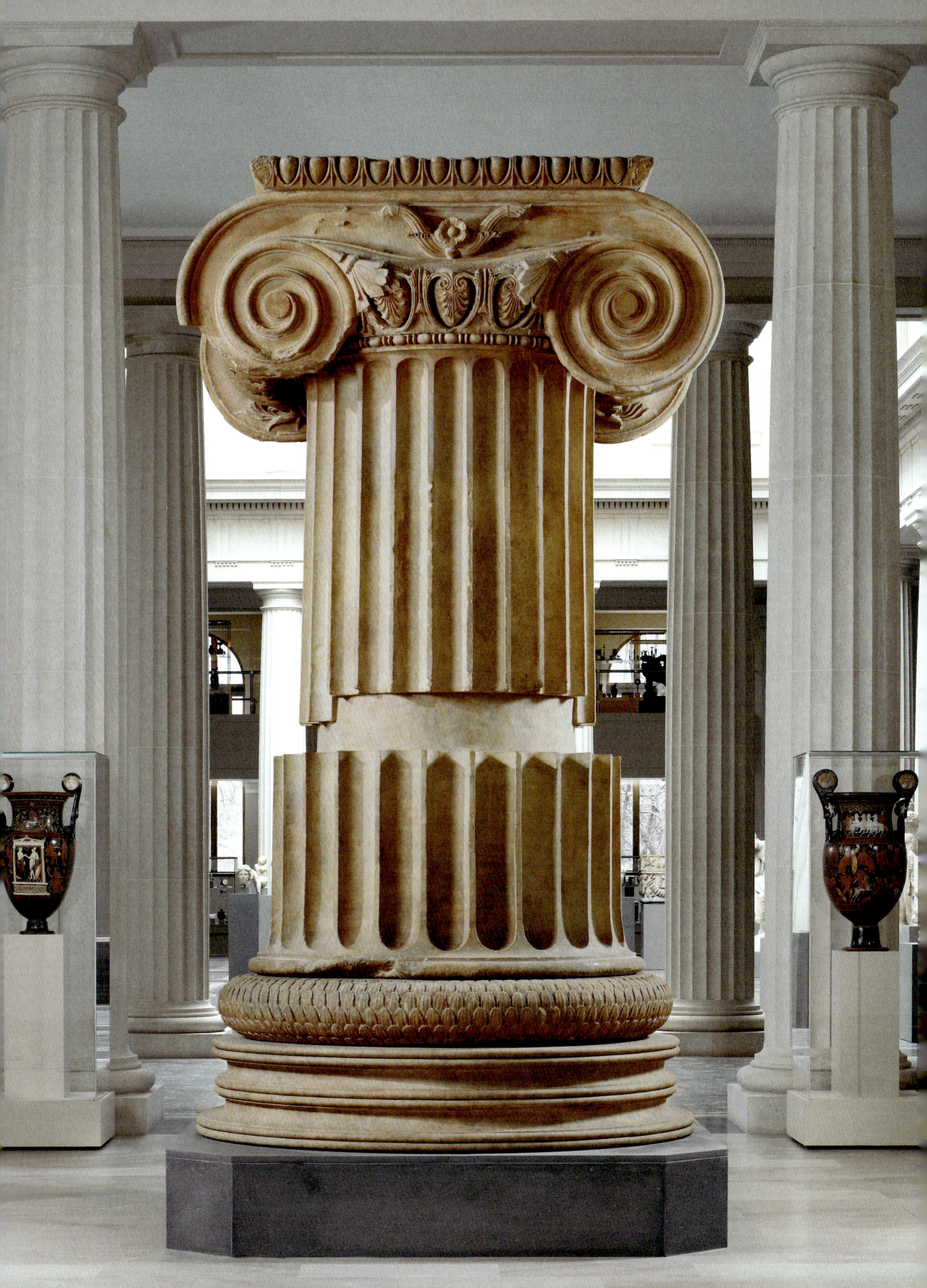

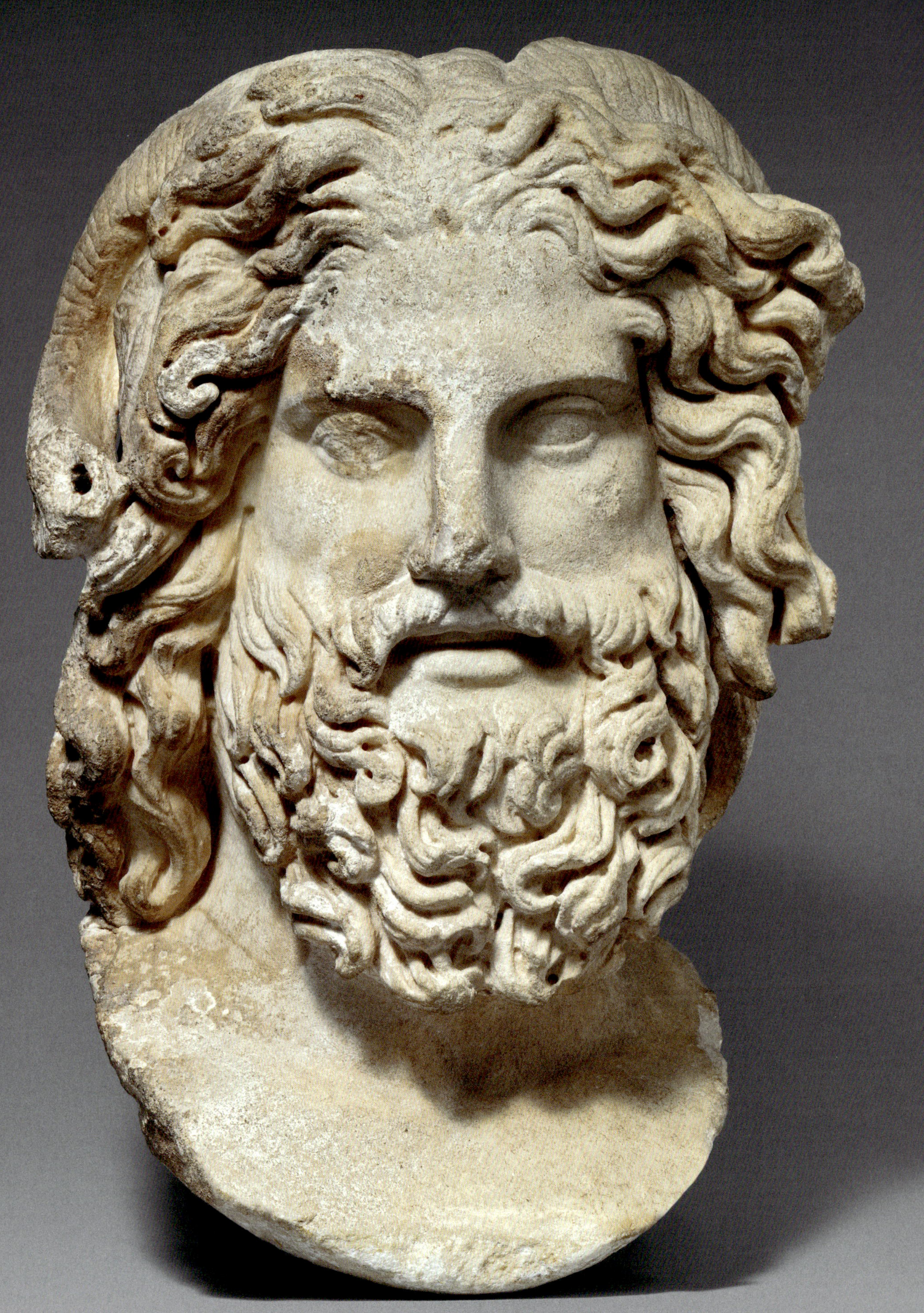

29

# Head of Zeus Ammon

Roman, Hadrianic or Antonine period, ca. A.D. 120–160
Marble, H. 19⅝ in. (49.8 cm)
Adaptation of a Classical or Hellenistic Greek statue
Purchase, Philodoroi Gifts, Acquisitions Fund, Mary and Michael Jaharis Gift, 2011 Benefit Fund, funds from various donors, Mr. and Mrs. John A. Moran, John J. Medveckis, Nicholas S. Zoullas, Mr. and Mrs. Frederick W. Beinecke, Leon Levy Foundation, Jeannette and Jonathan Rosen, Judy and Michael Steinhardt, Malcolm Hewitt Wiener Foundation and Aso O. Tavitian Gifts, 2012 (2012.22)

Zeus Ammon is a Hellenized form of a powerful Egyptian deity, Amun, who was syncretized with Zeus, father of the Olympian gods. The divinity is known to have been worshipped in various Greek city-states, including Thebes (in Boeotia), Sparta, and Cyrene, but his most renowned oracular sanctuary was at a remote oasis in the Libyan desert called Siwa. Sculptural representations from Cyprus during the Archaic period emphasize the deity's association with the ram. Zeus Ammon can appear with a human body and a ram's head (fig. 50) or more typically with ram's horns alone (fig. 51). A Classical Greek statue of the god with large ram's horns and ears, known from a series of Roman marble copies and sometimes attributed to Pheidias, also emphasizes the deity's animalistic appearance.

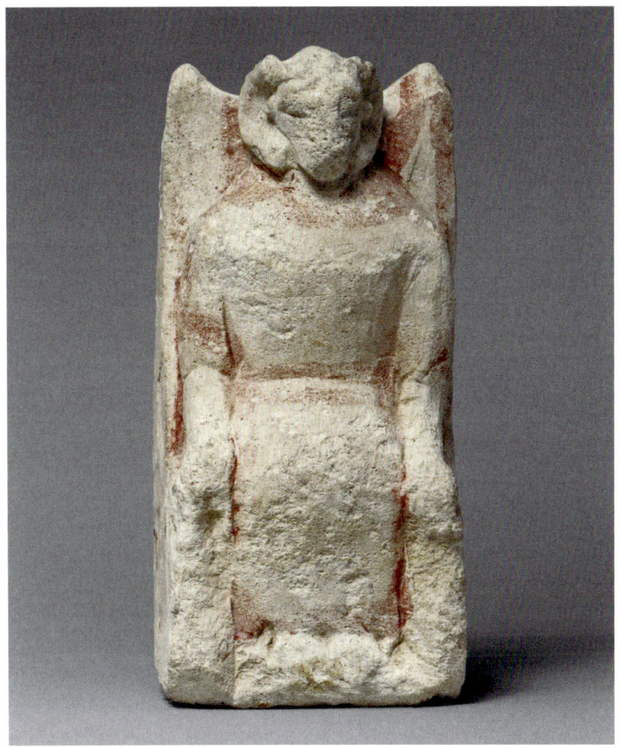

Fig. 50. Statuette of seated Zeus Ammon. Cypriot, Archaic period, second quarter of the 6th century B.C. Limestone, H. 3¾ in. (9.5 cm). The Cesnola Collection, Purchased by subscription, 1874–76 (74.51.2560)

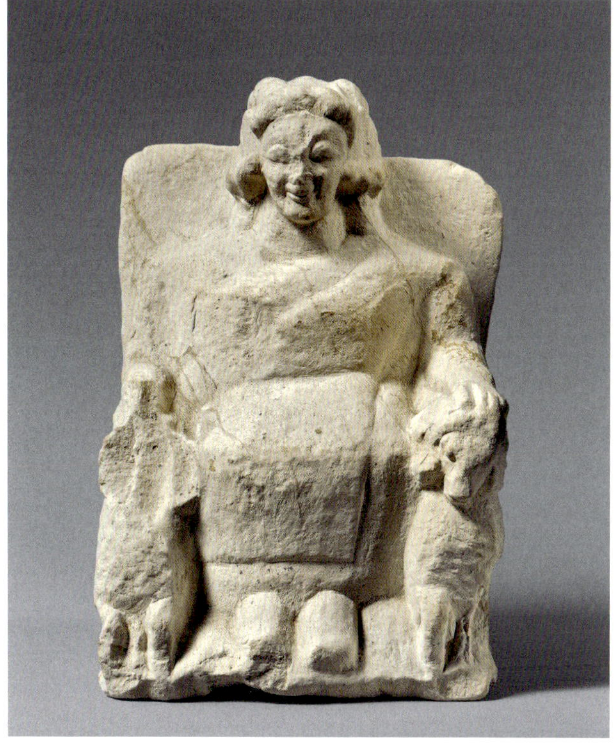

Fig. 51. Statuette of seated Zeus Ammon. Cypriot, Late Archaic period, early 5th century B.C. Limestone, H. 5¼ in. (13.3 cm). The Cesnola Collection, Purchased by subscription, 1874–76 (74.51.2675)

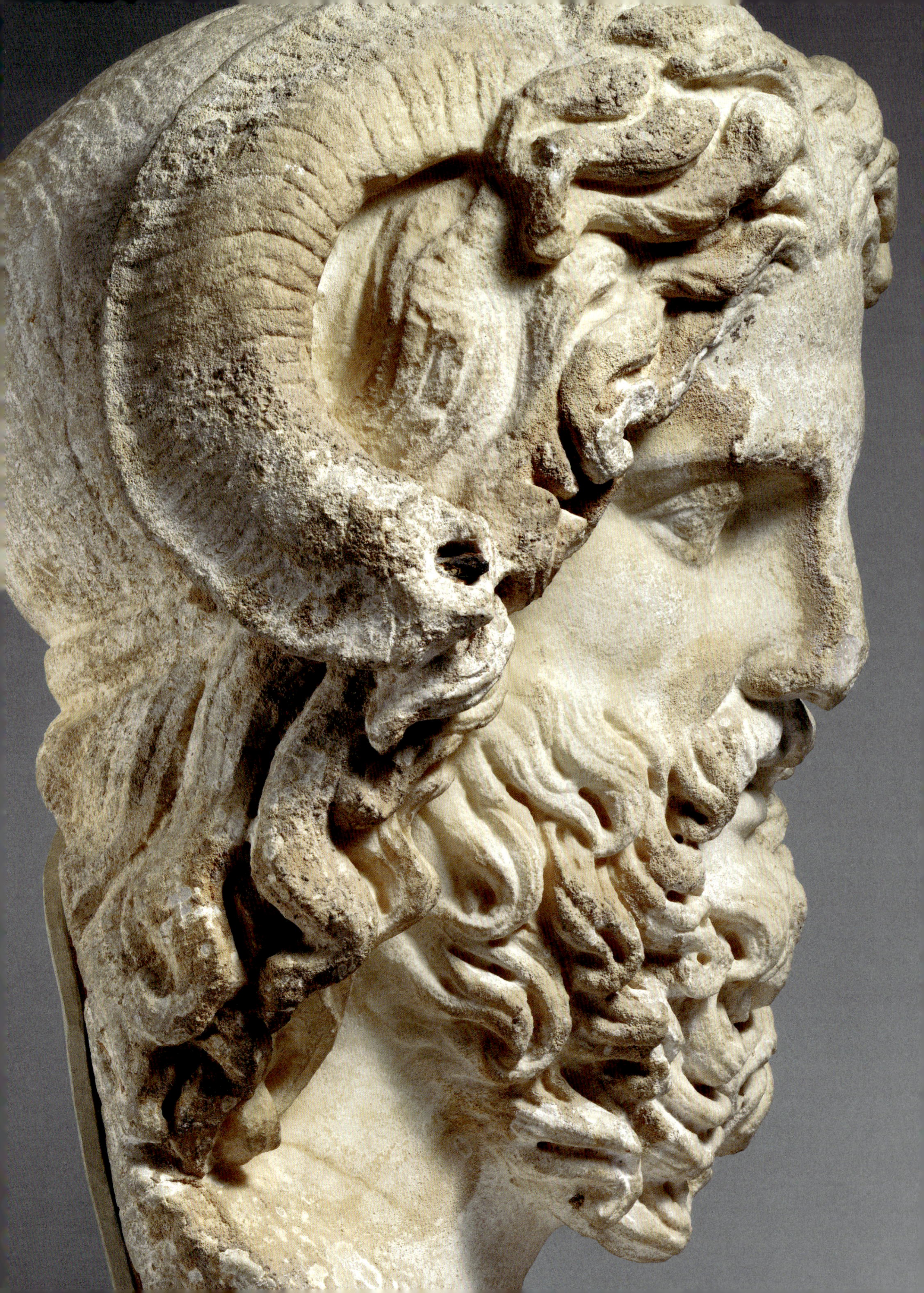

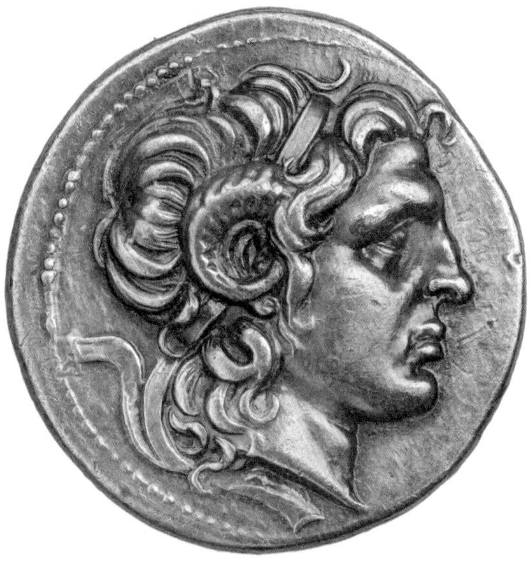

Fig. 52. Tetradrachm of Lysimachos of Thrace. Greek, Hellenistic period, 297–283 B.C. From the mint of Lampsakos in Mysia. Silver, Diam. 1⅛ in. (2.9 cm), Weight .6 oz. (16.93 gr). Harvard Art Museums, Bequest of Frederick M. Watkins (1972.186)

The majestic head in The Met collection presents a stately deity with a full beard and serene face in the tradition of Classical images of Zeus. Emerging from the long locks of hair above his forehead are two massive ram's horns, but his ears are entirely covered by his hair. The god wears a fillet, visible from the profile view, and looks down benignly, his head turned slightly to the right. The sculpture is said to have been discovered at the mouth of the Nile River in Egypt.

Zeus Ammon's sanctuary at the Oasis of Siwa was already famous by the time Alexander the Great made a pilgrimage there in 331 B.C. that proved to be a pivotal moment in the young king's extraordinary life. The details of the visit are shrouded in mystery, but legend has it that the oracle at the site proclaimed Alexander son of Zeus Ammon and answered his questions "to his heart's desire." Alexander was sometimes represented with the ram's horns of Zeus Ammon, especially in the coin portraits minted by his Successors (fig. 52). Although the present monumental portrait of the god looks strongly to the Classical tradition, its massive, lively locks follow Hellenistic style. It may well reflect a sculpture created in Egypt under the Ptolemies in the years after Alexander's historic visit to Siwa.

## 30

# Head of a horned youth wearing a diadem

Greek, Hellenistic period, late 4th or early 3rd century B.C.
Marble, H. 13⅞ in. (35.2 cm)
Gift of Renée E. and Robert A. Belfer, 2012 (2012.479.10)

The youth represented in this fine portrait has two significant attributes: a rolled fillet, or diadem, in his hair—the primary indication of kingship in Hellenistic royal portraiture—and the remains of two dowels, cemented with stucco and set into the hair above the forehead, that indicate horns were inserted there. The addition of horns, the subject's highly idealized youthful appearance, and the fillet suggest that this is a divinized portrait of a Hellenistic ruler.

One possible identification of the subject is the young Demetrios Poliorketes (Besieger of Cities), who was among the first of Alexander the Great's Successors to mint coins bearing his own portrait. Demetrios also liked to represent himself with bull's horns to signal his association with the god Dionysos, whose most common animal manifestation was the bull (fig. 53). The portrait might even show Demetrios's son Antigonos II Gonatas, but the image is too idealized to be certain. Since the archaeological provenance of this piece is not known and since bull's horns were a popular attribute among the early Hellenistic rulers, many of whom identified with Dionysos, a secure identification remains impossible.

Of great interest is the fact that the portrait has been recut from an earlier one, a common occurrence in antiquity because fine marble was a valuable commodity. This is evident in many places on the head. If you look at the profile view, you will see its elongated shape, which is the result of having been cut down from a larger head. Other indications of recutting are evident in parts of the hair and on the left earlobe as well as in the small size of the head in proportion to the neck. The way that the horns are set into the hair indicates that they are part of the second use, the portrait we see today. The back of the head is not carved as carefully as the front. The head is turned dramatically to the right and would have been part of a full-size statue. Despite the obstacles that the artist faced, the overall effect is most successful. The supple appearance of the flesh, evident in the freshness of the surface, and the careful attention to the strong, idealized countenance make for an impressive portrait.

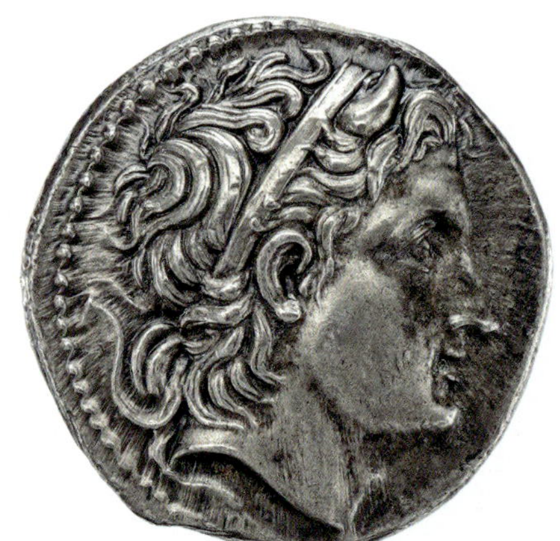

Fig. 53. Tetradrachm of Demetrios Poliorketes. Greek, Hellenistic period, ca. 289–288 B.C. From the mint of Amphipolis. Silver, Diam. 1³⁄₁₆ in. (3 cm). Gift of C. Ruxton Love Jr., 1967 (67.265.30)

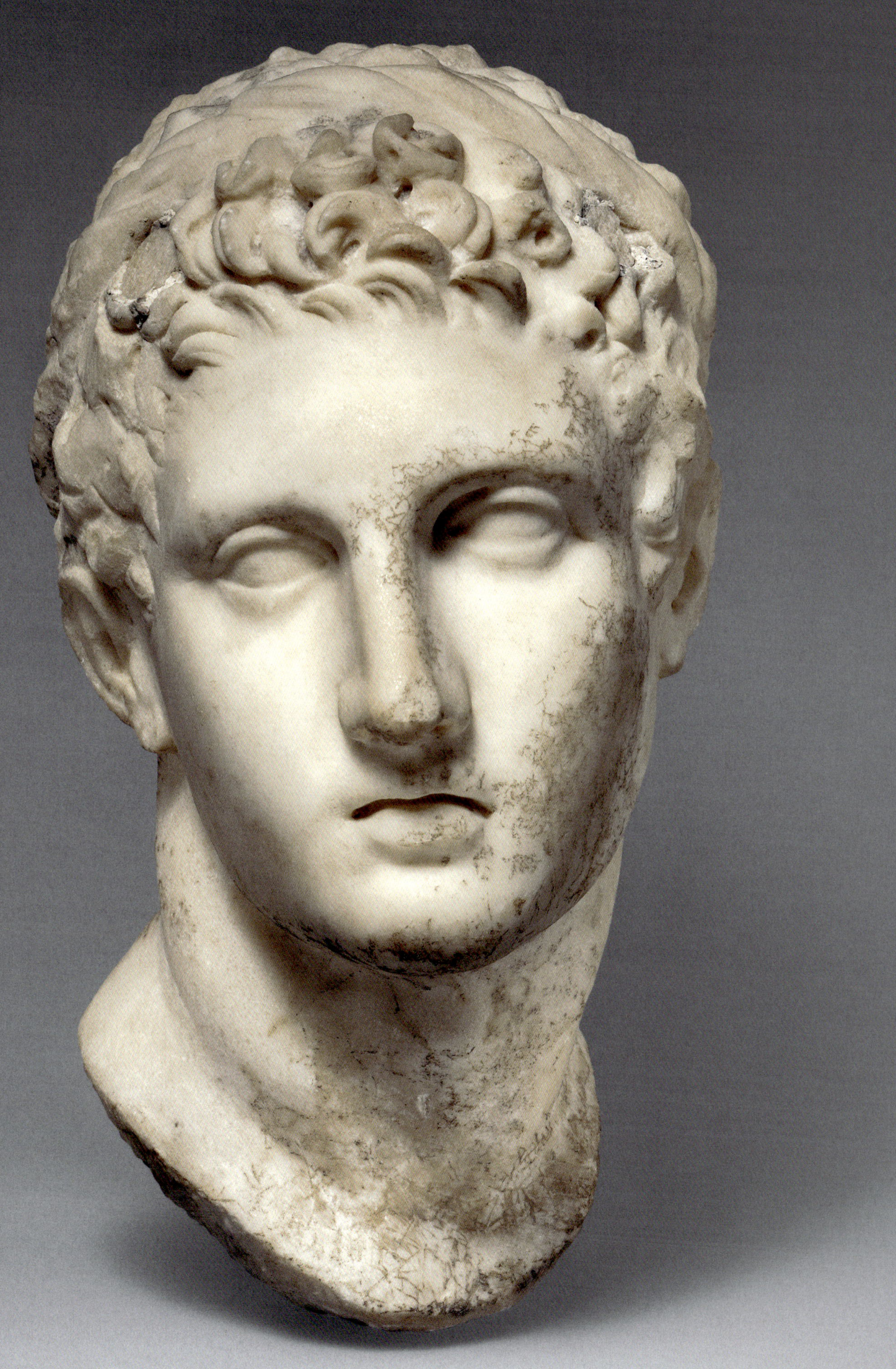

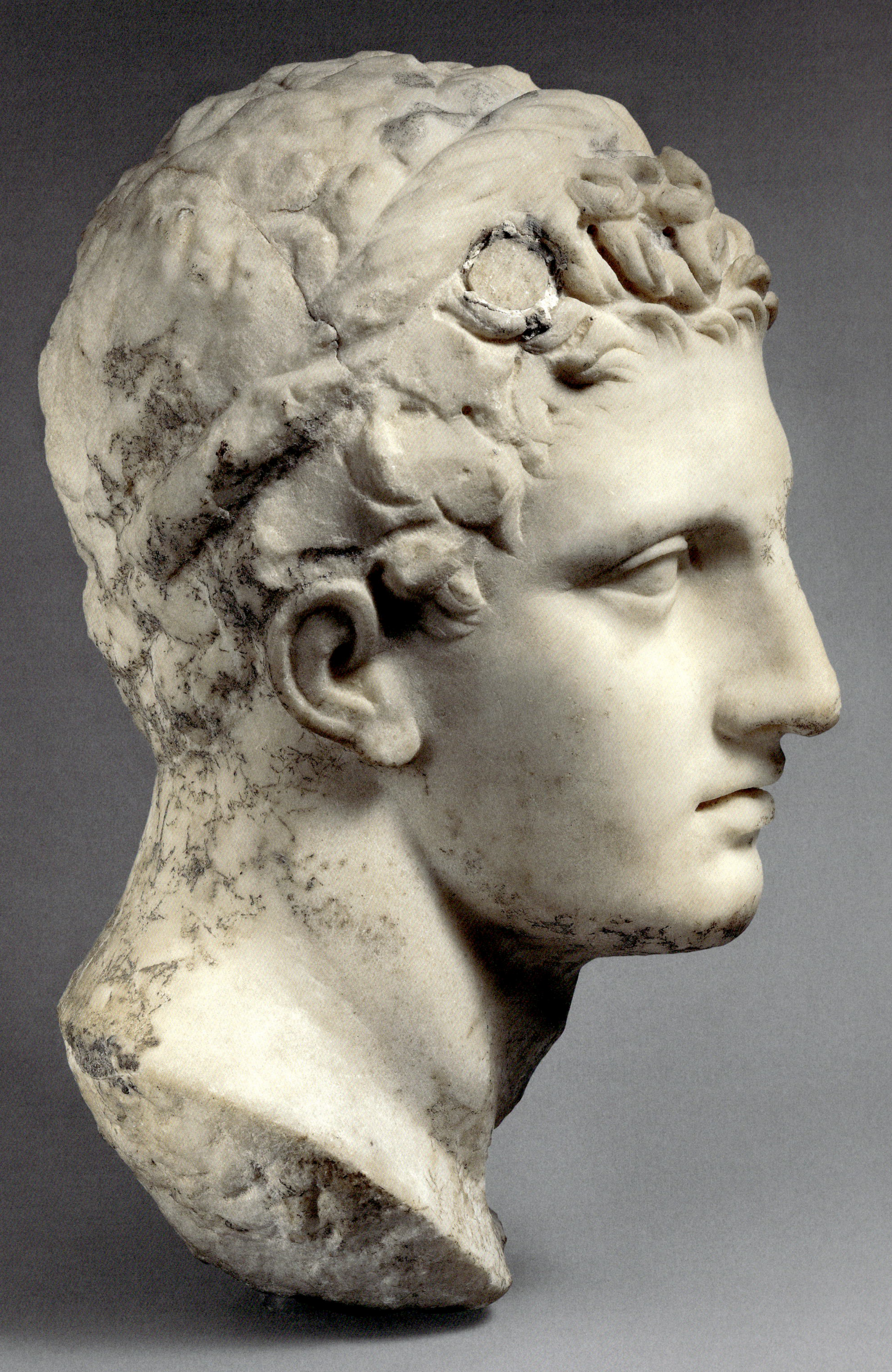

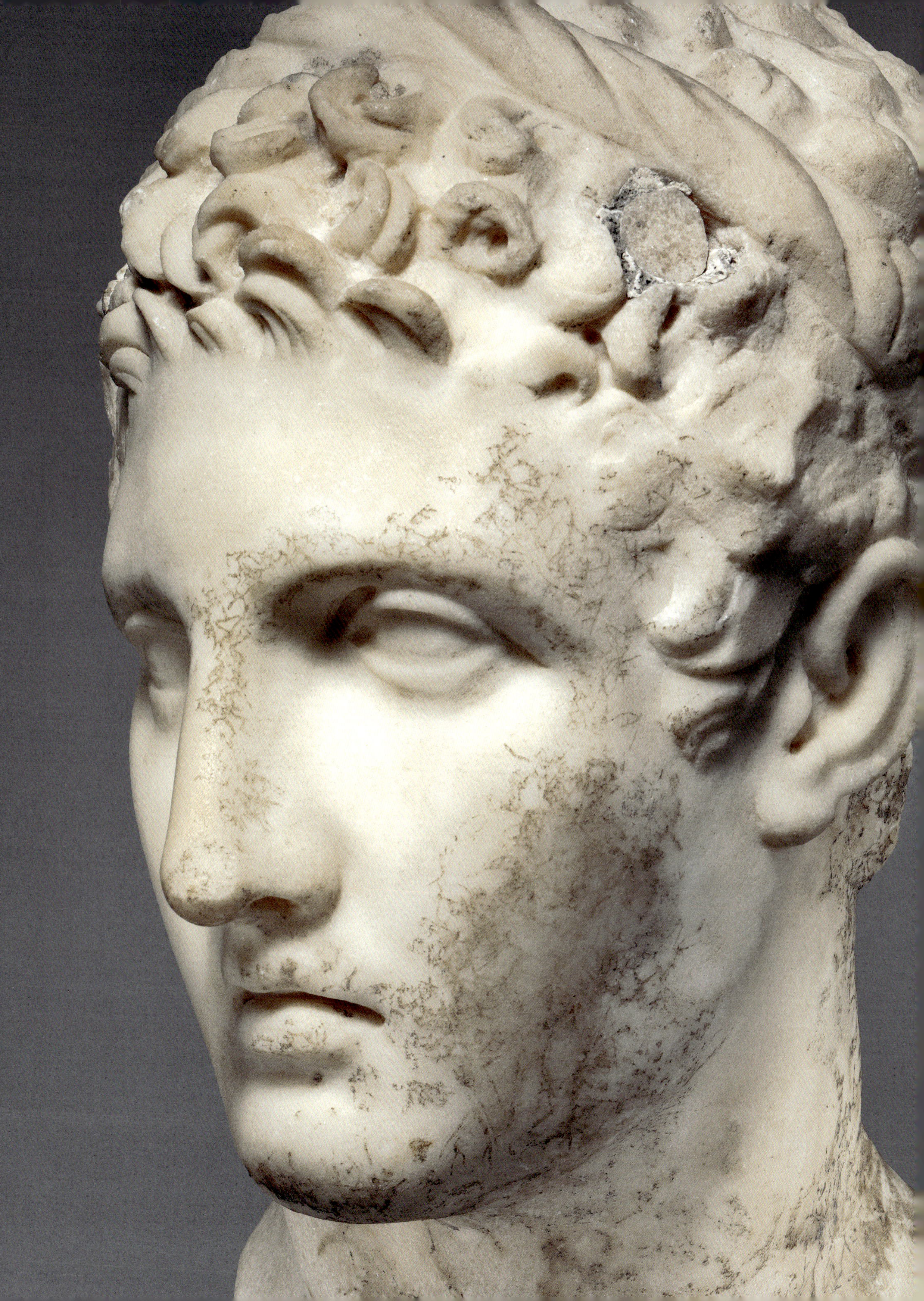

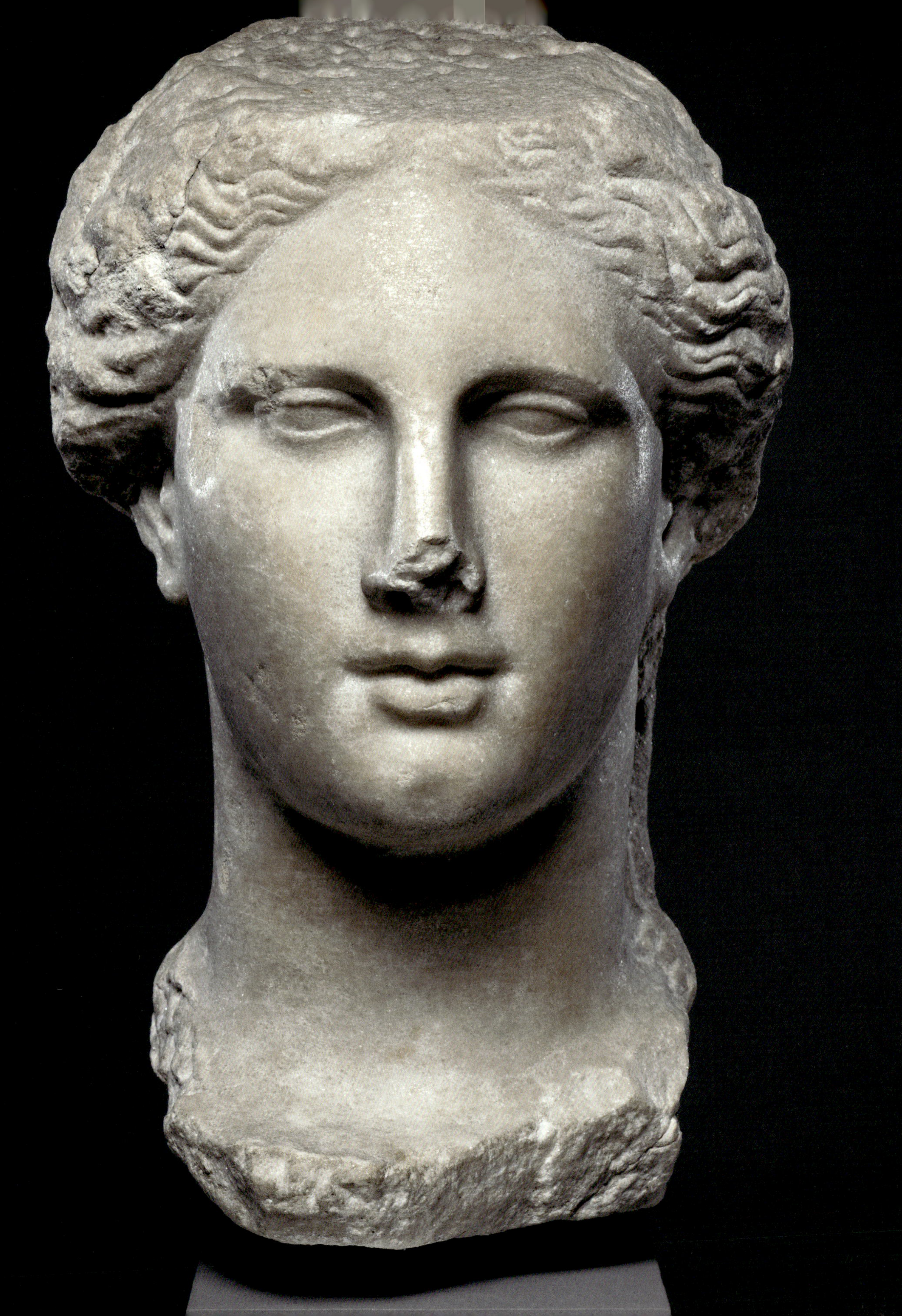

31

# Head of a Ptolemaic queen

Greek, Ptolemaic, Hellenistic period, ca. 270–240 B.C.
Marble, H. 15 in. (38.1 cm)
Acquired in Egypt by George Baldwin, British Consul-General, 1785–96
Purchase, Lila Acheson Wallace Gift, The Bothmer Purchase Fund, Malcolm Hewitt Wiener, The Concordia Foundation and Christos G. Bastis Gifts and Marguerite and Frank A. Cosgrove Jr. Fund, 2002 (2002.66)

When Alexander the Great's empire was divided upon his death in 323 B.C., the general Ptolemy, one of the Successors, took Egypt and its surrounding territories and made Alexandria the royal seat of his kingdom. The longest dynasty to rule during the Hellenistic period, the Ptolemies endured for nearly three centuries until the death of Cleopatra VII in 30 B.C., when Egypt became part of the Roman Empire. This fine portrait head representing a Ptolemaic queen comes from Egypt, and although its archaeological provenance is unknown, its history can be traced back to the late eighteenth century.

Since the members of the Ptolemaic royal family often bear strong resemblances to one another, even in their official portraiture, secure identifications of their portraits can be difficult when the inscription naming the subject is not preserved. Elements of the present portrait, such as the treatment of the hair and the idealized countenance, adhere closely to the Classical style of the late fourth century B.C., while other details, like the high cheekbones, small pointed chin, and long nose, indicate that a specific portrait is intended. Various identifications for the queen have been suggested. She may be Berenike II or, more likely, Arsinoe II (fig. 54), who ruled together with her brother Ptolemy II Philadelphos from 278 B.C. until her death in 270 B.C. The portrait was probably carved in the period following Arsinoe's death, when Ptolemy established her divine cult. She was worshipped both as a Greek goddess and as an Egyptian deity in association with Isis.

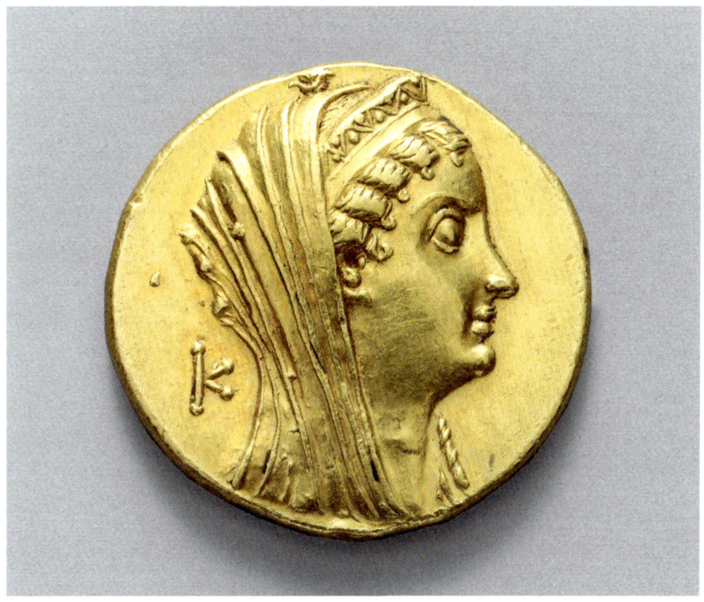

Fig. 54. Octodrachm of Ptolemy II Philadelphos representing Arsinoe II. Greek, Ptolemaic, Hellenistic period, ca. 262–246 B.C. Minted in Alexandria, Egypt. Gold, Diam. 1 1/16 in. (2.8 cm). Theodore M. Davis Collection, Bequest of Theodore M. Davis, 1915 (30.115.23)

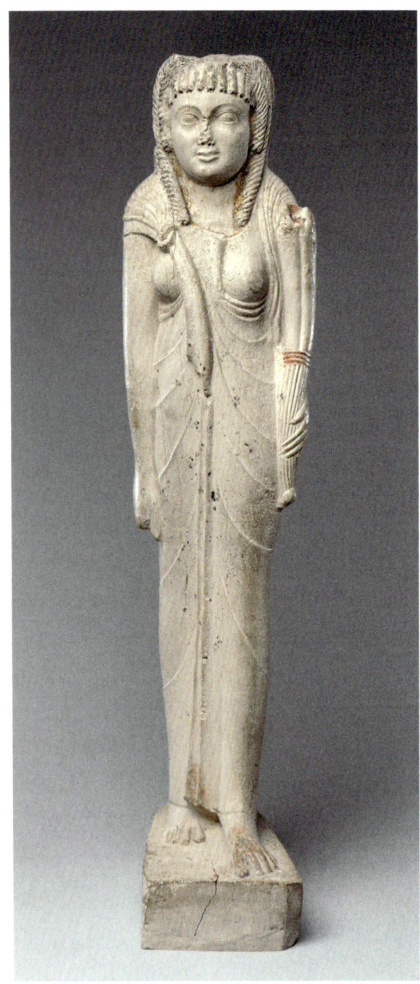
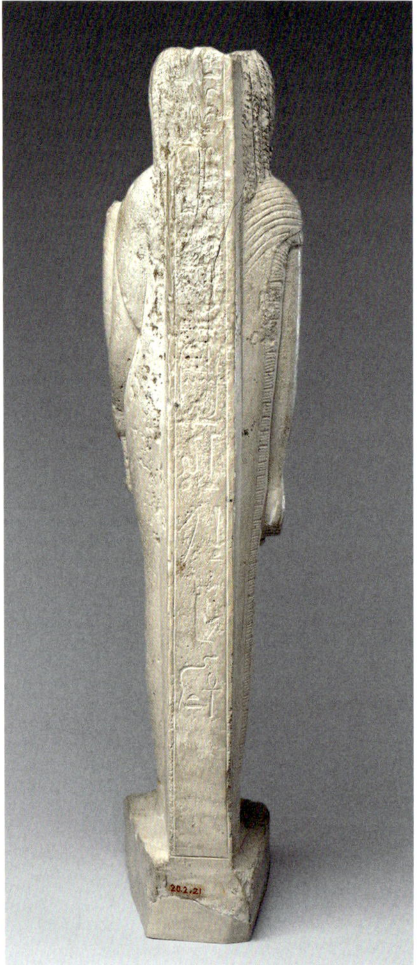
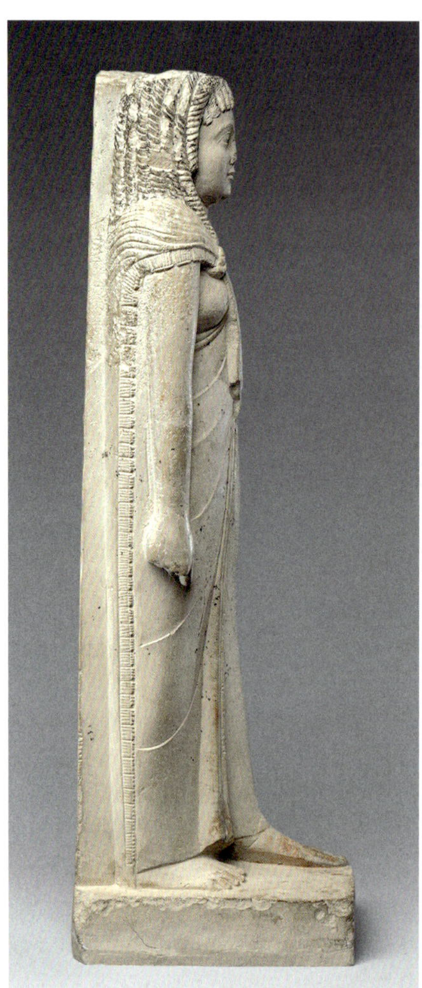

Fig. 55. Statue of Arsinoe II for her posthumous cult. Egyptian, Ptolemaic, ca. 150–100 B.C. Limestone, paint, and gold leaf, H. 15¼ in. (38.7 cm). Rogers Fund, 1920 (20.2.21)

Marble, the stone preferred by ancient Greek sculptors, was scarce in Egypt and needed to be imported. As a consequence, rough-cut and unfinished areas around the head, like those here, would have been covered by a veil and locks of hair made from plaster stucco, and then the head would have been inserted into a draped body fashioned from a different piece of marble or another material. The combination of marble for the delicate features of the portrait with plaster for subsidiary elements is found on a number of Hellenistic portrait sculptures from Egypt and the Greek East. Ptolemaic sculptors sometimes combined marble and plaster to great effect, although the plaster is rarely well preserved owing to its fragility.

In Greek sculpture of the Hellenistic period, various styles converged as a result of many new cultural connections in a greatly expanded world. One of the fascinating aspects of Ptolemaic sculpture is how it was made in styles and materials that were both purely Egyptian and strongly Greek, as seen here. The Museum's Ptolemaic statuette of Arsinoe II, identified by a hieroglyphic inscription on the back, makes for a good comparison (fig. 55). Its overt Egyptian style—with rigid frontal pose, use of local materials, and hieroglyphics—predominates, while a few Greek elements, such as the cornucopia and the corkscrew curls on the forehead, reveal the melding of cultural elements. The Ptolemies were able to harness both of these starkly different sculptural traditions to appeal to different sectors of the population.

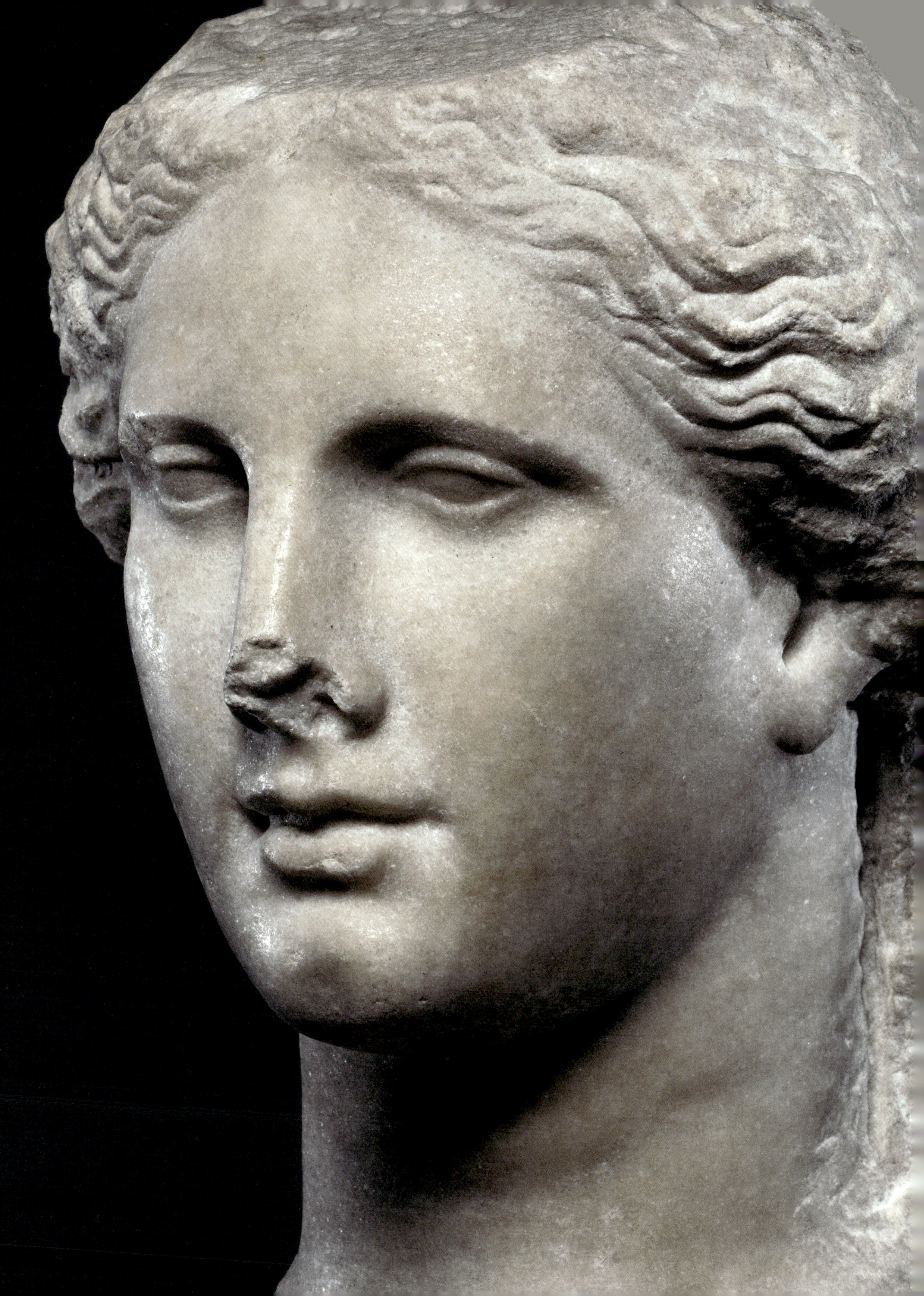

32

# Statuette of a dancer

Greek, Hellenistic period, 3rd century B.C.
Bronze, H. 8 1/16 in. (20.5 cm)
Bequest of Walter C. Baker, 1971 (1972.118.95)

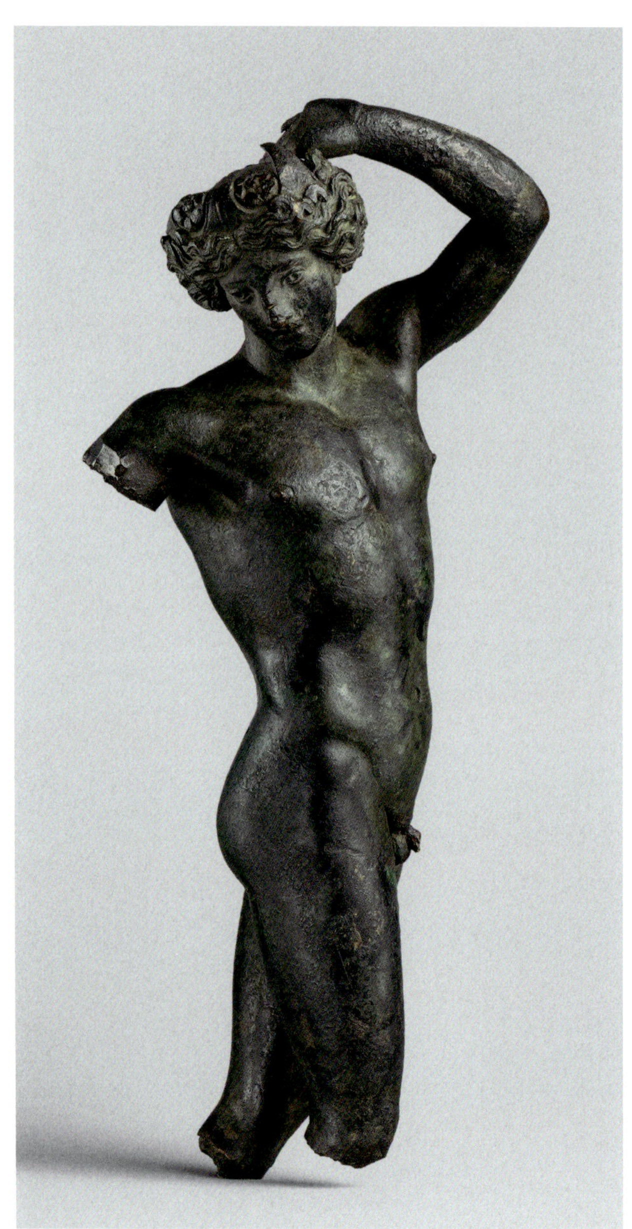

At first glance, this dancer might look to be a modern creation—so real is her appearance. However, the statuette is very much a product of its time and place, arguably the third century B.C. in Alexandria, Egypt. Although the figure is only slightly more than eight inches tall, its elegant details and exquisite manufacture give the impression of a much larger sculpture. People who have not seen it in the flesh are often surprised by its intimate scale. Yet this was clearly part of its original appeal: she is a private dancer, meant for personal enjoyment. Despite the fact that only her left hand and her eyes are exposed, the artist has managed to convey the sensuality of the woman's beautiful figure beneath layers of dress made visible through the movement of her dance. She is performing a mantle dance, which has a long history in the ancient Greek world. The thin himation is pulled tight over a full-length chiton as she dances, her left foot extended to reveal her laced slipper raised in the air; she wears the sheerest of veils with cutouts for her eyes.

Capturing the dancer in midmotion is a very different approach from that found in a slightly earlier statuette of a dancing youth, in which the pose looks to be one in a series of dance steps (fig. 56). It has been suggested that the woman here is doing the *baukismos* (meaning "playing the prude"), a specific mantle dance mentioned by the ancient writer Pollux. She is thought to be a professional entertainer, for which the metropolis of Alexandria was famous in antiquity. Although there are no exact replicas

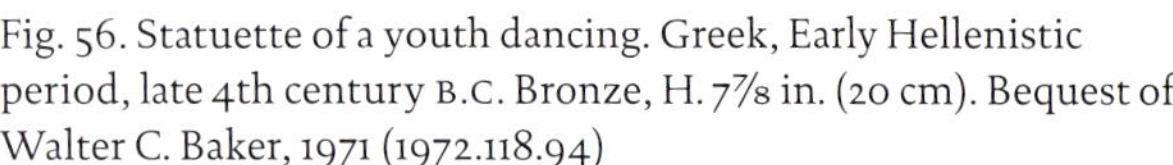

Fig. 56. Statuette of a youth dancing. Greek, Early Hellenistic period, late 4th century B.C. Bronze, H. 7⅞ in. (20 cm). Bequest of Walter C. Baker, 1971 (1972.118.94)

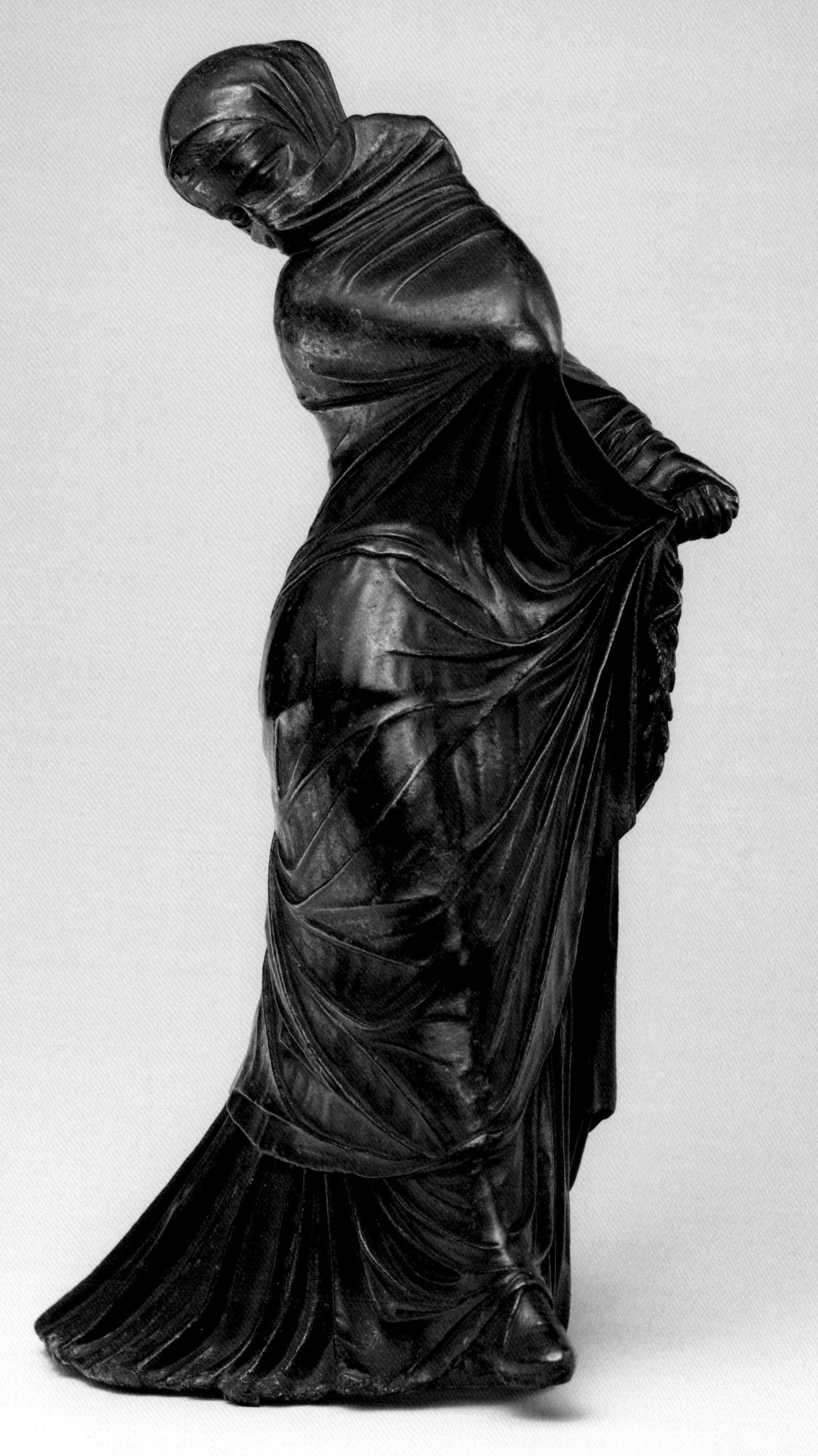

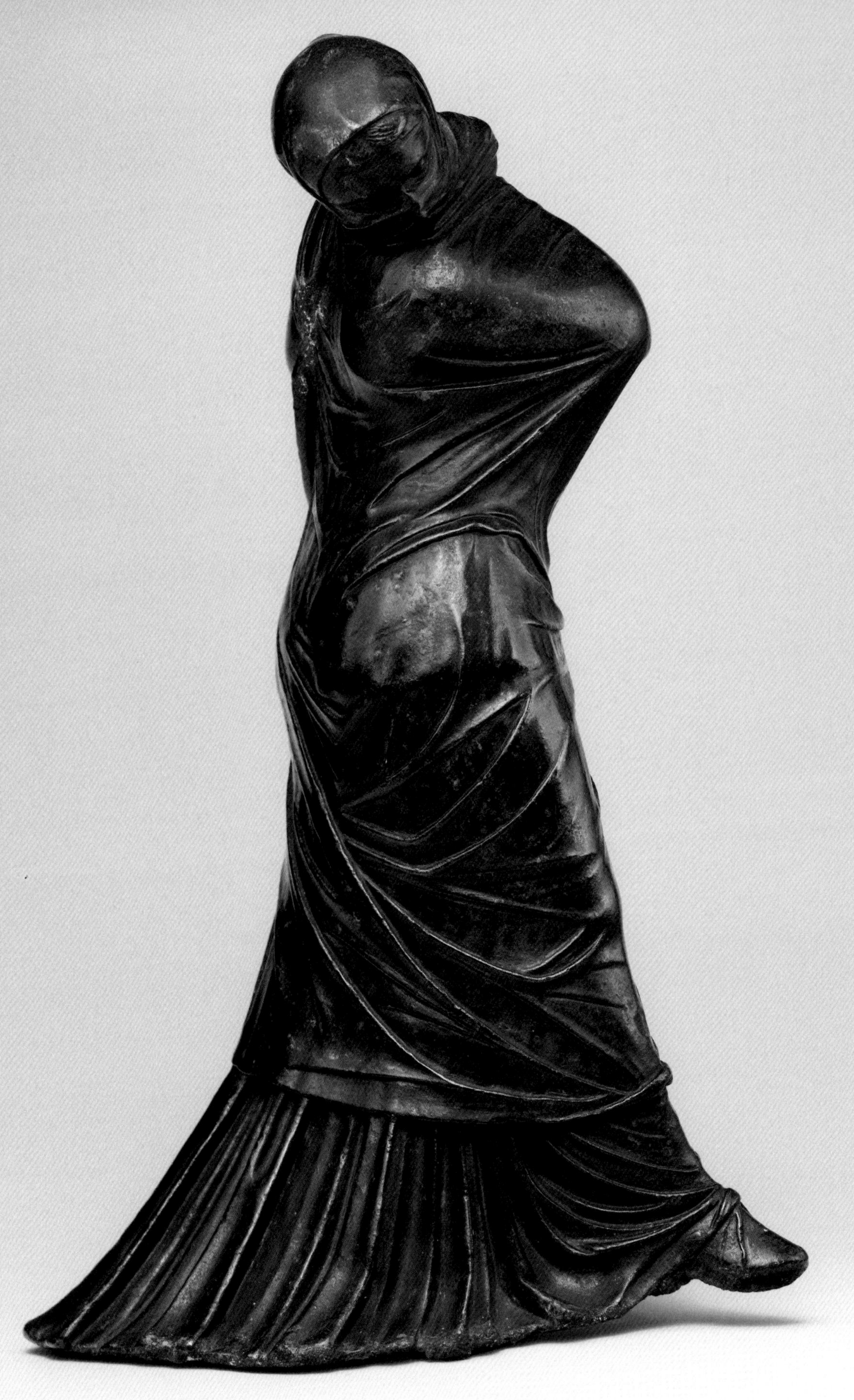

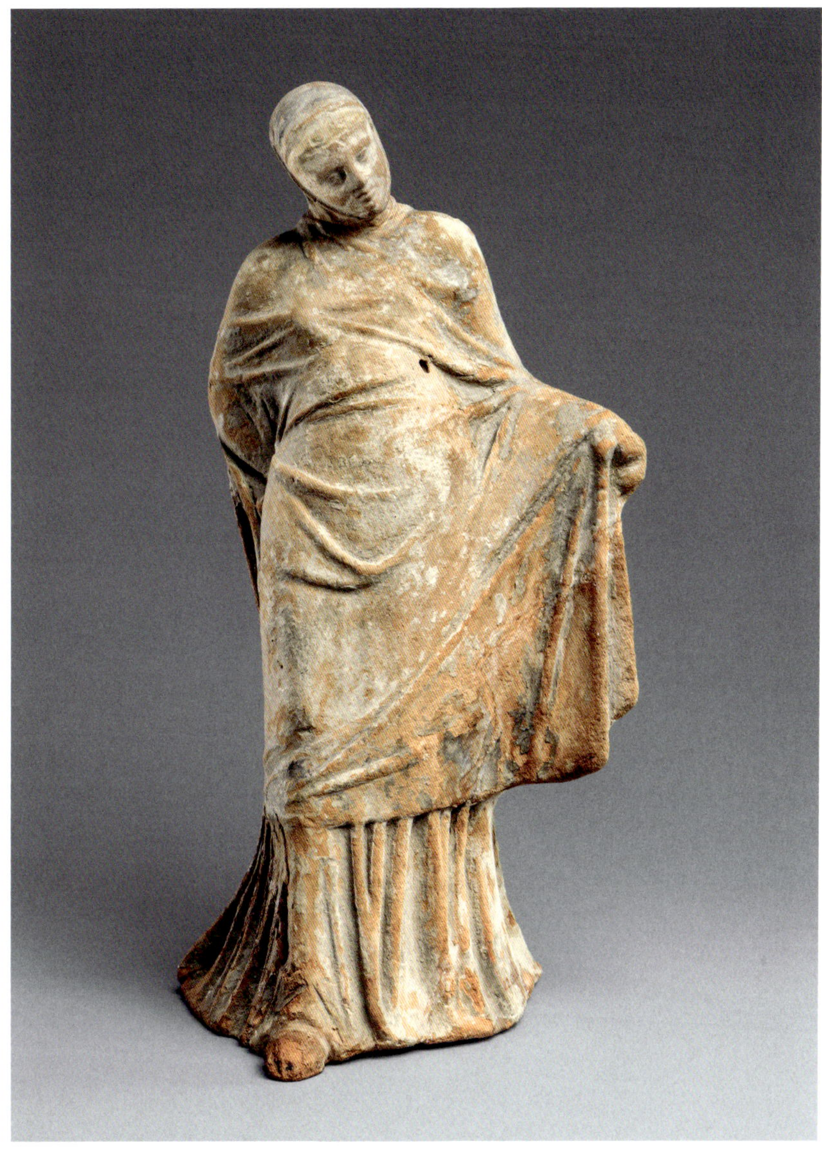

Fig. 57. Statuette of a veiled dancer. Greek, Pontic, Hellenistic period, 3rd century B.C. Said to be from Trapezus (Trebizond) on the Black Sea. Terracotta, H. 7⅞ in. (20 cm). Rogers Fund, 1922 (22.139.38)

of this statuette from antiquity, many similar representations of women dancing are known from diverse parts of the Greek world (fig. 57).

The technical quality of this statuette is outstanding. It is hollow and was cast in a single piece. Ironically, in order to show the many sheer layers of the garments, it is a very thick casting. Aside from a lost casting plug that has left a square hole in the back, the figure is remarkably well preserved and exhibits a black patina. Inside the statuette are greenish tinges of corrosion acquired over centuries.

33

# Statuette of a Black African youth

Greek, Hellenistic period, 3rd–2nd century B.C.
Bronze, H. 7 3/16 in. (18.3 cm)
Rogers Fund, 1918 (18.145.10)

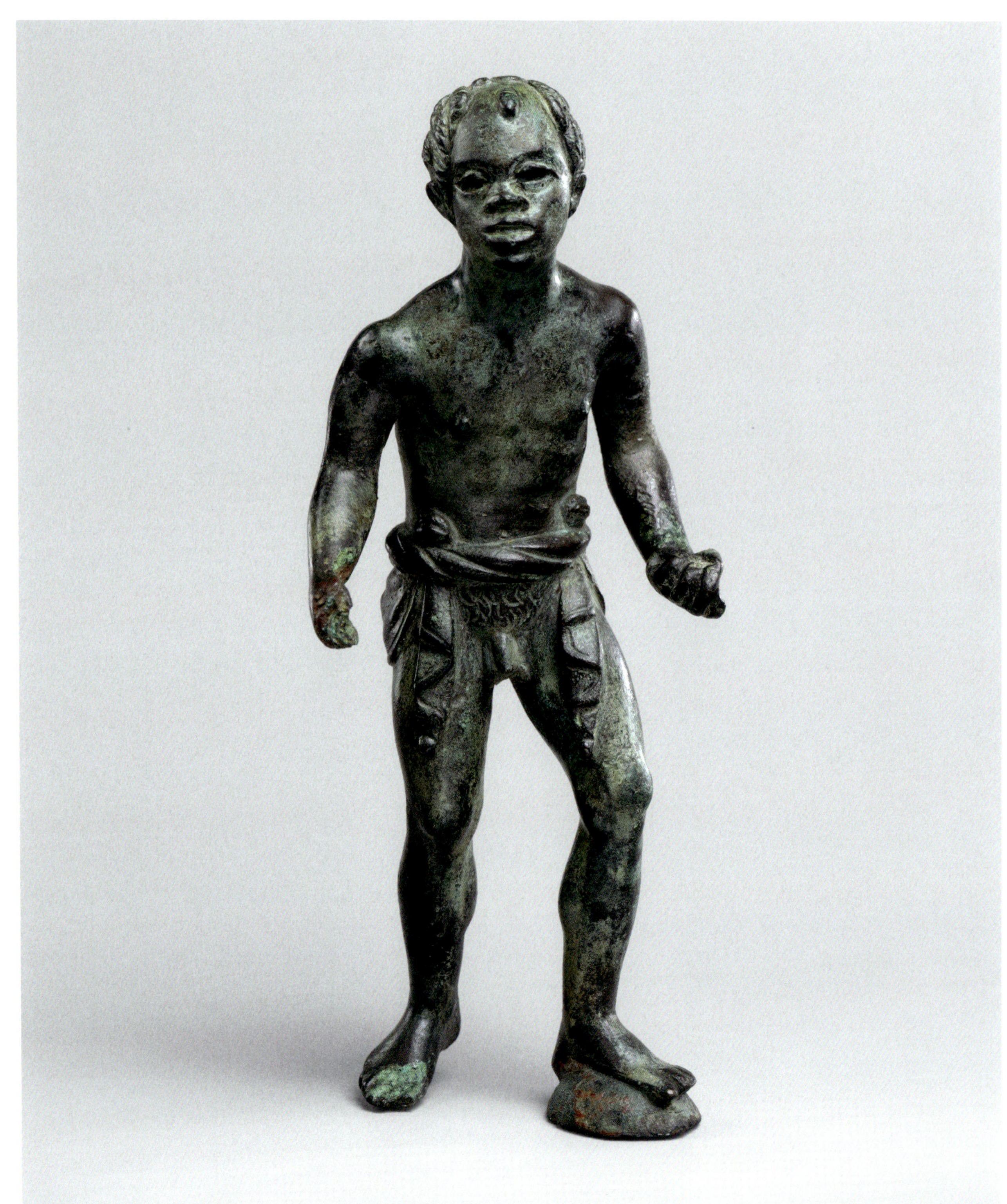

Aside from its northern coastline, the geography and peoples of the African continent were not well known to the ancient Greeks. The lands south of the Sahara Desert were called Ethiopia by the Greeks. In Greek mythology, the kings of Ethiopia were believed to descend from Aurora, goddess of the dawn, and their country lay on the fringe of the known world, an idea reinforced by the rarity of Black Africans living in classical Greece. During the Archaic and Classical periods, the iconography of sub-Saharan Africans was likewise narrowly defined in Greek art. An Athenian sculptural vase of the fifth century B.C. presents a typically stylized representation (fig. 58), with features that differed dramatically from the Greeks' own well-established perception of themselves.

The picture changes significantly in the Hellenistic period, however, when there was a greatly expanded repertoire of Black Africans in Greek art. While their images are less common in Greek mythology, an increase in other types of representation suggests that they made up a larger minority population in the Hellenistic world than ever before. Images of sub-Saharan Africans as artisans, athletes, entertainers, and scholars give an indication of some of their occupations. The existence of large-scale statuary, along with images on high-quality jewelry and

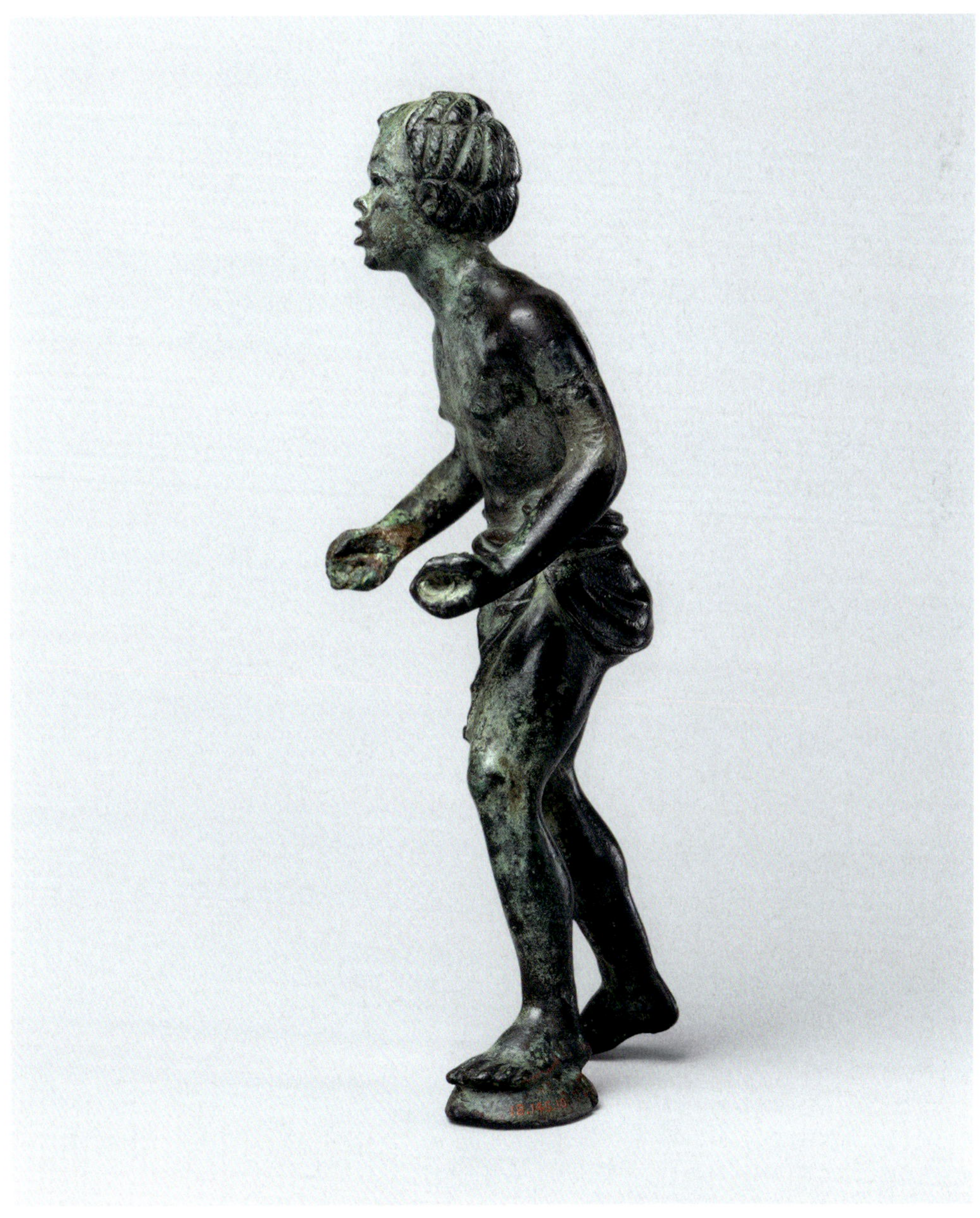

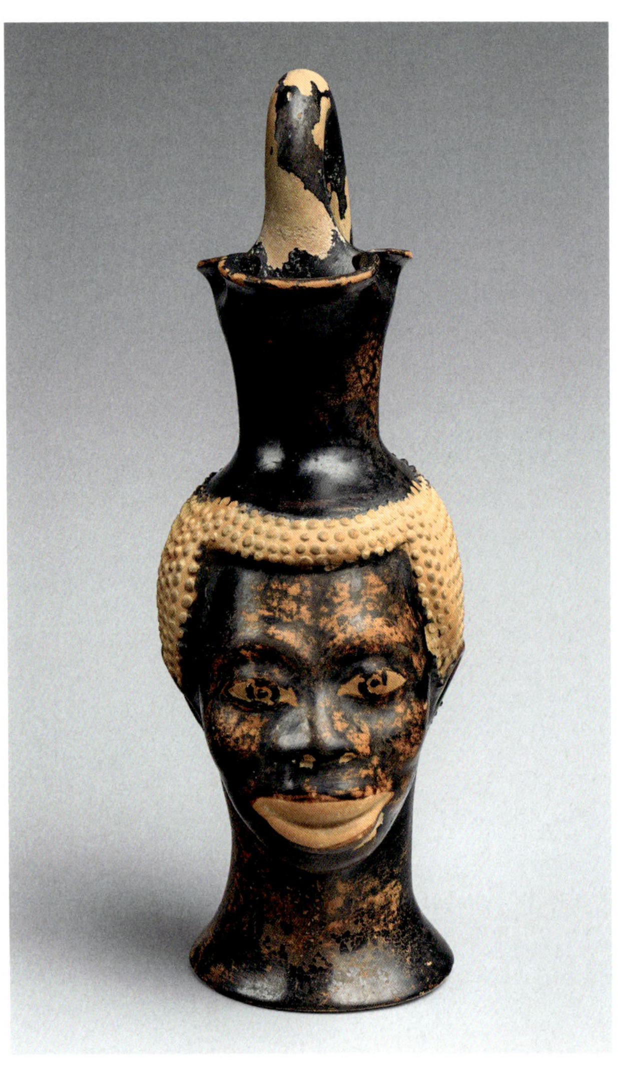

Fig. 58. Oinochoe (jug) in the form of a Black African's head. Greek, Attic, Early Classical period, ca. 480 B.C. Terracotta, red-figure, H. 6 1/16 in. (15.4 cm). Purchase, 1900 (00.11.1)

fine bronzes like the one seen here, is tangible evidence of their integration into various levels of Hellenistic society.

This excellent statuette depicts a Black African youth with a sensitivity that reflects firsthand observation. Moving ahead with both arms extended and hands clasping a now-missing object, the young man leans forward slightly under the weight of his load. A simple cloth is wrapped around his waist and tucked on both sides at the front of his thighs in a carefully ordered fashion. The distinctive garment, which leaves his genitals and the cleft of his buttocks exposed, is the kind of clothing worn by an artisan working in the heat of a foundry, forge, or brazier. The youth's eyes are hollowed out to receive inlays now lost. His hair is carefully arranged in tight curls. He has a broad nose and full lips. His physique is slim, and his muscles toned. Although the surface of the bronze now has a greenish tinge, from its patina's having been transformed after centuries of exposure to the elements, the bronze surface of his skin originally would have been tinted black.

An interesting comparison can be made with a remarkable scene found on a Late Classical Greek vase from Apulia in southern Italy (see fig. 21). On the vase, a sculptor's assistant prepares pigments mixed with wax on a brazier. Although the assistant's skin color is not differentiated, certain physical characteristics indicate he is a Black African or a person of Black heritage. The sculptor applies the pigment to the skin of the Nemean lion belonging to a marble statue of Herakles and, humorously, the hero himself approaches to admire their work.

34

# Statue of Eros sleeping

Greek, Hellenistic period, 3rd–2nd century B.C.
Bronze, 16½ × 33⁹⁄₁₆ × 14 in. (41.9 × 85.2 × 35.6 cm)
Rogers Fund, 1943 (43.11.4)

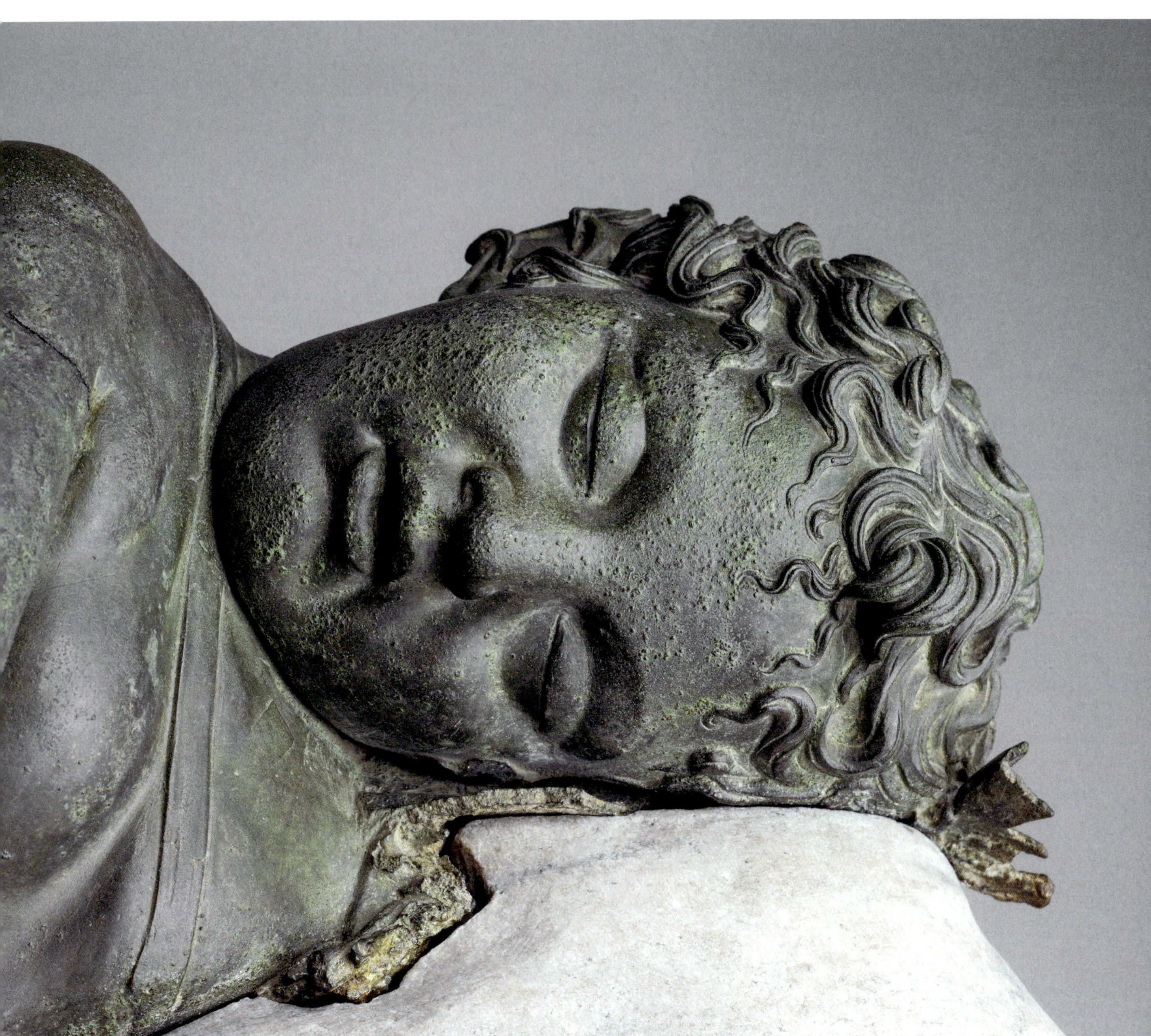

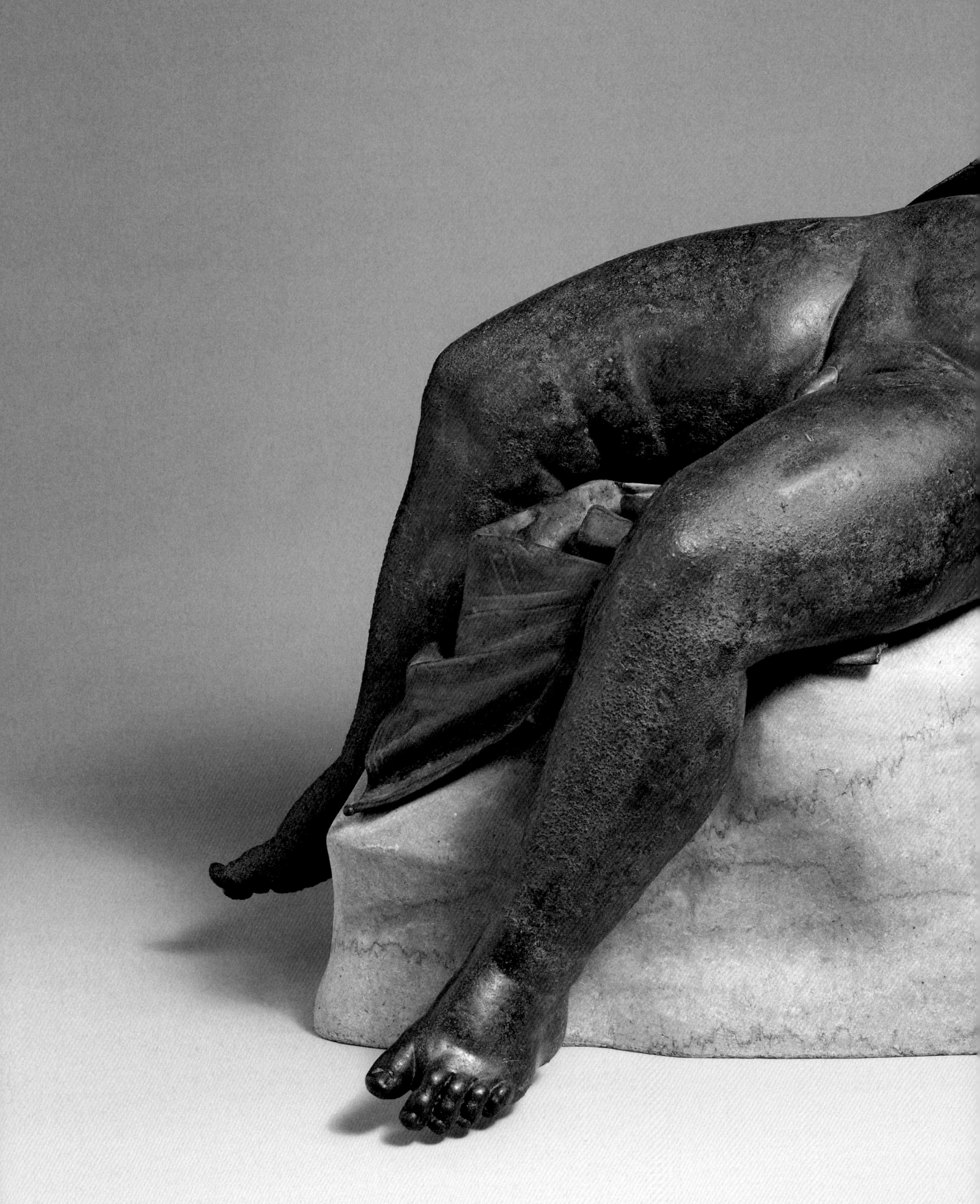

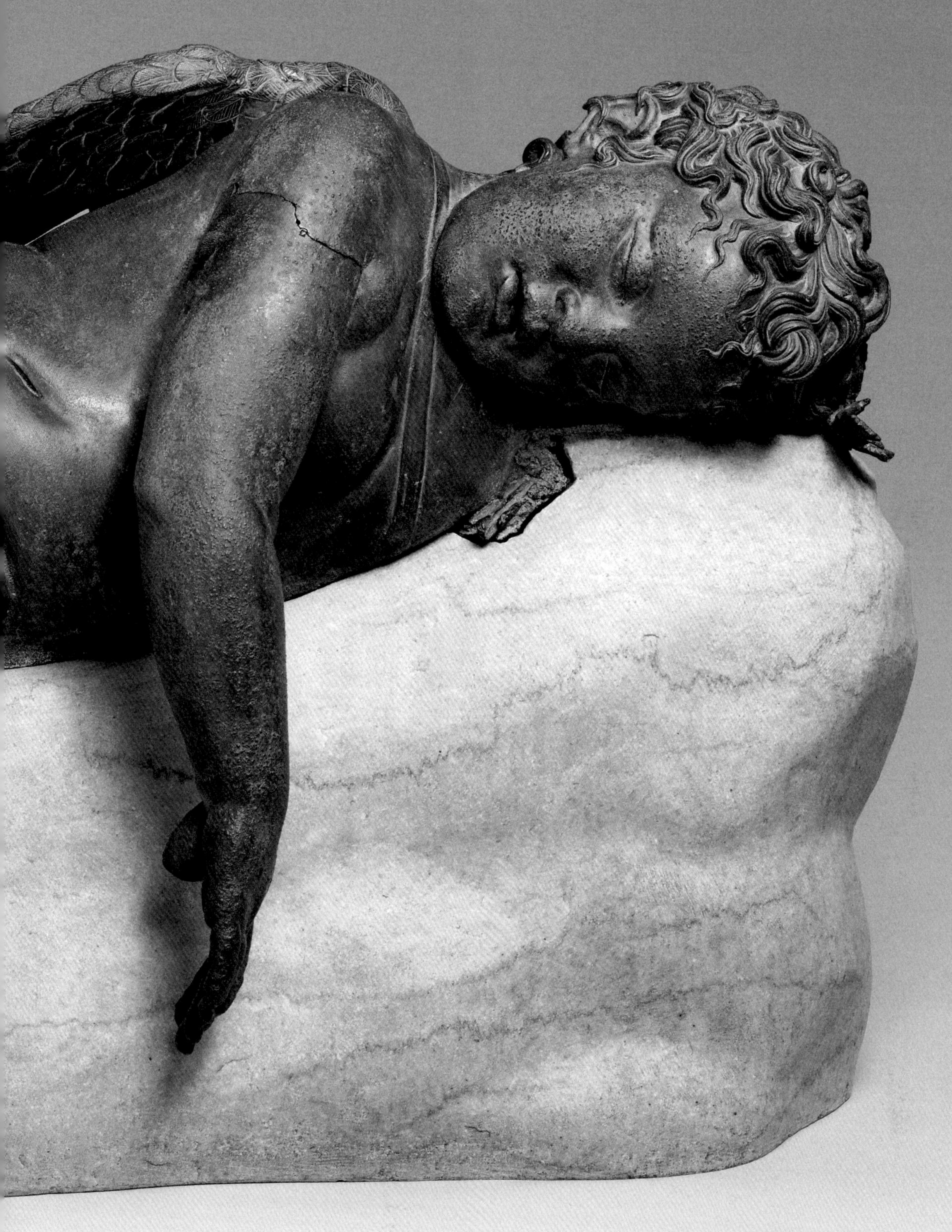

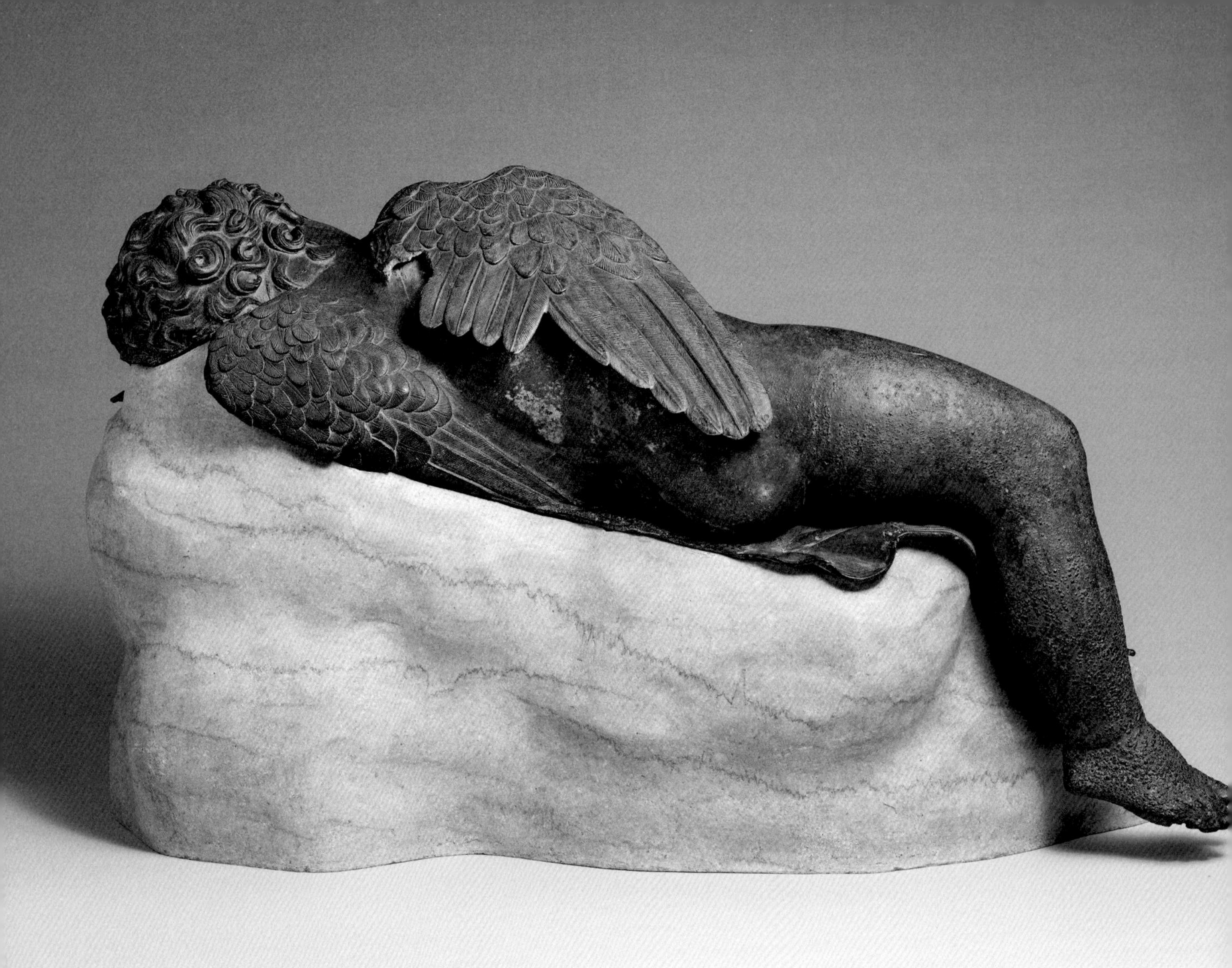

Although bronze was the preferred medium for large-scale Greek statuary during the Classical and Hellenistic periods, very few ancient Greek bronze statues survive today. Judging from the large number of its replicas and variants, this statue is the finest example of a type that was extremely popular in Hellenistic and especially Roman Imperial times. It provides an excellent opportunity to look closely at a Hellenistic bronze statue.

The sculpture represents Eros, the god of love, asleep on a rock after stopping to rest in the midst of his labors. His right hand hangs limply open, and his small bow must have rested just below it, as can be seen on other variants of the type. He is missing his left arm and his quiver, the latter indicated by the strap around his chest. The feather of an arrow preserved by Eros's head adds to the momentary nature of his nap, for his quiver was still open from recent use. The way his soft belly slumps, his delicate little feet with toes curled, and his angelic face present an incredibly accurate and endearing characterization of the god's tender age—a new stylistic development in the Hellenistic period. His gently folded wings are rendered with precise detail.

In earlier Greek art, Eros is typically represented as a youth, described in poetry as a powerful, capricious being who could cruelly wound with his arrows, causing his victims to fall in and out of love. The poet Hesiod considers

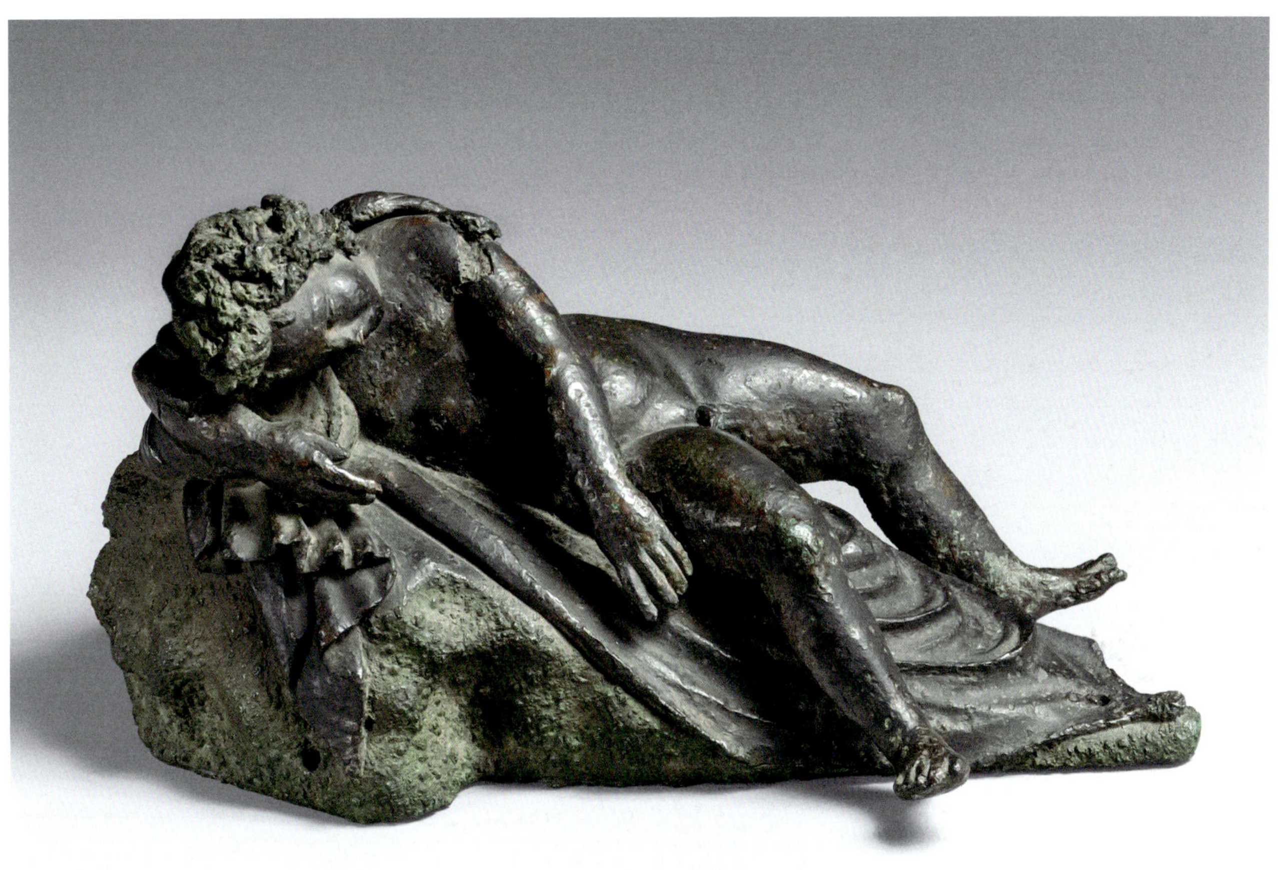

Fig. 59. Statuette of Eros sleeping. Greek or Roman, Late Hellenistic or Imperial period, 1st century B.C.–2nd century A.D. Reduced version of a Hellenistic statue of the 3rd or 2nd century B.C. Bronze, L. 8¼ in. (21 cm). Rogers Fund, 1913 (13.225.2)

him to be a primordial deity, all creation originating from his union with Chaos. In Hellenistic times, the myth of Eros as the son of Aphrodite, goddess of love, and Ares, god of war, gained currency, and it became popular to represent Eros as a baby. Such an impressive statue would most likely have been made as a dedication at a sanctuary to the god or perhaps to Aphrodite.

A tour de force of bronze casting, the statue is said to come from the island of Rhodes, a major center for bronze work in the Hellenistic period. Careful scientific and technical examination has shown that, as preserved, it was made in seven pieces: head, body, left arm, left leg, right leg, drapery between the legs, and right wing. Each piece was expertly joined metallurgically by means of flow welds, most of which are still not visible from the exterior. It has very few casting flaws. The drapery between the legs was restored in antiquity, most likely centuries after it was made. The rock on which Eros rests is a modern restoration based on other examples of the type (fig. 59). A groove along the bottom cast edge of the bronze indicates that the original base was made from a different material, most likely stone, which would have added to the realistic impression intended by the sculptor.

35

# Head of Epikouros

Roman, Imperial period, 2nd century A.D.
Copy of a Greek statue of the first half of the 3rd century B.C.
Pentelic marble, H. 19⅝ in. (49.8 cm)
Rogers Fund, 1911 (11.90)

The ancient Greeks did much to further the field of philosophy, which studies the fundamental nature of knowledge, reality, and human existence. The most important Greek philosopher of the Classical period was arguably Sokrates (fig. 60), who was known for his method of cross-questioning those whom he encountered. Sokrates was the son of a sculptor and practiced stone carving himself. He had a distinctive appearance, likened to that of Silenus, a minor woodland deity and companion of Dionysos.

In the early Hellenistic period, Epikouros, the founder of Epicurean thought, was among the truly influential Greek philosophers of his generation. Born on the island of Samos in 341 B.C., he moved in about 307/6 B.C. to Athens, where he established a philosophical school known as the Kepos (Garden). It became one of the three most important schools of philosophy in Hellenistic Athens, together with Plato's Academy and the Lyceum, which was founded by Aristotle. Although Athens was no longer the preeminent city-state in the Greek world, as it was in the fifth century B.C., it remained a major center for learning throughout the Hellenistic period.

This portrait is among a number of Roman copies of a statue of the philosopher that is believed to have been commissioned and set up at the Kepos soon after his death in 270 B.C. Epikouros is represented as an old man with a prodigious beard, leaning forward, his eyes alert and open, his mind deep in thought. The ability of Greek sculptors to render the impression of the inner workings of the mind is one of their great contributions to sculpture. The sculptor of this fine copy has captured some of the subject's original intensity. From various copies, it is understood that Epikouros was seated on a chair in the original composition.

Epikouros's teachings were held in high esteem in antiquity and gained a large following far beyond Athens, especially in the Late Hellenistic and Roman Imperial periods. His philosophy of living well and focusing on the pleasures of this life had tremendous appeal. A bronze statuette in The Met collection presents a skillful portrait of one of his followers (fig. 61). Once identified as Hermarchos, who led the school after Epikouros, the subject is now better understood as a later practitioner. His ample belly exhibits the well-fed physique that came to be a feature of Epicureanism, since an important part of living well was eating well. The statuette appropriately decorated a lampstand, most likely for a banqueting table.

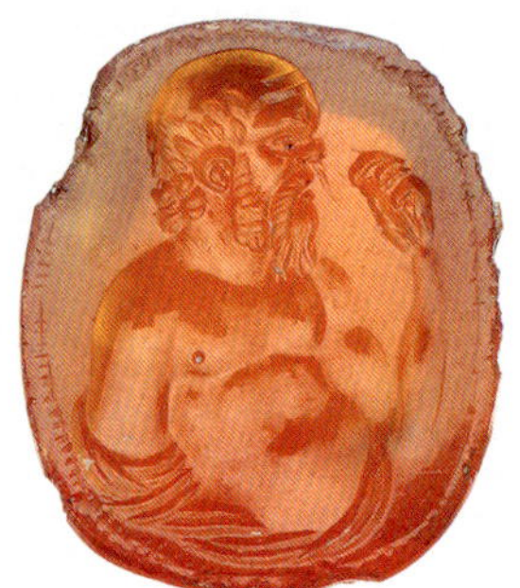

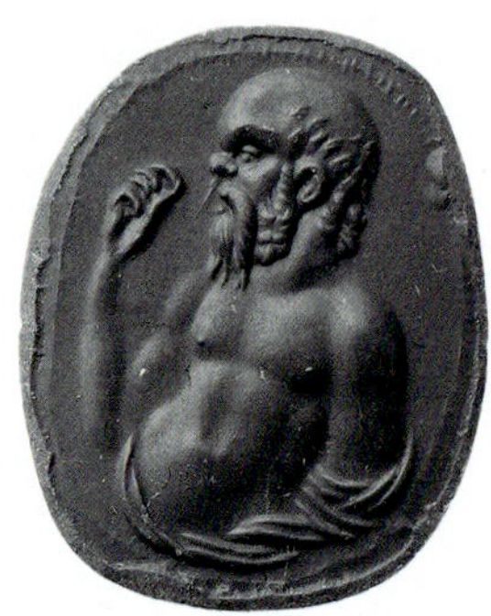

Fig. 60. *Left*: Gem with a portrait of Sokrates; *right*: impression of gem. Roman, Late Republican or Early Imperial period, ca. 1st century B.C.–1st century A.D. Carnelian, 9/16 × 7/16 in. (1.4 × 1.1 cm). Gift of John Taylor Johnston, 1881 (81.6.81)

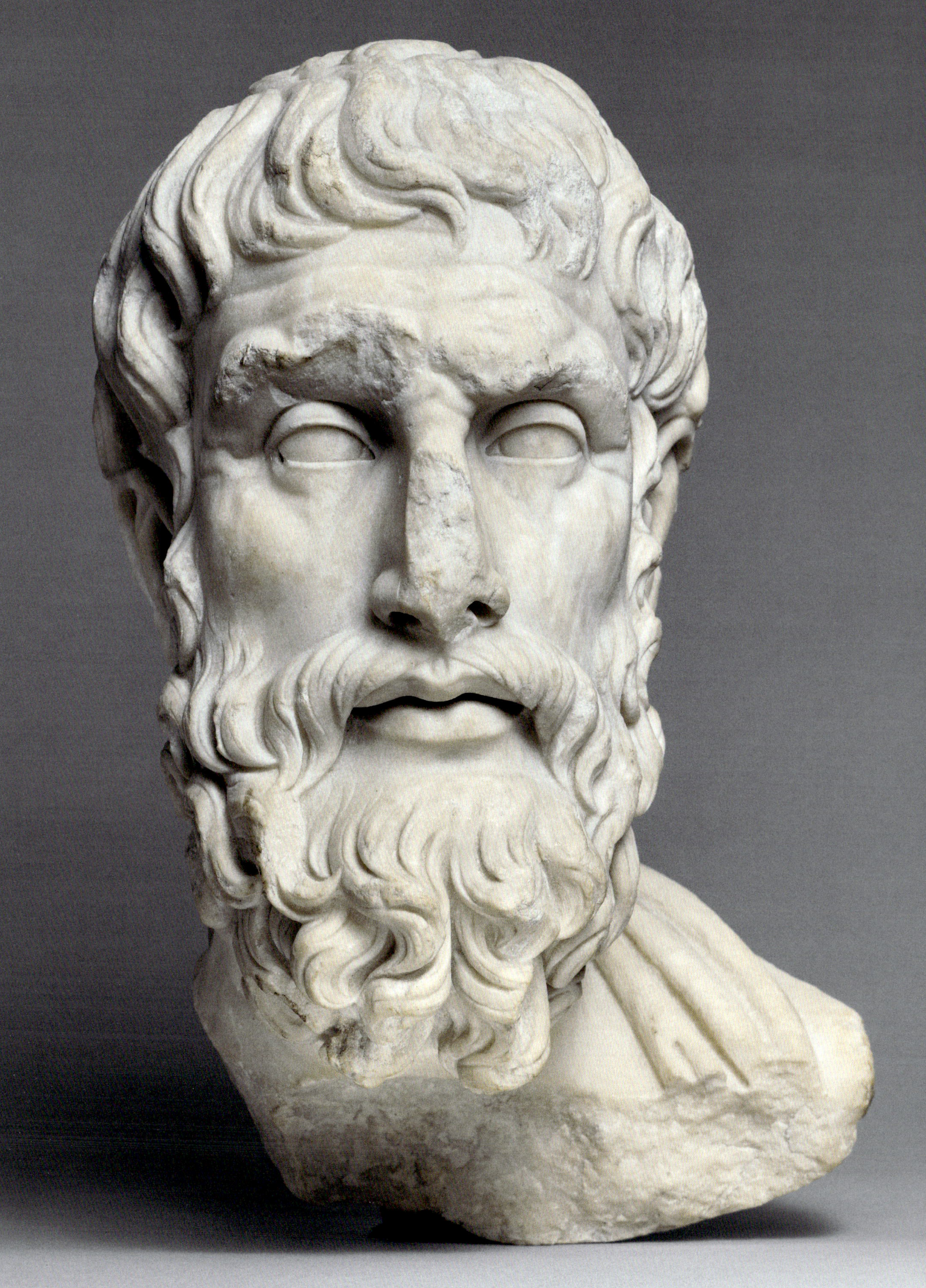

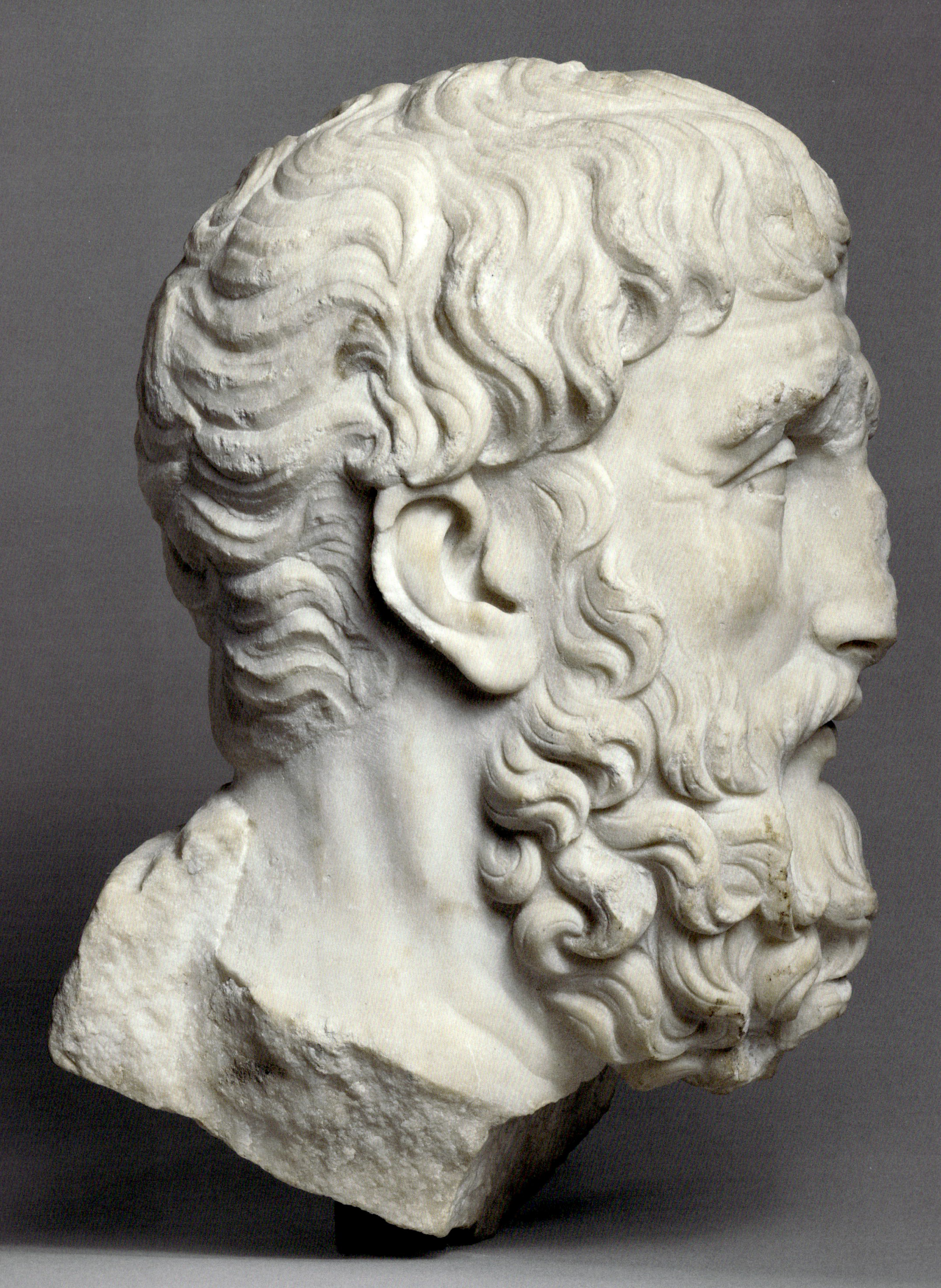

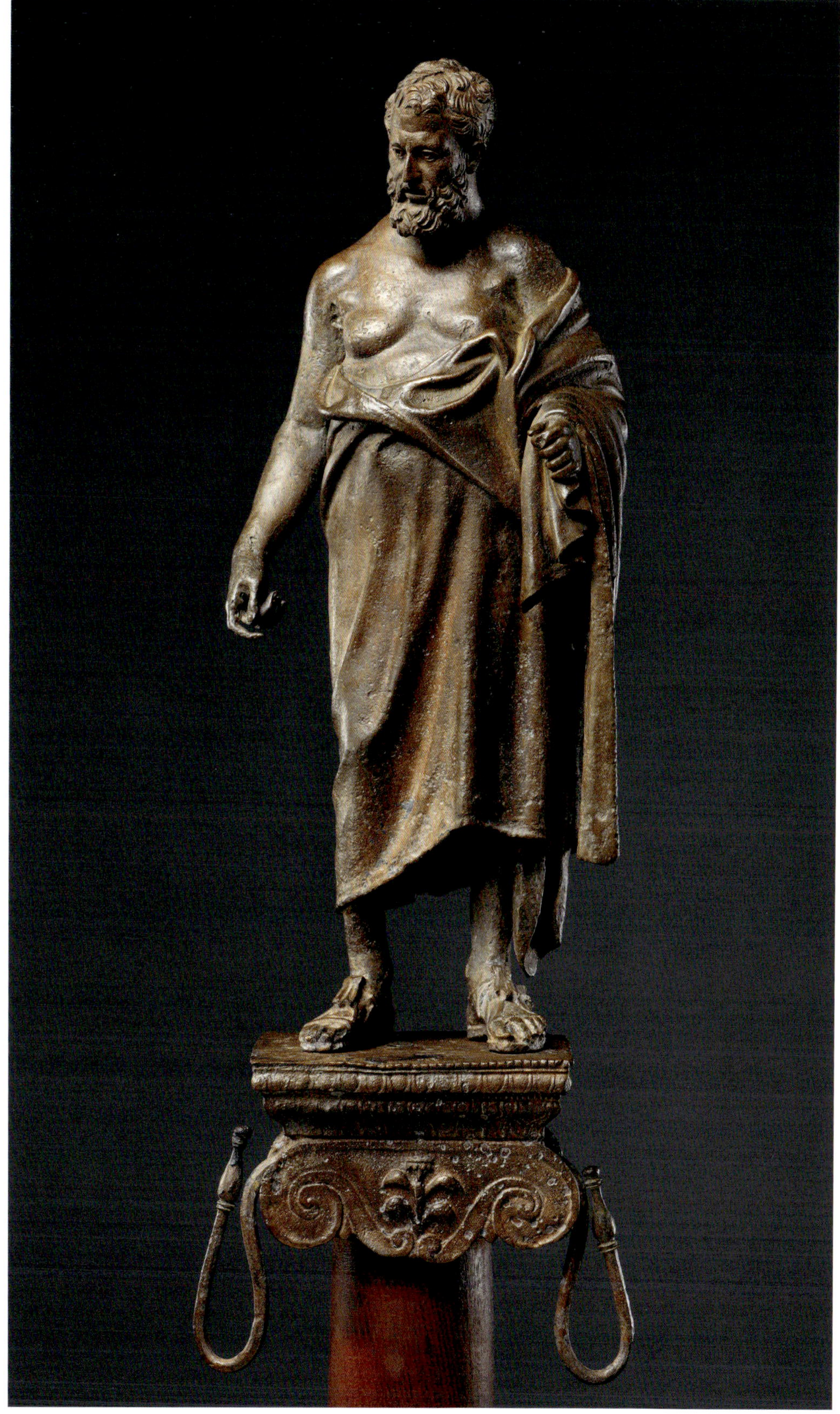

Fig. 61. Statuette of a philosopher on a lampstand. Roman, Augustan period, late 1st century B.C. Adaptation of a Greek statue of the 3rd century B.C. Bronze, H. 10¾ in. (27.3 cm). Rogers Fund, 1910 (10.231.1)

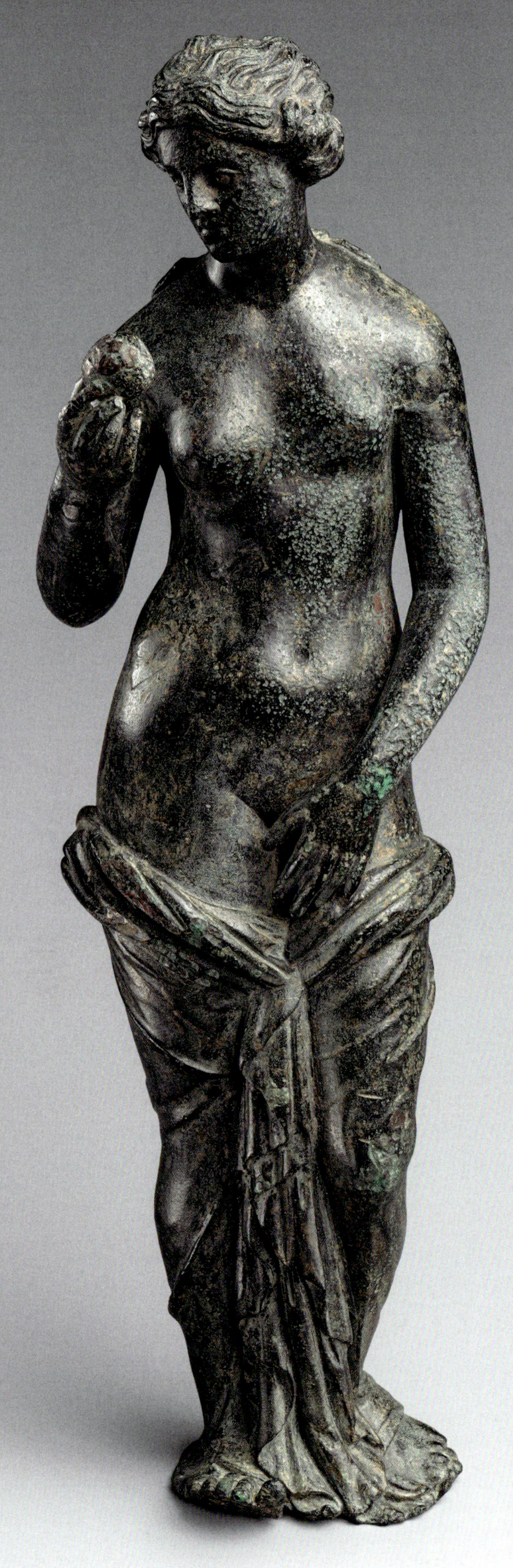

36

# Statuette of Aphrodite

Greek, Hellenistic period, ca. 3rd–1st century B.C.
Bronze with silver inlay, H. 8 3/16 in. (20.9 cm)
Bequest of Walter C. Baker, 1971 (1972.118.96)

In this carefully wrought statuette, Aphrodite contemplates the Apple of Discord, which was given to her by the Trojan prince Paris as a prize for being the fairest of the Greek goddesses. The goddess of love is portrayed half naked, her garment draped around her thighs as though it were slipping from her body. Her pose, covering her genitals and looking to one side, derives ultimately from Praxiteles's famous fourth-century-B.C. nude sculpture from Knidos, hailed by Pliny the Elder as the finest statue in the world. After the creation of this masterpiece, nude or seminude sculptures of Aphrodite became hugely popular in the Hellenistic period, and many variations like the present statuette appeared.

While reinforcing the idea of Aphrodite's quintessential beauty, the poignant image also evokes the cause of the Trojan War. In exchange for the apple, Aphrodite offered Paris the most beautiful woman in the world, Helen, who was the wife of the Greek king Menelaos. When Paris brought Helen to Troy, Menelaos assembled a vast army drawn from his many alliances, and a ten-year epic battle ensued between the Greeks and the Trojans. In Classical Greek art, scenes of the contest do not illustrate the apple, which appeared first in the Hellenistic period, but instead focus on the competition between Aphrodite, Athena, and Hera with Paris as judge (fig. 62).

The statuette is remarkably well preserved, its greenish black patina having formed over centuries and its eyes still inlaid with silver. The original context of this statuette is not known. Such accomplished small-scale statuettes often functioned as votives, dedicated to the gods in thanks for some granted prayer. In the Hellenistic period, they were also used in the home, where they could have served as private devotional sculptures or sometimes even as decorative objects.

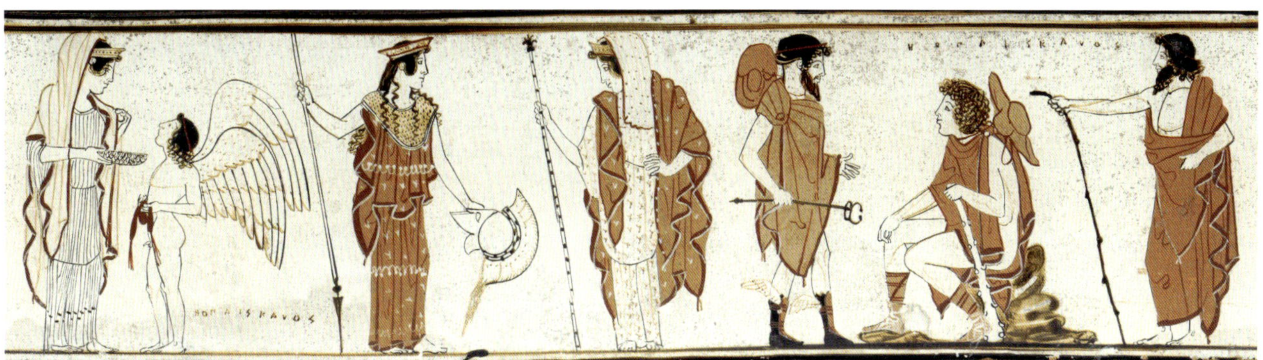

Fig. 62. Rollout image of a pyxis (box) with the Judgment of Paris. Greek, Attic, Classical period, ca. 465–460 B.C. Attributed to the Penthesilea Painter. Terracotta, white-ground, H. 4 3/4 in. (12.1 cm). Rogers Fund, 1907 (07.286.36a, b)

37

# Statue of an old woman

Roman, Julio-Claudian period, A.D. 14–68
Copy of a Greek work of the 2nd century B.C.
Pentelic marble, H. 49⅝ in. (126.1 cm)
Rogers Fund, 1909 (09.39)

This slightly under-lifesize statue shows an old woman walking gingerly and carrying a basket full of fruit and three chickens trussed in a rope satchel. Since its discovery in Rome in 1907, it has been known as the Old Market Woman, a peasant genre figure from daily life. However, close examination has revealed details that have led to other interpretations. The woman's elegant clothes indicate she is a person of status, and she wears delicate sandals. Her voluminous chiton with a high belt is carefully knotted at the front, while a mantle draped over her right shoulder hangs down her back. On her head is a veil held in place by a crown of ivy. Hunched over considerably, she probably grasped a staff in her right hand to steady her. Under the mantle, her garment has slipped, and her right breast heaves forward as she walks. Her attire and the items she carries indicate that she is setting out to a religious festival. The provisions may be votive offerings to the gods or food to share during the celebration.

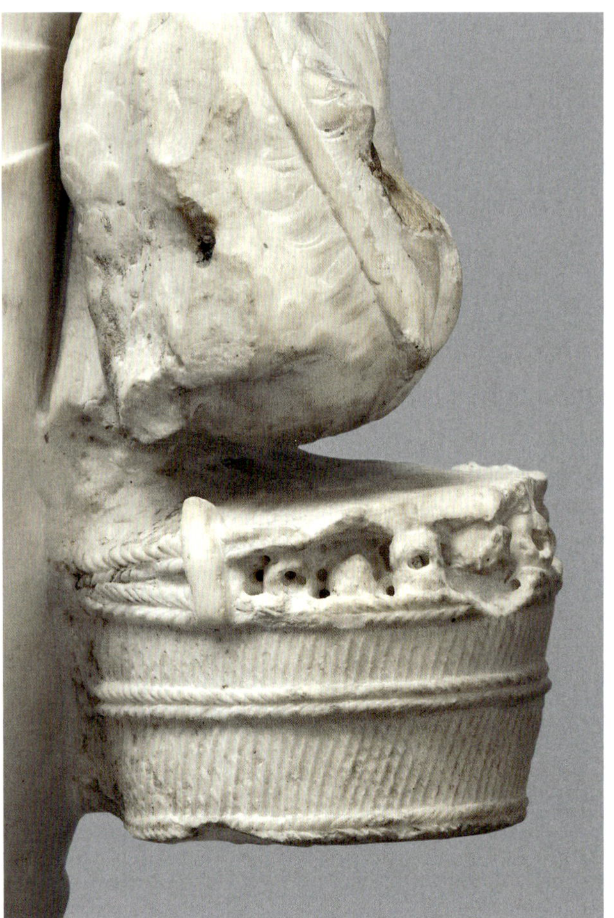

Festivals in honor of the gods were an important part of the religious calendar. In the third century B.C., the Hellenistic king Ptolemy IV Philopator established an elaborate Dionysian festival in Alexandria. This festival, the Lagnophoria, is described by the ancient writer Athenaeus in *The Banqueters* (V. 197–198):

> In the Dionysiac procession, there marched Silenoi who kept back the crowds. . . . These were closely followed by Satyrs, . . . ornamented with gilt ivy leaves. After these came Victories with gold wings, . . . after these came a four-wheeled cart, twenty-one feet long and twelve feet wide, drawn by one hundred and eighty men; in this stood a statue of Dionysos fifteen feet tall, pouring a libation from a gold goblet. . . . In front of him lay a gold Laconian mixing bowl holding one hundred and fifty gallons.

And the wonders continue for pages.

Another marble statue similar in theme to this work, now in the Munich Glyptothek, shows a seated old woman grasping a large wine jug and laughing in Dionysian inebriation. It has been suggested that the sculpture may represent an aged hetaera, or courtesan. A recent interpretation proposes that it may have been a dedication in the temple

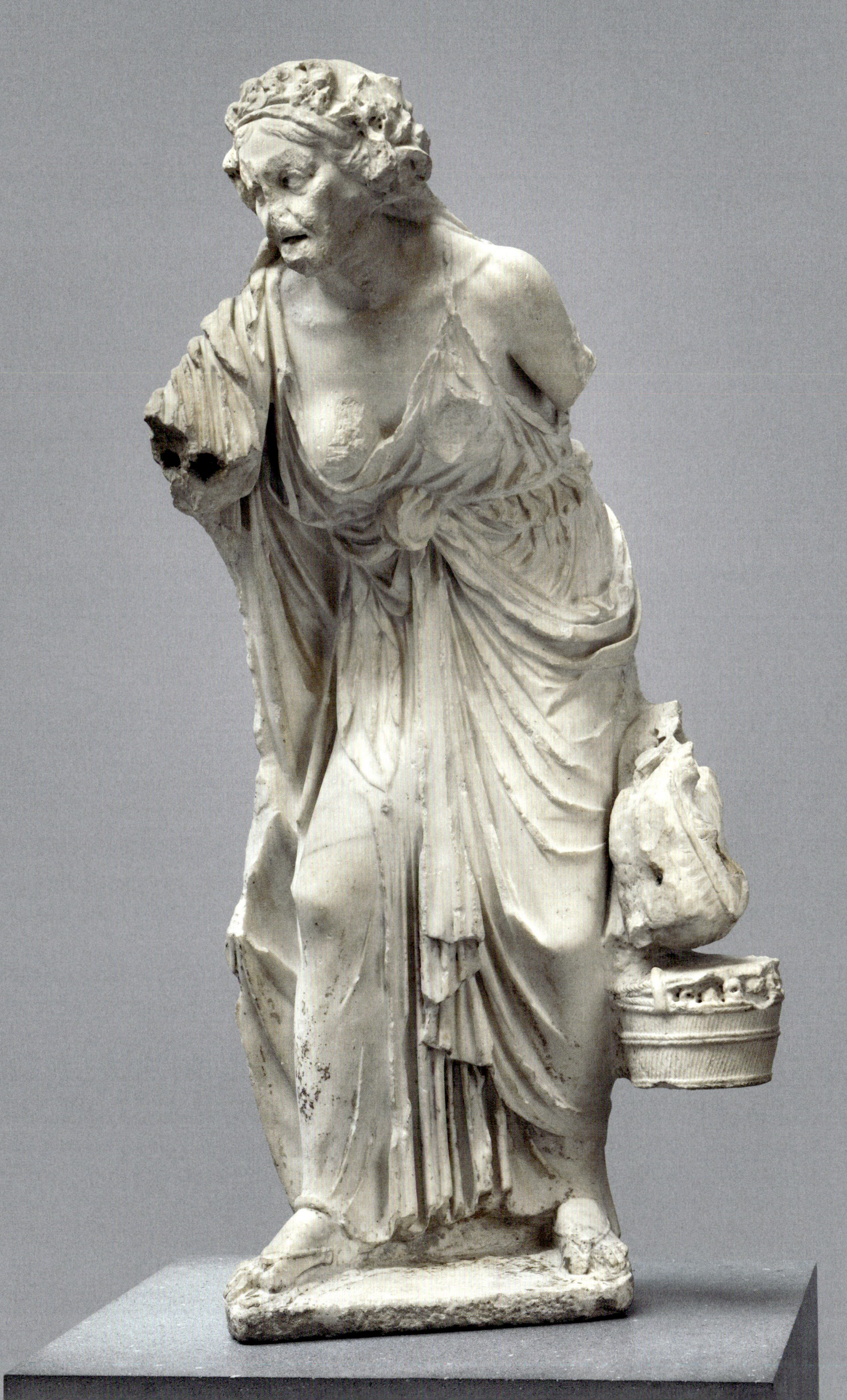

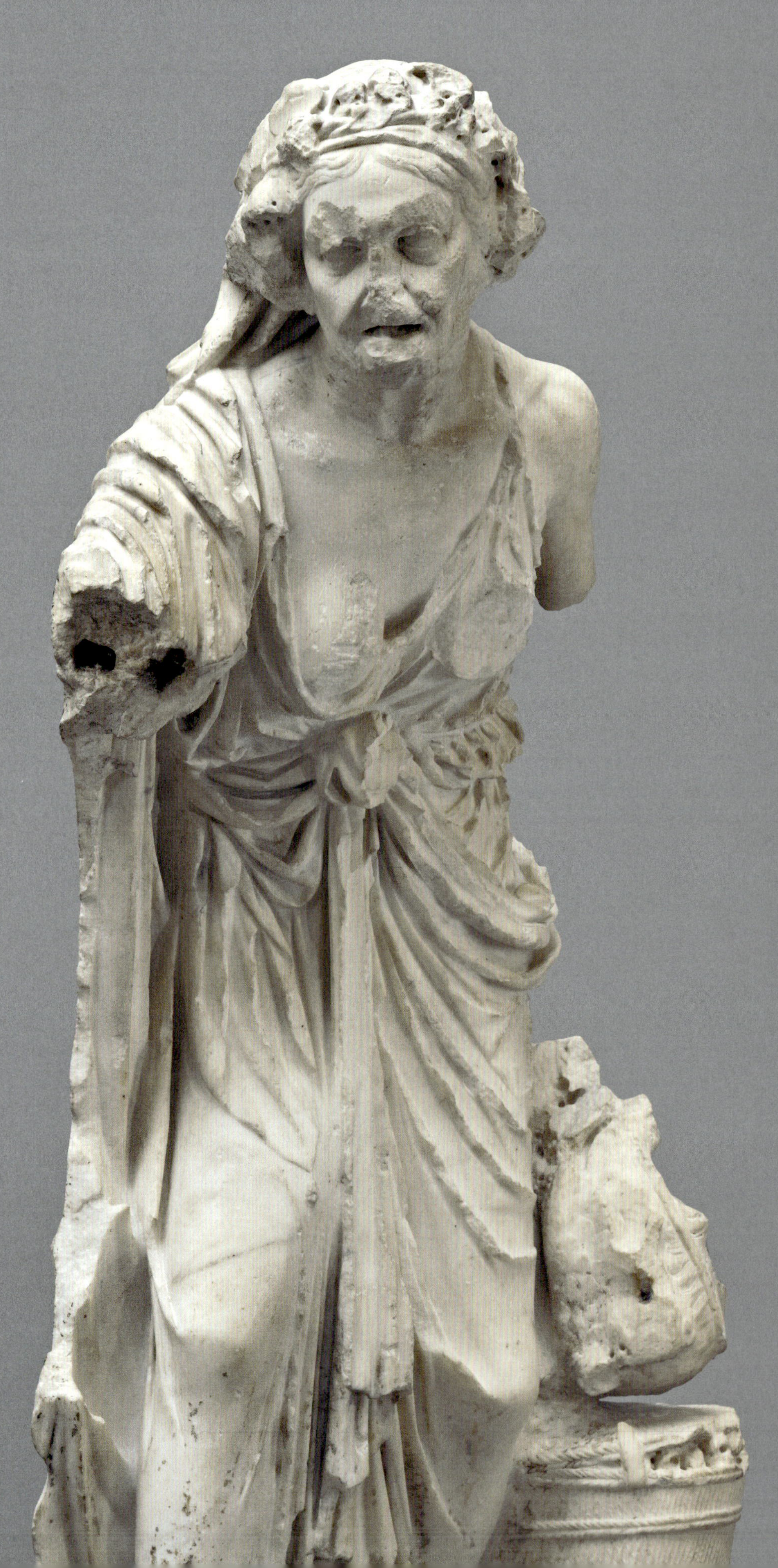

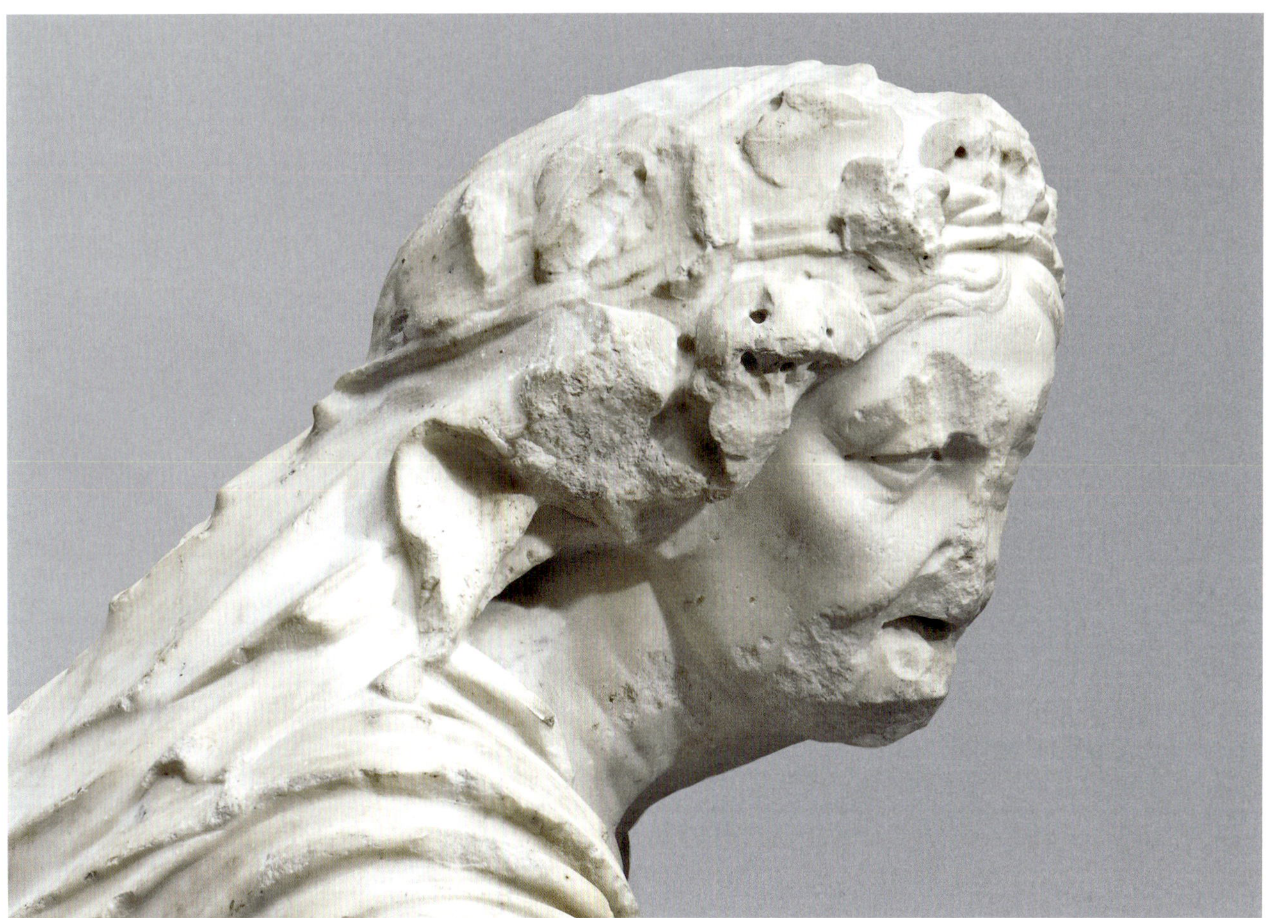

of Fides, the goddess of trust, or Ops, the goddess of agriculture, both on the Capitoline Hill in Rome.

This work illuminates the complex issues surrounding the interpretation of adaptations of Greek sculptures from the Roman Imperial period. Dated to the Julio-Claudian period based on stylistic considerations such as the sharp folds of the drapery and the soft modeling of the body, it is thought to be an adaptation of a Hellenistic work of the late second century B.C. However, such realistic depictions began much earlier, in the third century B.C., so the date of the original is open to debate. Hellenistic sculptors employed a variety of styles concurrently, and there are few closely dated Hellenistic sculptural monuments preserved today.

The original sculpture would most likely have been a dedication at a sanctuary to Dionysos. In order to appeal to his Roman clientele, the copyist has made some changes to the figure, most notably the smoothing out of some features, like the skin of her left shoulder, arm, and chest, which appear less ravaged by time—something arguably not the case in the Hellenistic original. Other details, including the crow's-feet around her eyes, her sunken cheeks, and the poor state of her teeth, suggest the original's emphasis on her old age. The way the sculptor has oriented the statue from a three-quarter view is characteristic of copyists during the Roman Imperial period. Traces of bright pink on the edge of the chiton and fugitive remains of dark green pigment on the left sandal strap indicate that the figure was originally painted.

The statue was brutally damaged in either ancient or medieval times. The head was purposefully defaced, and successive chisel marks on the exposed breast also denote intentional damage, quite likely by early Christians offended by the pagan subject.

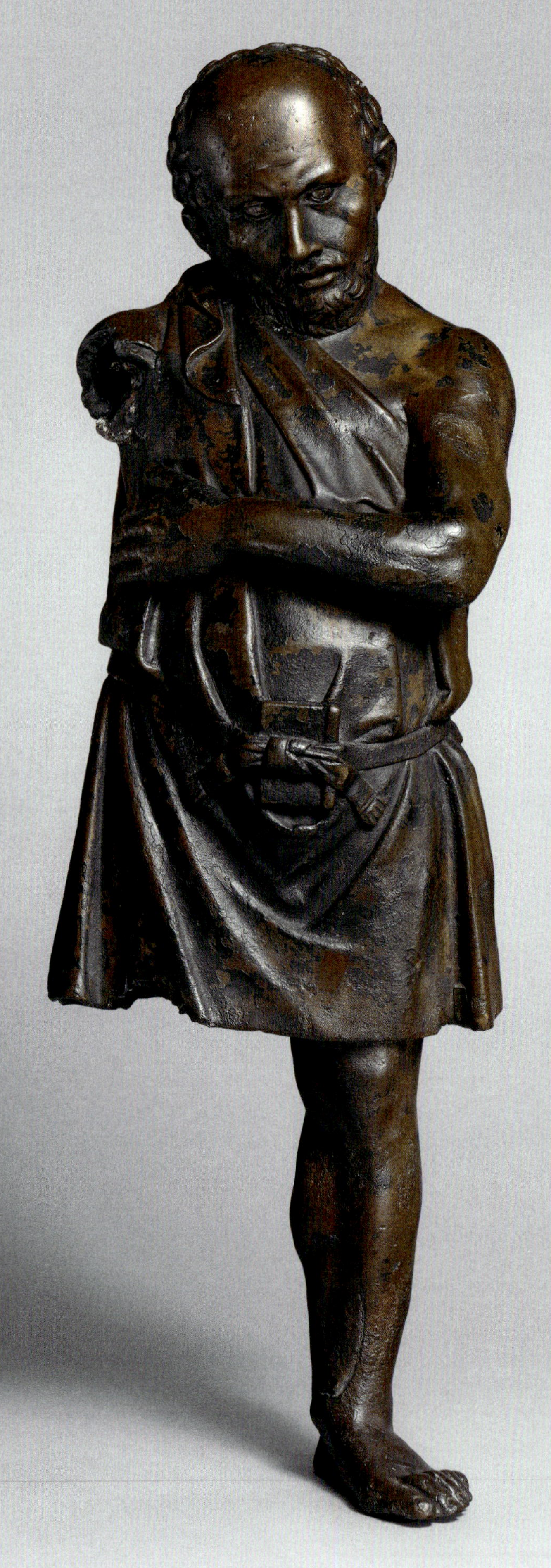

38

# Statuette of an artisan

Greek, Late Hellenistic period, ca. mid-1st century B.C.
Bronze with silver inlay, H. 15⅞ in. (40.3 cm)
Rogers Fund, 1972 (1972.11.1)

This statuette depicts a truly remarkable personage, if only we knew who he was. Although the figure is missing his right arm and right leg, what is preserved conveys the presence of a significant, self-composed individual. His short tunic, known as an exomis, his stocky build, and his muscular legs and arms identify him as an artisan. Tucked into his belt is a small wooden tablet made to hold two wax sheets, which he could use to make notes or sketches with a pointed stylus. His large head, receding hairline, and slight paunch add to the impression of seniority. Head tilted to one side, he looks down with a furrowed brow and appears deep in thought.

Imbued with great psychological power, the person depicted here was most likely a well-known historical or mythological figure. According to one suggestion, this is an imaginary portrait of the Classical Athenian sculptor Pheidias, famous for his chryselephantine sculptures of Zeus at Olympia and the Athena Parthenos on the Acropolis. An argument has also been made that he is Hephaistos, the craftsman god, but the figure's strong realism and stark individuality seem more appropriate to a mortal man. More likely, we are looking at a mythological craftsman. One possibility is Epeios, the Homeric hero who with Athena's help carved the Trojan Horse, a monumental wooden structure in whose belly the Greeks were finally able to breach the walls of Troy and sack the city. However, there is no clear iconographic tradition for representing this famous legendary artisan.

Arguably the best identification is that this is the master craftsman Daidalos, who built the Labyrinth at Knossos and escaped from Crete to Sicily with his son Ikaros by flying with wings of their own design. Ikaros did not heed his father's advice and flew too close to the sun, tragically plunging to his death in the Mediterranean. Daidalos appears in Roman art as a short, older man with a receding hairline and a paunch not dissimilar to this figure's. With his intense gaze, he may be devising one of his extraordinary creations. The portrait manages to combine the strong physical characteristics essential to craftsmen with the intellectual machinations of a gifted artist at work.

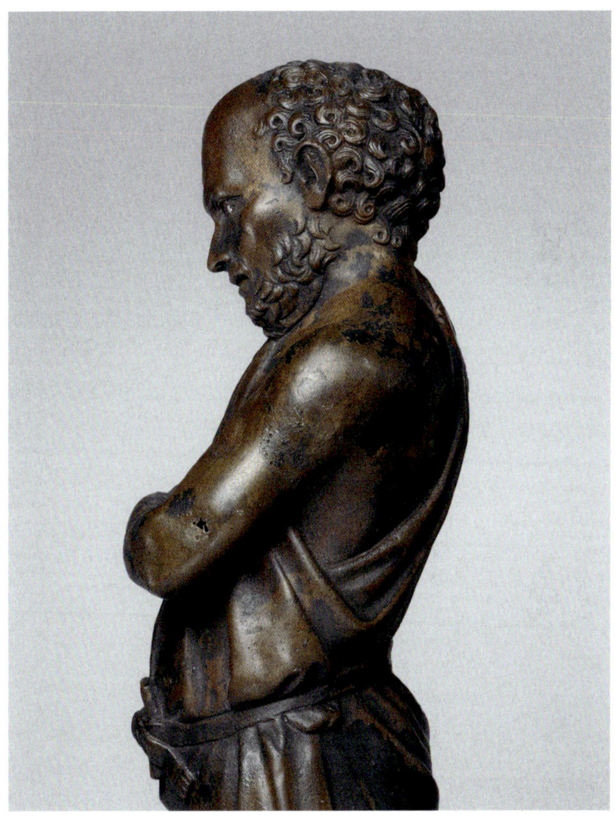

This large statuette is said to have been found in the sea off the northern coast of Africa or possibly at Cherchell, Algeria. It was originally cast in at least five sections (one for the head and body and one for each of the limbs) by means of the lost wax process, much in the same way that ancient Greek bronze statues were made. The eyes are inlaid with silver. The bronze has a warm, golden-brown surface, with black encrustations, and is worn in places, notably on the forehead and parts of the hair.

39

# Statuette of the Diadoumenos (Fillet-Binder)

Greek, Late Hellenistic period, 1st century B.C.
Copy of a Classical bronze statue of ca. 430 B.C. by Polykleitos
Terracotta with gilding, H. 11 7/16 in. (29 cm)
Fletcher Fund, 1932 (32.11.2)

In this clay statuette, a youth ties a fillet around his head to commemorate an athletic victory. The work is a small-scale version of a famous bronze statue known as the Diadoumenos attributed to Polykleitos of Argos, a renowned fifth-century-B.C. Greek sculptor. The original probably stood in a sanctuary such as Olympia or Delphi, where Panhellenic games were held on a regular basis and victors were allowed to erect statues in their own honor.

Traces of gilding appear on the fillet, and it is likely that the missing parts of this ribbon, which he would have grasped in both hands (also now missing), were made from gilded metal. The way he stands with his weight on one leg, a contrapposto stance, is a well-known innovation by Polykleitos that had a wide influence on later Greek sculptures. To accommodate the stylistic preferences of his time, the artist who made this statuette has slightly elongated the proportions and made the head smaller.

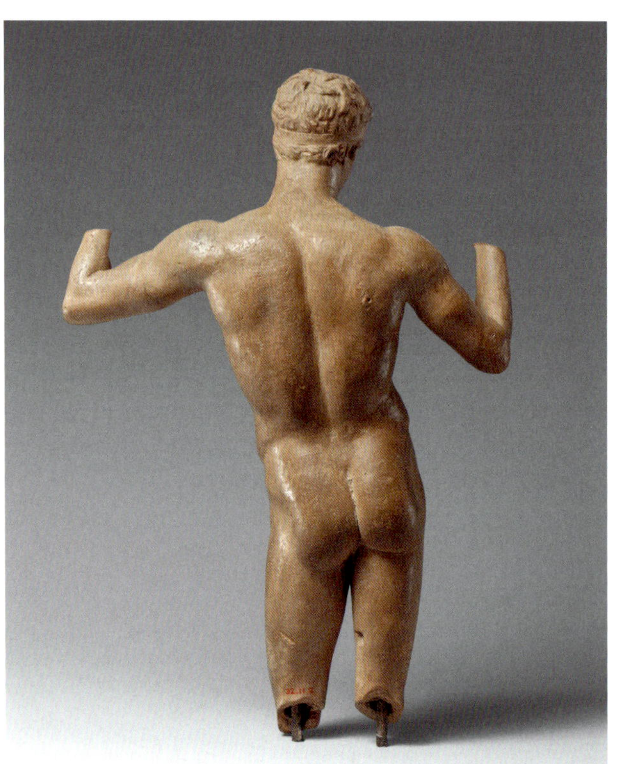

The statuette was acquired in Smyrna on the west coast of Asia Minor in the 1880s by W. R. Paton, a distinguished British epigrapher, and was displayed for many years in the Louvre before its acquisition by The Met. It has been attributed to a workshop from ancient Smyrna, where other small-scale replicas of Classical Greek statues were made. While terracotta was widely available and inexpensive, the relatively few surviving replicas suggest that their production was limited. The interest in and production of small-scale replicas of Classical sculpture grew in popularity during Roman Imperial times, as the Romans were great admirers of Classical Greek sculpture. Ancient Roman miniature copies in bronze and marble of the Diadoumenos are also known.

The field of art history began in the Hellenistic period. The first books about the history of art, as well as artist biographies, were produced, and earlier Greek statues, especially those of the fifth century B.C. by sculptors such as Myron, Pheidias, and Polykleitos, were sought out and replicated. Among the earliest preserved copies of the Diadoumenos is a large-scale marble statue of about 100 B.C. excavated in a Late Hellenistic house on Delos. It is arguably a one-to-one copy of the bronze statue by Polykleitos represented in this small replica. The Met collection contains fragments from another copy of this type, from the late first century A.D., that includes the head, arms, and parts of the lower legs. The missing parts were restored in plaster using the Delos copy (see fig. 17), which was shown to be nearly identical in its scale and proportions, demonstrating that Hellenistic and Roman sculptors had a reliable system for creating close copies.

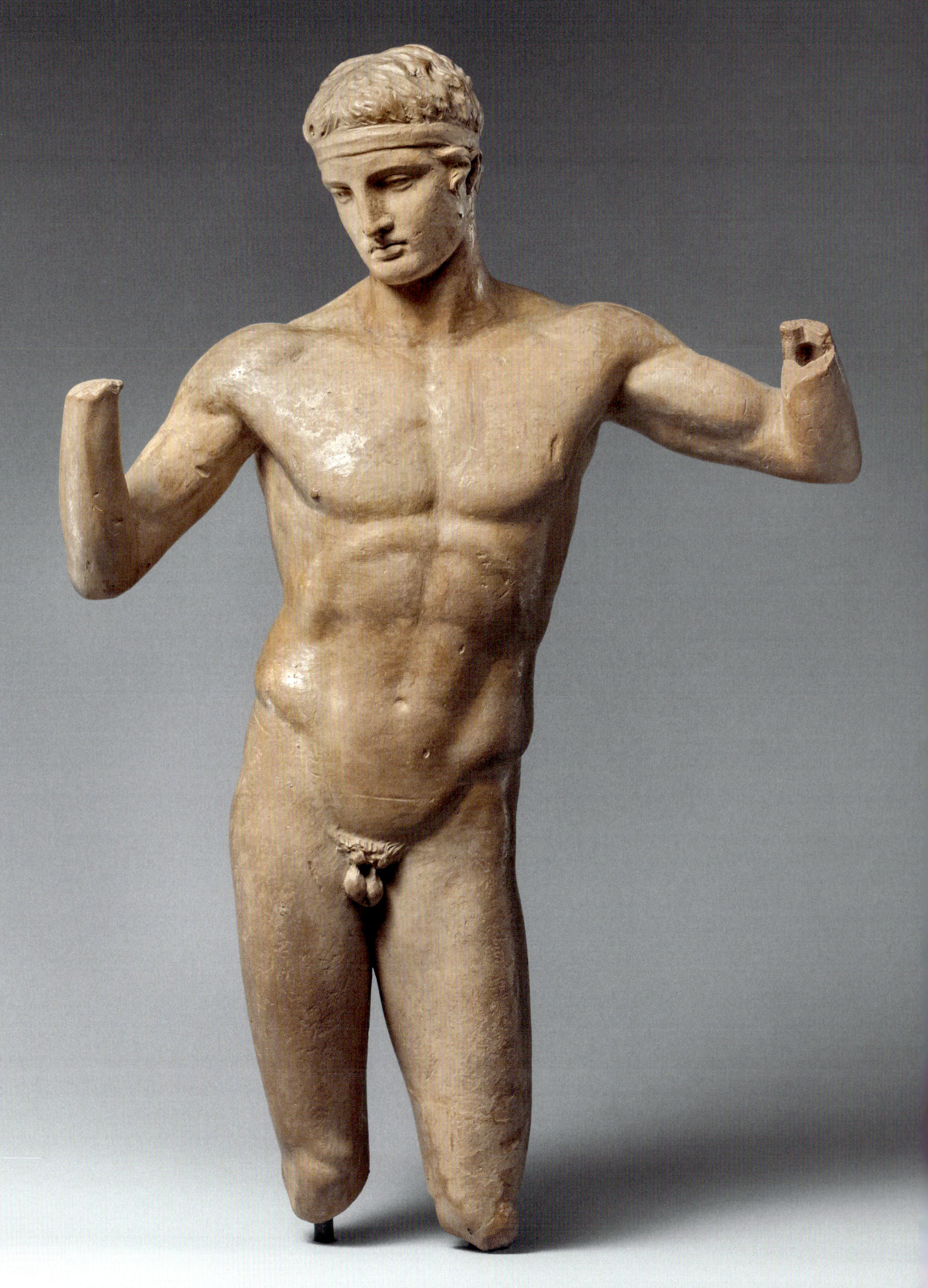

40

# Statuette of a horse

Greek, Late Hellenistic period, late 2nd–1st century B.C.
Bronze, H. 15 13/16 in. (40.2 cm)
Fletcher Fund, 1923 (23.69)

The direct method of lost wax casting was employed to make this impressive large statuette, which would have had inlaid eyes that added to its vitality. Since this technique involved destroying the original model from which the work was cast, the present sculpture is essentially unique. When it was first acquired by The Met in 1923, it was thought to be an Early Classical masterpiece of the fifth century B.C. and was long considered to be the single most important sculpture in the Museum's collection of Greek antiquities. In the 1960s, however, questions regarding its authenticity sparked intense scholarly debate. Extensive scientific and technical examination, including X-radiography and thermoluminescence dating of its clay core, led to its vindication, but with a later dating in the Hellenistic or Early Imperial period, a date since narrowed.

The pose, while not entirely natural, gives the impression of the animal's walking methodically forward. Its mane is trimmed, and the tuft of hair on its forehead is carefully coiffed; the tail and three feet are missing. Although at first glance the work is similar in style to Classical sculpture, its proportions are much too slender for a Greek horse of that period; its primary viewpoints are clearly the profiles. The reuse and adaptation of earlier styles were common in Hellenistic times, the period in which this statuette was most likely made. Such refined classicizing works were especially popular in the late second and first centuries B.C., when there was a significant market for them in Rome. The ancient Romans admired Greek culture, especially their arts, and liked to display Greek sculpture in their private houses and villas.

While the archaeological provenance of this statuette is unknown, one suggestion is that it may have come from the shipwreck off the coast of Tunisia, near Mahdia. That ship, which foundered in the second quarter of the first century B.C., was carrying a large cargo of bronze and marble sculptures from Greece for the Roman art market. The horse would have fit in well with the works found among the Mahdia shipwreck's cargo, which included earlier sculptures as well as classicizing creations of the Late Hellenistic period. Given the horse's closeness in style to Classical models, it is even conceivable that it was made as a forgery in antiquity. Ancient Roman collectors paid huge sums for Greek bronze sculptures from the fifth century B.C., and demand surely outstripped supply.

In Classical Greece, such a statuette would probably have been created to commemorate a victory in one or more of the horse races that were among the most celebrated events at the Panhellenic sanctuaries of Olympia, Delphi, Isthmia, and Nemea as well as at regional festivals such as the Panathenaic games of Athens. The sculptures made to commemorate Panhellenic equestrian victories were among the most prestigious honors allowed to citizens throughout the Greek world.

We began the selection of artworks for this book with a bronze horse statuette of the Geometric period, and we end, appropriately enough, with this horse sculpture made some seven centuries later. It is difficult today to appreciate the importance of the horse in ancient Greece, so completely has our dependence on this animal changed in the last centuries. Yet horses remained a fundamental part of many civilizations until the industrial age began in the late eighteenth century. This noble animal is celebrated here in a style that harkens back to Greece's golden age. Its sculptor has both subsumed the essential elements celebrated in the Geometric statuette and incorporated his own mannered approach to the Classical style, most evident in details of the pose and hairstyle. As a result, the statuette has a decorative quality quite different from that of previous Greek sculptures but one clearly valued at the time of its creation.

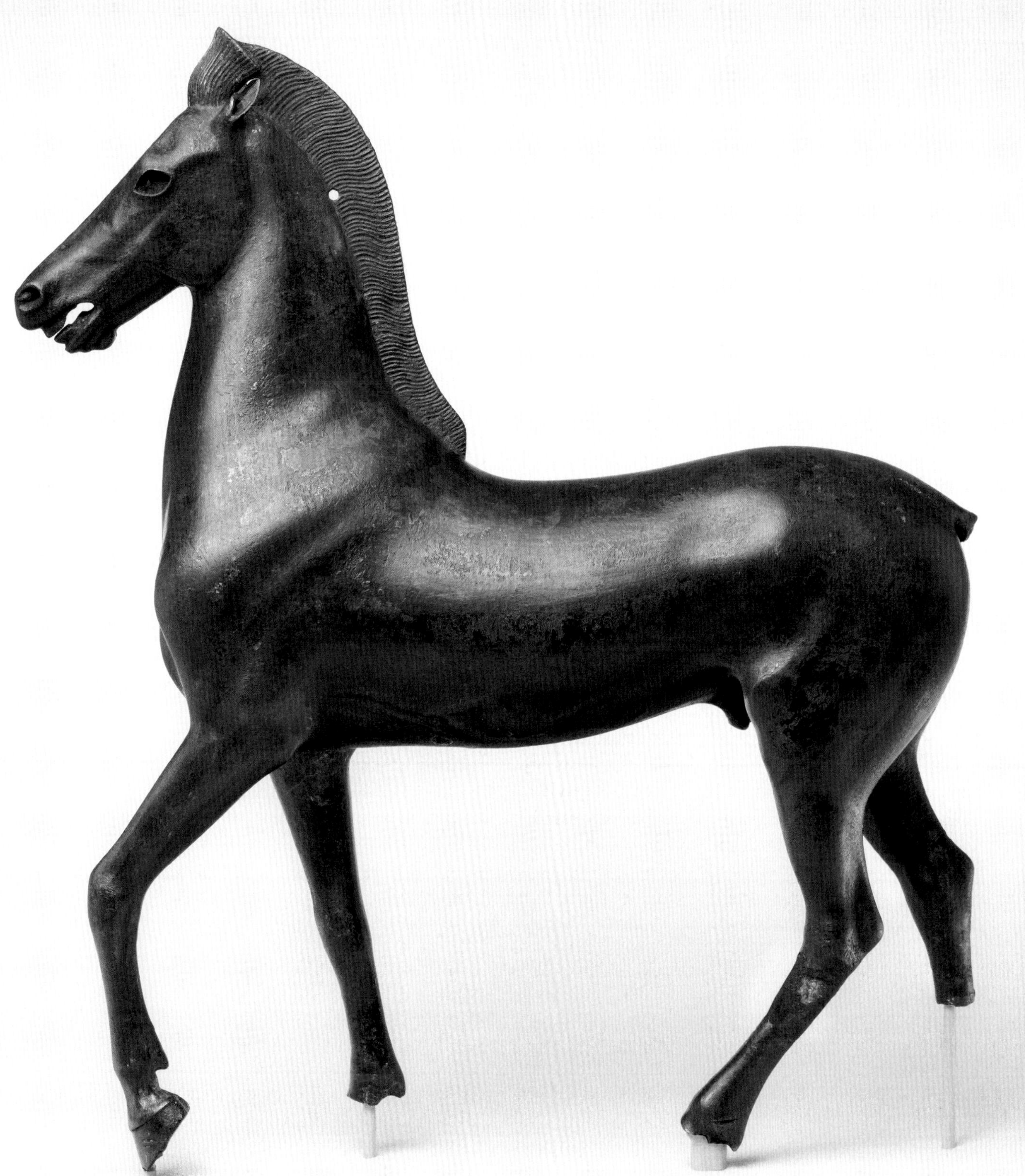

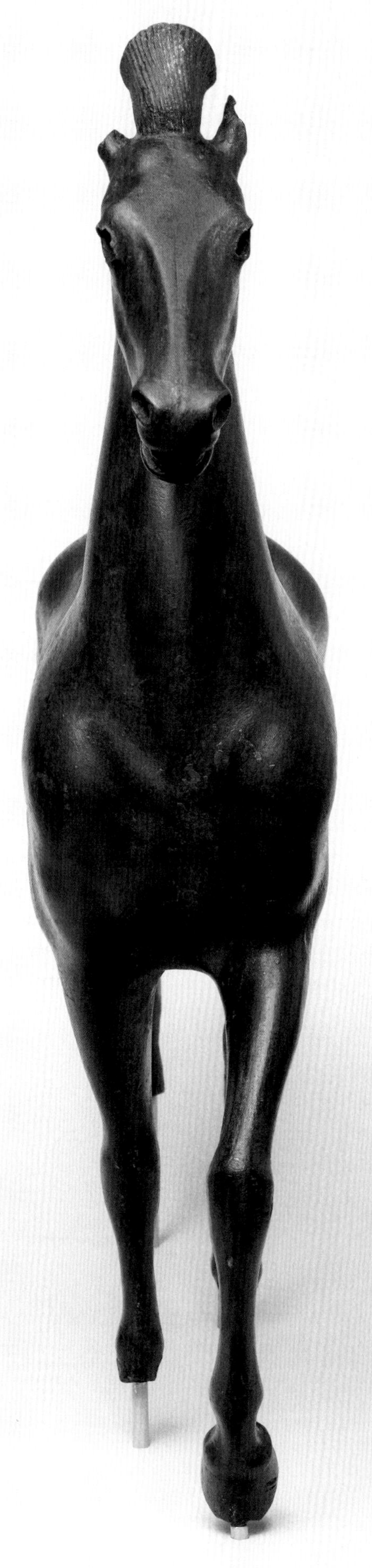

# SUGGESTED READING


## GENERAL INTRODUCTIONS

Fullerton, Mark D. *Greek Sculpture*. Oxford: Wiley Blackwell, 2016.

Hölscher, Tonio. *Visual Power in Ancient Greece and Rome: Between Art and Social Reality*. Oakland: University of California Press, 2018.

Jenkins, Ian. *Greek Architecture and Its Sculpture*. Line illustrations by Kate Morton. Cambridge, Mass.: Harvard University Press, 2006.

Palagia, Olga, ed. *Handbook of Greek Sculpture*. Berlin: De Gruyter, 2019.

Richter, Gisela M. A. *The Portraits of the Greeks*. Abridged and revised by R. R. R. Smith. Ithaca, N.Y.: Cornell University Press, 1984.

Rolley, Claude. *Greek Bronzes*. Translated by Roger Howell, with a foreword by John Boardman. London: Sotheby's/Chesterman, 1986.

Spivey, Nigel. *Greek Sculpture*. Cambridge: Cambridge University Press, 2013.

Stewart, Andrew. *Greek Sculpture: An Exploration*. 2 vols. New Haven: Yale University Press, 1990.

## GEOMETRIC PERIOD

Bennett, Michael. *From Chaos to Order: Greek Geometric Art from the Sol Rabin Collection*. St. Petersburg, Fla.: Museum of Fine Arts, St. Petersburg, 2020.

Hampe, Roland, and Erika Simon. *The Birth of Greek Art: From the Mycenaean to the Archaic Period*. Foreword by John Boardman. New York: Oxford University Press, 1981.

Langdon, Susan. *Art and Identity in Dark Age Greece, 1100–700 B.C.E.* Cambridge: Cambridge University Press, 2008.

Schweitzer, Bernhard. *Greek Geometric Art*. Edited by Ulrich Hausmann in cooperation with Jochen Briegleb. Translated by Peter and Cornelia Usborne. New York: Phaidon, 1971.

## ARCHAIC PERIOD

Karakasi, Katerina. *Archaic Korai*. Los Angeles: J. Paul Getty Museum, 2003.

Richter, Gisela M. A. *Kouroi: Archaic Greek Youths: A Study of the Development of the Kouros Type in Greek Sculpture*. 3rd ed. New York: Phaidon, 1970.

Ridgway, Brunilde Sismondo. *The Archaic Style in Greek Sculpture*. 2nd ed. Chicago: Ares, 1993.

## CLASSICAL PERIOD

Boardman, John. *The Parthenon and Its Sculptures*. Photographs by David Finn. Austin: University of Texas Press, 1985.

Childs, William A. P. *Greek Art and Aesthetics in the Fourth Century* B.C. Princeton, N.J.: Princeton University Press, 2017.

Palagia, Olga, and J. J. Pollitt, eds. *Personal Styles in Greek Sculpture*. New York: Cambridge University Press, 1996.

Pollitt, Jerome J. *Art and Experience in Classical Greece*. Cambridge: Cambridge University Press, 1972.

## HELLENISTIC PERIOD

Burn, Lucilla. *Hellenistic Art: From Alexander the Great to Augustus*. Los Angeles: J. Paul Getty Museum, 2004.

Daehner, Jens M., and Kenneth Lapatin, eds. *Power and Pathos: Bronze Sculpture of the Hellenistic World*. Exh. cat. Palazzo Strozzi, Florence; J. Paul Getty Museum, Los Angeles; National Gallery of Art, Washington, D.C. Los Angeles: J. Paul Getty Museum, 2015.

Ma, John. *Statues and Cities: Honorific Portraits and Civic Identity in the Hellenistic World.* Oxford: Oxford University Press, 2013.

Picón, Carlos A., and Seán Hemingway, eds. *Pergamon and the Hellenistic Kingdoms of the Ancient World.* Exh. cat. New York: The Metropolitan Museum of Art, 2016.

Pollitt, J. J. (Jerome Jordan). *Art in the Hellenistic Age.* Cambridge: Cambridge University Press, 1986.

Smith, R. R. R. *Hellenistic Royal Portraits.* Oxford Monographs on Classical Archaeology. New York: Oxford University Press, 1988.

———. *Hellenistic Sculpture: A Handbook.* London: Thames and Hudson, 1991.

Stewart, Andrew. *Art in the Hellenistic World: An Introduction.* Cambridge: Cambridge University Press, 2014.

Uhlenbrock, Jamiee Pugliese. *The Coroplast's Art: Greek Terracottas of the Hellenistic World.* Exh. cat. The Art Museum, Princeton University; College Art Gallery, The College at New Paltz, State University of New York; Arthur M. Sackler Museum, Harvard University, Cambridge, Mass. New Rochelle, N.Y.: Caratzas, 1990.

## POLYCHROMY AND SCULPTURAL TECHNIQUES

Brinkmann, Vinzenz, Renée Dreyfus, and Ulrike Koch-Brinkmann, eds. *Gods in Color: Polychromy in the Ancient World.* With contributions by John Camp, Heinrich Piening, and Oliver Primavesi. Exh. cat. Legion of Honor, Fine Arts Museum of San Francisco, 2017. Munich, New York: DelMonico Books, Prestel, 2017.

Ling, Roger, ed. *Making Classical Art: Process & Practice.* Charleston, S.C.: Arcadia, 2000.

Mattusch, Carol C. *Classical Bronzes: The Art and Craft of Greek and Roman Statuary.* Ithaca, N.Y.: Cornell University Press, 1996.

Palagia, Olga, ed. *Greek Sculpture: Function, Materials and Techniques in the Archaic and Classical Periods.* New York: Cambridge University Press, 2006.

## ROMAN COPIES OF GREEK SCULPTURE

Jenkins, Ian. *The Discobolus.* British Museum Objects in Focus. London: British Museum Press, 2012.

Marvin, Miranda. *The Language of the Muses: The Dialogue between Roman and Greek Sculpture.* Los Angeles: J. Paul Getty Museum, 2008.

Mattusch, Carol C., with Henry Lie. *The Villa dei Papiri at Herculaneum: Life and Afterlife of a Sculpture Collection.* Los Angeles: J. Paul Getty Museum, 2005.

Settis, Salvatore, ed. *Serial/Portable Classic: The Greek Canon and Its Mutations.* With Anna Anguissola and Davide Gasparotto. Exh. cat. Fondazione Prada, Milan; Fondazione Prada, Venice. Milan: Fondazione Prada, 2015.

Zanker, Paul, Seán Hemingway, Christopher S. Lightfoot, and Joan R. Mertens. *Roman Art: A Guide through the Metropolitan Museum of Art's Collection.* Translations by Alan Shapiro. New York: Scala, in association with The Metropolitan Museum of Art, 2020.

## PROVENANCE AND THE HISTORY OF COLLECTING

Anderson, Maxwell L. *Antiquities: What Everyone Needs to Know.* New York: Oxford University Press, 2017.

Cuno, James. *Who Owns Antiquity? Museums and the Battle over Our Ancient Heritage.* Princeton, N.J.: Princeton University Press, 2008.

Picón, Carlos A. "A History of the Department of Greek and Roman Art." In *Art of the Classical World in the Metropolitan Museum of Art: Greece, Cyprus, Etruria, Rome,* by Carlos A. Picón, Joan R. Mertens, Elizabeth J. Milleker, Christopher S. Lightfoot, and Seán Hemingway, with contributions from Richard De Puma, pp. 2–23. New York: The Metropolitan Museum of Art, 2007.

Thompson, Erin L. *Possession: The Curious History of Private Collectors from Antiquity to the Present.* New Haven: Yale University Press, 2016.

Valavanis, Panos, ed. *Great Moments in Greek Archaeology.* Translated by David Hardy, foreword by Angelos Delivorrias, essays by George F. Bass et al. Los Angeles: J. Paul Getty Museum, 2007.

# INDEX

All featured works (nos.) are illustrated; *italic* page references indicate illustrations of other works.